Religion
in the Multi-faith School
A Tool for Teachers

edited by

W. Owen Cole, B.A., B.D., M. Phil., Ph.D., Dip.Ed
Senior Lecturer, West Sussex Institute of Higher Education

Hulton Educational

Colour is no longer an indication of national origin. It has often been claimed that the Commonwealth is multi-racial and multi-religious, but until this century most racial and religious groups remained concentrated in their homelands. Today, almost every country of the Commonwealth has become multi-racial and multi-religious. This change has not been without its difficulties, but I believe that for those with a sense of tolerance the arrival and proximity of different races and religions have provided a much better chance for each to appreciate the value of the others.

Her Majesty Queen Elizabeth II
Christmas, 1982
(by gracious permission)

First published in Great Britain 1983
by Hulton Educational Publications Ltd
Raans Road, Amersham, Bucks HP6 6JJ

© Hulton Educational Publications Ltd 1983

ISBN 0 7175 1159 6

Printed in Great Britain by
Richard Clay (The Chaucer Press) Ltd
Bungay, Suffolk

CONTENTS

5

FOREWORD

I have great pleasure in writing a few words by way of foreword to this new edition of Dr Owen Cole's excellent book, *Religion in the Multi-faith School*. I wrote a foreword to the first edition, and it was a privilege to be asked to do so. The demand for the book has fully justified the publication of another edition.

The book, to which Owen Cole has devoted so much hard work, might well be regarded as a practical memorial to the Yorkshire Committee for Community Relations, which for ten years played a leading role in the development of good community relations in that county and beyond. The book reiterates the need for education to play a full part in creating a harmonious multi-cultural Britain. I recall the occasion when the late Lord Boyle, who showed such a genuine understanding of the subject, commended me for using the expression 'multi-cultural' rather than 'multi-racial'. I claim no originality, but the distinction is important. I hope those in authority will learn to appreciate and to persuade others that we are living in a multi-cultural society.

As to religion, I feel that I cannot do better than repeat a phrase in my earlier foreword: 'Religion has sometimes brought men together, sometimes its influence has been divisive. It is to be hoped that through this book the teaching of religion in our schools will be a means of bringing children of various faiths and of none together in an atmosphere of understanding, respect and tolerance.'

All those who have contributed to the writing of this book will, I know, wish to join with me in expressing appreciation to Hulton Educational Publications for undertaking the publication of this new edition. I wish the book and its authors continued success.

LORD WADE

(Lord Wade was chairman of YCCR until it dissolved itself in 1979. Under his leadership it undertook many projects, one of which resulted in the publication of *Religion in the Multi-faith School*.)

List of Contributors

Vimal Khadke, teaches science at The Walsingham School, Orpington. A well-known and authoritative speaker on aspects of Hinduism.

Hazel Broch, a leading member of the Jewish community of Leeds. Much of her time is devoted to speaking to Christian groups about Judaism and organising synagogue visits.

Muhammad Iqbal, teaches science at Huddersfield Polytechnic. A research chemist, also one of Britain's leading Muslim educationists. Author of many books on Islam. Commissioner of the Commission for Racial Equality.

Piara Singh Sambhi, trustee and registrar of the Sikh Temple, Leeds. Author of a number of books on Sikhism.

Horace Lashley, senior educational officer of the Commission for Racial Equality. An experienced teacher and youth worker.

Jack Austin, Anglican cathedral chorister as a boy, later became a Roman Catholic. Joined Buddhism at the end of the war, being initiated into Zen and then Shin. Ordained Shin priest in Japan, 1977.

Raymond Trudgian, has taught in Africa and Britain. Formerly head of religious studies at West London Institute of Higher Education, London. Member of the British Council of Churches Committee for Relations with People of Other Faiths. Author of books on religious studies.

Clive Lawton Former comprehensive school teacher of English and Drama. Now Executive Director of the Education and Information Department of the Board of Deputies of British Jews.

Marjorie Gee, teaches at Alverthorpe Church of England Primary School, Wakefield.

Elizabeth Wilson, founder member of the Shap Working Party on World Religions in Education. Teacher. Locally active in community relations in Yorkshire and nationally for Oxfam.

Pat Lord, former primary school teacher, now employed by the Youth Service of Kirklees Education Committee.

David Baldwin, headmaster Havelock Middle School, Southall.

Barry Swain, headteacher Broadgate Lane Junior School, Horsforth, Leeds.

Arthur Ravenscroft, senior lecturer in English Literature, Leeds University. Has also lectured in South Africa and Zimbabwe. Founding editor of The Journal of Commonwealth Literature (1965–79).

Mewa Singh Bussan J.P., former secretary of the Guru Nanak Temple, Bradford.

8

Nila Pancholi, teaches in Leeds and is very much involved in the educational work of the Leeds Hindu Temple. Author and speaker on Hinduism.

Ewart Thomas, former advisory teacher in religious education in Bradford.

Vida Barnett, Principal Lecturer, City of Liverpool College of Higher Education. Information officer of the Shap Working Party on World Religions in Education.

Geoff Fenwick, Senior Tutor in-service education, City of Liverpool College of Higher Education. Former primary school deputy headteacher.

Graham McFarlane, Head of Bedfordshire Multicultural Resources Centre.

Ursula King, Senior Lecturer, Department of Theology, University of Leeds.

All the sections and chapters not attributed to other contributors are written by W. Owen Cole.

ACKNOWLEDGEMENTS

I am greatly indebted to my friends who contributed to the original edition of *Religion in the Multi-faith School* for revisions and additions which they have made to their pieces. The Christian Education Movement has been similarly helpful in permitting the use of material which first appeared in one of its mailing for teachers in primary schools. My wife, Gwynneth, and Debbie Mutton have struggled very successfully with my handwriting which deteriorates over the years, and Ron Hawkins, Tony Short and James Shepherd of Hulton Educational Publications have dealt with me with great patience and turned a very awkward manuscript into an attractive book. However, my greatest debt is to children, students and teachers who provoked me to work on this book, and to the multi-cultural society which has so enriched my life.

OWEN COLE

INTRODUCTION

All teachers are educating children for life in a multi-faith and multi-cultural society — because that is the society that we live in. There may be those who face this reality with distaste or apprehension, but only the wilfully blind can pretend that it does not exist.

When I studied history at university it might not seem to have mattered very much if I had been taught that the Arabs were cruel savages without honour or honesty. Today such teaching would prejudice my encounter with Muslims, who are to be found in most of our large cities, and would probably cost my firm valuable contracts were I to be let loose on the large and growing Arab world market! In the last thirty years times have changed beyond all imagining. Now, we are all educators for life in a multi-cultural Britain and a multi-cultural world — whether we live in Leeds or Chichester.

A kindly intentioned college lecturer some years ago once excused my views on religious education to a group of clergyman by saying that my close contacts with the religious pluralism of Leeds had unbalanced my judgement. I can only reply that after two years living in the Deep South, in Chichester, I have lost only my day-to-day contact with Jewish, Sikh, Hindu and Muslim friends; my conviction that religious education has perhaps the greatest contribution to make in educating everyone for the multi-cultural reality has increased, not diminished. When Hulton Educational Publications showed interest in a new edition of *Religion in the Multi-faith School* which I edited for the Yorkshire Committee for Community Relations in 1972 I was more than pleased to give the task of revision my priority. The need was great ten years ago; today it is even more urgent. I can only hope that this book will have some worth, giving to some a vision, and to all practical guidance. There will be those who do may not like what they find within these pages, yet the next generation may damn this book as much I have condemned the literature of white colonialist paternalism. I am less bothered about particular reactions than I am to challenge the teacher, the parent, the minister of religion or the politician to recognise society as it is, to consider what it should be or to realise that the school has a role to play — but not in isolation. I pray that this book might make a small contribution to the peaceful curriculum and social revolution which must take place if something less pleasant is to be avoided.

PART 1: BACKGROUND

INTRODUCTION

The complexities of family life cannot be covered in a few short articles: think how impossible it is to speak of *the* English family! If these introductory sections, written by members of the communities concerned, awaken the sensitivity of the teacher, give initial help and prompt him to turn to Morrish, *The Background of Immigrant Children* and other books, as well as to members of the various faiths, they will have served their purpose.

A few pertinent observations might be made as preface to the articles.

First, the Asian or Caribbean family system operating in Britain is often incomplete and one key member is missing — Grandma, in the Asian home the paternal, in the Caribbean often the maternal grandmother. Consequently, the young child growing up in Britain may be linguistically or culturally deprived compared with children of the same age in the homelands. To the West Indian child the grandmother may give stability and may be almost completely responsible for his upbringing while mother goes out to work. For the Asian child she is the most important source of religious education, as she has the time for telling the stories and, free from many domestic concerns, for performing *puja* which the children observe and imitate.

Probably mosque education compensates totally in the case of the Muslim child; indications are that Sikh and Hindu parents are aware that the religious and cultural heritage is not being transmitted adequately, but they have yet to make an urgent communal as opposed to individual response.

In reading the Caribbean articles it should be remembered that by no means all West Indians are Pentecostalists. Many are Roman Catholics, Anglicans or Methodists. Besides Christians, there are Hindus and people of other faiths as well as those of none at all. There is no such thing as a West Indian church. Many Caribbean Christians attend English churches; others for a variety of reasons, colour sometimes being one, feel happier in the company of fellow West Indians.

THE RELIGIOUS UPBRINGING AND EDUCATION OF A HINDU CHILD

Religion is not taught in school but imbibed from the daily routine of life. In the sectarian sense, Hinduism is not a religion but a way of life which the child learns through the family — the extended family.

The first teacher is the grandmother, with whom the children sit in the evening. They wash their hands and feet and get ready for the evening prayers. First they bow to God and then to the elders. The grandma chants Sanskrit verses — which she knows by heart. She may not be able to read or write but has learnt them by word of mouth. The children listen and slowly attempt to imitate and chant and thus learn them. Then she tells the stories from the epics — *Ramayana* and *Mahabharata*, emphasising the victory of good over evil, truth over untruth, and kindness over cruelty.

Children are told that early to bed and early to rise is healthy and that morning is the best time for learning. Hence they get up early, bow to the rising sun — in gratitude for the removal of darkness — and sit down to learn. They have a bath every morning and change into clean clothes. They do not take shoes into the kitchen, and must wash hands and feet before sitting down for a meal. They must bow to God and the older members of the family as a mark of respect. They must not be rude to parents and elders of the extended family.

At about the age of seven, the thread ceremony (*Yagyopavit* or *Upanayana*) is performed[1] and then the child (male) is ready to receive the religious knowledge. He chants the Sanskrit *Gayatri Mantra* morning and evening with the priest until he knows how to pronounce it correctly. After the thread ceremony the child observes certain rules, such as not to eat the food tasted by others and not to eat till he has chanted the *Gayatri Mantra*.

Festivals, fasts and rituals are the best teachers of all. Every festival symbolises the code of life, so *Dasehra, Diwali (Deepwali)* and *Holi* are all celebrations of the victory of right over wrong. During this time the epics are enacted which leave a deep impression on the tender mind.

Besides the thread ceremony there are other rituals, such as those for the deceased forefathers. In a particular month the ceremony is performed by the priest to remember them. When a person dies there is a ritual on the 10th, 11th, 12th and 13th day. The bones of the dead (after cremation) are usually taken to a holy place, like Banares, to immerse in the holy river Ganges and a cow is presented to a priest, as well as clothes, gold or silver, depending upon the financial status. A grand feast is given to eight priests, to couples and to relatives. In this way one recognises that death is inescapable and the fact is to be accepted philosophically. It also signifies the sharing of possessions and,

14

by pleasing others, pleasure will be mutual and the soul of the deceased will rest in peace.

PUJA AND PRAYER

Every house will have a shrine, small or large. Perhaps even a commercial illustrated calendar will be there in a hut and it will be treated with reverence. *Puja* is a ritual performed every morning after having a bath, either by a priest or by the head of the family (usually a man). Children watch *puja* being performed and join in the prayers. Every day a share of food is offered to the sacred cow. At every stage the importance of sharing and giving away with a smiling face is emphasised as a good act.

On important fasts, festivals, eclipses and auspicious days there are special *pujas* and prayers in the temples. People visit the temples on those days, if not every day. There are sermons — *Puran, Katha Kirtan,* etc — every day in the temples and one is free to go and listen or join them. These promote the essential feature of Hindu religious thought — tolerance for other faiths. This is underlined in the *Bhagavadgita*, which says 'All paths lead to me', and again 'Whosoever offers me with devotion a leaf, a flower, a fruit or even water, with love in his heart, that offering is dear to me'. Hindus find their harmony in action without attachment, in enjoyment without desire.

During the thread ceremony, marriage, festivals, pilgrimage (when the people set out for the Himalayas, Vrindaban or other pilgrimage centres) or death in the family, all the relatives — the members of the extended family — gather together. This is an ideal opportunity for the children to meet and know all of them. Children also learn comradeship, family loyalty, respect and the ways of the family. Thus festivals and other important occasions have considerable social as well as religious importance, and are a means of binding together the extended family.

Children are told about *OM*, the symbol of God who is omnipotent and omnipresent and every watchful. One can deceive others but cannot deceive oneself and God, as He perceives what goes on in every mind and keeps an account of all deeds, good or bad.

VIMAL D. KHADKE

The Walsingham School,
St Paul's Cray,
Orpington, Kent

---

1. *This ceremony is confined to male members of the twice-born castes (Brahmins, Kshatriyas and Vaisyas) and observed most strictly by Brahmins.*

THE RELIGIOUS UPBRINGING AND EDUCATION OF A JEWISH CHILD

There is a river in the ocean. In the severest droughts, it never fails, in the mightiest floods it never overflows. The Gulf of Mexico is its fountain and its mouth is in the Arctic Seas. It is the Gulf Stream. Its waters are so distinctly marked that their line of junction with the sea-water may be traced by the eye. There seems to be a reluctance on the part of the waters of the Gulf Stream to mingle with the waters of the sea.

There is a lonely river in the midst of the ocean of mankind. The fiercest fires of human cruelty have never caused it to dry up, although its waves for more than 2,000 years have rolled red with the blood of its martyrs, in Rome, in Greece, in Spain, in Russia, in Germany. The line which divides its billows from the ordinary waters of humanity is also plainly visible to the eye. It is the Jewish race.

Throughout the centuries, the Jewish people have wandered from country to country, seeking refuge from persecution — a persecution which miraculously accentuated their individuality. Three hundred years ago, a few found a haven and tolerance in England. Today, there are four hundred thousand Jews in Britain, accepted as citizens with full rights and privileges. In their everyday mingling with their fellow citizens, they appear to have lost their individuality. The Gulf Stream seems to have merged completely with the surrounding waters, the only outward sign of difference being that, on Sunday, their Christian friends go to Church, whereas on Saturday, they themselves go to the synagogue.

But the Jewish stream has not been swallowed up, and in the orthodox Jewish home, in its family life, the torch handed down by Abraham and Moses is still very much alight, in the practice of the Mosaic Code. Even before one actually enters a Jewish home, one sees on the right hand side of the doorpost a small case, a *Mezuzah*. Inside the case is a small parchment scroll on which are written two paragraphs of a special prayer known as the *Shema*. These paragraphs refer to the love of God and loyalty to His Commandments. The *Mezuzah* is the distinctive sign of the Jewish home.

The orthodox Jewish home is different, especially in the kitchen, where meat and milk are not mixed. The Jewish housewife has separate sets of china, pots and cutlery, one set for meat meals and another for milk. There are two washing-up bowls and even different coloured tea towels, one for meat utensils and the other for milk. No milk foods are served with meat meals and one has to wait not less than three hours after a meat meal before one can partake of any milk foods.

The Jewish housewife buys only Kosher foods. The word 'Kosher' means 'Proper', and when the word is applied to food, it means fit and proper and obeying all dietary laws. The Jewish mother often takes her children with her when she goes shopping. From very early childhood they see that their mother buys all kinds of vegetables and fruit, but that she is careful not to purchase foods containing animal fats or meats unless they are specifically marked Kosher. Certain foods, for example, pig in any form, and wild fowl, are forbidden, and so are all kinds of shellfish and snails. The only fish permitted are those that have both fins and scales. Meat and poultry may be bought only from Kosher butchers or poulterers who are authorised by the Rabbis to sell Kosher food — from the killing of the animal to the sale to the housewife, everything is supervised.

When the housewife takes home the meat and poultry, she must soak it in a bucket of cold water for half an hour to remove any remaining blood. The meat is then put on a wooden box and sprinkled with coarse salt and there it remains for one hour, after which the housewife washes it off before cooking it.

To the orthodox Jew, everything leads to the *Shabbat*, the Sabbath, the most important day of the week. The Jewish housewife makes a special effort for the *Shabbat*. In her home, she is a queen and her home must shine with the spirit of the *Shabbat*. Her children see that, though she takes care every day of the week, she makes special arrangements in honour of the *Shabbat*. So it is that from their early childhood the children are imbued with the principles of Judaism which they themselves can put into practice when in their own Jewish homes.

The *Shabbat* actually begins on Friday evening. For the account of Creation in Genesis, it says 'And it was Evening and it was morning of the first day' — and the second day, and so on. So the *Shabbat* begins at sunset on Friday evening and ends with sunset on Saturday evening. All preparations for the *Shabbat* food are begun on Thursday as no cooking is permitted on the *Shabbat*.

Early on Friday the housewife, helped by her daughters, sets the table — a special white tablecloth, candelabra, two loaves of bread covered with a special bread cover, Kosher wine and goblet and prayer books, table settings for all the family. Just before the commencement of the *Shabbat*, when the menfolk are at a synagogue service, the housewife offers up a prayer. She lights the candles and makes a blessing over them. The lights of the candles are reflected in the eyes of her daughters as they realise that *Shabbat* is now in their home.

Father returns home and blesses each of his children. He then turns to his wife and quotes Proverbs 31 'A woman of valour who can find for her price is far above rubies'. He sings *Kiddush*, a sanctification over the wine. Each one washes his or her hands and all are given bread from the special *Shabbat* loaves. Between the various courses of the meal which follows, hymns are sung, and finally at the end of the repast, Grace.

Shabbat morning, a walk to the synagogue for services from 9.15 a.m. to 11.45 a.m. All the prayers, which are led by the Cantor, are chanted in Hebrew, with the exception of the Loyal Prayer for the Royal Family, which is recited in English by the Rabbi. The service is divided into two parts and, before the second part, the Cantor leaves his *Bimah*, a kind of dais from which he has been leading the service, and, accompanied by the wardens and two male members of the congregation, he walks to the Eastern Wall of the synagogue where the Ark is situated. The curtains of the Ark are drawn, a scroll of the law is taken out and the Cantor returns to the *Bimah*. The Scroll is opened at the portion of the week and eight men are called up to sing a blessing between each of the eight parts of the portion, which are usually chanted by the Rabbi. The scroll is returned to the Ark and the second half of the service is completed. During the service men and women do not sit together: the women sit in the gallery of the synagogue.

The service ends, and all the congregation goes to another room for *Kiddush* and wine and coffee and cakes. A walk home for a mid-day *Shabbat* meal and in the afternoon the children return to the precinct of the synagogue grounds where there is a Youth Centre. Here they join their friends of the Synagogue Youth Group and have discussion, sing Israeli songs and dance Israeli dances.

Back home — and as the evening draws to a close, the family gather round Father again, this time for *Havdalah*, a farewell to the *Shabbat*. This ceremony is performed both in the synagogue and at home. A plaited candle is lit, a sweet-smelling spice box is passed round for all to inhale the fragrance and a blessing is sung over a cup of wine.

And so as the stars appear one by one in the sky outside, the Jewish family bids farewell to the *Shabbat*, for on the morrow begins the first ordinary weekday. But though it is farewell, it is a happy ceremony, for the happy Jewish family knows that whatever trials and responsibilities will come in the next six days, the *Shabbat* will return again, bringing with it the close family atmosphere and a day of rest for themselves and for all their people and, for that matter, for all people. For family life and the day of rest are two of the most valued contributions given to the children of Israel, the Jewish people, not only for themselves but for all mankind.

HAZEL BROCH

Some records which may be found in a Jewish home but cannot be bought in Britain and are instructional as well as enjoyable, are:

Enjoy Your Festival (in Hebrew), AN11–71. Available from USA.

Chasidic Song Festival 1971 (in Hebrew), BAN 14203. Available from Israel.

Jewish Ethics Through Story and Song (in English), LP 222. Available from USA.

The Mitzvah Tree (songs and stories) (in English), LP 615B. Available from USA.

K'tonton by Sadie Rose Weilerstein, an American book about a Jewish imp or 'Tom Thumb,' is popular with Jewish children. It may be available in some London bookshops.

THE RELIGIOUS UPBRINGING AND EDUCATION OF A MUSLIM CHILD

INTRODUCTION

The average Englishman who comes to know of the existence of a number of Muslim mosques in his country might well wonder what is going on within. Primarily these are places of worship for all, and especially for the religious instruction of children. The mosques in England, however, have taken on extra responsibility of providing social education and instruction in language and religious essentials. The main reason for this is that Muslim children attending English schools receive little education in Islamic theology, whereas in schools such as those in Pakistan this is part of their school curriculum and syllabus, and the timetable is built around the prayers. The day starts with prayers (which has a special relevance to education), or with national songs in primary and secondary schools.

HOME

From birth, Muslim children grow up at home with the Muslim faith and traditions in practice. If not all, at least one member of the family is seen praying five times a day. The children are there to hear some of the calls to prayers daily and they would notice the difference in the construction of their own homes and the mosque. Thus environmental influence alone may help them to learn a great deal about their faith.

The daily work begins with early morning prayers preceded by washing or ablutions, loud recitation of the *Qur'an* by the female members, followed by breakfast. The children visit the mosque to learn from the *Imam*, the religious leader. They have ample opportunities to watch the common ceremonies and customs attendant at the time of birth, circumcision, marriage, and death; and festivals of fasting, *Eid-al-Fitr, Eid-al-Adha* and *Eid-Milad-al-Nabi* (the Prophets' Day). The extent of their activities in these events is determined by their age. Whilst the children are away at school, mother looks after the household duties and father sets off to the farm, reciting the *Qur'an*. Every home has two or three copies of the *Qur'an*, which is handled with great respect when carried to the mosques and back home.

All kinds of work stop at noon during summer and in the early afternoon during winter. The early and late afternoon, evening and late evening prayers are short periods of worship for both men and women. Preferably men go to the mosque for their prayers. Older children also attend. *Lota* (a utensil for ablutions), rosaries and prayer-carpets are ubiquitous and are offered as presents to young ones and family friends.

THE MOSQUE

The *Imam* in the mosque does not finish his work until an hour after the early morning prayers. The boys and girls come to the mosque before they eat their breakfast and memorise the Arabic text (and its meanings) of the prayers at the age of four to six. After this age they read the *Qur'an*. The visits to the mosque continue until a child can say the prayers and read the *Qur'an*. Some may embark upon learning it by heart. The process entails a good deal of skill and labour and is conducted in special schools called *Madrissahs*.

The older boys and girls attend to the cleanliness of the younger ones and help the *Imam* in teaching them. The *Imam* reports to the parents on matters concerning progress and discipline. In his time between the prayers he looks after his own family and attends to the religious ceremonies for all in the area. Usually, he invites the learned men to lecture on Muslim history, law and doctrines. The *Qaris* (those who can chant the *Qur'an* sweetly) recite the *Qur'anic* verses and also sing Urdu-Punjabi poems, which cover the reappraisal of the Prophet Muhammad's and his followers' lives. Such events last overnight and even for days, especially during the fasting month of *Ramadhan*. The young boys also participate in singing and recitation.

MUSLIM FESTIVALS

In addition to the five daily prayers, special prayers are said on special festival days. The festivals are subject to the lunar calendar, beginning on AD 16 July 622, marking the first of *Muharram*, the month during which the Prophet Muhammad migrated from Mecca to Medina. The year is 10–11 days shorter than the solar year and consists of 12 months:

1. Muharram
2. Safar
3. Rabi-al-Awwal
4. Rabi-al-Thani
5. Jamadi-al-Awwal
6. Jamadi-al-Thani
7. Rajjab
8. Sha'ban
9. Ramadhan
10. Shawal
11. Dhu-al-Qadhah
12. Dhu-al Hijjah

The tenth of Muharram marks the killing of Hussain, Muhammad's grandson who fought against the evil forces of the day. The event is remembered every year throughout the Muslim world. The next date in the calendar is the 12th *Rabi-al-Awwal* i.e. *Eid-Milad-al-Nabi* (The Prophet's Day), which is also the day when the Prophet died. This is the 71st day of the lunar year. Besides popular celebrations, special lectures and remembrances are arranged. Not much attention was paid to this day in the early days of Islam but it is gaining more appeal because of the uniqueness of the messages the Prophet had brought to mankind.

One hundred and sixty-six days after the Prophet's Day is the fasting month of *Ramadhan*, the successful completion of which is marked by the happiest day in a Muslim's life, *Eid-al-Fitr*, which is celebrated on the first *Shawal*. *Ramadhan* is a month of physical sacrifice and a lot of prayers. *Eid-al-Fitr* is also the day of prayers. No work must be done on this day. The children must start fasting at the age of 12.

Two hundred and sixty-four days after the Prophet's Day, the festival of *Eid-al-Adha* on the 10th *Dhu-al-Hijjah*, is celebrated. It commemorates the near-sacrifice of Ishmael, the Prophet Abraham's son. An animal is sacrificed and prayers are said. The usual rejoicings, as for *Eid-al-Fitr*, are presents for children, good food and clothes and participation in communal games.

The events of *Eid-al-Fitr* and *Eid-al-Adha* are significantly important to Muslims throughout the world. All work stops in all Muslim countries. Teachers of Muslim children in schools may find the following chart of special interest to them. Even if the parents do not absent themselves from work on these days in Britain, the children are likely to be away from school.

Hijri Year	1st Muharram	The Prophet's Day	1st Ramadhan	Eid-al-Adha
1402	30 Oct. 1981	8 Jan. 1982	23 June 1982	29 Sept. 1982
1403	19 Oct. 1982	30 Dec. 1982	12 June 1983	18 Sept. 1983
1404	8 Oct. 1983	19 Dec. 1983	1 June 1984	7 Sept. 1984
1405	28 Sept. 1984	8 Dec. 1984	20 May 1985	28 Aug. 1985
1406	17 Sept. 1985	27 Nov. 1985	10 May 1986	18 Aug. 1986
1407	7 Sept. 1986	16 Nov. 1986	29 Apr. 1987	7 Aug. 1987
1408	27 Aug. 1987	5 Nov. 1987	18 Apr. 1988	27 July 1988
1409	15 Aug. 1988	24 Oct. 1988	7 Apr. 1989	15 July 1989
1410	4 Aug. 1989	13 Oct. 1989	28 Mar. 1990	4 July 1990

A difference of a day on either side of the dates given above can be taken into account, subject to the appearance of the moon. All Muslim festivals are subject to the phases of the moon and one has to allow for the sighting of the new moon. This is sometimes impossible because of the English climate. Low clouds can obscure the moon altogether. The religious leaders confirm the time by telephoning religious institutions which are based in Muslim countries where there is a likelihood of the moon being sighted. Help from the Royal Greenwich Observatory can often be of great service.

It is advisable to obtain the lunar calendar for the current year which is sold in every Pakistani shop nearer the time. There are also very picturesque calendars given away by airlines and cultural consulates of Muslim countries in Britain. The *Hijri* dates can be converted to Gregorian dates by using the following formula:

$$CE = AH - \frac{3 \times AH}{100} + 622$$

For example, the *Battle of Karbalah*, when the Prophet's grandson Hussain (may Allah the Almighty be pleased with him) fell martyr, took place during the 40th year of the *Hijri* calendar. Accordingly, if we insert this figure in the above equation, it will give us the equivalent year in the Gregorian calendar as follows:

$$CE = 40 - \frac{3 \times 40}{100} + 622$$

$$= 40 - 1 + 622 \quad \text{(by bringing the middle figure to the nearest whole number)}$$

$$= 661$$

Alternatively, as the lunar year is shorter by about 10–11 days than the solar year, the former gains an extra year after the passage of every 35 years of the latter (that is, 365 days divided by 10–11 days will give the figure of 35, approximately). Furthermore, the above calculations can be further confirmed from the literature on history through the knowledge of chronometry. Herein every letter of the Arabic alphabet is allotted a specific number which does not alter at all. These numbers are then added up having been substituted in the name of an event, battle or an incident. Sometimes a poet coins a verse on the death or birth of someone, which helps to give a figure giving the actual date of death or birthday.

SCHOOLS

In schools, a compulsory subject of Islamic Studies is introduced for all until entering a degree course at the age of 16. The comprehensive syllabuses available from the directorate of education and various universities in Pakistan consist of Islamic history, Muslim theology and worship. Study during the early schooldays is made easy because of the visits to the mosque.

In the sixth year of their school life children learn to speak English and Persian (or Arabic) as second languages just as French or German is taught to English children. As the language improves, books including extracts from the famous Muslim writers such as Rumi, Saadi, Al-Hariri and Umar Khayyam are introduced. The older children enjoy the extracts from Shaikh Saadi Shirazi's (d. AD 1292), *Gulistan* (The Rose Garden) and *Bustan* (The Orchard), because of their *sufic* subtleties explained through short stories. Both these books, which are regarded as masterpieces of Persian literature, are available in English and other major languages.

The moral stories of Saadi (of the type given below) and others are written in Urdu or Persian, but are often of no use to Muslim children educated in Britain who may only have a limited knowledge of Urdu script however hard they try at the mosque, and may not find time in their later life to read the difficult translations in English.

A dog bit the foot of a Bedouin with such fury that poison dripped from its teeth and the pain at night was so great that sleep could not comfort him. Now in his household he had a little daughter who upbraided him and was very angry. 'Did you too not have teeth?' she asked. The unhappy man ceased his wailing and said, laughing: 'My darling little mother, even though I had the power and a spear too, yet it would revolt me to use my own jaws and teeth. It would be impossible for me to apply my teeth to a dog's leg even if a sword were held at my head.' The nature of dogs is evil, but man cannot (in defence) act like a dog. (Adopted from Reuben Levy's translation.)

The collection of Muslim religious stories (at the end of this book) are true historical events. It is becoming increasingly obvious that there is a definite need for a good selection of moral stories from Islamic literature for both teachers and pupils.

THE BRITISH MOSQUES

The mosques in England partly resemble the ones of the Islamic countries in the eleventh century, when these institutes of learning were responsible for the social, cultural, religious, scientific and artistic education of the people at that time.

With a number of objectives in mind Muslim parents send their children to the mosque regularly during the evenings and during the day over the weekend. The average attendance per week for all age groups, after the age of four, is three to four hours, but there are those who do not put in an attendance at all, and others who put in as much as ten to thirteen hours per week.

The first British mosques were dwelling-houses adopted for use as places of prayer. More recently, purpose-built mosques with customary designs have been constructed in such places as London, Birmingham, Coventry, Preston and Keighley. Others are planned.

The governing body, usually called the Mosque Committee, employes a religious leader well conversant with the languages of the East, whose duties are many and manifold. He teaches the children the rudiments of language and religion, conducts prayers five times a day and funeral prayers when the occasion demands.

SOCIAL TEACHINGS

A function that has only recently been introduced into a number of mosques is the teaching to the children of certain sections of the Highway Code; this has been brought about by the increasing concern of the Road Safety Departments of the Borough Police and by the Welfare Department of the Local Education Authorities at the alarming rise in road accidents to immigrant children, especially those between the age of three and five years. To assist the New Commonwealth Communities to become road-safety conscious a section of the Highway Code has been translated into Urdu — the *lingua franca* of the majority of immigrants from India and Pakistan — and presented in the form of a booklet (Reference: West Yorkshire Constabulary).

The children themselves are bridging the gap between the Eastern and Western worlds they are absorbing things from both the mosque and the state school and in this way are helping their parents to broaden their outlook of life in a changing situation. The religious leaders of some of the mosques have made it a permanent feature of their sermons to the children to ask their parents to attend local English classes for adults. In this way they prove very helpful to the Further Education Departments in their endeavour to help the non-English-speaking immigrants. Once the English classes have begun, the religious leaders' sermons are geared to maintain interest in the classes and uphold their motives. Still another function of the mosque is to introduce the cross-section of the Muslims attending the large Friday afternoon prayers to such current events as 'The Year for Racial Harmony', 'Human Rights Charters', and 'Relationship between Muslims and Christians' in different towns.

PUBLICATIONS

Some mosques are producing printed matter, varying from small occasional papers and bulletins to voluminous monthly magazines, purely on Islam in all its facets and different prospectives. The Shah Jahan Mosque at Woking, Surrey, the oldest in this country, is publishing *The Islamic Review* — an English monthly in its 75th year of publication in 1982. A number of other mosques in the country are contemplating producing literature in both English and Urdu to help parents to teach their children the basic tenets of Islam from the modernist's point of view. The UMO National Muslim Educational Council, which has recently been set up in London, is looking into the needs of the English-speaking children, and has, in fact, produced a few useful books in English. A graded series of primers is being prepared and should be published shortly.

THE *IMAM*

The *Imam* can often be of great help to the head teachers of schools with a high proportion of Muslim children by explaining the principle of ritual slaughtering of animals and the reasons why children refuse to eat pork at school. To avoid confusion, the pre-school children are being taught at the mosque what to eat and what to refuse. Sometimes the difficulties that arise with regard to dress and dietetic customs are caused by confusion over what is religious and what is non-religious and purely a social habit.

With both day and evening study it might appear that these children are being grossly overworked, but the fact remains that the education they receive in the mosque covers all the aspects of social education which an English teacher might find great difficulty in imparting to the Muslim child.

EXAMPLE OF THE MOSQUE TEACHING

There are certain aspects of Islam which are of intense interest for the Muslim children alone. The following extract, for example, is from the authentic collections of the sayings of Prophet Muhammad (peace be upon him) by Al-Tirmidhi (d. 888 CE), and Abu Duad (d. 888 CE), the famous reporters, and is often repeated and common narration for Muslim children in the mosque by bringing home certain lessons.

Saad (may Allah bless him) was one of the Prophet Muhammad's companions. Once the Prophet visited him. He stood by the side of the door and greeted him saying, '*Assalam-o-Alaikum*', meaning 'peace be on you.' Saad replied, rather quietly, '*Wa-Alaikum-Salam*', meaning 'and peace be on you.' Qais (may Allah bless him), one of Saad's sons, remarked that the Holy Prophet was coming and would he please call him in. Saad said to him, 'Be quiet, let him greet us again. The Prophet's well wishing brings a lot of wealth. The more he wishes the better it is.'

The Prophet was standing at the door and he greeted Saad for a second time. Again Saad replied only quietly. The Prophet greeted him again but did not hear Saad's soft reply. Having greeted the man three times without receiving any reply, the Prophet turned away and was about to go when Saad ran to him and said, 'May Allah help me to sacrifice my life for you, the fountainhead of Islam. I heard all your *Salams* [blessings]. But I craved for more blessings from you. Is it not good fortune that you, the exalted Prophet of Allah, pray for peace for us? O, Prophet! The human beings do strange things for love and this gesture of mine was in love for you. Please forgive me for this rudeness and walk in and bless us with your presence.'

The Prophet walked in. It was one of the hot days of summer. Saad prepared a bath for the Prophet. After his bath he put on a saffron-coloured sheet, which his host had offered him, and prayed to Allah for his blessing for the family.

Saad brought some food, which the Prophet ate. After a short while when the Prophet asked Saad's permission to go he offered him his horse to ride. He put a red cloth on the back of the horse and ordered Qais to go with the Prophet. Qais walked alongside the riding Prophet. They had gone off only a little when the Prophet asked him to sit on the horse. When Qais would not agree the Prophet told him to go back home. Qais said *salam* to the Prophet and went away.

The story brings home such points as that greeting holds the status of a prayer and is a meaningful blessing which has now become a part of Islamic civilisation. The answer to the greeting holds equal importance. The simple permission to enter a house may be refused if the greeting is not given. If greeting three times does not bring any reply then entering a house is not allowed. Returning home happily is the only alternative. People should not stand right in the middle of the doorway while asking permission to enter. Peeping inside is strictly forbidden. Hospitality of the guest is a sacred task and walking a few steps with a departing guest is a part of the farewell gesture. The host comes back only when the guest tells him to do so. Offer transport if you have any. Don't be cross if the host does some funny thing out of respect, but instead appreciate it. Disclose your name when asked by the people inside the house. Love is enhanced by short interludes of absence in your visits.

Such are the stories which one comes across quite frequently in the Islamic textbooks in use in Pakistani state schools catering for the religious educational needs of all age groups. They are of varying length and depth, obtained from the sayings of the Prophet and the biographies of the Rashidin Caliphs and the just kings/Caliphs of other dynasties such as Umar bin Abdul Aziz, Haroon al Rashid, Mahmud Ghaznavi, Qutab-ud-Din and Aurangzeb Alamgir. Their lives are similar to that of the Prophet, and their practices are highlighted by narrating stories to the students in the classroom. The events devoid of inter-religious encounters can be usefully incorporated in books on world religions without giving offence to any other religious group.

EXCLUSIVE MUSLIM TEACHING

Experience has shown that the study of the Islamic theology devised for all ages of schoolchildren throughout the Muslim world also includes incidents where superiority of the Muslim faith is emphasised. In the mosque everybody, indiscriminate of age, listens to sermons voicing both Islamic-orientated and egalitarian views, particularly on Fridays. People will listen to these stories again and again, and the meanings become clearer each time.

One example of the superiority of the miraculous powers of the Prophet Muhammad follows.

Abu Bakr, the first Caliph of Islam, reported that when he and the Prophet Muhammad (peace be upon him) were forced to leave Mecca, a man named Saraqa bin Malik chased us. I could see that he was closing upon us so I said to the Prophet, 'Now we are, indeed, caught by this person'. The Prophet replied, 'Do not worry, Allah is with us'. Then he prayed and to our amazement we saw Saraqa's horse sink down into the hard earth till only its body and head were above ground and Saraqa's legs were stuck fast. Saraqa called out, 'I know that you have both prayed for my misfortune. Now pray that I may get out again. In return, I promise that I will stop all those who are out searching for you.' The Prophet returned to his prayers and soon Saraqa was a free man. Saraqa kept his word and turned away all those who were chasing the Prophet and his companions.

This event may be compared with the sinking of Qaroon and his palace. It is reported that Qaroon made the Prophet Moses' (peace be upon him) life hell on earth. But as he was the Prophet's cousin the Prophet always forgave him.

When the Prophet had the Divine Call to ask people to pay *Zakat* (the giving of compulsory alms to the poor) he demanded that Qaroon should pay *Zakat* if not at the standard rate of 2·5 per cent of the savings at least one Dirham out of one thousand. Qaroon estimated that even at the reduced rate he would have to pay to the poor a huge sum of money. He thought of a plan to turn the Israelites against Moses.

All the same, Qaroon bribed a bad woman to accuse the Prophet of immoral relations with her.

It was the day of *Eid*. Before the *Eid* prayers the Prophet Moses preached a sermon which prescribed the just punishment of thieves and adulterers. The latter were to be stoned to death. Qaroon interrupted and shouted, 'What if you yourself have committed adultery?' The Prophet answered that he should be punished likewise. At this, Qaroon announced that the Prophet had committed adultery with an Israelite woman.

The Prophet called for the woman, who swore under oath that Qaroon bribed her to accuse him of this sin. Hearing this, the Prophet fell onto his knees and prayed to God to decide Qaroon's punishment. His prayers were met, and a revelation commanded him that the earth was made subservient to Moses in order to punish Qaroon. The Prophet Moses said, 'Oh, Earth! catch hold of Qaroon'. Qaroon slowly sank into the earth up to his knees. At the second command he was swallowed up to his waist, at the third up to his neck until he sank completely.

As soon as the earth started swallowing Qaroon, he repeatedly asked the Prophet for his mercy, but he would not forgive him. Allah, the Compassionate and Merciful, told Moses that had Qaroon asked Him for mercy only once he would have been forgiven.

After this happening the Israelites accused Moses of taking Qaroon's wealth. He became angry, and in a rage ordered the earth to swallow Qaroon's palace and wealth. Thus everything sank.

Although the events are similar yet the Prophet Muhammad showed mercy and forgave the accused. Not only that, Saraqa was given a certificate of peace and told that he would have good fortune later in life.

MUHAMMAD IQBAL

THE RELIGIOUS UPBRINGING AND EDUCATION OF A SIKH CHILD

HOME

The Sikh child's first experience of religion will be in the home. In this respect the Sikh is like the child of any faith. In the Punjab, people rise before 6 a.m. A Sikh will take a bath in running water and then should meditate upon the Name of God. After saying morning prayers, especially reading the *Japji Sahib* of Guru Nanak, he should then make a visit to the *Gurdwara* where he will listen to *gurbani kirtans* (hymn-singing), or quite often bow before the *Guru Granth Sahib*, perhaps read from it, and make an offering before returning home or going to his work.

The work of most Sikhs living in the villages of the Punjab is related to agriculture. The way of life differs from that of the typical inhabitant of Britain in two ways. First, it is not geared to time, clocking in, being at the office from 9 a.m. to 5.30 p.m., or working in shifts. Second, the hotter climate almost compels a person to rise by 6 a.m. Consequently there is less rush, the schoolboy beginning his day at 10 a.m. in winter, 8 a.m. in summer. The office worker (10 a.m.) will have had ample time for a bath, morning devotions and going to the *Gurdwara*.

Women, of course, have the running of the home. They may not have time for a bath as soon as they rise. They will, however, recite, or rather one should say sing, the *Japji Sahib* as they go about the task of lighting the fire and preparing a meal. Young children will soon begin to imitate them and are encouraged to say their prayers before breakfast.

In the evening a Sikh should pray before going to bed, this time using the *Sohila* (vespers).

It is fairly rare to find a copy of the *Guru Granth Sahib*, the Sikh scripture, in the home. It contains 5,894 hymns, being a collection more like the Psalms than any other book of the Jewish–Christian scriptures. It is treated with such respect and ceremonial that many Sikhs feel that they cannot meet their responsibilities adequately. Most Sikhs possess a small book containing about seven of the most important *Shabads* (hymns), among them the *Japji Sahib*, the *Anand*, *Ardas* and *Sohila*.

THE *GURDWARA*

The Sikhs have no weekly day of worship corresponding to the Jewish Sabbath or Christian Sunday. They will go to the *Gurdwara* in the morning, as has been mentioned, or in the evening. There they will sometimes hear discourses or explanations of the *Japji* or some other *Shabad* (hymn) or of material from one of the *Janam Sakhis*. (These are accounts of the life of Guru Nanak written by his followers.) There are no priests or ministers in the Sikh religion: talks will be given by members of the community or by visiting musicians (*Ragis*).

There are certain times of the year when Sikhs will assemble at the *Gurdwara* and the *Guru Granth Sahib* will be read from beginning to end. These *Gurpurbs* (holy festivals) celebrate important anniversaries associated with the Gurus and are occasions upon which Sikh children learn much about their historic faith.

SIKH FESTIVALS

India is a land of fairs and festivals which give vivid colour to the texture of our lives and enhance the joy of living and spiritual security. The Sikh festivals comprise the observance of the anniversaries of the Sikh Gurus and a few other events relating to the development of Sikh religion and history. The Gurus' anniversaries are termed as *Gurpurbs* — the holy festivals in honour of the Gurus — while the others are simply called *Melas* (fairs). It is interesting to note that *Baisakhi Diwali* and *Holi*, which are principally the Hindu festivals, are also celebrated by the Sikhs, though in a different way and for different reasons.

The birthdays of Guru Nanak and Guru Cobind Singh, the first and the last ten Gurus of the Sikh respectively, the martyrdom days of Guru Arian Dev and Guru Tegh Bahadur and Baisakhi, the day of the founding of the *Khalsa* (brotherhood of arms) are celebrated by the Sikhs all over the world wherever they are, while *Hola Mohalla* is chiefly celebrated at Anandpur, *Diwali* at Amritsar, the Martyrdoms of Guru Gobind Singh's sons at Chamkaur and *Fategarh Sahib* in the Punjab.

The death anniversary of Maharaja Ranjit Singh in June is also commemorated every year with great pomp and show. An important aspect of this anniversary is a poetry competition.

GURPURBS

The content of each *Gurpurb* depends upon the particular anniversary being celebrated. Two days before the *Gurpurb*, a continuous reading of the *Holy Granth* is commenced and is completed in the early hours of the day of the celebration. This is followed by hymn-singing by the musicians. Eminent theologians and speakers on Sikh religion are also invited to address the assembly. As a large number of people are expected to participate in the function a huge *Pandal* (marquee) is usually erected either in the precincts of the *Gurdwara* or elsewhere near it on open ground for accommodating the public. Arrangements for the distribution of free food for all from the Guru's Kitchen (called *Guru ka langar*) are also made on such occasions.

In the afternoon it is customary to take the *Granth Sahib* in procession through the city. The Holy Book, covered with costly pieces of cloth, i.e. Zari or silk, is carried in a *Palki*, placed on top of a vehicle decorated with flowers and coloured bunting. Two Sikh gentlemen carrying golden yellow Sikh banners (*Nishan Sahib*) constitute the advance guard while five others representing the first five initiates (*Panch Pyares*) march in front of the vehicle with drawn swords. The women walk behind the van and sing hymns.

The procession stops for a while every now and then at crossroads and the main city centres where the speakers address the spectators and the poets recite poems suitable for the occasion, while the sword and stick experts find opportunities to show their skill. In the evening everything comes to a close and the people go back to their homes.

The celebrations outside India are, however, held only in the *Gurdwara* and the procession of the *Holy Granth* is conspicuous by its absence.

HOLLA MOHALLA (MARCH)

The origin of *Holi* is as obscure as that of *Diwali* and a large number of myths and legends are associated with its inception. The festival is, however, quite popular in the north of India. People sprinkle coloured water on one another with syringes. Much of the fun and merrymaking is, however, lost when people resort to the use of mud, grease, charcoal or paint in place of coloured water or powder. Sometimes the situation takes a very bad turn when this is sprayed on any unwilling participant, a wayfarer or a stranger. The position was much the same during the time of Guru Gobind Singh. He therefore provided an alternative celebration for the Sikhs, a three-day fair held at Anandpur Sahib, beginning on the eve of *Holi*.

Tents are pitched and stalls erected. Crowds assemble for a variety of activities, singing, talks about Sikhism and political conferences. On the day of the *Holi* itself there are exhibitions of horse riding, tournaments and athletic competition, for Sikhism has always placed importance upon physical health.

BAISAKHI (APRIL)

Baisakhi is one of the few famous festivals which are celebrated by both Hindus and the Sikhs, though for different reasons. It combines the spirit of festivity with that of religion. *Baisakhi* marks a turning-point in the development of Sikh religions with the creation of the

Khalsa brotherhood by Guru Gobind Singh. The new organisation of the saint-soldiers changed the course of history by ushering in a revolution not only in the minds but also in the physical appearance of the Sikhs. The day is commemorated by administering Sikh baptism to the prospective candidates of the faith.

DIWALI — FESTIVAL OF LIGHTS (LATE OCTOBER/NOVEMBER)

Diwali is another Indian festival which is shared by the Sikhs, though no definite date can be assigned as to when the festival of lights was first observed.

More than half a dozen historic events that took place on this day can be recollected. As far as Sikh history is concerned, Guru Amar Das — the third Guru of the Sikhs made it one of the bi-annual gatherings of the Sikhs (the other being *Baisakhi*), Guru Ram Das had laid the foundation stone of *Darbar Sahib* Amritsar,[1] and Guru Hargobind, who was imprisoned by the Emperor Jehangir in the fort of Gwalior, was released from captivity on this day. The Golden Temple was profusely illuminated there and the custom continues today. Sweets and presents are distributed to friends and relatives, homes are illuminated with rows of lights and children make merry with fireworks.

SCHOOL

In India there are a number of different types of schools, besides those provided by the government. In state schools there is no compulsory religious instruction but, of course, in history periods Sikh children will learn about the events which have influenced their religion so considerably and without which it would not have come into existence.

In Sikh (*Khalsa*) schools the religious element will be fairly strong. There will be school assembly in the open air at which the appropriate hymn will be chanted. There will be *Gurdwara* in the school and important *Gurpurbs* will be observed. The Punjabi lesson will often be a medium for teaching the faith. At festivals the school will be represented in the processions and children join in *Kirtan*, the praise of God, in the school *Gurdwara*.

SIKHS IN BRITAIN

Life in a north European industrialised society has influenced the religious life of the Sikh in a number of ways. First, he had to live by the clock. The early rising, bath, meditation and visit to the *Gurdwara* have given way to a quick breakfast and the rush-hour. For men working on the night shift (and there are many) the problem is even more difficult. They cannot go to the *Gurdwara* in the evening as many other people do, especially women.

Second, *Gurpurbs* celebrated on the precise day in the Punjab are now moved to the weekend, Friday night, Saturday and Sunday. Sunday has, in fact, become the day of weekly worship through necessity.

The religious upbringing of Sikh children in these circumstances is causing considerable anxiety. Sunday schools have been established in many *Gurdwaras* where children are instructed in their faith and also in Punjabi, for many a second language spoken with a strong Birmingham or Yorkshire accent!

Other experiments are also being undertaken. For example, in one town an English Sikh conducts a service in English for Sikh children whose Punjabi is not adequate for them to share properly in the normal service. The Sikh Missionary Society based at Gravesend exists not to convert the British but to produce literature about Sikhism in English for use by young Sikhs. Often Sikh children will bring copies of these booklets to school and perhaps small books containing the more famous *Shabads*. One should not, however, ask a child to bring a copy of the *Guru Granth Sahib* to school. Even if the family possesses a copy, it is treated with such respect that its removal from the house would entail a special service, a procession and its ceremonial installation in the building to which it was being taken. At least the occasion would be memorable in the history of the school and in the life of the unfortunate teacher! The *Guru Granth Sahib* is not merely a book, it must be remembered; it is the living word of God, it is the Guru's voice.

PIARA SINGH SAMBHI

1. The *Darbar Sahib* or *Harimandir* is the name given to the building known today as the Golden Temple because of the lavish appearance of the temple as rebuilt by Maharaja Ranjit Singh in the nineteenth century.

WEST INDIANS AND RELIGION

INTRODUCTION

Here I wish to focus on the relevance of religion to the West Indian community, to trace the historical experience and interest in religion of West Indians in the 'islands' and to show how that development affected them as immigrants in Britain. Additionally, I will refer to the contextual situation of religion in the Caribbean both at the time when the majority of West Indian immigrants came to Britain — mainly during the period of British rule— and the post-colonial and contemporary developments which have taken place in some of the major islands of the Caribbean.

HISTORICAL BACKGROUND

One must start with the movement of African slaves from the West Coast of Africa to the Caribbean and other territories of the New World. The islands which eventually became the British Caribbean were not always British but were subjected to the rule of different countries at different periods. It is not surprising, therefore, that with a variety of European colonising countries their own particular established churches eventually effected what more recently would be accepted as the West Indian religious development Malcolm Cross[1] argues, 'It is hardly surprising to find that Roman Catholicism dominates the religious observance in islands subject to Spanish or French colonialism or that Protestantism predominates in most former British or Dutch colonies'. At the same time Elizabeth Thomas Hope[2] suggests that religion reflects the heterogeneity of the Caribbean more than any other cultural phenomenon. 'It reflects the differences in the traditions and colonial policies of Spain, Britain, France and Holland and . . . the common experience of slavery . . .'[3]

Religion was an important aspect of West African culture. Such religions were not, as a rule, monotheistic. The majority of Africans who were taken as slaves to the Caribbean came from the West Coast of Africa, and here the religions were particular to the different tribal or ethnic groups. However, religions in the area consisted of a pattern of worship which, like many others, praised a deity or collective of deities. Family and ancestors also formed a part of the ideological structure of their worship. In this way it was thought that the soul of ancestors played a significant part in determining the position that the living would ultimately enjoy and the experience to be endured after death. Religion in this context therefore had a strong additional appeal, being based on a deification of ancestors. There also was a hierarchy of supreme beings to whom dead ancestors were believed to have access. Worshipping and pleasing ancestors therefore guaranteed those who were still alive a place prepared for them after death. Regular sacrifices and offerings to ancestors were important ceremonies in the religions of West Africa. Additionally, one devoted one's life to the pleasure and acceptance of one's departed ancestors. These observances were carried out in a variety of rituals, some individual, others family, while others were collective, of which singing and dancing formed a part. The offering of food was also an important part of such rituals.

These religions required a variety of artifacts manufactured by certain members of the tribe, who did so as a family tradition. Additionally, there were other members of the tribe who traditionally performed specific functions in the rituals. Items such as ceremonial drums, masks and special utensils were manufactured by special individuals and very often in conditions which were a mystery to the rest of the tribe. When the slaves were taken to the Caribbean, religiously the selection was of a random nature, and perhaps special functionaries who would have been important in providing different aspects of the religious ceremonies and manufacture of artifacts were selected who were able to ensure that the technologies, knowledge of the rituals, etc. were taken intact. This may therefore be one of the reasons why, in spite of the break in the continuation of the open practice of African culture and religion, many of the most secret rites have survived.

The major factor which prevented the wholesale continuation of aspects of traditional African culture among the slaves was the extent of cultural control and repression imposed by the European slave-masters. This control was based entirely on the fear that, if the slaves were able to communicate freely with each other, they would be more likely to plot revolts against the bondage in which they found themselves. They were therefore subjected to a very stringent process of deculturation while at the same time exposed to a new process of acculturation. The penalties for slaves found practising their religions as well as speaking their African mother-tongues were very severe indeed. Those found guilty of such transgressions were put to death in full view of the other slaves. The consequence was the loss of their African culture to a very significant extent and all of their mother-tongues. At the same time it is arguable whether the process of acculturation was based on default rather than design, since the slaves were not actually introduced to European values and norms.

Obviously, having had their native languages taken away from them and being placed with other slaves who did not speak or understand the same language, it became necessary for them to develop forms of communication which their masters were able in some way to understand as well. Therefore, in the case of English-speaking territories they developed an English dialect which we have come to know as Creole.

A similar development also occurred in territories which were controlled by the Dutch, the Spanish and the French. The result in linguistic development in the Caribbean was a rich variety of new languages. These, at one extreme, approximate to the standard form of the original European language while also being forms of those original languages which can be considered as totally new languages. The extent of the approximation to the European standard form correlated with the standard of education of the individual.

The slaves were prevented not merely from communicating in their traditional mother tongues but were also debarred from following other aspects of their culture. However, a significant number of Africans preserved some aspects of their culture, through secret societies, their children, the telling of legends and even open revolution (for example, the Maroons in Jamaica and the slave revolt of Haiti).

Religion played an important part in the life of Africans. It was therefore not surprising that many of them attempted to keep alive their religion and beliefs even under the threat of death. They continued to perform the rituals of homage to their ancestors in strictest secrecy and from the earliest days of slavery syncretised it with the religious celebrations observed by their European masters.

The early slaves were also excluded from the observances of the Christian religions, although there were variations in the islands. In some cases it has been argued that certain priests from the Catholic faith were particularly worried about the souls of these unfortunate people. The Catholic Church encouraged the baptism of all slaves and therefore did show some interest in saving their souls. However, in the case of many of the British territories the concern was mainly with what commercial use could be made of the Africans. Territories which had the longest relation with Britain had larger numbers of Europeans as members of the established Church, which was the Anglican Church. In other territories where there was a preponderance of Spaniards or French the Catholic Church predominated and in islands like Trinidad, which at first was Spanish and later in the eighteenth century became British, there were well-established communities of Catholics and subsequently Anglicans.

As slavery developed and as the movements for abolition took hold, an increasingly active Christian lobby began to emerge. An early concession which was made to slaves was to offer them the Sabbath as a day away from the field. Increasingly, missionaries argued for the right of Christian worship for the slave, and the Bible became an important factor in these processes.

CLASS STRUCTURE

A slave plantation had three categories of slaves: first, there were the field slaves, who formed the majority; second, there were skilled and unskilled slaves who were carpenters, mechanics, etc.; third, there were the house slaves. Another category followed which was based on the complexion of the slave. Status in the three categories of slaves depended on their complexion, a result of the female slaves having been subjected to sexual relations by either a white master or his overseers on the plantation.

The slaves who lived in nearest proximity to an organised social European structure, i.e. the family, adopted the culture of such families more easily. Additionally, it was known that masters took an indirect responsibility for their offspring by ensuring that such slaves became married and were set up in units that had some degree of social stability. Some of these more privileged slaves lived in the same main house as their masters, but in separate quarters. This gave them an insight into their masters' culture which made imitation of such culture patterns much easier. These privileged few were able to practise the teachings of Christianity in a far more organised way both in adopting the beliefs of Christianity and in performing its rituals.

The division of slaves persisted subsequent to the abolition of slavery in the form of social class. The former field slaves continued to make up the bulk of the lower classes, the skilled and semi-skilled slaves developed into a middle class and the light-skinned slaves, through education and inheritance from many of their white ancestors, moved on to an upper middle class. This affected the development of Christianity in the ex-slave societies. It also meant that the established churches continued to be supported both by the middle class and the upper-middle class, while to a large extent new churches of non-conformism and cults, combining aspects of Africanism and Christianity, emerged.

The religious leadership of the working class group tend to produce very radical leaders in the Caribbean. These developments occurred outside of the state or established churches, and were centred among the revivalist Protestant groups. The antipathy between working classes and the lighter-skinned ruling classes of the Caribbean has also had its effect in, if not necessarily driving many people away from the established churches, at least restricting their membership. Social and cultural experience also made it inevitable that most of the darker-skinned peoples would in many respects retain some elements of Africanism in a far more coherent and deliberate way than the lighter-skinned blacks. The latter attempted quite consciously to develop a closer approximation in their culture to their European ancestry, and in some respects they deliberately rejected any contact with their African ancestors. The established churches contained a membership which participated significantly in the commerce and government of the Caribbean. In areas like Trinidad, which became a British colony in the late eighteenth century, there was a conflict between the Catholic and the Anglican Churches based on the fact that Catholicism was still seen to some extent as a threat against the rule of the English. Missionary societies, on the other hand, established non-conformists and revivalist Protestantism, and contributed significantly to social reform and education in the territories.

WEST INDIAN RELIGION TODAY

For West Indians, religion is an important part of their existence. They are monotheistic in the main, although for many of them there would be vestiges of an African tradition which was polytheistic. West Indians in Britain are most active in non-conformist churches and revivalist movements. There is still a significant number who are members of the established Churches and continue to exercise their membership.

In recent years in the Caribbean religion has had a somewhat different experience to that prior to independence, which was gained by the larger islands in the earlier part of the 1960s. In Trinidad in particular, as one can also argue for Jamaica, subsequent to the gaining of independence the islands and their peoples explored the possibility of creating a local identity. In other words, in Trinidad there was a determination to find an identity of 'Trinidadianness' about most things and most activities, while the same would be for Jamaica, Barbados and the more recently independent territories of Grenada, Antigua, etc. In the large islands the Church was as much a part of this endeavour to find a national identity as other aspects, such as language and music. This has been so much so in Trinidad in particular that during the early 1970s in the period of the black consciousness movement the Catholic Church had to make specific efforts to bring about certain changes to its structure. It was forced to re-examine the appointment and training of its priests and nuns, its social relationship with the community and how it perceived the black community which dominated its membership. Bishops and other dignatories of the Church in the Caribbean began to be selected from local priests, mainly as a result of direct action during the black power uprisings in Trinidad in the 1970s.

On a recent visit to Trinidad I was astounded at the change which has taken place. Revivalism seemed to have occurred at a period of great social upheaval. The crime rate has been rising and other forms of social chaos have taken hold of the society. It was with some comfort, therefore, to see this revivalism, which was very marked, particularly among many Trinidadian youth. Additionally, the revivalism was not confined to Afro–Trinidadians only but was also increasingly gaining members from Trinidad's Indian population. There has been a marked growth in the building of churches all over the island, the majority being controlled by revivalist movements which are not connected with any specific established denominational church.

THE SHOUTER BAPTISTS

In Trinidad, the local revivalist movement consisted mainly of what were called the 'Shouter Baptists', who were almost entirely all working-class blacks. They have now established themselves as an island-wide cohesive church which is largely, if not entirely, Trinidadian and Tobagonian, and is a major part of the revivalist movement, with a hierarchy of bishops and other pastors copied from the established churches. The Shouter Baptists have retained many aspects of Africanism which have been incorporated into their own Christian practices. One of their major rituals is the process of *calling*. Someone who is called is pointed out by the preacher or, as will now be acceptably termed, the pastor. On being called, such a person must go through a *mourning* period, which consists of a fast which lasts for about seven days. At the end of this period the called person is placed on a throne of grace. The mourning journey undertaken by the Shouter Baptist is made by the mourner lying on a bare floor of a mud hut. The hut, generally situated well away from any houses, has a total absence of any decorations and is kept spotlessly clean and sometimes whitewashed. During the seven days they are believed to experience a spiritual journey, during which they are given the 'gifts' for which they were called. Such gifts may be to heal the sick, to exorcise demons or to perform a variety of other functions in the service of the Lord Jehovah.

As the mourning fast is observed the called person is only allowed to drink milk and to have nothing else. The traveller is also attended by a 'nurse', who has received the gift of healing and caring at a previous calling. The nurse comforts and also records the experience that the called person expresses throughout the spiritual journey. On emerging from the spiritual journey the called is very weak, and this weakness will have been further aggravated by the eyes of the traveller having been blindfolded for the seven days of mourning. If at the end of the period the traveller has not understood what gifts have been received, then a further period of mourning may be undertaken. However, on completion of the journey and receipt of the gift the traveller is then returned to the flock in order to carry out the work he is gifted to do and to 'preach the word of God throughout all the land'. The gifts received by the traveller are identified by the colour of robes worn — the head tie in the case of women, and the cord or sash that is belted around the waist when in service. In this way people knowledgeable about the Shouter Baptists are able to identify whether such a person is a preacher, a nurse, or whatever gift such a person would have received on his or her spiritual journey.

The Shouter Baptists are monotheistic in essence. Despite this, there are noticeable signs of African traditionalism. Additionally, the syncretism that exists also shows elements of Catholicism. Many of the ceremonies that have evolved in, for instance, the Shouter Baptist movement can also be found in similar religious groups in South Africa, which emerged independently and at about the same time.

PENTECOSTALISM

The other major Africanist revivalist movement in Trinidad has been Pentecostalism. An indication of their popularity is the use they make of both the local radio and the television. These media are used to expose to all Trinidadians the practice of Pentecostalism, and the services consist of much melodic singing accompanied by vigorous movements of the body. Instruments such as tambourines are also used. At one particular church that I attended in Trinidad there was also a band which accompanied the singing. They certainly made a 'joyful sound unto the Lord' with as much enthusiasm as a carnival band.

A factor common to the Africanist revivalism Pentecostals is the use of trance and ecstasy, attained by vigorous singing and preaching, which apparently brings to those in the audience the visitation of the Holy Spirit. When the spirit enters they are alleged to speak 'in tongues'. I witnessed such speaking on my visit to a Pentecostal church in Trinidad. There appeared to be a fluency in whatever language the person in the trance was speaking. It is questionable as to whether this was gibberish or a proper language. It has been claimed that understandable foreign tongues have been spoken by individuals who were not previously conversant with such languages, and it has been verified that they have, during these trances, spoken words from languages of which they had no previous knowledge. Many of the revivalist movements which have taken hold in Trinidad have had contacts with American revivalist churches, and there are regular visits from revivalist preachers from the United States.

THE RASTAFARIANS

The other major religious movement to evolve from the social and industrial experience of the people of the Caribbean is the Rastafarian cult. The Rastafarians have their origins in Jamaica, and are said to have emerged as a direct result of the teachings of Marcus Garvey in the 1910s and 1920s. Like most of the revivalist movements which have emerged from the Caribbean, the Rastafarians are also a sign of the times in which we live as well as a product of the fact that lower working-class blacks in the Caribbean have been subjected to not only slavery in the past but more recently to other forms of oppression. The more recent rise of the Rastafarian movement coincided with the black power movement which swept the Caribbean and much of the black world during the 1960s and 1970s. On my recent visit to Trinidad I was impressed by the extent to which the Rastafarian movement has taken hold there and the large number of black young people who have joined the movement in an endeavour to gain dignity for themselves as Africans in exile and to draw on the commercial success Trinidad has recently gained through its oil economy. Rastafarianism had its origin in a 'Back to Africa' philosophy. More recently it is beginning to play a more specific political organisational and commercial role. Despite many common factors, the West Indians are not a homogenous cultural and religious group. On the one hand, there has been an acceptable type of religious development in that these developments have not varied greatly from the norm. On the other hand, we have seen the development of the Rastafarian movement throughout the Caribbean and in Trinidad in particular, with even more extreme aspects of this development with the 'Friends of the Earth'. To the older black population this trend seems to be a retrograde step, and is not accepted by the majority of the community. This dichotomy to a large extent indicates the change that has developed in the search for a black identity within the social and religious framework over the years. It is also mirrored in the Caribbean community in Britain.

THE CARIBBEAN FAMILY

The black West Indian family in Britain has been subjected to these developments in microcosm, unlike in the Caribbean, where the macro-society is black and a loose extended family structure provides a 'cushion'. Therefore the changes taking place, although socially disruptive, are not as pointedly focused, as has been the case with West Indian family life in Britain. Additionally, the desire to migrate to Britain entailed values and unfulfilled expectations in employment and opportunity for the betterment of the family, of which education was considered to be a major aspect.

The Caribbean family is both matriarchal and matrilineal. The men migrated and the women were therefore left in charge of the children. When the mothers, or girl friends, migrated, grandmother was then left in charge. This migration caused severe breaks in the pattern of family life and administration. In the traditional African experience grandmother has played an important stabilising role in the West Indian family, which has therefore become extremely vulnerable in Britain, where these customs have been discontinued. Thus there is a much greater pressure on mothers and fathers to retain family traditions.

Long working hours and a disproportionate number of working and single-parent mothers have further aggravated the family disruption experienced in Britain.

In addition to the extended family, where grandmother was important, the Church also played a major role in family life, including discipline. Two major differences were observed when the family migrated to Britain from the Caribbean. First, the extent of the importance of the Church and religion in British society differed. Second, the importance of discipline in school life and in the home has less emphasis than in the Caribbean. Therefore, when this is added to other West Indian customs and unfulfilled expectations the stress on the family unit is further compounded. For this reason, the West Indian community is now developing its own churches and is strengthening the social support that these churches can lend to family life in the Caribbean community. On the other hand, the Rastafarian movement is trying to bridge the gap between a cult and an organised acceptable religion. The West Indian community has always been a religious community, and it hopes to preserve its religiousness.

1. M. Cross, *Urbanization and Urban Growth in the Caribbean*, Cambridge University Press, 1979.
2. E. Thomas-Hope, *The Pattern of Caribbean Religions in Afro-Caribbean Religions* (ed.) B. Gates, Ward Lock, 1980.
3. M. Cross, op. cit.

HORACE LASHLEY

A SHORT USEFUL BIBLIOGRAPHY

Bastide, R., *African Civilizations in the New World,* Hurst, 1967.

Braithwaite, E., *Development of Creole Society in Jamaica 1780–1820*, Oxford University Press, 1971.

Caldecott, A., *The Church in the West Indies*, Frank Cass, 1970.

Calley, M., *God's People*, Oxford University Press, 1965.

Clarke E., *My Mother who Fathered Me*, Allen and Unwin, 1966.

Cole, W. O. (ed.), *World Religions: A handbook for Teachers*, CRE 1977.

Cross, M., *Urbanization and Growth in the Caribbean*, Cambridge University Press, 1979.

Femor, P. L., *The Traveller's Tree*, John Murray, 1950.

Gates, B. E. (ed.), *Afro Caribbean Religions,* Ward Lock Educational, 1980.

Gerber, S. N. (ed.), *The Family in the Caribbean*, Institute of Caribbean' Studies, Puerto Rico, New Beacon Books, 1974.

Herskovits, M. J. (ed.), *The Myth of the Negro Past: 1*, Beacon, Boston, (1958).

Hill, C., *Black Churches: West Indian Sects in Britain*, British Council of Churches, 1972.

Horowitz, M. M. (ed.), *Peoples and Cultures of the Caribbean*, Natural History Press, 1971.

James, C. L. R., '*The Middle Classes*', in Lowenthal, D. and Comitas L. (eds), *Consequences of Class and Colour: West Indian Perspectives* pp. 79–92, Doubleday, New York, 1973.

Kilson, M. L., and Rotberg, R. I. (eds) *The African Diaspora: Interpretive Essays,* Howard University Press, 1976.

Lowenthal, D., *West Indian Societies*, Oxford University Press, 1972.

Mitchell, D. I. (ed.), *With Eyes Wide Open*, CADEC, Jamaica.

Salley, C., and Behr, R., *Your God is too White*, Lion, 1973.

Sherlock, P., *The West Indies*, Thames and Hudson, 1976.

Simpson, G. E., *Religious Cults of the Caribbean: Trinidad, Jamaica and Haiti*, McGill, 1970.

Watson, B., *Magic and the Millennium Paladin*, 1975.

RESOURCE GUIDE FOR BOOKS
Materials, Artifacts and Information Concerning Peoples of an Afro–Caribbean Background in Britain

Afro–Caribbean Education Resource Project, Director, Len Garrison, Centre for Learning Resources. 275 Kennington Lane, London SE11 5QZ	01–582 2771
Africa Centre, 38 King Street, London WC2	01–836 1973
Commission for Racial Equality, Elliot House, 10/12 Allington Street, London SW1E 5EH	01–828 7022
Commonwealth Institute, Kensington High Street, London W8 6NO	01–602 3252

Bookshops

Bogle-L'Ouverture Publications, 5a Chignell Place, Ealing W13	01–579 4920
Grass Roots, 61 Golbourne Road, London W10	01–969 0687

Grassroots Bookshop,
1 Newton Street,
Manchester M1 1HW

061–236 3112

Harriet Tubman Bookshop,
27 Grove Lane,
Handsworth,
Birmingham B21 9ES

021–554 8419

Headstart Bookshop,
25 West Green Road,
London N15

01–802 2838

New Beacon Books,
76 Stroud Green Road,
London N4

01–272 4889

Sabarr Books,
121 Railton Road,
London SE24

01–274 6785

Shanti Third World Centre,
Waterloo Place,
178 Oxford Road,
Manchester 13

061–273 5111

NAME (National Association for Multi-Racial Education)

23 Doles Lane, Findern, Derby DE6 6AX

Branches of NAME can be found in most areas with large ethnic minority pupil-populations.

Catalogues can be obtained on application from the following publishers: Nelson Caribbean; Gins Caribbean: Hulton Educational Publications; Longman Caribbean; Macmillan Publishers Ltd. Most other publishers also carry catalogues of multi-cultural books.

Journals

GENERAL

Race and Class; Race Today; West Indian World; Afro–Caribbean Post; Grass Roots; Root; Ebony (USA); *Jamaica Gleaner; Tempo* (free from British West Indian Airways); *New Equals* (CRE).

Caribbean Journal of Education: Roots: Journal of Negro Education
(Howard University, USA): *Black Scholar: CRE Education Journal.*

Caribbean High Commissions

Barbados High Commission	6 Upper Belgrave Street, London SW1	01 235–8686
East Caribbean High Commission	10 Kensington Court, London W8	01 937–0854
Grenada High Commission Horace Lashley *Education Officer, Commission for Racial Equality*	102–5 Grand Buildings, Trafalgar Square, London WC2	01 839–5922
Guyana High Commission	3 Palace Court, Bayswater Road, London W2	01 229–7684
Jamaica High Commission	50 St James St, London SW1A 1JS	01 499–8600
Trinidad and Tobago High Commission	42 Belgrave Square, London SW1	01 245–9351

BRINGING UP CHILDREN THE BUDDHIST WAY

Whilst we in Britain live in a multi-racial and multi-religious society, there are considerable differences between the Buddhist community and others such as the Christian, Islamic Jewish, Hindu or other minorities. The immigrants and descendants of immigrant groups brought with them or retain their distinctive religious and cultural traditions, and they also have children who have grown up in these. As a general rule, there are few immigrant Buddhists (these tend to be adult anyhow), and the Buddhist population consists largely of people of British origin who have converted to Buddhism in adult life.

So, in brief, we may say that the religious minorities are family groups, usually of foreign origin, whereas the Buddhist population is made up of indigenous Englishmen, Welshmen or Scotsmen, who, when they are married, have to face the instruction of their children as a fresh issue, with no previous experience to guide them.

In these circumstances, which are quite different from those faced by Buddhist communities in the United States, where there are *Dharma* schools (Sunday Schools) and *Dharma* classes organised by the Buddhist Churches of America, the task of bringing up children in a Buddhist way is beset with great difficulties. In the first place, apart from the total lack of organised classes as in Buddhist countries or countries with long-established Buddhist groups, there is the matter of making a child feel unhappy and 'out of things' if he or she is subject to any exclusion from the activities of friends and those in the immediate home or school surroundings. Nothing is calculated to upset children more than being made to feel strange or peculiar. So very often Buddhist parents simply do nothing about Buddhist religious instruction in schools or colleges, where it is practically never available anyway, and confine themselves to the attempt to convey something of the Buddhist spirit day by day.

In the United States there are well-thought-out programmes of *Dharma* schools, and many handbooks are produced to help teachers in these classes. But there is no religious instruction in *schools*, and since this applies to most children there, it is not a problem, since all religious communities have to cope with such teaching in out-of-school hours one way or another. Here Christian education, or, at any rate, religious instruction, is compulsory, and from the nature of our residual Christian traditions it consists mainly of biblical or Christian subjects, except where the parents can make arrangements for their children to be withdrawn from the class for that period. As observed above, however, this makes the child feel isolated, and is very seldom done. In

47

any case, Buddhists think that it is a good thing for children to know something of other religions.

In fairness to teachers these days, there are now many attempts to introduce into religious classes some idea of faiths other than the Christian one, and efforts are often made to be fair to minority groups by touching on all religions instead of restricting everything to conventional Christianity, as used to be the case in my own schooldays. Bodies like the Shap Working Party, the standing Conference for Inter-Faith Dialogue in Education and several others, mainly of an *ad hoc* or unofficial nature, are making strenuous and diligent efforts to produce material on all the world religions.

Whereas some Christians and others, notably Muslims and Sikhs, still feel strongly that instruction should only be given in their own faiths, it is also true that many are willing to have their children taught the elements of all faiths, to lessen the barriers between people and to broaden the outlook of children who have to live with those of another life-view. There is a natural tendency for parents of strong religious conviction to want their children to follow them, and to fear the introduction of 'alien' religious customs or ideas.

Buddhists do not believe that any religion has a monopoly of truth, but that reality is to be found everywhere and in all people, though naturally, for themselves, they feel that the Buddha, the Supremely Enlightened One, taught the realities more directly and more effectively than other teachers, or they would not be Buddhists. They are so, in Britain, by deliberate choice rather than upbringing as yet. So it is fair to say that Buddhists feel secure in the belief that what the Buddha taught is true and will lead from ignorance to Enlightenment. He made it clear that all men are potential Buddhas and could undergo the same experience.

Perhaps, apart from extensive reading of the many Buddhist books now available in English (many of them published in London), Buddhists may feel that their families will absorb the teachings over the years in this way, coupled with the example and influence of parents.

So as formal Buddhist education in Britain is unlikely in the near future and as children of Buddhist families are often quite indistinguishable from others ethnically or by language, it would be unrealistic to expect more than a mention of Buddhism in schools along with other faiths under the new syllabi. Whereas the ethnic minorities, and the 'imported' religions (imported in the sense that they were brought over by immigrants) will feel a need to maintain themselves and their identity, for some time, and possibly permanently, British-born Buddhists feel themselves part of the community at large, retaining some of the underlying traditions but having an *interior* conviction in the truth of the *Dharma*. This relieves them from the need to overstress their differences, but, by the same token, it also makes them less of a distinguishable community.

What is then needed in bringing up children by Buddhist parents? First, there should be a sense of always looking for the realities behind the appearances. The All-Enlightened One, the Buddha, taught us to look at things not as they seem to be, but as they are in their essence. He also taught us not to accept ideas on hearsay or mere tradition, but only if they accorded with our experience and with reason. Blind beliefs of any kind were firmly ruled out.

Second, followers of the All-Compassionate One (another name for the Buddha) will try to be kind to all living beings, human or animal. This quality, like most vital human characteristics, can only be caught rather than formally taught, and the influence of parents is again vital here. It is in the home environment that the non-harming and questioning attitudes are first and most effectively learned.

There are those who doubt the validity of the religious, denominational schools, and there has been much controversy on the matter in the Catholic press. It has been asserted that many of those attending Catholic schools, and being indoctrinated in Catholicism, fall away from the faith in later life, whilst many of those who attended non-Catholic schools retain their beliefs. My own experience at church schools confirms this every time I attend a reunion! I am far from being the only one to have changed faiths or abandoned faith and practice altogether. So we need not exaggerate the importance of religious teaching in schools as such, though a knowledge of the main ideas of all faiths is bound to be useful in a general educational and social sense.

Formal teaching of religion always has its drawbacks. In many instances the teacher is not especially interested in the subject, sometimes, as I have found in visiting schools, being 'saddled' with religious education because the headmaster could not find anyone else to do it! In any event, no teacher could possibly understand deeply all faiths, even if conversant with his own or one particular one. So the most we can realistically expect is that an open-minded teacher will try to convey general beliefs held by the various religions, and not make any attempt to push one of them at the expense of others. In this atmosphere, the more dispassionate and, later on, academic the tone, the better. The 'religious' content of the individual's thinking is the prerogative of the parents and the ministers concerned.

The main truths of the Buddhist religion are simple enough to grasp and memorise — such simple lists as the Four Noble Truths, the Eightfold Path, the Twelve *Nidanas*, the Six Perfections and the Three Signs of Being. Above all, perhaps, the Three Poisons are to be eradicated — those of greed, anger and selfish illusion of a permanent and separate soul. Beyond these simple and elementary statements lies a vast hinterland of development philosophy, expanded religious thinking, scriptural and commentarial literature and personal and public devotions. But these have to be acquired gradually and naturally, and cannot be made the subject of classroom study except in a very general way.

It is very likely that for some considerable time the majority of Buddhists will come from those who have left other faiths, or never had any very definite faith. In other words, adult converts, who consciously choose to take refuge in the Buddha, His Teaching and His Community. Such people have not been affected by scholastic considerations, nor by any one particular religious tradition. They are unlikely to concern themselves very heavily with school training in Buddhism, though they may well try hard to pass on to their children the basic tenets of their faith, and encourage them in the main virtues of the Buddha's *Dharma*. A smile may do more than a sermon in this respect, and children, above all others, detect the genuineness of what people profess to believe. So, in the last resort, the quality of their parents' lives will determine what children really think, hopefully reinforced and expanded by the teaching of ministers (or monks in one tradition) and those who arrange Buddhist groups and meetings, or give private instruction in the deeper aspects of the *Dharma*.

SELECT BIBLIOGRAPHY

A Program of studies for Buddhist Sunday Schools, Buddhist Churches of America, 1960.

Buddha Loves Everyone, Buddhist Churches of America, 1970.

Lord Buddha is with Me, Buddhist Churches of America, 1970.

Lord Buddha Speaks to Me, Buddhist Churches of America, 1973.

Children in the Church, Iris Cully, Westminster Press, Philadelphia.

Creative Teaching in the Church, Mossison and Foster, Prentice-Hall, New Jersey.

The Teaching of Buddha (Teachers' Guide Series), Buddhist Churches of America, 1962.

Buddhist Reader for Several Years, (for primary, intermediate and junior), Research Dept, Seattle Buddhist Church, 1967.

Crystals of the Dharma, Seattle Buddhist Church.

Buddhism for Youth. Part one — Buddha and His Disciples Buddhist Churches of America, 1962.

Nursery Stories, Research Dept., Seattle Buddhist Church, 1961.

Many painting books, readers and other material published by the Buddhist Churches of America.

The Dhammapada, Jack Austin, The Buddhist Society. The most famous and simplest of the Scriptures.

A Short History of Buddhism, Edward Conze, Allen and Unwin, 1980.

(There are so many hundreds of books in English on the subject that it is impossible to do more than give a sample.)

JACK AUSTIN

THE RELIGIOUS BELIEFS AND CUSTOMS OF HINDUS, JEWS, MUSLIMS AND SIKHS AS THEY MAY AFFECT THE SCHOOL SITUATION

Although in Bradford, Leicester, many London boroughs and other parts of Britain the communities listed above are of longstanding and highly respected, this section is included because each year some young teacher will be coming into a multi-faith school. Also, schools which used to represent one cultural tradition are themselves likely to discover one September morning that they have become multi-cultural.

The first requirement of the teacher is that of informed sensitivity. To call a Muslim a 'Muhammadan' is to betray ignorance and so undermine one's status just as much as one would by offering a Jew (or a Muslim) a ham sandwich! To pour extra gravy on the plate of an Indian child who has refused meat might be kindly meant but it has probably made the whole meal inedible. To ask a Jewish child his 'Christian name' is a very common slip. It may be a natural reaction to say when a new child says he is called 'Satnam' (or in the case of a West Indian 'Beauregard') 'What a funny name': it can also hurt. To conclude that all West Indians come from Jamaica is no less thoughtless and demonstrative of ignorance.

It is important to recognise that in the faiths under discussion the separation of culture and belief is not as distinctive as it often is in Britain. This is particularly true of people recently come from Asia. To ask whether the wearing of the *shalwar* is simply cultural or whether it has anything to do with religion is to ask a Western question which may be meaningless to a person from the East. Consequently, the girl who is told she must wear a skirt and not the *shalwar* is likely to conclude that her religious beliefs are under attack.

Other faiths are no less complex than Christianity. There are orthodox Jews and many liberal Jews. There are some for whom the term 'Jewish' has no real religious significance but refers to a valued heritage. One can meet Muslim atheists, Pakistani Christians, and people whose religion apparently means nothing in terms of ethics. The teacher needs to guard against stereotyping human beings. All are different, in spite of generalisations which may be made in this article.

It is in areas of food and clothing that the difference of culture is most likely to be encountered.

FOOD

The Jewish child may prefer not to eat school meals at all because the religious requirements refer to much more than not eating pork. Hindus will not eat beef, and this includes beef extract gravy of course! They may also be vegetarians, in some cases refusing to eat eggs. For others, fish and eggs may be acceptable. The Sikh, because he has lived as a minority group among Hindus and Muslims may avoid eating both beef and pork, though many Sikh children in Britain will have no such reservations. Muslims will not eat pork but also, like Jews and Jehovah's Witnesses, and some West Indian groups, they will not eat meat with the blood in it (or such foods as black pudding), that is, meat killed by some process of stunning the beast rather than severing an artery. The usual method of slaughter found in England is that which is contrary to Muslim practice and therefore, often, Muslim children will not eat meat in school.

The Western use of the knife and fork is regarded as odd by many people who come from the Indian subcontinent and teachers of small children may have to assist them in coming to terms with such implements, though nowadays many Asian parents prepare their children for eating school meals the Western way so they have the experience of older brothers and sisters to guide them.

The left hand is normally used for toilet purposes by Asians; therefore food is eaten with the right hand and things are usually given or received with that hand. (One would not give a Delhi bus conductor one's fare with the left hand!)

CLOTHING

The Muslim is encouraged to dress modestly, and in thinking of the Pakistani child all thoughts of 'Turkish Delight' should be dismissed from the mind. A girl's clothes should not define her physical features and often red and silken garments are avoided. Although small girls may wear dresses or skirts long before they reach puberty Muslims will adopt the *shalwar* (trouser reaching to the ankle) and a tunic called the *kameez*. This will often be the dress of Sikh girls, as their Punjab homeland has been under strong Muslim influence for over five hundred years. Hindu girls are much more likely to adopt mini-skirts or school uniform, though, as with diet, this can vary from family to family.

The Muslim emphasis on modesty is likely to show itself in a number of other, sometimes related, ways. As she approaches puberty a girl might be sent back to Pakistan rather than be allowed to grow to womanhood in our permissive society. If she remains, her parents are unlikely to let her go out at night to clubs or dances even on the school premises and may not wish her to find employment upon leaving school.

Some will demand their immediate return home at 4 p.m. Boys may be protected rather less than daughters, but Asian parents generally are horrified at the way in which British parents let their children do what they like and don't know where they are half the time!

Mixed swimming and PE lessons can be embarrassing, but often solutions have been found along the lines of avoiding mixed swimming or allowing girls to do PE in slacks. The adoption of the trouser suit by English society has come at a fortunate time; many schools permit their Asian (and English girls) to wear the *shalwar* or trousers in the school colour or one of several colours, and everyone is happy.

The attitude of Sikh parents to the dress their girls adopt and to their social activities is variable, and often they have professional aspirations for their daughters. However, the school should attempt sensitively to enable the girl and her family to make their own response to British society rather than seeming to be attempting to alienate her from her traditional culture.

A few comments follow about each other group in turn.

THE JEWS

Most Jewish children are third-generation members of British society. Their parents have decided upon their attitudes and responses, and at a social level they are no longer finding their way. Few difficulties should arise in school, though anti-semitism in the playground and, sometimes, the classroom is not unknown.

HINDUS

Hindus may come from Gujarat, the Punjab, East Africa or other places. They may speak Gujarati, Hindi, Punjabi or some other language. They may only be able to speak to one another in English! Some may have more in common with an Englishman than with another Indian.

Caste is not likely to be of considerable importance in school for people who have left the sub-continent, though sometimes social mixing may be avoided, and two Indian boys might not wish to sit together or necessarily be in the same team. (However, in this respect English society is not free of class, and children from 'poor' homes have been known to suffer at the hands of classmates and teachers in our schools.) Sometimes a boy will be found to be wearing the sacred thread of his caste, and this might present a danger in PE. However, it is not something he should be asked to take off, like a watch. Wearing a sports vest or a football shirt, or the avoidance of body-contact games may be the solution. Some, though not all, Indians may find body contact sports repugnant, but one hopes that in games we are reaching the position where those who do not like football or cricket can play tennis or badminton, or volleyball, go for a run or a walk, even perhaps play chess!

MUSLIMS

Often Muslim children come from backgrounds in which education may have been optional, very formal and perhaps religious — the memorising of the *Qur'an*. The 'play way' of British primary schools may be suspect, and the whole education system seem as an attempt to supplant Islamic faith and culture with Christianity and Western permissiveness.

The month of *Ramadhan* (see section on festivals, p. 00) is one in which Muslim adults should fast; it is observed even by Muslims whose religion is generally most casual. Often very young children will follow parental example, refusing school milk or meals during this period.

The drawing of the human face or form, and sometimes of animals and birds, is often disliked by Muslims, and the case has been known of a Muslim child drawing pictures in school and depositing them in large numbers at a Christian friend's home because they would be unwelcome at home! Geometrical patterns may be more appropriate art forms for Muslim children than pictures of people and animals, despite the Mogul miniatures in the Victoria and Albert Museum!

SIKHS

The steel bracelet (*kara*) on the right wrist of the Sikh boy or girl is not an ornament but a reminder of the unity of God and of the Sikh brotherhood. The teacher should not demand its removal. The long hair is also of religious significance and, especially when the boy is young and not yet wearing a turban, it may be necessary for the teacher to defend him from ridicule. The short sword (*kirpan*) need cause no alarm. If carried, it is likely to be merely in the form of an outline of a dagger 1 cm long embedded in the comb worn in the hair!

Sikh names may cause confusion. Sikhs take the name *Singh* (boys) or *Kaur* (girls) and may use it as a surname. So Khushwant Singh may have a sister Manjit Kaur and their father may be Mr Dandi! In fact, the children's full name is Kushwant Singh Dandi or Manjit Kaur Dandi.

Difficulties can arise, and there are a number of ways of overcoming them. Often the matter can be taken to an older brother or sister who has faced and overcome the difficulty, or the advice of a colleague experienced in multi-cultural education can be obtained. The parents might be invited to school and consulted. They will be found extremely understanding and helpful. The Community Relations Officer is someone else who can provide assistance. The *Imam*, president of the *Gurdwara*, or some other senior member of the child's community might be approached.

Normally, once parents or community leaders realise that the teacher and school is as concerned for the wellbeing and happiness of the child as they are, co-operation will be assured.

Sensitivity cannot be learned from books but they can provide knowledge. A few are listed below.

Scope, Handbook 1, Butterworth & Kinniburgh, Longman.
New Backgrounds, R. Oakley (ed.), Oxford University Press.
Chapter 6 of *Comparative Religion in Education*, J. R. Hinnells (ed.), Oriel Press.
Comparative Religions, Charing, Cole, El-Droubie, Pancholi and Sambhi, Blandford Press.

FESTIVAL DATES

Children love festivals, with their opportunities for dressing-up, exchanging gifts, singing songs, old and new, and acting out familiar stories.

This enjoyment need not be limited to Christmas. It may be possible, with the help of children in the school and local religious leaders and parents, to stage a festival from another culture. Just as children from other faiths share in our festivals so we can help British children to share in the joy and excitement of those special days which mean so much to their friends.

Even if it is difficult to celebrate these festivals it is hoped that these notes will help the teacher and children to understand why their friends may sometimes be absent from school on one of their festival days.

Where there are no children of other faiths the children could be helped to know more about children in other parts of Britain and throughout the world by telling the stories and acting out the situations described.

The festivals listed below are set in the context of religious communities in this country. Details of further material about each religion is contained in the resource and book lists.

Table of Jewish Holy Days

		1983	1984	1985	1986	1987	1988
PURIM							
Passover *(Pesach)*	1st day	27 Feb.	18 Mar.	7 Mar.	25 Mar.	15 Mar.	3 Mar.
Pentecost *(Shavuot)*	1st day	18 May	6 June	26 May	13 June	3 June	22 May
		5744	5745	5746	5747	5748	5749
New Year *(Rosh Hashanah)*	1st day	8 Sept.	27 Sept.	16 Sept.	4 Oct.	24 Sept.	12 Sept.
Day of Atonement *(Yom Kippur)*		17 Sept.	6 Oct.	25 Sept.	13 Oct.	3 Oct.	21 Sept.
Tabernacles *(Sukkot)*	1st day	22 Sept.	11 Oct.	30 Sept.	18 Oct.	8 Oct.	26 Sept.
PURIM		1989	1990	1991	1992	1993	1994
Passover *(Pesach)*	1st day	20 Apr.	10 Apr.	30 Mar.	18 Apr.	6 Apr.	27 Mar.
Pentecost *(Shavuot)*	1st day	9 June	30 May	19 May	7 June	26 May	16 May
New Year *(Rosh Hashanah)*	1st day	30 Sept.	20 Sept.	9 Sept.	28 Sept.	16 Sept.	6 Sept.
Day of Atonement *(Yom Kippur)*		9 Oct.	29 Sept.	18 Sept.	7 Oct.	25 Sept.	15 Sept.
Tabernacles *(Sukkot)*	1st day	14 Oct.	4 Oct.	23 Sept.	12 Oct.	30 Sept.	20 Sept.

THE JEWISH FESTIVALS

The Jewish New Year is in September, and instead of 1983 it will be 5743, the number of years from the Creation according to calculations based on the book of Genesis. When Jews and others use our time-scheme which is reckoned from the birth of Jesus, they refer to BCE (before the Common Era) and CE (Common Era, ie AD).

The New Year, or *Rosh Hashanah* means the 'Head of the Year.' The *Shofar* (ram's horn), is blown in the synagogue to awaken the conscience to new effort. It is a day of reflection, combining repentance with prayer for the future. The period lasts for ten days and ends with

The Day of Atonement. During the ten days quarrels will have been made up and on *Yom Kippur* all but the children and the sick will fast and remember those who have died as well as their own wrong-doings.

The Feast of the Tabernacles. The *Sukkah* is a little hut built in the garden out of branches, leaves and twigs. Where this is not possible a trellis is erected on a window-ledge which can be decorated. It is both a harvest festival of thanksgiving for the completed harvest and a reminder of God's care for his people when they lived in 'booths' in the wilderness.

The Feast of Lights, or *Hanukkah*, sometimes spelt *Chanucah*, means 'dedication'. In practice there are many similarities to Christmas such as the exchanging of gifts and the holdings of parties. It marks the cleansing and re-dedication of the Jewish Temple by Judas Maccabeus in 165 BCE. The Temple had been desecrated by Antiochus Epiphanes of Syria. When Judas re-entered the Temple they celebrated for eight days. Throughout this time the Temple candelabrum was lit from a miraculous supply of oil. Today in the synagogue and home eight candles are lit on a special candlestick (the *Menorah*), one for each day of the feast. Children are reminded of the heroes who died for the faith to enable the light of truth to shine in the darkness. It has become a symbol of Jewish education as the children are encouraged to dedicate their own lives to the service of God. You will find the story in the Apocrypha which contains the books between the Old and New Testaments, in 2 Maccabeus, chapter 10.

Purim is a time of great rejoicing in Israel in February or March. The story is told in the book of Esther in the Old Testament. Haman, a Persian leader, cast lots (*Purim*) to decide the way on which he would attack the Jews. The Jews were saved and today Haman is carried in effigy and burnt and the story is enacted by the children.

The Passover is the feast of deliverance recalling not only how the Jews were set free from slavery in Egypt but the continued persecution throughout their history. The story of the Passover night (Exodus 12) is repeated in the home through the traditional words of the *Haggadah*. In the special meal there are bitter herbs to remind them of suffering, roasted shank of lamb to remind them of the lambs sacrificed, a sweet mixture of honey and nuts to symbolise the joy of being set free and an egg to symbolise the new life on which they are entering.

The Feast of Weeks, Pentecost or *Shavuoth*, is a reminder of the giving of the law on Mount Sinai. It is interesting to note that on the second day the book of Ruth is read, reminding Jews that an ancestress of David was not a daughter of Israel but a foreigner from Moab. It is also a harvest festival giving thanks for the harvesting of the wheat and the first of the grapes and other fruits.

MUSLIM FESTIVALS

Muslim festivals are linked with the *Five Pillars of Islam*, especially No. 4 *Saum* (or fasting) and No. 5 *Haji* (or pilgrimage to Mecca). The prayers are led by an *Imam* who may deliver a sermon on the Friday. Although he is a layman and not ordained, he is often compared in this country to the Jewish Rabbi or Christian clergyman, as he also performs marriage and burial ceremonies, gives instruction to Muslim children and looks after the mosque.

Saum

This 'pillar' is compulsory to all but children and the sick. The month of fasting is called *Ramadhan*, the month when it is believed the *Qur'an* was given by Allah. Between sunrise and sunset for every day of the month Muslims abstain from all food and drink. This 'abstinence' enables young Muslims to appreciate the gifts which God has given them. The fast lasts for 29 to 30 days, depending on the sighting of the moon. It ends with the festival of *Id-ul-Fitr*. The festival lasts for three days and begins with prayer in the mosque. Gifts must be given to the poor and children wear new clothes and school books, clothes and toys are given to them. Friends visit each other or send special festival cards.

Hajj

This should be made at least once in a lifetime. The pilgrim must first go to Mecca to kiss the Black Stone in the wall of the Kaaba and walk around it seven times, and then go to Mount Arafat and ask forgiveness. This should ideally be carried out in the 8th–13th day of the last month of the Islamic calendar. The feast of *Id-ul-Adha* is held on the tenth day of this month.

In addition the Festival of *Id-ul-Adha* is connected with the sacrifice of Ishmael, reminding Muslims that they should not hesitate to sacrifice anything for the glory of God. Instead of alms, the sacrifice of a goat or lamb is usually made during this festival.

Muhurram

Muhurram marks the death of Hussain who was killed in battle exactly 40 years after the death of Muhammad. Muhammad also fasted on this day to celebrate the victory of Moses over Pharoah when the Egyptians were drowned in the Red Sea. One group of Muslims, called Shias, trace their group back to Hussain, and therefore this festival is most important to them. For the main group (*Sunnis*) it is regarded as the New Year.

DATES OF FESTIVALS

	1983 (1404)	1984 AH (1405)	1985 AH (1406)	1986 (1407)	1987 AH (1408)	1988 AH (1409)
Muhurram	9 Oct.	28 Sept.	17 Sept.	7 Sept.	26 Aug.	15 Aug.
Prophet's Day	18 Dec.	12 Dec.	27 Nov.	16 Nov.	6 Nov.	24 Oct.
1st *Ramadhan*	13 June	2 June	22 May	11 May	30 Apr.	19 Apr.
Eid-ul-Fitr	29 or 30 days after beginning of *Ramadhan*, depending on the sighting of the moon					
Eid-ut-Adha	20 Sept.	9 Sept.	29 Aug.	18 Aug.	7 Aug.	27 July

HINDU FESTIVALS

There are many festivals celebrated throughout the regions of India, but two of the main ones are as follows.

Holi

Holi or festival of Colour, usually in February or March. Like Trinidad's 'Carnival', this festival is celebrated with great gaiety. It is the time of 'wild childish pranks' and red powder and water is thrown over everyone up to midday. It is a harvest thanksgiving as the spring wheat is harvested in the country at this time with much singing and merrymaking. In the orthodox Hindu tradition the Lord Krishna, symbolised in popular pictures as a 'Blue God', returns to the temple city of Gokul near Delhi, playing his flute and dancing with the milkmaids (*gopis*). One of the cow-herds dancing for joy, smears the *gopis* with curry powder mixed in milk. They in turn take red cosmetic powder and sprinkle it on the men.

Diwali

Diwali (the New Year Festival of Lights) is celebrated in October or November. Rama was one of the avatars of Vishnu. In the story which lies behind the festival he is depicted as a model prince. He was born into a noble family and married a beautiful girl called Sita. Through family intrigue Rama went into exile with Sita, his wife. She was sitting alone in their cottage when she was attacked by Ravana, the Demon King, who was disguised as a wandering monk. He carried her off to Ceylon. After a long journey and many adventures Rama reached the coast opposite Ceylon. He was advised by the monkey god, Hanuman, to build a bridge. This was done by throwing rocks into the sea. Rama crossed over with his 'army of righteousness', rescued the queen and returned to India. The people welcomed him with shouts and cheers and asked him to rule over them again. From that day the occasion is remembered as a time when good overcame evil, and when light triumphed over darkness.

At the present time lamps are ceremonially lit, housefronts are illuminated and presents are exchanged. Homes are given a thorough cleaning and outlined with tiny clay lamps to welcome into the home Lakshmi, the goddess of prosperity and wife of Vishnu. Some make an effigy of the Demon King, Ravana, and burn it on a bonfire; fireworks and crackers are set off to frighten away the evil spirits to the great enjoyment of the children. Shopkeepers not only light up their shops but open new account books on this day and everyone eats sweets and cakes.

SIKH FESTIVALS

The festival of *Diwali* is celebrated by Sikhs as well as Hindus and is the second of the large Sikh assemblies during the year. The first is *Baisakhi* (13 and 14 April), each year. This is the first day of the Sikh and Hindu New Year. For the Sikhs it is a reminder of the founding of the Khalsa by Guru Gobind Singh. The story is that on this festival day in 1699 the Guru came out of his tent demanding the head of one of his followers. The people were horrified but eventually one volunteered. He was taken to the tent, the sword was heard to fall and the Guru came out with a blood-stained sword demanding another head! In all there were five volunteers! Then the tent flap was drawn to reveal five beheaded goats and five very happy Sikhs, alive and well. These five had been chosen in this way to form the basis of the new order of the Khalsa. They were then baptised by the Guru who was himself baptised by them into the Order. In these days it is a great time of festivity for all Sikhs.

A note on calendars and systems of dating

In this book CE, standing for Common Era, is used instead of AD, which, in a sense, is a Christian affirmation 'The Year of our Lord' which one cannot expect people of other faiths to share.

61

In many books about Guru Nanak or Indian history the *Bikram* dating is used, year one being 58 years before the Common Era, (BCE). In this year King Vikramditya, according to legend, won a great victory and commemorated it by inaugurating a new era.

The Hindu religious calendar of twelve lunar months, necessitating the insertion of a leap month periodically, begins in March–April.

The Muslim era dates from the migration (*hijra*) of Muhammad and his followers from Mecca to Medina in 622 CE. Again Muslims use the lunar calendar of 354 days for religious purposes but do not insert leap years or leap months. Consequently Muslim festivals and anniversaries vary by eleven days from year to year, according to the Western calendar and a mathematical calculation is necessary if the AH (after Hijra) equivalent of CE date is to be discovered.

$$CE = AH + 622 - \frac{AH}{33}$$

$$AH = CE - 622 + \frac{CE - 622}{32}$$

The Jewish religious calendar dates from a biblical calculation of the beginning of creation.

Although a lunar calendar is used it is adjusted so that festivals and anniversaries vary within limits of about six weeks, as for example, the Christian Easter does.

For further information see *Shap Book of Religious Festivals*, W. O. Cole, (ed.) Longman (provisional title). and the Calendar of Festivals which forms part of the annual Shap Mailing.

BOOKS ON THE HOMELAND, CULTURAL BACKGROUNDS AND CUSTOMS OF ASIAN AND CARIBBEAN COMMUNITIES IN BRITAIN

Comparative Religions, Charing, Cole, El-Droubie, Pancholi and Sambhi, Blandford Press, 1982. In this book a Jew, a Christian, a Muslim, a Hindu and a Sikh introduce their religions to the general reader. Useful for teachers and social workers, ministers of religion and nurses as well as in the classroom.

The Background of Immigrant Children, I. Morrish, Allen and Unwin, 1971. Provides information about education and society in the 'sending countries'. It may be a little dated, as the title is, but the best book of its kind.

East Meets West, M. Iqbal (ed.), CRE, 1982. The successor to *East Comes West*. Covers Hinduism, Islam and Sikhism. A book for teachers.

Between Two Cultures, J. Watson (ed.), Blackwell, 1977. Studies of various communities in Britain including Chinese and Caribbean but not Hindu. A useful book for teachers.

Between Two Cultures, M. Anwar, CRE, 1976. A study of relationships between generations in the Asian communities of Britain. Especially useful for any who work with Asian teenagers.

Colour and Citizenship, E. J. B. Rose (ed.), Oxford University Press, 1969. Somewhat dated, but, for those wishing to understand the origins, reasons and consequences of immigration to Britain, still important.

At the time of compiling this brief list materials prepared for the Open University course, *Ethnic Minorities and Community Relations* (E354), are not available to the general public. When they are they will provide valuable additional reading.

COMING TOGETHER — A PERSONAL VIEW

The previous sections have been written in order to provide readers with accurate information about upbringing of children in the Hindu, Jewish, Muslim and Sikh faiths. My purpose now is to focus more precisely upon the coming together of cultures so that misunderstandings may be avoided and the opportunities which a multi-cultural society offers may be enjoyed as fully as possible. In many respects this is a personal view, but it is the product of fourteen years of mixing with and learning from Hindus, Muslims and Sikhs, as well as Jews and West Indians.

MIGRATION AND SETTLEMENT

If this section could have only one beneficial result it might be that we cease to use the word 'immigrant' when referring to Asian or Caribbean members of our society. One head teacher, when asked about the 'immigrant intake' into his secondary school in September 1976, conceded that only one child had been born outside Britain. Asked when he would stop calling these children 'immigrants' he said 'When their English is good enough!' Often one suspects it will be when their skins turn white, for it seems to be a term reserved for certain ethnic groups, but applied much less to Poles or Hungarians (this headmaster was himself Irish). Migration from the Indo–Pakistan sub-continent or the Caribbean needs to be put into its historical context, otherwise it will seem odd and be inexplicable.

The fact is that Jamaicans, Gujaratis, Sikhs and many other people who have found their way to Britain since 1945 already enjoyed a reputation as migrants. Sikhs, for example, are to be found in East Africa, California, Canada, Australasia, the islands of the Pacific and the East Indies as well as Singapore, Thailand and now the Arab Gulf states. You can meet West Indians from Guyana or Trinidad who are Hindus or Muslims. Their ancestors went to the Caribbean one hundred and fifty years ago. Once the European, as ruler, colonised their countries, and they are now settling in the mother-country, just as Indonesians have gone to Holland and Algerians to France.

A careful reading of history will show that as far back as knowledge goes, man has been a migrant. The movement of people is as natural as the seasonal migration of birds. Often the process has been accompanied by pain and suffering, but frequently the migrants have been the most enterprising members of the land from which they came, and their settlement, though seldom welcomed at the time, has proved to be to the social, economic and cultural benefit of the indigenous population. Perhaps we might remember that Britain is like a massive Heath-

row Airport. Its arrivals have been from other parts of Europe —
Saxons, Vikings, Normans, Huguenots, Jews, Irish, Poles, Serbians,
Hungarians and Italians — and its departures have been to North
America, the Caribbean, Australia, New Zealand, most of Africa, India
and even to the Argentine — the Welsh of Patagonia! Asians, including
Vietnamese, and West Indians are only the latest, but probably not the
last, arrivals.

The reason for their coming was largely economic. In their own
countries they were not the very poor, otherwise they could not have
afforded the passage to Britain. They were not the very rich, who
seldom have any incentive to uproot themselves. They were people in
the middle, seeking opportunity but frustrated in their homelands.
Britain was known to be wealthy and in need of labour. These were
the years of the slogan 'You've never had it so good'. Industry even
advertised and made other efforts to recruit workers from the Indian
sub-continent and the Caribbean. This was at a time when some British
industries were running down, but quite naturally the ship-worker on
the Wear or the miner in South Yorkshire or the Welsh valleys was not
prepared to move to Leicester and retrain as a textile worker or change
one underground job for another, with London Transport. The Asians
and West Indians who came to Britain in the 1950s came to meet a
need Britain could not supply from within. The places in which they
have settled and the forms of employment they took say much about
the economic situation in Britain at that time. Besides undertaking jobs
no-one else wanted and avoiding increasing high unemployment, Asians
and West Indians occupied houses and districts which the indigenous
population was vacating. They did not make such areas as Chapeltown
in Leeds into what they are; they were already in decline. Often they
stopped the rot. The grim exteriors and unswept streets often disguise
homes which are in good repair, well furnished and friendly. One old
lady (white) told me that her house, in which she was living until only
a few months ago, had been condemned in the 1950s long before any
'blacks' moved into the neighbourhood.

'They've come to take our houses and our jobs' is a lie which is in
danger of becoming part of British folklore. If children undertake an
objective study of man as a migrant and of the social and economic
history of their own city in environmental studies, fact may replace
malicious gossip. No bad thing, even if changing attitudes is far more
difficult.

Sikhs and Muslims certainly had little intention of bringing their
wives and families to Britain. The climate may have deterred them to
some extent, but more important was the fact that they would be part
of a society in which white western Christian culture was dominant.
Many Asians say that they never intended to stay, and they still express
an intention to go home one day. A major reason for staying was the

immigration legislation of the early 1960s, which closed the door, giving them the choice to stay alone or bring their families, or, if they left, not to be able to return. They had not yet saved up enough to establish themselves back home, so the natural choice was to stay.

The establishment of complete Asian households in Britain has had a number of consequences. There is a tug-of-love between the home country and Britain. Parents will always long for their own country, as my father did for Wales. For their children this is the only country they know, and as they grow up and marry they will bind their parents emotionally to Britain. There is a gradual replacement of the extended family by the nuclear family of mother, father and children, partly because the head of the extended family may still be in India, Pakistan or Bangladesh, but also because the physical closeness of the Indian family, to be successful, requires something other than a three-bed-roomed semi. When the womenfolk joined their husbands a revival of culture and religious observance took place. If the Indian or Pakistani's family is to be saved from beans on toast it will be as a result of the energy of the wife. Hindu temples and Sikh *Gurdwaras* began to appear to meet many needs of Indian families, and gradually Britain became aware that three 'new' religions existed in its midst. Perhaps the greater consequence, however, was the emergence of a new generation growing up between two cultures. On the one hand, there are children like my own, to whom little attention has been given, but whose experiences of Asians and West Indians is as old as mine and in many ways more profound, for they have been educated with them and have grown up unaware of a Britian that was ever white. On the other hand, there is the well-known 'between two cultures' Asian child, in some danger because his own cultures are strong and distinctive but that of the host community is dominant.

The rest of this section will concentrate upon real consequences, actual or potential, of the Jewish, Hindu, Muslim and Sikh culture meeting a dominant Western culture, but first a word must be written about numbers and about the view which Asians are likely to have of Britain.

NUMBERS

The numbers game is notoriously dangerous to play, and we embark upon it with much trepidation. Scaremongers will double the numbers to allow for illegal immigrants! The 1971 and 1981 census figures do not discriminate between a white Christian child born in New Delhi or, Nairobi or Kingston and one who is black Christian, Hindu or Muslim. Allowing for the exaggerations of religious minorities seeking to em-phasise their strengths and for the fact that some 40 per cent of these minorities are children and young children who were born in Britain,

I would estimate the totals as: Hindus 300,000, Sikhs 300,000 Muslims 700,000 and Jews 400,000. A special problem exists with Sikh and Hindu statistics; immigration statistics merely list people of Indian origin. Some will be Muslim, a few Christian, but the majority seem to be Sikh. In future censuses the government might ask people (voluntarily perhaps) to list their religious affiliation, if any.

EXPECTATIONS

Asian expectations of the British are mixed. The Britons many of them had met or heard about were missionaries, doctors and nurses, teachers and ministers or administrators. The Englishman was therefore stereotyped as honest, just, hardworking and Christian. The permissiveness seen in our inner cities and on television and read about in our papers, and the racial hostility of some members of the indigenous population, together with a readiness to exploit them, has been a sad revelation. Religious education and school worship has often been seen as an effort to convert because Christianity, as experienced in the subcontinent, has been a missionary faith. Also religious education as taught in Muslim, Sikh or Hindu schools in India and Pakistan has had as its motive the desire to nurture children in the faith of their community. It is therefore expected that religious education in British schools will exist for the same purpose. School worship confirms this expectation. Open-ended, objective religious education often causes confusion; it must be the sugar-coating concealing a well-hidden but very real pill! The ecumenical movement after generations of denominational rivalry in the mission field, and interfaith dialogue, can also provoke more bewilderment than open attempts to convert. It might be asked why Muslims in particular do not withdraw their children from religious education and school worship. Sometimes they are unaware of their legal rights; more often they wish to be accepted and are unwilling to do things which might provoke hostility by drawing attention to differences. They want the best for their children and do not wish to appear ill-mannered. Acquiesence, however, must not be mistaken for satisfaction. Older Asians still have a great respect for the British. Some of us have experienced the consequences in the subcontinent and in Britain as men and women have attempted to treat us with reverence which neither our years nor our personality deserve. It is disconcerting to be offered a seat on a crowded bus in Pakistan by a sixty-year-old lady! Sadly, young Asians, just like young West Indians, are rejecting their parents' image of the white man. Their experiences are often replacing goodwill with distrust, and chances to create a harmonious multi-racial Britain are being thrown away

The next few paragraphs will deal with particular situations in which cultural differences can cause friction, but the reader must beware of regarding all Muslims, Sikhs or Hindus as alike, all equally religious, all equally kind and honest. Just as a nursing sister cannot be sure that a Jew admitted to her ward will require a Kosher diet, so not all Hindus will prove to be vegetarian. Some Sikh men will be clean-shaven and not wear the turban, and it is possible to find a so-called Muslim frequenting a public house. However, Hindus, Muslims and Sikhs are more conformist than Westerners, because the areas from which they come are not yet secularised, because acceptance by their community is important to them and this is the price they must pay for it, because family pride and respect for elders requires them to meet certain norms of behaviour and because many of them as individuals choose to do so anyway. 'I can do as I like' is a very Western way of looking at life, and a very recent one at that. For the Asians there are more important things than self-gratification; the honour of the family, the respect of the Muslim, Sikh or Hindu community and the teachings of his religion. Added to this, Asians often come from villages which are highly struc-tured socially and in which there is little documentation. Not long ago a friend discovered himself to be six months older than he is. He thought his birthday was in October, but the family priest assured him it was the previous May. The October date arose from the fact that it was in this month that he began school. When in doubt, the teacher recorded month of entry and added five years! Lack of documents also causes difficulties in getting dependants into Britain, a major source of distress among Asians in Britain.

Hinduism, Islam and Sikhism, like Judaism, are three strong and independent religions, each with long and proud traditions. Culturally they may seem very similar to one another from an English point of view but their individuality soon becomes apparent as knowledge grows.

For most adults contact with Asians may be minimal, confined to working hours from 8 a.m. to 5 p.m. and the relationship may simply be one of live and let live. If by this means we discover one another to be human, trustworthy and good-humoured much has been learned. A chat over a cup of tea about Pushpa's new baby or Peter's 'O' levels may be more beneficial than hours of academic dialogue conducted by sociologists, anthropologists and theologians. However, once cultures meet involuntarily in hospital, through health visitors or other members of the social services, or in the form of the police or school, difficulties can begin to appear. The next few paragraphs are intended to help people who meet Asians in these situations.

DIET

Diet is a source of great irritation: wrongly, people with special needs are seen as nuisances. Bacon and egg, a quick ham salad, beefburger and chips — things easy to prepare — are all rejected with profuse apologies! It upsets the busy school dinner lady, nursing sister or hostess! It can be frustrating because it is not simply a matter of Jews or Muslims not eating pork and Hindus not eating beef. The extremely orthodox among these groups are very chary of any foods they may be offered. Lard may have been used in making cakes or greasing the baking tin, and the lamb which the Jew or Muslim may be offered might not have been slaughtered in the approved manner. Sikhs traditionally behave similar to Hindus in matters of diet, avoiding cow meat, even though they do not respect the cow as Hindus do. Some Sikhs, like many Hindus, are completely vegetarian, occasionally to the point of refusing eggs.

When preparing a meal for Jews or Asians in school or hospital a sensible rule is to provide a vegetarian alternative, including boiled potatoes, and to remember that gravy is made of meat extract. It can render a child's meal completely unacceptable and should not be added to the dry-looking two veg.! The fact that some Jewish or Asian children will eat anything that is put before them should not make us think that all are lax in their observance of food laws. Sad to tell, some schools with good multi-cultural curricula do not enjoy good reputations when it comes to catering for children's dietary needs or in home economics lessons.

Fasting at certain times of the month is common among Hindus, Muslims fast during the month of *Ramadhan*. Younger, primary school children should not observe these fasts but often they do, to be like the rest of the family. Anxious teachers should consult the parents or community leaders.

CLOTHING

Many Hindu ladies still retain the sari in England and so brighten our street on grim winter days. Sikh women wear either the sari or the *shalwar* (trousers) and *kameez* (a blouse-like top). This is the normal dress of Muslims, though some women wear saris. One feature common to all is modesty of dress. Mini-skirts or low-cut blouses and dresses are regarded as distasteful. This same modesty causes some Asian parents to dislike their daughters going to swimming baths where mixed bathing takes place or taking part in mixed games and athletics. The *Qur'an* requires a woman to cover her body from the wrist and neck to the ankles and in some schools Muslim girls do PE and games in tracksuits. When one sees international goalkeepers and other athletes dressed in this way it is impossible to argue that it impedes performance!

Sikh women, as well as men, should never cut their hair, which usually reaches to the waist but is often tied in plaits. Young Sikh boys, therefore, constantly run the risk of being mistaken for girls, and strangers, including student teachers and Santa Claus in big department stores need to be very tentative before saying 'You're a nice little girl, what would you like for Christmas?' Careless talk costs confidence and respect.

The turban is part of the personality of a Sikh man. It is not worn to keep the hair in place — a bald Sikh should still wear one! It is worn as an outward observance of Guru Gobind's Singh's 'Be like me!' and should therefore be regarded as something worn to meet a religious requirement. It is more than an article of clothing.

Visitors to Hindu temples, *Gurdwaras* and mosques will be expected to take off their shoes like worshipping members of the congregations and in the *Gurdwara* and mosque as well as synagogue they will be asked to cover their head. Because they will be sitting on the floor in mosques, temples and *Gurdwaras*, trousers are a more sensible form of clothing for women to wear than skirts!

GREETINGS

To shake hands or not to shake hands is quite a problem. Hand-shaking is not as common among the indigenous population as it was a generation ago, and I am never sure what to do. Some people leave us in no doubt that it is a nasty middle-class habit that I should get rid of! Asian men shake hands whenever they meet and they embrace male relatives and friends with a hug. Sometimes an Asian lady will shake hands with us when we are introduced to her and once, in Amritsar, this caused me some embarrassment. I held out my hand to a friend's wife only to be told — 'This isn't England. You may shake Sikh ladies by the hand there but we don't do it here!' Equally disturbing was the day when I introduced a Muslim scholar to a group of teachers. The Muslim custom is to shake hands only with men so he shook hands warmly with them, and did not even speak to the women. The meeting which followed was very difficult to chair, and I was left feeling that I had done badly by both the Muslim and the ladies. If the occasion were to arise again I still do not know how I could totally avoid the embarrassment. Perhaps the *Imam* would have adjusted himself to British ways and I should have invited him to take his seat before introducing him generally, so that no hand-shaking was needed!

Asian politeness is likely to be mentioned more than once in these pages. It is not a politeness of words but of manner and actions. 'Thank you' is not used anything like as often as it is used by Englishmen. Once in Pakistan someone asked me 'Why do you keep saying thank you? We know you are grateful, you don't need to keep on saying that you are!' 'Please' and 'thank you' may be the hallmarks of politeness in British culture. They have not the same place in Asian cultures or languages, which usually imply them in the inflection of the voice rather than in specific words.

FAMILY

If I invite a friend to bring his family to lunch with us it is not usual that his mother and a number of other relatives will come too. Family means husband, wife and children. This is not so in the subcontinent. At marriage a bride will leave her own house and go to her husband's, where she will live with his parents, unmarried sisters, his other brothers and their wives. This is the extended or joint family. Its members are expected to subordinate their own individual interests to the needs of the family, which has a head with whom ultimate authority lies. Among Hindus and Sikhs the head may be a woman, the widow of the senior member. One of the practical reasons for assisted marriage (perhaps a more accurate term nowadays than 'arranged', at least in Britain) is that the bride is not marrying a husband, she is marrying into a family. More has to be considered than the personal feelings of two people. These are considered, to an increasing degree, but it must also be remembered that the couple will live with the boy's parents, sharing his family life, and if the bride's temperament or family background makes it unlikely that she will fit in, it is unwise to encourage the marriage. Assisted marriages have to be understood within the context of the Asian family; so has the custom of marriage by proxy. The family has to be seen as a tightly knit unit in society which lacks unemployment and sickness and universal pension benefits. It supports the elderly and cares for the young orphan as well as the chronic sick. It clubs together to put someone through college or pay his passage to England. It guarantees what the individual promises. In Britain the extended family is having to adapt to new circumstances. It is fairly unusual, to find two or three sons, their wives and children and the sons' mother and father living under the same roof. More probably, the sons have houses of their own in the same street or nearby, but still the family acts as a unit in other matters. If someone is ill they look after the children, they buy a shop jointly and run it together. They pay their parents' fare to visit other relatives in Canada, East Africa or India. Success always makes some people envious or suspicious. The success of many Asian businessmen in Britain lies in their willingness to work hard and, through the family, to muster very effectively human and financial resources.

The family is under strain in the subcontinent as people seek their fortunes in the big cities and as Western-style individualism penetrates Asian society. It is under greater strain in Britain, especially when families may be split between East Africa, India, Pakistan or Bangla Desh or scattered in Britain, some living in Leicester and others in Manchester. However, it is likely to survive. Young people may sometimes find it frustrating but they also see its value, and emotionally their sense of family is very strong. Weekend reunions are so important that a rumour once circulated that the motorways were built to help

Asian families from London, Leeds, Birmingham, Leicester, Manchester, Bristol, Preston and Liverpool to keep in touch! Just as the purpose of the sick and London commuters is, no doubt, to keep West Indians employed!

The family can also have considerable influence upon the careers of its members. It often has high aspirations for its young people, both male and female, encouraging them to go to university or enter one of the professions. There was a time when Muslim women rarely went out to work, in Britain, but this is certainly less true of the younger generation.

DEATH

Hindus cremate their dead, Jews and Muslims bury them, Sikhs prefer cremation but, in countries where this is not possible, inhumation has been practised. The main difficulties which are experienced in Britain are associated with preparations for the funeral which, in every case, should take place soon after death. Post-mortems or the delays experienced in obtaining the release of a body after an accident are particularly distressing, and should be avoided unless they are absolutely essential, Muslims like to undertake the preparation of the body from the moment of death to the interment, and usually have arrangements with undertakers who have become conversant with their needs. As they become more established, presumably Muslim communities will establish the same relationships with hospitals that Jews have in some of our cities. Muslims have also managed to arrange for some cemeteries to be moved so that Muslims may be buried in the same part. Full details of Muslim requirements are contained in the pamphlet *Muslim Burials,* which is available from CRE.

SOCIAL WORKERS

Police

It is often forgotten that the British policeman spends more of his time on work unrelated to crime than he does catching thieves and other criminals. In many respects he is a social worker. To this extent he is unlike his counterpart in many other areas of the world, and therefore the image which an Asian or West Indian has of him may be a false one. In a variety of ways the police are making contact with ethnic minorities. Sometimes they build up links with schools, helping with sports, teaching the Green Cross Code, swapping stamps, establishing human relationships casually and unobtrusively. This is time-consuming, and makes heavy demands upon an undermanned force, but the work of these contacts cannot be over-emphasised, especially when the middle class (perhaps because the motor car sometimes brings them into dispute with the law) is often alienated from the very people it created to protect its interests!

By now courts should have enough experience not to hand a Jew the New Testament or to give the Muslim witness a Bible. Jews should be given a Hebrew Bible for preference, but will usually swear on a copy of the Old Testament in English. Muslims should be asked to place the right hand on a *Qur'an* wrapped in cloth and handled with reverence. Hindus will swear on a copy of the *Bhagavad Gita* and Sikhs will use a little book of daily prayers, pronounced in English as 'Nit-Name', or *Gutka,* which contains some of their scriptures. If asked, most communities will be willing to supply courts with an acceptable copy of the scriptures upon which an oath can be taken.

Teachers and social workers, including the police, can be met with a mixture of respect and suspicion, usually accompanied by considerable politeness. Tea and biscuits, or more, is likely to be offered in the most unsociable situations, and the invitation is not merely polite, it is expected to be accepted. Such visitors will receive the respect due to a professional person and a white man, or woman, but just as the police can be the government's oppressive right arm in some parts of the world, so social workers have sometimes been associated with the enforcement of political decisions like compulsory sterilisation. Also family pride and honour suffers if a family is seen to be unable to sort out its own problems.

If a family is being interviewed it might be helpful if the interviewer were a woman rather than a man. The discussion should be conducted in the presence of the husband or father, for he will be answerable in the community for the womenfolk of his household, no matter how senior they may be in age. For a long time I would arrogantly go to friends with a question about their religious phrases in the 'You believe . . ., don't you?' manner, and they would reply with a 'Yes'. On a number of occasions I discovered from further reading that my original conclusions were wrong. When I tried to check my new solution my friends again agreed with me. It was only when I learned to ask 'What do you believe about . . .?' and put myself in a position of total ignorance that I was given correct answers. Such is Asian politeness! I remember seeing a television play in which an Indian was being interrogated by the police, who interpreted his agreeable answers as a pack of lies. A simulated, fictional situation perhaps, but the playwright had been accurate in his observations on this occasion.

EDUCATION

The school is the place where greatest contact takes place. Here children form friendships and are likely to learn about each other's cultures, though all too often such exchanges occur in the playground and during the lunch hour rather than in class.

When teachers discuss the education of children from the sub-continent two considerations often dominate their conversation. The first is language and the second the education of Muslim girls. However, two other issues may be more fundamental. The first is the worth of formal education, the second is effect. We who are teachers or have come through the educational process unharmed, or even improved, are convinced of its value. Not everyone is. A relative of mine who was a school governor and a farmer was once threatened with prosecution for employing a boy to drive a tractor during school hours. He explained to me that the boy was going to work on his farm when he left school, that nothing he learned in school would be of any use to him and even in the short term if I wanted green peas with my lamb someone had to do the ploughing and drilling. Who would if the boy was sitting at a desk all day? I have heard similar views expressed in villages in India and Pakistan. Energetic government literacy programmes were faced with the problem of convincing villagers that the ability to read was not only a good thing but a necessity. Despite compulsion, not all boys went to school, and apparently only a minority of girls. Though education is highly prized in the subcontinent and the educated person is respected, there is still a credibility gap. Coming to England has not necessarily removed it. Certainly, there are some families who wonder whether the risk they run by allowing their teenage daughters to continue at school are outweighted by the advantages.

The effect of education in Britain is to encourage children to become autonomous thinking adults, making up their own minds, taking their own decisions. I do not think teachers are always aware of the revolution they are provoking. We teachers still seem to expect children to do as they are told, even when we ask them to think for themselves. Society as a whole is certainly unaware of what is happening. Perhaps an important cause of the social unrest which manifests itself in trades union leaders being out of step with the rank and file or in the break-up of families and the outbreak of violence is our emphasis upon individualism. This is alien to Jews, Hindus, Muslims and Sikhs. Family before self, communal loyalty before individual liberty are important principles. Some of my Asian friends see the effect of British education upon their children as the undermining of these values. It is the whole trend of British education, not the content of a particular lesson or school worship, which really makes them anxious. Here they are not alone in their concern. Many members of the indigenous population lack confidence in the philosophies which are determining the direction in which education and society is going. When we come to straightforward practical matters in education, language learning, religious education, the Western culturally based curriculum, school meals, PE and swimming can all create difficulties.

When a child whose parents come from the sub-continent, Africa, a Jewish home or even from Eastern Europe, enters school at the age of five he is stripped of his possessions and given a new language, a new history perhaps, new manners and codes of conduct, possibly an unaccustomed diet and introduced to a new religion. Of course, this is an exaggeration, but it is well known that the first day of a child's school life can be traumatic, and often remains in the memory when everything else related to school has faded from the mind. If this is true of the white English child it is even more likely to be true of the Asian, who frequently comes from a closely knit, affectionate home where his parents, aunts and older brothers and sisters have lavished attention on him and let him have his own way to a considerable extent. It is unlikely that he will have been allowed to run wild in the streets, almost his only contacts hitherto will have been members of his family. Now he becomes one child among thirty or more for the first time in his life, he is called 'Paki' or Jew, or told he has a funny name, looks like a girl, smells and is black. Child development courses for trainee teachers and social workers might give more attention to the Asian and West Indian child, so that those who work with them in nurseries and reception classes are informed about ways of child-rearing which differ from the English patterns.

Language causes many heartaches. Asian parents know that English is necessary if their children are to succeed in British society, whatever that phrase means — usually a good, possibly university, education with a professional qualification at the end. They also feel, in common with some Welsh people and French Canadians, that if a child loses his mother-language, Urdu, Punjabi, Gujarati or Bengali, he will lose his culture. Retention of language is deemed essential to cultural survival. Consequently, there is pressure upon schools to let children study their own languages for CSE or 'O' levels and to take some of their lessons in these languages. Rather than analyse this debate let us point to the other consequences. First, teaching English as a second language is often seen as a specialist task to be undertaken by teachers in language or reception centres and infant schools, whereas it is a continuous task. The teachers of mathematics, science and geography, as they introduce concepts and terms which are new to all their pupils, are also teachers of language. Secondly, girls who only acquired limited English at school and who did not go out to work or mix socially with English people are now marrying and having children who are entering schools with no English. Reception centres and the teaching of English as a second language have still a considerable future. Third, many Asian children are growing up deceptively bilingual. They can chat with their parents in their mother tongue, they can get by in the playground or classroom but they are unable to discuss serious matters, demanding an advanced vocabulary, with their parents. There is a danger of linguistic estrangement.

Religious education has been mentioned earlier. For a variety of reasons it, and home economics, seems to have made more response to the multi-cultural nature of Britain than most other subjects. The curriculum is still geared to Western culture. This is understandable and proper. In most countries, probably all and especially Pakistan, education is charged with some responsibility for transmitting a cultural heritage. However, one feels that some quite simple response might be made which would not turn the curriculum on its head but would make it more relevant to Britain as part of a world which is a global village. For example, India and Africa have civilisations which go back beyond the days of the white man's 'discovery' of them, the story of the Crusades is far more than that of Richard the Lionheart, the Old Testament might be studied as the scripture of a living faith of Judaism, rather than merely the first part of the Christian Bible. There are a number of African, West Indian and Indian writers in English as well as Jewish authors whose works might find a place in the school library and in English literature lessons. After the 'World of Islam Festival' of 1975 one would hope to find the Islamic contribution featuring more prominently in art appreciation courses. Amazingly, our museums are enriched by cultures which our schools tend to neglect. They are part of our world heritage and the direct tradition of many children in our larger cities. A shift in balance from the Black Hole of Calcutta, recently downgraded by historians anyway, to Muslim Spain or the achievements of Akbar the Great and Ashoka need not harm British pride, might do something for the self-esteem of children of Jewish, Hindu, Muslim and Sikh faiths, and could present a more accurate picture of world history. The curriculum needs to be broadened, rather than overturned, to reach towards the new extended horizons resulting from the development of television and easy air travel.

Difficulties over diet and the clothing of girls for PE and games and the wearing of skirts as part of uniform are perhaps diminishing as schools have sorted them out after a decade or more of experiencing minority groups. However, dispersal sometimes means that a head teacher finds himself faced by this new 'problem', as he is all too eager to call it. There is sufficient experience available now for him to call upon. Old mistakes need not be repeated except by the proud who refuse to seek guidance.

Trends towards co-education seem likely to provoke confrontation in some authorities in which hitherto there have been single-sex secondary schools. It is disliked by Muslims, being contrary to their way of life in which social mixing between the sexes is very restricted, and is not really congenial to Sikhs and Hindus. There are mixed secondary schools in India and Pakistan, but only the most Westernised families send their children to them, and certainly in Pakistan, mixing is carefully supervised after the age of twelve or thirteen. As one head teacher said, 'We are like a family, the children have been together since they were five or six. We would have to think very carefully before letting someone new join us at the age of thirteen'. The case for co-education does not seem overwhelming and no-one seems to have asked parents for their preference. The doctrinaire introduction of co-education any-where seems hard to justify. In areas with large Asian populations it seems to be unnecessarily thoughtless and insensitive.

Re-entering the classroom, I still cannot forget that the first piece of information my younger daughter picked up at school was 'Jew, Jew, dirty old Jew', in the playground on her first day! By sharing festivals, talking about greetings and different languages, encouraging national costume days (what would the English wear?), inviting an Indian mum to bring her new baby to school and in a host of other ways the prejudice which children bring from home can be dealt with at least to some extent. Teachers who say that they treat all their children in the same way and avoid emphasising differences are certainly well-meaning, but they are also, arguably, unrealistic. The children know they are different, their classmates sometimes tell them that they are quite nas-tily, and in some respects they need to be acknowledged as being different. For good or bad, we are who we are not because of our similarity to other people but because of our distinctiveness. Sometimes teachers are lazy, some have refused to pronounce my own daughter's name (Eluned), others, like the one who told an English child who moved from Kent to the commuter belt of Wharfedale 'The sooner you learn to speak like us the better', are just unprofessional. At least these examples show that white children can be treated thoughtlessly.

NAMES

Names create confusion as well as pronunciation difficulties. I have met teachers who thought children were trying it on when confronted with Mohan Singh, Manjit Kaur and Mahinder Gill, who claim to be brothers and sisters. With Muslims it can be even more complicated, with Sikhs the number of possible permulations is only three — though Mahinder may be a girl or a boy! The British Nursing Council has been known to stand for none of this nonsense, as the number of women called nurse Singh or Sister Singh testifies. If Manjit Kaur's father is Singh on her birth certificate that is good enough for them, she is Manjit Singh! An insensitive solution, as simple ones often are.

RELIGIOUS OBSERVANCE

Frequently the question is asked 'Is the turban, (or wearing the *shalwar*) part of their culture or their religion?' This is a Western question to which there is no easy eastern answer. Religion and culture are virtually one in practice to Hindus, Muslims and Sikhs and, to a considerable extent, Jews. Christianity became separated from its Jewish cultural roots and in turn moulded a culture which, it might be argued, has in turn become separated from its religious origins, leaving Christianity to wither or discover a new vitality. Sikhism may be a distinctive religion, but it has never succeeded in severing its connections with Hinduism, partly because it is in the nature of Hinduism, no matter how strongly Sikhs protest. Sikhs are often vegetarian because of this Hindu connection, and they never serve meat in the *Langar*, the dining room of the *Gurdwara*. Custom rather than a written code determines many of the practices of both religions and therefore, in Britain, both have made Sunday their main day for congregational worship, as most people are free on that day, and they celebrate their great festivals in the evening or at the weekend. Only the turban issue has caused any ill-feeling on religious grounds.

The *Qur'an* and Jewish Bible, unlike the revealed scriptures of Hinduism and Sikhism, lays down very precise rules of conduct. These are as much part of the spiritual life of a Jew or Muslim as going to synagogue or the mosque, making the pilgrimage to Mecca or giving a portion of one's income to the poor. To pray five times a day within prescribed periods of time and to observe the holy days is not something optional, it is obligatory. To see Muslims in Pakistan praying on a railway platform or at the roadside cafe when they break their bus journey for a meal is to become aware of the importance of religious observance in their lives. It is not unusual to find a mosque built into a factory complex, just as Titus Salt built a church opposite his factory at Saltaire, Bradford, a hundred years ago. Lack of opportunities to attend the mosque for noon prayers on Friday and to observe holy days cause Muslims in Britain difficulties, especially with regard to the latter, because the two great annual festivals are related to the actual sighting of the new moon. The Jewish community has settled for specific times for the beginning and ending of Sabbath which you can find in Jewish diaries. Why, it is sometimes asked, cannot Muslims do likewise? In Lahore I visited a school and met a man who was preparing to visit his parents to celebrate the *Eid* after *Ramadhan*. In the hills in the north of Pakistan the moon would be sighted a day earlier than on the plain. He had therefore begun the fast a day before his colleagues and would be starting his holiday a day earlier. The emotion was strong in his voice when he spoke of the joy of being with his parents to watch for the new moon. Feelings play an important part in our lives, and Muslims will not quickly, if ever, shed a cherished tradition going back to the time of the Prophet.

For a number of years some businesses and schools have closed to enable Jewish workers, pupils and teachers to observe the Day of Atonement. As time passes it is to be hoped that Muslim needs will be met in the same way, but not reluctantly. To Explain *Eid* at assembly and wish Muslim pupils 'Eid Mubarak' is far better than to hear teachers complaining of 'Another Saint's Day! Mrs Flynn will be away so I'll be using my marking period to teach her class —— Catholics!' What price goodwill! Such off-the-cuff remarks have far more impact upon children than enlightened lessons about the ecumenical movement or world religions.

CASTE

Caste has not been mentioned in this section. It is a very ill-understood subject to which people react over-hastily. Discrimination based on caste is now illegal in India, and many of the worst practices which we have heard about have gone. Among Hindus and Sikhs in Britain caste plays a minor role as far as East–West contact is concerned. The most observant Hindus with regard to caste would not defile themselves by crossing the *Kali Pani,* the black ocean, to live in a foreign land. Caste should play no part in Sikhism, it is against the spirit and letter of the religion, but Sikhs are not entirely free of this Hindu influence. It is like racial and sexual prejudice and discrimination in Christianity, easily denounced but still practised. In Britain caste plays a part in deciding who may be an acceptable marriage partner, it could explain disagreements among members of the Asian workforce in a factory and why a city has two Hindu temples or Sikh *Gurdwaras* though national and regional differences are likely to be more important. However, this simple and attractive conclusion is not one that social workers should jump to too easily. A father's insecurity at having his authority and public standing threatened by a daughter finding a boyfriend of her own may be a far more likely reason for family disagreement than the fact that he comes from another caste.

THE FUTURE

I have no crystal ball with which to gaze into the future, but I feel a need to look towards the year 2000. After all, a child entering school in September 1985 will only be twenty at the end of the century, though we often seem to think that 1945 is not only nearer but more important.

A number of facts seem clear. Britain will be multi-ethnic and multi-faith. Hinduism, Islam and Sikhism will still exist in Britain, the survival of the Jews as a minority in every country from 70 CE until

79

1947 is something of an indication of the strength of established religions. How the other religions, Christianity for that matter, will cope with the experience of being minority faiths in a secular society is unpredictable, but they will. Already farsighted Hindus, Muslims and Sikhs, like the Jews, recognise that transmitting their beliefs and cultures to the next generation is their responsibility. They are launching cultural programmes to teach their children music and dance, as well as classes in language and religious instruction. Some cities have established community relations festivals which are bringing the cultures Britain ignores to public attention.

Numbers are less important than quality, but so far politicians and the media have been more concerned with how many non-whites will be living in Britain in 2000 than with the quality of the population. One of my ablest students qualified as a teacher in 1976 and within a year had taken her family back to St Kitts. She felt a sense of discrimination, and did not think that her children would get a fair chance here. One knows of Asians who have already moved on to Canada from Britain. We could become a land of poor blacks and poor whites — poor in terms of quality, enterprise and spirit. This is a gloomy prospect, but one which can be avoided by social engineering and social reconstruction which demands insight, policy and effort. The implications of multi-racialism for television, radio, employment, housing and espeically school organisation and the curriculum of schools and universities have yet to be worked out. The multi-racial debate has not even begun.

It may be that Asians and West Indians came to Britain at an auspicious time. Britain itself is undergoing a change of role, and more positive attitudes to ethnic minorities exist than hitherto. Generally, the response to Jewish settlers was negative when it was not indifferent. No community relations machinery was set up, schools made little response in religious education and only slowly did the Council of Christians and Jews gain support — and it was a long time coming into existence.

The chances of achieving a harmonious multi-racial Britain cannot be estimated. Whether we shall succeed better in becoming a multi-cultured nation than we did in establishing and taking seriously a multi-racial commonwealth, time alone will tell. Because one chance to make history was lost it does not mean that the other need be frittered away. Britain could become a model of multi-cultural harmony. Meanwhile I hope that this section, will help readers not only to cope with day-to-day realities but also consider long-term aims.

W. OWEN COLE

PART 2: RELIGIOUS EDUCATION IN THE MULTI-FAITH SCHOOL

RELIGIOUS EDUCATION IN A MULTI-FAITH SOCIETY

My aim is to produce an approach to religious education which might be applicable anywhere — in Coventry, Chichester, Leeds, Lahore or Kingston, Jamaica. However, education in school should be related to the children we teach and to the world in which they live, so the strategies may not be identical everywhere.

The first need is to agree on the purpose of religious education. In recent years something of a revolution has been taking place. It is based upon three principles.

(1) The purpose of religious education should be to study religion in order to understand its place and function as an aspect of human activity and its importance in life. This replaces the traditional aim of RE, which has been to nurture children in the culture of their parents. Whilst denying that the purpose of RE should be to undermine faith, religious educationists would argue that the home and religious institutions have responsibility for a child's religious development.

(2) The study of religions should draw on material from a variety of religions, using the most appropriate examples available. In other words, instead of being a study of Christianity, or of Islam, it will be a study of religion — using Christian baptism and confirmation, as well as Jewish *Bar Mitzvah* and the *Sikh Amrit* ceremony in probing initiation rites. A study of how religions express their sense of corporate unity would include not only the service of holy communion but also the Jewish Passover meal and the Sikh institution of the *Langar*. Religious studies are also seen to be the study of many dimensions of religion — practices as well as beliefs and historical development — not only the study of scriptures, as hitherto.

(3) The role of the teacher is that of a go-between, bringing the students (whether child or adult) into contact with the religion being studied.

81

Traditionally, the teacher has been an authority figure, behaving in such a way that it was natural for the pupil to assume that he or she was a believer. Consequently, the religious education lesson was an embarrassment to the humanist or agnostic teacher or pupil.

The 'revolution' in religious education, as outlined very briefly above, is intended to take the subject beyond such considerations as the religious composition of the class and the beliefs of the teacher. It should enable a model to be created which is as capable of being used in Lahore, Jerusalem, Peking or Southall, by a Muslim, a Buddhist or an agnostic, as by a committed Christian in West Sussex. The requirement of the revolution is not faith, but knowledge, respect for religion as a realm of meaning worthy of serious study, and the readiness to let the student and religion meet rather than an eagerness to compel him to undertake a personal search for meaning and to predetermine the goal of such a quest.

Certain skills and attitudes have to be acquired by both teacher and pupil if the religious studies is to be based upon these principles. Among the skills are:

(1) To recognise and respond appropriately to religious phenomena. There are inappropriate responses — regarding Judaism as legalistic, Hinduism as idol worship, Roman Catholic Christianity as superstition, all priests as lazy, exploiting hypocrites. Proper responses are understanding the place of priests in religions, how Sikhs regard their scripture, how and why Hindus use statues of Krishna, Radha and other forms of deity.

(2) The ability to enquire appropriately into religious issues, for example, why the place of Jesus is different in Islam than it is in Christianity.

Key attitudes are those of fair-mindedness — willingness to observe openly without feeling a desire or need to make personal comments or judgements of the kind already cited as inappropriate above, respect — for the holy ground of others, whether you possess a holy ground or not.

These skills and attitudes may be particularly difficult for people from semitic cultural backgrounds to acquire. They seem to have an inbuilt inclination to regard things as right or wrong, good or bad, whereas those from Indian backgrounds seem more prepared to acknowledge the validity of beliefs and practices other than their own.

The study of religion should bring both student and teacher in touch with a number of concepts, such as:

(1) The dimension of mystery — in existence itself, in self-consciousness, in good and evil, for example:

(2) What constitutes a religious approach to life:

(3) Insights and motivations provided by religious faith and experience:

(4) The place and significance of religion in human life:

(5) The chief forces influencing form and content of religious beliefs and practices:

(6) The symbolic use of words, objects and gestures — for example, the removal of shoes:

(7) The use and meaning of religious language — for example, saying 'Jesus saves, or 'Islam is true':

(8) What is meant by religious experience.

The main ingredient of any syllabus may seem to be information, knowledge, but the emphasis should be upon understanding, not on becoming a religious 'Mastermind'. It is far more important to know what the *Hajj* means to a Muslim who has experienced it than to be able to describe the sequences in perfect detail from start to finish. Similarly, to know what the Easter experience means to a Christian is more a religious studies goal than being able to recite the events of Easter Day in chronological order, if such an arrangement is possible.

Religions consist of many ingredients or dimensions, all of which have their place in religious education syllabuses.

First, there is the mythological element. The word 'myth' is often abused in ordinary English. We say something is a myth when we mean that it is untrue. The teacher needs to remember that this may well be what children conclude when they hear or read the word in the religious studies lesson, where it has a technical meaning. A myth is a story which may be the story of the creation in Genesis or that of the death of Jesus or that of the Exodus of the children of Israel. It is the narrative dimension in religion. Where we speak of the myth of Jesus dying on the cross we are not making any judgements about what happened — but if the word myth is going to be misunderstood by children or by other people in whose presence we use it, perhaps we should prefer to talk about the narrative element.

Second, there is the ritual dimension, worship, celebration of festivals, and other activities. These may be as elaborate as a coronation or as simple as a handshake, for ritual is not confined to religion, of course. Meditation as well as pilgrimage or High Mass could be included under the heading ritual.

Third, there is the social dimension of religion, the way it manifests itself in the community of believers — the Sikh *sangat*, the Christian church or the Muslim *umma* — and, especially in Hinduism and Judaism, in family life.

These three areas are the ones most attractive to younger children,

83

the ones which the teacher of fives to thirteens is probably most eager to use. Each has its plan, but mythical or narrative material needs to be used with considerable care. Take, for example, the story of Jesus feeding the five thousand. Told as it stands, it appears as farfetched as Aladdin's lamp or Ali Baba's cave — a story likely to create doubt as children grow older and incredulity in some eight-year-olds. To avoid presenting Jesus as a 'magic man' some teachers reduce the story to an example of sharing. When the young boy offered his picnic snack to Jesus the rest of those who had brought something to eat shamefacedly brought out their food and shared it with their neighbours. Such an explanation does violence to the biblical accounts, which either ex- plicitly state that the people had no food (Matthew 15:32: Mark 8:2) or in every case emphasise the action of Jesus as provider (e.g. the above plus Luke 9:16–17; John 6:11).

The point that this act was a messianic declaration, an anticipation of the messianic banquet, is completely lost. Almost without exception, the miracles of Jesus (and of Guru Nanak and others) have a theological meaning, which is the real reason for their inclusion in the Bible and other books. If this is ignored, the miracles become trivial or fanciful. The miracles stories are not, then, tales to be told to young children — I would save them for thirteen-plus.

The same can be true of such stories as Noah's Ark and David and Goliath. The first includes complex ideas about the nature of God which are beyond children. Reduced to a well-told story it may be fun and could have a place in the afternoon story slot — but not as religious education, as a folk tale. As for David and Goliath, does the fact that it is in the Bible justify us in pretending that it is religious?

What of stories of the birth of Jesus or many of the myths of Krishna? There is a compulsive element present which influences us to tell the former. Christmas is universally celebrated in Britain! Let the story be told well, in an atmosphere of joy and wonder so that it is felt to be significant long before its theological meaning can be appreciated. So with similar stories about Krishna, the Buddha or Guru Nanak, or the *Diwali* narrative. Perhaps they are best appreciated if embedded in the ritual and social dimensions of religion — how the birthdays or Jesus or Krishna, or other events, are celebrated by the believing community and in the home.

What a synagogue is like, how Muslims say their prayers, the *puju* shrine in a Hindu home, baptising a Christian child or adult — these ritual and social aspects of religions and many others can almost natu- rally fascinate primary children and those in their middle years. They capture the imagination and enable pupils to enquire into religions in ways which suit their capacities.

The remaining three dimensions of religion belong largely to the thirteen-plus part of the syllabus and are therefore often in danger of

84

being squeezed out by social studies courses and the many forms of non-RE which are to be found in upper schools. These, however, form the essential parts of religions. To ignore them is to eliminate the relevance of religion to daily life or to providing people with a sense of purpose.

The doctrinal dimension of a religion is that which explains the meaning of the myths or the significance of worship. The place of Muhammad in Islam, the meaning of the Crucifixion of Jesus, the significance of the Exodus or the Passover *seder* in Judaism are all doctrinal. Unless, eventually, children learn what Christians believe about the life, death and resurrection of Jesus, the accumulation of knowledge in earlier years will have been meaningless, if enjoyable.

The ethical element is the fifth area of religion for study. If the doctrinal examines what it means to be a Jew or Muslim, for example, in terms of belief, this considers what it means in terms of conduct. This relates both to everyday life, such as how a Muslim should dress and what foods a Jew may eat, as well as to attitudes to such issues as vegetarianism, pacifism, abortion or stealing. A person who has grown up within Western culture may need to bear in mind the fact that his way of life which puts things like dress and diet or attitude to parents into one compartment marked 'secular' and others, such as euthanasia or adultery, into one labelled 'religious' is doing something which many or almost all Jews, Muslims, Hindus and Sikhs might find are ways of life embracing every aspect of life. Consequently, though vegetarianism may be a matter of conscience for a Christian it may be the *Dharma* of a Hindu, acquired as part of his heritage, though no less personally important for that. The ethical dimensions of religions other than Christianity seen often to be neglected in religious education courses, implying that only Christians care or possess consciences! Not surprisingly, kind Jews or Muslims have been told, 'You're a real Christian!' The compliment may have been well intended, but what did it imply?

Sixth, and finally, religions have an experiential dimension. Study can be made of those experiences through which new religions have begun — the call of Muhammad, or Guru Nanak, the Enlightenment of the Buddha, the experience of Moses at the burning bush. There are also the experiences of people like St Paul or John Wesley, and many from all religions which have made personal for them or authenticiated the experience or the message of the teacher who has pointed them to ultimate reality. It is this dimension which, in the last resort, gives meaning to the rest and brings religion to life. Though it may be the most difficult to explore and study, a religious education course which neglects it can only hope to be limitedly intelligible to the pupils.

In those few paragraphs in which I have broken religion down into six dimensions I have also suggested that some — the ritual, social and mythical — are more promising for exploration with young children than the others. However, there is always a likelihood that children may encounter, say, the experiential in studying worship or the doctrinal together with the mythical. Religions cannot be comparmentalised adequately, and teaching should never let structural syllabus considerations dominate circumstances and common sense.

In later sections particular issues will be raised, but here is probably the place to make some general points.

(1) In schools which includes Muslims or Sikhs as well as (supposed) Christians there is a need to work out ways of including all the religions represented in the school, beginning in the reception class. This can often be done through cross-religions topics. Failure may prompt the children to conclude that religions neglected in the syllabus are not worth knowing about. This can deprive the adherent of self-esteem and foster prejudice or paternalism in the other pupils.

(2) The approach can often be cross-subject. For example, I recently saw a fascinating topic on St Paul's Cathedral which included aspects of art, history, language, mathematics and science, and resulted in building an excellent model. The Taj Mahal, Regent's Park mosque, or the Golden Temple at Amritsar could prove equally exciting focuses — or even the local synagogue, church or Hindu temple, even if they are less spectacular.

(3) There is a need to recognise latent prejudices — between Protestant and Roman Catholic Christian, or between Muslim and Sikh. In the religious education lesson the concern should be for sound, accurate and open learning, and teachers as well as pupils need to be educated to engage with religion in this way. It isn't easy. I myself find it easier to use the word 'sister' when addressing a Buddhist *bhikkuni* than when speaking to a Roman Catholic nun, and to use 'priest' or 'father' of an Anglican or Roman Catholic clergyman is very demanding! Children need to be helped to cope with such gut reactions of which they may be unaware. There is a need for Islam, therefore, to be taught in schools where there may only be Sikh and Christian pupils — and probably Judaism, for anti-semitism seems to be a universal phenomenon. I have encountered it in Asian children who have never met Jews!

(4) Differences must be honestly faced, at the appropriate time. Religions do not all teach the same thing. In fact, if they did, Christianity, Islam, Buddhism and Sikhism would probably not have come into existence, for to some considerable extent they are critiques of and protests against Judaism, Christianity, brahminism and Hinduism. If one is teaching about Jesus or the Crusades to a class which contains Muslims and Christians it would seem impossible to ignore areas of disagreement. It would also be wrong, for

maturity comes from recognising, accepting and coping with differences. Sadly, this seems alien to the semitic tradition, which is often inclined to suppress contrary views.

(5) Mother Teresa or Christian Aid exemplify another issue. They represent caring Christianity. Can they also imply feckless or uncaring Hinduism? Is it wise to include Mother Teresa in the religious education syllabus of a school with children from Indian backgrounds in it? Were I to include her, it would be in a topic on Christianity, perhaps to demonstrate Christian commitment, and I would make sure to include Gandhi and other Hindu social workers in my syllabus. As for Christian Aid Week, I would avoid it, and any other appeals which might embarrass Asian or Afro–Caribbean youngsters or encourage racist views that they are inferior and a drain upon the wealth of hard-working Westerners!

(6) This, of course, raises the whole question of our approach to the 'recovering world', that is, the areas which are emerging from the effects of colonialism!

(7) Care needs to be taken to avoid triumphalist Christian missionary approaches. These can appear by accident — as well describe Mother Teresa's work enthusiastically, for example.

(8) There is also the danger of stereotyping a religion — 'Islam teaches', 'Christians believe. . . '. We know that even in areas of belief there are differences; regarding rituals or ethical conduct, there is also considerable variety.

(9) The hidden curriculum is even more important than what is taught in the classroom. If the dietary needs of Muslim pupils are ignored in the dining room they are likely to regard the presence of Islam in the religious education syllabus as mere tokenism. Not long ago I heard of a school which enthusiastically used the broad Hampshire Agreed Syllabus but refused a Jewish teacher a holiday to celebrate *Rosh Hashanah*!

(10) Finally, we have to consider how to teach Christianity in all its dimensions, with no assumptions about general knowledge. Sometimes writers assert that the teacher can assume that all five-year-olds will come to school with some knowledge of Jesus. I doubt whether this is true — or that it ever has been. With her Muslim, Sikh, Hindu or Jewish pupils the task of presenting Christianity is virtually as considerable as that of introducing Islam into a West Sussex primary school — possible, but the exercise is one which requires thought and planning.

Few, if any of these issues are exclusive to multi-faith schools. Elsewhere they are often mistakenly ignored. In multi-faith schools the challenges and opportunities are apparent and obvious.

FURTHER READING

The Religious Experience of Mankind by Ninian Smart (Collins/Fontana), Chapter 1, explores the notion of the six dimensions of religion. My debt to that chapter and his approach to religious studies in general is one which I gladly acknowledge. *The Study of Religion* by Jean Holm (Sheldon Press) will also be helpful to teachers wrestling with some of the matters raised in this section.

TEACHING RELIGION IN THE MULTI-FAITH SCHOOL

This section will confine itself mainly to aims and approaches with children under thirteen years of age, because, in the upper school, the teaching of religious studies is something which can only be done by the trained expert. However, there are a number of general needs common to all multi-faith schools.

(1) The need to recognise that this world is multi-faith. Whilst every school in Britain must recognise that it is preparing children for life in a multi-faith world, this section will concentrate upon particular needs of the school in which a number of religious traditions are represented.

(2) The need to recognise the needs of Jewish, Muslim, Sikh, Hindu and Caribbean children as well as other Christians of various traditions, including Eastern Orthodox. It is not the duty of the school to induct them into their particular faith; this is the work of the home and church, *Gurdwara*, mosque or synagogue, but the children do need to be shown in a tangible way that their faiths are acceptable, by having them taught in class.

(3) The need to inform the indigenous children so that they may be able to face the reality of a pluralistic multi-cultural, multi-faith world and may gain cultural enrichment from membership of a truly multi-cultural school.

(4) The need to attempt to meet the needs of the various groups constantly. Whereas, for example, in an all-white school where children come from a Christian background it may be possible to study Christianity this year and Islam next, in a school which has Muslim pupils the teacher has to find ways and means of introducing Islamic content much more frequently.

The teaching of religion in multi-faith schools might be divided into three tiers.

THE DIRECT CONCRETE (5 years to 8 or 9 years)

Themes and topics within the direct experience of the child might be explored and used as opportunities for certain knowledge to be acquired, for example, that Sikhs do not cut their hair so that boys wear a topknot, as they get older they will wear a turban; that some people do not eat pork, others do not eat beef; that we have times of rejoicing — festivals — that we eat different foods and dress differently.

Outlines of one or two topics are given later. The aims of the teachers will have been at various times

(1) To satisfy the needs of the various groups for cultural recognition.
(2) To help the children understand and accept the differences of which they will already have been aware to some extent. Difference, be it red hair or black skin, wearing spectacles or a turban, is not something we accept naturally. The attitude that difference means odd, peculiar, funny or even nasty, will, it is hoped, have been dealt with.
(3) To help the children become aware of the specific contribution of the various groups of which it is composed so that their experience may be enriched and positive attitudes towards one another's cultures developed.
(4) To share, as far as possible, the various festivals.

In schools where only one culture or religion appears to be present (though there will usually be many sub-cultures), teachers will be respecting the pluralism of the school in many ways — by looking at the different things people do on Sunday, the various ways they celebrate Christmas, or accepting that some couples marry in church and others in registry offices. One hopes that honesty and a recognition of reality will prevent teachers from pretending that *everyone* practises Christianity either through active membership of the Church or in terms of morality. One would hope that a teacher's respect for the children would discourage them from marking those who spend Sunday at the seaside or with grandma from being made to feel guilty because they don't go to church!

In this context of pluralism, or even in the rare denominational school where every family is observantly Christian, young children can be introduced to the multi-cultural world through stories of other lands or being introduced to the facts climatic, cultural, dietary or dress differences. The teacher who describes her holiday in Spain using some Spanish music, perhaps teaching a Spanish greeting and putting pictures of Spanish costumes on the wall or bringing a costume doll to school, is doing precisely that. Even the less fortunate teacher who has not been abroad can acquire the same information and bring Spain into her classroom. Why not India, Egypt, or Israel then, even in West Sussex!

THE VICARIOUS CONCRETE (9 to 13 years)

By the age of nine children are ready and eager to explore the world which lies beyond their immediate experience, though not in a systematic and academic way. The past (but not dates), the wider world (but not maps), is exciting their imagination. So with religion practices, but not systems of belief, and stories about real people and events can be used.

Clothes, fabrics and foods, customs, places of worship, festivals, still provide the foundation materials. The child is still in need of descriptive material and more detailed information. He is only in the position of being prepared for later thinking about history, geography or science. Perhaps the topics outlined later will indicate what is meant more clearly.

The teacher's aim at this stage will be much the same as at stage one, but horizons will be widened as books, filmstrips or radio and television programmes add to the child's personal direct experience.

THIRTEEN-PLUS ONWARDS

What the festivals mean, how religous material (myths, miracles, parables) is to be understood, ideas about God, the meaning of life, what Hindus, Muslims, Sikhs and Christians believe about life after death, these are tasks which only a person adequately trained in theology and in the teaching of religious education should undertake. Professor Ninian Smart in *Secular Education and the Logic of Religion* and *The Religious Experience of Mankind* has outlined six areas with which religious studies should concern itself. They are the mythological, the doctrinal, the experiental, the ritual, the ethical and the social. Although religion in schools should not fall into the trap of aping the universities, yet one may argue that certainly all children should be helped to understand the religious material in which doctrine is enshrined (for example, New Testament birth stories, creation myths of various religions, parables, miracles stories, and legends). They should also explore the ideas of worship and what is meant by prayer and meditation. Why religions have something to say about social and individual conduct, as well as what they say, is also an appropriate area of study.

Although religious studies in schools is moving away from attaching importance to agreed syllabuses, yet there is still, and increasingly, a need for programming curriculum content. It is hoped that this section and the subsequent examples will show that there are foundations which must and can be laid, and there is also an edifice to be built upon those foundations.

W.O.C.

LIVING WITH DIFFERENCES

The children swarming round the ice cream van come from several communities. This is clear because of differences of colour. All these children, as they grow up, will face the experience of being strangers, of belonging to a minority group whose cultural background is not wholly that of the country in which they are living. Most individuals experience being a stranger at some time or another because there are so many differences in our society. For example, the town-dweller may feel a stranger in the country, and vice versa; or northerners moving to the south of England; workers in industry as opposed to those in the professions; or simply the young and the old. Each person is an individual, and is only at home within certain, often narrow, limits. We need to consider how young people can be helped to deal with this experience of living in a strange milieu.

As far as citizens from the Commonwealth are concerned, we should begin by refusing to lump them all together. For instance there are Asians and Cypriots; West Indians from Trinidad, Guyana, Barbados, St Kitts and the Leeward and Windward Islands, as well as Jamaica. And surely it is time to stop using the word 'immigrant' of these children. We do not use it of Irish or Australian children, nor would we so describe an American boy in an English class. An increasing number of these children are British-born. They belong here and Britain is their home.

HOW DO THESE CHILDREN REGARD THEIR HOMELAND?

A child growing up in England may develop a love and interest for Wales though he has never been there Similarly, sons of Barbadians are likely to display a keen interest in Barbados and in Afro–Caribbean culture in general. This *hiraeth* is not necessarily symptomatic of a dislike of Britain; more likely it results from the conversations of parents and older friends, or from a desire to put down roots and establish identity. He will assume much of his identity and many of his attitudes from the minority group of which he is part. Minorities have always banded together in a strange land, as any Englishman who has lived abroad knows.

Experts have tended to identify various ways in which groups can live together:

(1) A group may be *assimilated* by the host society so that its identity is lost.

(2) A host society may help the newcomer to fit into the new community, which implies *accommodation* on both sides so that the host society and the newcomers *co-exist*.

(3) After some time, when the host society has accepted the newcomers and is prepared to live and work with them, the newcomers may be said to be *included* in society, taking part in politics, trades unions, etc.

(4) Some people feel that the newcomers should retain their culture and refrain from entry into the host society. This would lead to all-black clubs, all-Indian clubs, etc. — *a social pluralism*.

(5) Others would like to see the newcomers *integrated* into the host society, whilst retaining a measure of cultural identity. This requires real understanding and mutual tolerance, but it could bring enrichment to the whole community.

WHAT DO THESE YOUNG PEOPLE FEEL ABOUT ENGLAND?

To take an example, culture of the British West Indian is now predominantly European and his religion Christian. He finds it hard to realise that his homeland, his motherland, does not really want him. His bitterness begins at an early age. Few teachers will say in front of him, 'these children hold the rest of the class back. They are naughty, hard to teach and not very bright' (though some will). But sometimes the impression is received by the children, and it will be so as long as primary school classes remain too large. In downtown schools were most children are deprived, buildings are poor, books inadequate, it is all too easy to blame the immigrants when children make little progress. The 'blame', if that word must be used, lies more appropriately with those who believe that teachers in such schools can achieve adequate results with more than twenty-five children in a primary school class. Most teachers, the vast majority in fact, are fair and kind to their children — to all of them. Yet, in terms of what is learned through books and other media, the Asian or Caribbean child, often feels rejected. As an Asian sixth-former in Bradford put it, 'Tigers and poverty, that's all my white friends know about India'.

Even where the situation seems to be good, rejection may be felt. In the Manchester area a headmaster, new to his boys' secondary school, felt that the atmosphere among his young students was good. Asian, West Indian and Lancastrian English worked and played happily together. Talking to a West Indian teacher on his staff he was, therefore, surprised to learn from him that all West Indian boys would become white overnight if they could 'Why?' he asked. 'Because they hear what white Christians are doing in the world today, how the white man has civilised the whole world, how white science and technology are solving the problems of disease, poverty and overpopulation for which the black is apparently responsible, and how all music and worthwhile literature has been given to the world by the whites. Your black children are ashamed of the colour of their skins.'

The position must not be exaggerated, but the white curriculum can give the impression that only whites care, and stories of Livingstone, Damien or Wilberforce can produce the added conclusion that only white Christians care. It is all too easy for coloured Britons to learn that not only in the Caribbean but also in Africa and Asia there is no cultural heritage for them to learn about save for that transplanted by the West from Europe.

SOME SIGNPOSTS TO BETTER RELATIONSHIPS

Although the coloured Briton may ask that his culture may be represented adequately in the curriculum there is a respect in which he wants to be taken for granted. At a time when sociologists were surely running out of research fodder (there must be a limit to the number of books one can write about family and kinship in East London, or mothers without husbands!) along came the Sikhs and West Indians. Some children (and adults) in these communities have received the impression that they exist to be stared at like goldfish in a bowl, or for experimental purposes like guinea pigs, just as their forebears back home existed to provide Christians with opportunities to perform good works!

It would be wrong to suggest that all coloured Britons have a stereotype picture of white Britons. Their impressions vary and are based upon ideas implanted by their parents perhaps more than upon personal experience. They are impressed by the genuine liberal, tolerant attitude which they find in many people, but perplexed therefore by Immigration Acts — though some see these as measures giving them protection.

They are sometimes hurt by an insensitivity which after ten years in many cases can still result in a Muslim being asked his Christian name! Sometimes the lack of any provison of an alternative to pork sausages makes the Muslim, as it has the Jew, convinced that absorption, rather than multi-culturalism, is our aim. Our ignorance and lack of response to their ways of life convince many of our arrogance and feeling of superiority.

All coloured young people, as young people of all social groups, would like it to be known that besides possessing views they can also express themselves articulately and adequately. The next generation would like to state its own case. It does not have the language problems of its parents and, thanks to them very often, it has a leisure time which they often lacked, in which it can participate in meetings, write articles and represent itself in various ways. It has educated members who can write and speak for their communities and help them to find an identity unless our educational system has made them turn their back upon the culture of their parents (as English working-class lads were often accidentally educated to despise *their* parents).

As was suggested at the beginning of this section, at times everyone feels a newcomer, a stranger, in an unfamiliar environment. It is important right from the start of school life that children should learn to face and accept the fact of differences — of ability, culture, religion, social groups and race. They need to learn not only to be tolerant, but to be interested in differences and in the reasons for them; to be prepared to listen to the claims of injustice, and to accept stimulus which comes from opposing views.

Part of the primary school curriculum, at however simple a level, should be concerned with helping children to know and appreciate the contributions made by different civilisations, cultures and religions. To leave this to the secondary school is to wait too long. By then attitudes have been formed.

W.O.C.

SOME BOOKS ON RELIGIOUS EDUCATION

Approaching World Religions, R. Jackson (ed.), John Murray.
World Faiths in Education, W. O. Cole (ed.), Allen and Unwin.
Perspectives on World Religions, R. Jackson (ed.), School of Oriental and African Studies, London University.
World Religions: A Handbook for Teachers (plus 1982 supplement), W. O. Cole (ed.), Commission for Racial Equality.
India, Pakistan and Bangladesh, A Handbook for Teachers, P. Bahree, School of Oriental and African Studies, London University.
Young Children and Religion, C. Mumford, Edward Arnold.
Teaching Religion in School, J. Holm, Oxford University Press.
What Can I do in RE? M. Grimmit (2nd ed.), Mayhew-McCrimmon.
The Birmingham Handbook and 1982 Supplement. A valuable compendium of material produced by Birmingham LEA. Available for the education offices.
The Shap Mailing. This is a yearly publication containing articles, reviews and details of world religions courses. Available from Peter Woodward, 7 Alderbrook Road, Solihull, West Midlands B91 1NH. A good way of keeping up-to-date. The mailing includes a calendar of religious festivals.
Resource, University of Warwick Institute of Education. A new RE journal with a world religions emphasis.

THE CHRISTIAN TEACHER IN THE MULTI-FAITH SCHOOL

My period as International Secretary with the Christian Education Movement from 1968 to 1972 covered a period when Christian teachers felt threatened on at least two fronts. Many had been moving to an open-ended RE through the influence of Goldman and Loukes, supported in some cases by progressive Agreed Syllabuses and using ideas and materials produced by such agencies as CEM.

As Colin Alves points out in a most useful survey of developments in the *Christian in Education* (SCM Centre, 1972) these developments were 'not just a question of new methods, or even of new content, but of new aims, a new rationale'. He quotes the Durham Report which claims that the new-style teacher of RE is 'seeking rather to initiate his pupils into knowledge which he encourages them to explore and appreciate, than to a system of belief which he requires them to accept'. As Colin Alves pointed out, however, this presented no real problem for the Christian teacher because he was still concerned with what pupils believe. The purpose served by the 'exploration of religion is to make a distinctive contribution to each pupils' search for a faith by which to live'. *It is not merely to satisfy curiosity or extend cultural horizons,* says Alves (emphasis mine).

The Christian teacher still had a role to play in helping the children to find this faith by which to live. This is clearly set out in *Humanities for the Young School Leaver: An Approach Through RE.* 'What he is called on to do, as a teacher, is to make clear the available choices, and the grounds thereof: and to help his pupils make their choices and face the consequences of making them.'

Although this approach has been labelled 'neo-confessional' and was still basically Christian it was a long way from Scripture and RK and teachers who had made the adjustment in their approach and method felt that this new RE was here to stay.

During the 1960s many were thrown into confusion, if not alarm, almost before they had become accustomed to this new RE by the presence of significant numbers of followers of other faiths in their classroom. These were far from open-ended in their approach in religion, in fact they took it so seriously that it affected their approach to school dinners, undressing for PE and often led to withdrawal from Assembly and the RE period, thus making nonsense of the aim of the exercise. It soon appeared that some were attending Religious Instruction in their own faith both before and after school and also at weekends.

Both in their knowledge and attitude many Christian teachers found

96

it difficult to tackle the new situation. A Consultation in 1969 organised by the BCC Education Department in the West Riding found 'The majority of Christians regard Christianity as the completion of all other religions and often infer that it has nothing to learn from non-Christian traditions. RE specialists who accept this inference would find extreme difficulty in presenting a sympathetic and unbiased point of view'.

In 1970 a Birmingham group stated in their leaflet *R.E. in a Multi-religious Society,* 'It should be part of a general education today to become aware of the diverse forms of human culture and of religious faith. In the field of RE this means that children should not be ignorant (as too often they have been in the past) of the main features of the major world religions; and that in Birmingham, more specifically, Christian children should know something about the Hindu, Islamic, Judaic and Sikh faiths which are part of our pluralistic scene, just as children of these various faiths should know something both of Christianity as the majority faith of the country, and of other minority faiths.'

The West Riding consultation underlined the problem, however, when it stated, 'Many teachers, quite apart from personal convictions, consider themselves ill-equipped for such a demanding task'.

If the presence of pupils of other faiths with their mosques and temples down the road presented problems and even a threat to the Christian teacher so did the pressure from educationists to change their approach to RE yet again. This new approach in the minds of its advocates was separate from the 'immigration' issue but in the minds of many teachers I met were closely linked and formed a double threat.

This new approach encouraged teachers to explore the 'explicit' phenomena of religion. It is usually associated with the name of Ninian Smart of Lancaster and is supported by ginger groups such as the Shap Working Party, which has produced guides and materials. RE now became 'Religious Studies','providing a service in helping people to understand history and other cultures than our own'. It was felt by many of the teachers I met with that emphasis was on the descriptive, historical side and the 'spiritual growth of the child' and 'the exploration of a faith by which to live' was now swallowed up in a dry, factual approach, another kind of history lesson with Muhammad, Guru Nanak and Jesus ben Joseph being presented equally as 'religious leaders' to be excited by or bored with, depending on the teacher. This is a caricature of this approach which is set out clearly in the *Schools Council Working Paper 36,* but this idea that 'we now have to teach all religions as equal' was one of the common impressions I gained from teachers and this had obviously caused the committed Christian great heart-searching.

Colin Alves also states that the former open-ended approach should have caused few difficulties for the Christian teacher, but goes on to say: 'What strikes me as being a much more difficult matter for the

Christian R.E. teacher to come to terms with is the possible implication of open R.E. regarding faiths other than Christianity. It is logically necessary to accept the possible meaninglessness of existence as a valid alternative to the possibility of inherent meaning, but what does one say about the possible validity of *alternative grounds of meaning?* Is it logically necessary to accept all grounds of meaning, all faiths as having equally the possibility of validity?' He goes on to pose the agonising question I have heard so often, 'Open-ended R.E. would seem to imply that all faiths are equally valid. Can the Christian teacher really accept such an implication, or must he insist on the uniqueness (and the superiority) of Christianity? If Christianity is not the truth then why does he remain a Christian?'

Alves then looks at some of the Christian attitudes outlined in *Attitudes towards other Religions* by Owen C. Thomas (SCM Press) and ends this chapter with some controversial statements which need to be fully debated especially where the Christian teacher is in a multi-faith situation. 'Any R.E. teacher,' he states, 'who believed that Christianity was in any sense "the fulfilment or final refinement" of other religions would not be happy if some of his pupils rejected Christianity and turned say, to Buddhism or transcendental meditation.'

He does not go on to discuss, however, the situation which arises for many teachers who have Muslims and Sikhs in their classroom to start with. Would the teacher only 'be happy' if these became Christians? Should they be helped to be better Muslims or Sikhs, or should the proper Christian attitude toward other religions be summed up in the words of Owen Thomas as he outlines the Christian secularist approach. 'It is not that they should be replaced by the Christian religion. Rather Christians should help the adherents of other religions to free themselves from those aspects of their religion and culture which inhibit their freedom and responsibility, and which have caused them to accept their lot fatalistically and to turn to the eternal world for religious solace.'

Unless he is such a Christian secularist or a 'throughgoing relativist' prepared to accept with Toynbee 'that in some measure all the higher religions are also revelations of what is true and right; they also come from God and each presents some facet of God's truth' then the Christian teacher is in real difficulty.

'A Christian of any other persuasion,' says Alves, 'has to take the specific step of deliberately *setting on one side his own beliefs* about the comparative value of other religions before he can start to teach from a properly open basis. It may only be a "procedural step", inasmuch as it is a *suspension of his beliefs,* not a permanent abandonment of them but procedural or otherwise, it is a step which has to be taken' (emphasis mine).

Does this step have to be taken? Are teachers able to make this step? As Alves himself points out, some Christians 'will feel impelled to teach the truth to his pupils . . . and will not count his teaching as successful unless ultimately all his pupils come to see the truth as he sees it'.

It needs to be said, however, that a number of us who, committed to the 'Ninian Smart' approach in our teaching and lecturing and still remain committed Christians, have had to come to terms with the new RE and the new multi-faith situation without 'suspending our beliefs' which in my own experience would both be an impossibility and a denial of the wholeness of the teacher's personality.

Owen Thomas, in his book mentioned above, devotes a chapter to the thinking of William Hocking and, after twelve years involved in mission and education (four of them in Africa), maintaining close contact with followers of other faiths I still find the theory of 'reconception' as expounded by Hocking to be the most helpful. At least it enables me to lecture on world religions in what I hope is a factual and understanding way yet to live my life fully as a Christian *at the same time* without suspending my belief.

Hocking's views are described on pages 133–50 of *Attitudes towards other Religions*. William Ernest Hocking (1873–1966) was an American Methodist layman, a lecturer in comparative religion and philosophy at Harvard. He chaired a group taking a new look at missionary work in the 1930s and their work was published under the title 'Rethinking Mission'. He lectured at Oxford and Cambridge in 1936 and the lectures were published in 1940 under the title 'Living religions and a world faith'.

He states that there are three possible approaches to other faiths. First, the way of *radical displacement* which, put crudely, states that one religion is right and the others are wrong. Second, the way of *synthesis* which would seek to adopt bits of any and every faith and lead to a complete watering down of the given essence of the faith originally held by a person which would hardly be recognised as the original religion at all so far as it compromised its beliefs and practices.

Having dismissed these two methods as unacceptable, Hocking outlines what he feels to be the most helpful approach, which encourages both a tolerant attitude towards other faiths, and a deeper knowledge and enrichment of one's own faith through this inter-faith contact. He calls this approach the way of *reconception,* which he defines as 'a process by which every religion understands itself at a deeper level through contact with other religions, conserving what is best in them and developing into a deeper and wider conception of religion'.

Here there is no rigidity on the one hand or watering down on the other, but a deepening of the faiths that come into contact. As Christians we believe in the revelation of God in Jesus Christ, but we have also been given the Holy Spirit, 'who will guide us into all truth' and therefore through the confrontation of various faiths on these small islands and in the classroom we are being presented with a glorious opportunity of enriching and deepening our Christian faith rather than losing it. Canon Max Warren, former General Secretary of the Church Missionary Society, has expressed something of the role and attitude of the Christian teacher in the multi-faith school when he states, 'Our first task in approaching another people, another culture, another religion, is to take off our shoes, for the place we are approaching is holy. Else we may find ourselves treading on other men's dreams. More serious still, we may forget that God was here before our arrival. We have to try to sit where they sit to enter sympathetically into the pains and griefs and joys of their history . . . we have in a word to be present with them'.

It is only when we approach our pupils in this spirit that we will glimpse the vision of Peter in Acts 10:34: 'I now see how true it is that God has no favourites, but that in every nation the man who is God-fearing and does what is right is acceptable to him.' Such a vision will enable us to be true to our pupils, our subject and our own faith and to our Lord, for as the World Council of Churches statement has it, 'Christ draws us out of our isolation into closer relationship with all men'. It is *because* of faith in God through Jesus Christ and because of our belief in the reality of creation, the offer of redemption, and the love of God shown in the incarnation that we seek a positive relationship with men of other faiths.'

As we approach others in the true spirit of love we shall find a ready response from the members of other faiths. The most enriching experience in my work with CEM was the opportunity it gave to meet with pupils and educationists from a number of faiths, often in residential conferences. It was never held against me that I was a Christian, in fact, I was often invited in the first place for that very reason and even spoke at the formation of an Islamic Society in a north London polytechnic. They are anxious to explore with us the possible methods and content of education which will enable us to grow together in faith and understanding on these islands.

The multi-religious school is therefore a picture of our larger society presenting us with opportunities for enrichment as we explore the faiths represented in the school. The new RE will enable us to explore the prayer life, the worship and the experience of others which can only enrich our own prayer life, our own worship and experience.

We need have no fears then that Christianity will be 'pushed into the background' — it can now find a new and exciting role in the changed situation. Lessons about other religions will not be dull and boring as we discover together the faiths which have given meaning to life and there is no need to suspend belief. In fact, many of us who have faltered have discovered again our belief in God who has not left himself without witness, in every time and in every place.

RAY TRUDGIAN

BOOKLIST

Attention is drawn to the annotated booklist prepared by Eric Sharpe for the Shap bibliography, *World Religions: A Handbook for Teachers* published by CRC. The following books are cheap and readily available.

Religious Education in Secondary Schools, School Council Working paper 36. Contains an excellent summary of developments in RE, CH.VII, 'Non-Christian religions and the religious needs of minority groups' and Ch.XIII 'The Christian as R.E. Teacher' relate to this section.

The Christian in Education, Colin Alves, SCM Press (Centre Book), 1972. The main chapter on 'the Christian and Religious Education' has been discussed in this section but the whole book should be read by those who would call themselves Christian teachers.

Attitudes towards other Religions, Owen C. Thomas (ed.), SCM Press, Forum Books. This book looks at the various attitudes held by Christian theologians towards other religions and contains excerpts from their works. They include Schleiermacher, Troeltsch, Barth, Brunner, Hocking, Toynbee, Tillich, Hans Kung, Warren and Taylor.

Face to Face: Essays on Inter-Faith Dialogue, published by the Church Missionary Society. Essays include 'Christian Motivation in Dialogue', Taylor; 'A theology of Attention', Warren; 'Muslim and Christian dialogue', David Brown.

Christianity and Comparative Religion, J. N. D. Anderson, Tyndale paperback. A most useful contribution to the current debate from an evangelical point of view. The basic argument is that when a person of another faith truly seeks God he will find Him through the grace of God shown to us in Christ. Written from a deep Christian faith and knowledge of Islam.

The Finality of Christ, Leslie Newbigin, SCM Press, 1969. This book spells out what that 'finality' means in relation to other religions and contains a very important chapter on 'Conversion'.

Community Relations, Ray Trudigan, Probe No. 14, CEM. An attempt to bring the debate into the classroom. Looks at five religious communities and asks how they should relate to each other, raising issues such as the use of church buildings, conversion, etc.

RAY TRUDIGAN

TEACHING HINDUISM: ISSUES, APPROACHES AND RESOURCES

ISSUES

The religious studies teacher had been absent because of illness during Christian Aid Week. On her return she was met by a group of angry and sorrowful teenagers of Indian background. They took her round the school, showing her the photographs of life in poverty-stricken villages, many of them Indian, which decorated the walls. 'If you had been here, this wouldn't have been allowed to happen,' they said. 'No wonder people think we are poor, backward and unemployable.' This 'Third World' image is probably the most serious obstacle that the teacher of Hinduism has to overcome today, at least in the secondary school. Good intentions, in the form of concern for those parts of the world which are recovering from colonialism, can accidentally create the impression that India and places like it are inhabited by feckless people who are a drain on the resources of the wealthier nations inhabited by white Christians.

The solution of the Third World difficulty is not easily found. Ultimately it depends on a radically new and as yet unacceptable global strategy of development with the eradication of the notion of a 'Third World', an increasingly distasteful expression, in favour of the recognition that there is only one world. However, in the multi-faith school it is possible to light candles rather than only curse the dark. First, in terms of the hidden curriculum the staff might consider its attitude to Oxfam, Christian Aid and similar agencies. Banning Christian Aid Week might seem severe, but its observance can convey the impression that only Christians care. This must be avoided at all costs in any school, as must be the idea that poverty is a foreign disease, confined to Italy or Puerto Rico in the white areas of the world, but not found in Salford, Liverpool or London. Possibly the name Christian Aid is now too restrictive, especially as Jews, Hindus and others are to be found among collectors and givers. Second, the geography and history departments have a role to play in explaining the developmental situation in which the world finds itself today. Then the religious studies department can consider how to teach Hinduism.

Thirty years ago the first issue to have faced the teacher would have been that which is summed up in the words, 'The heathen in his blindness, bows down to wood and stone', or the line which I recently heard sung in Coventry cathedral, 'O'er heathen lands afar thick darkness broodeth yet'. In a more secular age it is probably the second issue in order of importance, though no less serious for that as it may well provide the Third World image with its theological justification — 'they are backward because they are not Christian and therefore lack a work ethic'. This belief is likely to be reinforced if we include Mother Teresa in a topic on India.

To counter the tradition that Hindus are idol-worshippers the course might include study of the work of Ram Mohan Roy and also the *Arya Samaj,* but, more important, an analysis of the Hindu concept of deity. As long as three thousand years ago the belief was stated, 'To what is One, sages give many a title; they call it Agni, Yama, Matarisvan' (*Rig Veda* 1:164:46). In the *Yagur Veda* (32:1) perhaps as a gloss on these words, it is written 'For an awakened soul Indra, Varuna, Agni, Yama, Aditya, Chandra — all these names represent only one basic power and spiritual entity.'

There may be Hindus who believe in many gods, just as some aspects of popular Christianity seem to be polytheistic, but the essential teaching of Hinduism is that God is One. Christianity and other religions use many names to describe God — Father, the Holy One, the Immortal, the Ineffable, Almighty, Lord . . . Hinduism dares to express this pictorially and by using female and animal symbols, not only male as in the semitic traditions.

As for idol-worship, the story is told of an iconoclastic prince to whose court came a Hindu sage. Seeing a portrait of the prince's father, the wise man threw it on the floor and stamped on it. The prince ordered him to be killed, but the Hindu retorted that he had only stamped on a piece of paper. Such an act scarcely deserved death. The prince, it is said, saw the point and stopped smashing religious statues. (This story is told on p. 178 of this book.) There is a need to sensitise children, especially in a country with a protestant heritage, to an understanding of the place of visual imagery in Hinduism.

But what of Mother Teresa and Christian missions? Their place is in the Christianity syllabus. Also, in a 'A' level course on Hinduism the consequences of Christian Hindu interaction provide an important topic for study.

The Indian village is quaint and exotic, even perhaps romantic to the Westerner who is just passing through, but all this can reinforce the impression of backwardness in the minds of children. India is not a museum where time has stood still, it is dynamic. Allusions to it being 'like Britain a hundred years ago' should be avoided, so should the use of black and white pictures which evoke none of the richness of Indian life.

The *varna-jati,* class and caste system, is something which the teacher of Hinduism must understand. One frequently comes across' simplistic remarks comparing it with the class structure of British society, or unhelpful comparisons with the feudal system (itself seldom explained anyway). It is something about which people delight in making value judgements — a response which is always easier than acquiring knowledge and understanding. Comparisons are to be avoided. *The varna-jati* system of India should be regarded as unique. It is not easy to suggest where the teacher should begin the task of understanding it. At this point Hindus often become unhelpful apologists and Sikh and Muslim tellers of horror stories which even outdo the anecdotes of missionaries! A. L. Basham's brief outline in *The Concise Encyclopaedia of Living Faiths* (R. C. Zaehner (ed.), Hutchinson) may be as good an introduction as any. His whole survey of Hinduism in that book repays study. Perhaps the real difficulty facing the teacher here, as with so much of Hinduism, is that Western writers have been interested either in Hindu philosophy, if they are specialists in religious studies, or in Hindu society, as anthropologists. Few seem to have studied Hinduism as a whole — and the class and caste system, like so much else that is Indian, combines dimensions which Westerners would compartmentalise as being religious, social and economic.

This finally brings us to two differences between Christianity and Hinduism, which the teacher (who is likely to be of Christian background) might consider. First, as has been intimated, Hinduism is a word which applies to a total life style, including diet, occupation, sex roles, ethical conduct, ritual practices and beliefs. The distinction between religious and secular is unfamiliar to the Hindu. The question 'Is that part of your religion or just part of your culture?' is a Western one which is likely to leave the Hindu baffled. It would also be meaningless to most Sikhs and Muslims, and many Jews. Secularisation may be creeping into all these cultures but it has not yet entered them as it has done British Christianity.

The second difference is between the semitic religions (Judaism, Christianity, Islam) and the religions which originated in India. The semitic religions are usually exclusive in that they refuse to take into their systems of belief doctrines or ideas from other traditions. Each has at some time claimed to be true in a way that implies that other religions are false. It would be unusual to hear a passage from the *Bhagavad Gita* read as a lesson in church, though it has happened, but it is quite a common sight to see a picture of Jesus in a Hindu temple. It has been known for a Hindu to complain at being called a non-Christian, 'Please don't call us that, we also revere Jesus'. The Indian tradition is eclectic and all-embracing. This openness has enabled India to survive Aryans, Greeks, Muslims and Christians, and retain its own characteristics. Much of the complexity of Hinduism is attributed to its ability to accept and absorb rather than be absorbed.

APPROACHES

The aim should be the humanising knowledge to enable pupils to understand what it means to be a Hindu in terms of belief and practice. There is no need to begin in India. We would not begin a course on Judaism in Israel but in the UK. The same place can be the starting-point for learning about Hinduism.

Younger Children

The casual but deliberate intrusion of Indian languages, dress and references to foods might be beginnings with younger children. Hopefully, the Wendy house, classroom objects and wall pictures are virtually taking the multi-cultural world for granted, with saris being available for dressing up and chappati-making being as normal a feature as baking bread. Indian words as well as English can appear under pictures of cows, babies, aeroplanes or ships. The clock, the piano, desks, chairs and tables can similarly be labelled in a number of languages as part of a pre-reading strategy. All this may seem to have little to do with Hinduism, but it is creating a situation of naturalness in which stories about Krishna or the celebration of *Diwali* will appear completely in place and not awkward, special exceptions to an otherwise Eurocentric education.

I would see a Wendy house which had Indian material from dressing up in saris, and Indian bracelets and garlands as preparing the ground for Hinduism. So, too, the reception class shop selling chappatis and burfi as well as sausage rolls and jam tarts. More directly, I would hope that a newly married Hindu bride might be persuaded to come to school dressed up as she was on her wedding day. If there is a helpful photographic specialist at the teachers' centre he might be able to provide enlargements of some of her wedding photographs for display on the classroom wall. Many Hindus and Sikhs have now taken to having their marriage ceremonies captured on video, and perhaps the film could be shown in school. Even more exciting might be the possibility of taking a school class to observe the wedding of a sister or brother of someone in the class. Most Hindus and Sikhs I know would be very happy for this to happen. Probably the class would be invited to stay for a meal — some thought would have to be given to that. Orange juice and biscuits, plus Indian sweets, might be preferable to introducing the children to curries! The class might be able to view the wedding presents at the bride's home. A fascinating experience; even more so in an Indian village!

Another visit might be that of a mother with her new baby with the school providing the transport, of course. In an all-white school this proved a very successful and intriguing experience. Children were sur-

106

prised that a baby born in this country was brown, and that he came complete with fingers and toes. The teacher discovered not only that older infants had funny ideas about Indians and skin colour, but also about babies. (Incidentally, someone overheard a nurse from the Caribbean telling a patient that she had four children, two born in St Kitts and two born here. 'Oh, so you've two white and two black', the patient said, in all seriousness!)

The major point that is being made so far is that much pre-Hinduism, pre-Islam and pre-Sikhism, as in a sense pre-Christianity and pre-Afro–Caribbean culture, can best be developed through links with the communities from which the children come. Just as a child bringing a young squirrel into my classroom in a rural school where I taught changed the whole day's programme, so might the return of a little boy from visiting his grandparents in India or Pakistan, or news of a little Roman Catholic girl's confirmation.

However, there is a place for structure. Things do not always happen and the ad lib speaker is usually found to be repetitive and lacking ideas if you hear him more than twice. There might be a need to simulate weddings or the arrival of a new baby. However, planning is more appropriate with regard to festivals and to storytelling. The Hindu festival of *Diwali* together with others celebrated by the local Hindu community would provide occasions for homing-in on Hinduism, through the telling of the story, its re-enactment and through dance and a party.

The stories which are told to young children need careful thought. I think they can discriminate between the miraculous (which I would not tell) and the fabulous (which I would), if the latter are told in a manner which evokes atmosphere. The purpose of such stories is affective, not cognitive. Indian myths and folktales should appear naturally among the stories told at storytime each afternoon. Art, puppetry and dance can also be invoked as aids.

The Middle Years

This is a time for building on what has gone before and for developing and extending it. If the infant school has done its work well the main difficulty may be that of avoiding repetition. A more observant look at the Hindu temple, at the Hindu extended family and the way it works, and at festivals should be possible and interesting. Certainly they should visit a Hindu temple and through its iconography be introduced to mythology and symbolism. But try to be sure that the temple is smart and bright. Some are still house-temples in need of renovation and reflecting the hard times many Hindus are facing through unemployment. The impression which visiting children would receive might not be the one the teacher had in mind.

The horizons of children in the middle years are continually extend-ing. As they approach other lands and other times the geography and history of India could be included, but with regard to the former comments already made about quaintness and backwardness have to be remembered. The use of the hydro-electric power and India's de-veloping industries are part of the story, as well as cycle rickshaws. As for tigers, elephants and snakes, the first acquaintance many Indians made with them was when they visited zoos in Britain. Stamps, coins and other things that pupils of this age are interested in can be used. The use of visual aids is essential.

The diagram of Hinduism content below is intended as a secondary school flowchart but some aspects can be included earlier.

The Secondary School

The study must include beliefs and ethics. The danger always is that it never goes beyond the description.

The greatest difficulty in Hinduism seems to be that of prising up an edge. With other religions it is apparently easy. Jesus, Muhammad, the Buddha, Guru Nanak seem to be obvious starting-points. Whether they are the best is irrelevant here. Hinduism has no 'founder figure' and no-one I know has begun with Krishna, though someone with flair might.

The home or the temple can provide introductions, hence their position at the top of the flowchart. The course can then develop as outlined. It will cover class and caste as well as Hindu 'polytheism' and the use of images in worship, but should also demonstrate the truth that Hinduism is self-critical through the study of such a personality as Gandhi.

Whichever route is chosen, all topics included in the diagram should demand attention. *Bhakti*, gurus and pilgrimage might provide a link with the village, and death and moksha if the temple route is taken. Village life can provide a taking-off point for any topic in the 'temple' column. Although the study of Hinduism need not begin in India and probably would not, it will eventually include the village and home in India and change in India (here Gandhi is important, though he died over thirty years ago, we must remember). Something of the wonder of India can be appreciated through its literature and architecture.

The content could also be used thematically over a number of years under such headings as:
Religion in the local community:places of worship;
Festivals and pilgrimages;
Religious teachers: gurus like Vallabha (whose modern followers are to be found in Britain in the *Pushti marga*), or Sai Baba, as well as the ancient *rishis* and the brahmin priests;

Hinduism Flowchart

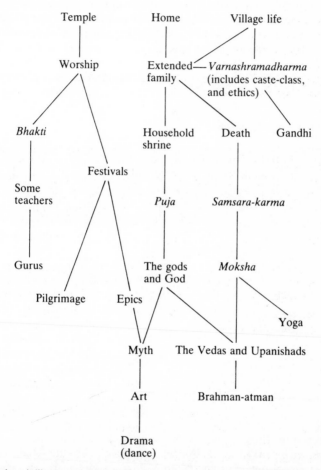

The flowchart indicates possible sequential development and provides checklist of content. It does not imply that the religion should be covered in a single course (see p. 153).

Scriptures, vedas, Upanishads, *Gita*, puranas, epics;
Rites of passage, birth, initiation, marriage and funeral rites;
Ethics, *varnashramadharma*;
Concepts of deity, links with worship and bhakti;
Paths to eternity, *moksha*, Brahman-atman.

These seem preferable to a one-term or one-year course on Hinduism. In a multi-faith school, as has been suggested elsewhere, the thematic approach may be the most practical, whether the teacher considers it the best or not.

RESOURCES

Books for the Teacher

There are number of introductory books which might be recommended but no single volume which is universally acclaimed. I would suggest that Nila Pancholi's section in *Comparative Religions* (Blandford Press, 1982) will be of greatest help to teachers coming to Hinduism for the first time. See also D. K. Vohra's contribution to *East Meets West*, M. Iqbal (ed.), (Commission for Racial Equality). These may be supplemented by other works such as:

The Hindu Religion Thought, T. K. Hopkins, Dickenson.

Hinduism, J. R. Hinnells and E. J. Sharpe (eds), Oriel Press. Includes sections on teaching Hinduism. Extensive bibliographies, though some of the books may be out of print now.

The Religion of the Hindus, K. W. Morgan (ed.), Ronald Press.

India: The Social Anthropology of a Civilisation, B. S. Cohn, Prentice-Hall.

The Sacred Thread, J. Brackington, Edinburgh House Press.

The Hindu Temple, G. Michell, Paul Elek.

Hindu Myths, W. D. O'Flaherty, Penguin.

The Hindu View of Life, S. Radhakrishnan, Allen and Unwin.

The Indestructible Soul, E. G. Parrinder, Allen and Unwin. A good introduction to the complexity of Hindu views on liberation.

Mind, Body and Wealth, D. Pocock, Blackwell. The sub-title, 'A Study of Belief and Practice in an Indian Village', sums it up.

Gods, Demons and Others, R. K. Narayan, Heinemann. Stories almost as told by the village storyteller.

Myths and Legends of India, J. M. Macfie, T. & T. Clark. A good anthology for the teacher's use. Useful notes and index. Difficult to obtain from bookshops. Still available from the publisher.

Cradle Tales of Hinduism, Sister Nivedita, Ramakrishna Vedanta Centre.

My Village, My Life, P. Mohanti, Davis-Poynter. Pen-portraits of his village by a famous Indian artist.
The Speaking Tree, R. Lannoy, Oxford University Press.
The Ramayana, R. K. Narayan, Chatto and Windus.
Hindu and Christian in Vrindaban, K. Klostermaier, SCM.
Hinduism in England, D. Bowen (ed.), Bradford College.
(See also the general booklist for encyclopedias or reference works.)

Books for the Classroom

The Hindu World, P. Bahree, Macdonald. A very sound and attractively produced book suitable for introducing any child from 9 to 15 to Hinduism.
Understanding Your Hindu Neighbour, J. Ewan, Lutterworth. Another good introduction for pupils in the middle years, especially to Hindus in Britain. Useful for CSE and pre-'O' level.
Hindu Family in Britain, P. Bridger, Pergamon (12–15).
The Way of the Hindu, Swami Yogeshananda, Hulton Educational (9–13).
Ramu, Rama Mehta, Angus and Watson (9–12). A story about *Diwali.*
Our Hindu Friends, Tony Perry, Denholm House Press (9–13).
The Hindu Way (part of the Schools Council *Journal in Religion* series), Hart-Davis (14–16).
India, Evan Charlton, Macmillan (10–14). (3 vols).
Thinking About Hinduism, E. J. Sharpe, Lutterworth (15–17).
Indian Tales and Legends, J. E. B. Gray, Oxford University Press.
The Story of Prince Rama, Brian Thompson, Kestral Books. A beautiful illustrated *Ramayana.*
(See also books in the general list.)

Audio-visual Aids

The Argus kit on Hinduism covers areas of Hindu practice not found in some other film strips or slide sets. Two very useful books and sound cassettes to go with the film strips.
Hinduism in India, Church Missionary Society.
Encounter with Hinduism, BBC Radiovision.
Hinduism, Educational Productions.
A Hindu Puja, Educational Productions (tape study available).
Hinduism, Concordia.
Holi, Slide Centre.
Hindu Worship, Slide Centre.
Hindu Wedding, Slide Centre.

Further studies especially of Hindu festivals are planned and should be published by the Slide Centre in 1983 and 1984.

Ghandhi Study Guides, Ian Wall (ed.) from Columbia Pictures, 135 Wardour St. London W1.

Approaches to Diwali, Multicultural Education Resources centre, Bristol.

Maps

India, Pakistan and Ceylon, Bartholomew; national and regional maps are sometimes available from India House, London and tourist agencies.

TEACHING JUDAISM: ISSUES, APPROACHES AND RESOURCES

ISSUES

One of the most provocative remarks that a teacher can make to the increasing number of Jews now participating in multi-faith religious education is 'of course we teach Judaism, we spend a whole year on the Old Testament'. Its primary school equivalent is 'of course we teach Judaism, we are always telling stories that Jesus heard, Noah, Abraham, David and Goliath . . .' The Old Testament is not Judaism. The very name suggests that it has been replaced by something else, something new and therefore better. The approach indicated by these two quotations is Christian, even if the content is Jewish; in the latter the focal point is clearly Jesus — 'stories Jesus heard'. The former suggests a biblical studies framework again with a Christian perspective. The emphasis is probably on the Prophets, for example, with no reference to the most important part of the Jewish Bible, the *Torah*.

By confining a study of Judaism to the Bible we not only distort it, we may also be giving the impression that it is a dead religion in either of two senses. First, that it is a 'fossil' religion, as one of my students described it. (My response was to take her to a synagogue to meet some of these fossils. She returned exhausted, impressed by their vitality and spirituality.) What she meant was that Judaism fossilised after the life of Jesus. It missed its chance and stagnated. How mistaken this conclusion is, but it is the natural one for children taught traditional Bible-based religious education to reach. However, taking down from my bookshelves a few books on Judaism which come most easily to hand, I find that *Judaism* by Isidore Epstein devotes 200 pages to the post-biblical period, out of 323; Leo Trepp has six chapters, ninety-three pages on the biblical period, and then another seventeen chapters, over 300 pages, on post-year 70 Judaism. Of course, even Epstein's book, which is subtitled 'A Historical Persecution', is not structured in such a way that his last 200 pages make no mention of the Bible, but I hope the point is clear. If Abraham lived about 1900 BCE more than half the story of Judaism belongs to the post-'Old Testament' times, if *Daniel*, the last book of the Jewish Bible to be written, is to be dated about 164 BCE.

At this point I am in danger of falling into another trap which it is not easy altogether to escape. We date our calendars from the supposed birthday of Jesus and divide time into BC and AD. These abbreviations, of course, stand from 'Before Christ' and 'In the year of *our* Lord' (*Anno Domini*), both of which are unacceptable affirmations for Jews to make. It is therefore customary to use BCE and CE (Before the Common Era and the Common Era, or Christian Era) in religious studies books. Nevertheless, even these abbreviations only modify the view that the most significant event in human history took place some 1980 years ago. In a study of Judaism, the year 1 CE, it might be said, was uneventful and unimportant; Jesus was only one of many messianic claimants. The pivotal event of Jewish history was the destruction of the Jerusalem Temple seventy years later. Somehow, when teaching about religions other than Christianity the historical perspective of those religions rather than that of Christianity must be maintained, despite the use of BC/AD or BCE/CE. This is a problem for history, too, of course. By saying that Guru Nanak was born in 1469, even if we use CE rather than AD, we are fitting him into our scheme of things rather than making the effort of entering his Indian world.

There is a second way in which Judaism is regarded as a dead religion. A rabbi was once speaking to a group of nuns in Ireland. One of them eventually asked him if he was a Jew. His reply surprised her; she confessed that until then she thought that they had become extinct with the ministry of Jesus. I once had a similar experience. A student asked me why I was teaching them about Judaism as though it was a distinct religion in its own right. She thought it was just another Christian denomination, 'like Roman Catholicism'!

Judaism is likely to have appeared in the school curriculum even before it is taught to the RE syllabus, in the form of Fagin and Shylock. It has been known for a teacher to say 'we don't teach Judaism in our school, it isn't a Jewish area', at the same time as *The Merchant of Venice* was being taught as an 'O' level English text. (Incidentally, the children studying the play had never met a Jew, but, when asked, they were sure that the portrayal of them as greedy and deceitful was accurate.) Anti-semitism has even been encountered among a group of Sikhs who had never met a Jew! In one way or another, then, the RE teacher is likely to encounter a bias when teaching Judaism similar to the bias which may still exist against Roman Catholics, but worse, because it combines racial and religious prejudice.

Judaism's claim to be included in a religious studies syllabus just so that the record can be put straight is strong; but the proper and primary reason for including it is for its own distinctive worth. It is an important religion in its own right. In the religious studies context it also provides valuable examples when one is examining religion in the home, the place of ritual and symbolism, the significance of scriptures and the celebration of festivals. It is an exciting religion to teach, full of things which are tangible and fascinating — there is therefore a danger of distorting it and failing to explore the spirituality of Judaism. Perhaps because of the richness of its rituals and the New Testament portrayal of Judaism as legalistic in the worst sense of the word (though we usually applaud people who are law-abiding), it is possible to hear Christian preachers asserting that Jesus brought God close to man; in Judaism he was always remote and far off. Have they never read *Jeremiah* or *Job*, not to mention the stories of Abraham, God's friend, Moses, and most of the other Prophets?

Judaism is, of course, the womb from which Jesus was born. Jesus was a Jew. He was circumcised on the eighth day. Perhaps he was not able to express a view on the rite just then, but if, as an adult, he had disapproved it is unlikely that Paul would have deemed it proper to circumcise Timothy. Often one hears Judaism being condemned by Christianity for its sacrificial system but there is no evidence of Jesus doing this. At Passover, when every Jew could be his own priest, Jesus may have sacrificially killed his own lamb; if not someone else did it for him. Throughout the *Acts of the Apostles* there is explicit evidence of Christians continuing to worship in the Temple, and nowhere in the New Testament is the sacrificial system criticised on moral grounds. When, eventually, Christians did reject it their reason was theological; the sacrifice of Jesus rendered all others ineffectual, unnecessary and redundant. Those who speak from a position of superiority against blood sacrifice in Judaism or in Hinduism not only fail to recognise that there was a growing emphasis upon sacrifice of the heart, the offering of one's personal devotion and commitment as a living sacrifice, but also that many agnostics and Humanists have been disgusted by a Christianity which can speak of Jesus' death on Calvary as a sacrifice.

Judaism is so much on the agenda of Christianity that it is hard to see how, in a country in which the dominant religion is Christianity, Judaism can be excluded from the syllabus. To omit it is probably to teach it in a distorted and inaccurate manner: to paint the New Testament portrait of Pharisaic legalism and imply that it is Judaism, then and now — forgetting, incidentally, that the theology of Jesus was probably pharisaic. The relationship of Judaism and Christianity can be explored at various points in secondary school courses. Before this, however, Judaism needs to be taught as a religion discrete in itself. Should it precede Christianity in the syllabus? Opinions differ, but on two points there is agreement. First, it should be taught in its own right, not as the handmaid of Christianity. (In any case, the practices of Judaism have not stood still and are not precisely the same as they were in Jesus' day.) Secondly, it should be taught as a living faith, not as Jewish biblical studies. So how much attention should be given to the Jewish Bible? As much as is needed to make the Judaism of today intelligible.

APPROACHES

The starting-point, as with all living religions, should be with the here and now. With younger children, aspects of family life and festivals, especially accompanied by pictures and artifacts, provide interesting topics. The prayer shawl, the *mezzuzah* on the door, miniature scrolls with Hebrew script, all add reality and interest, though better still may be the synagogue, which can be visited, and meeting the friendly minister. Some Jewish biblical stories might be added if the teacher wishes, under the kind of heading 'Stories that Jewish Children Hear'. However, I would hope the teacher would be more discriminating than has usually been the case in selecting them. Not David and Goliath, please. Some Joseph, Moses, David material is suitable (his selection as king and friendship with Jonathan especially), but there are also Ruth, Jeremiah and others.

With pupils in the middle years and older the significance and symbolic meaning of many aspects of the Jewish religion can be explored, such as *Bar Mitzvah*, the meaning of the festivals, especially the Passover, the use of Hebrew in orthodox worship, reverence for the *Torah*, and the importance of the Sabbath.

With still older pupils there is the place of woman in Judaism, anti-semitism and the Holocaust, and the messianic age. Negative attitudes should be allowed to surface (which is not the same as provoking them by asking 'Why do some people dislike Jews' — do you ask 'why do some people dislike school, teachers, me?'). However, hopefully, by the end of the course people like myself will have to spend less time educating the man in the street and the Christian in the pulpit as well as the pew out of distorted views of Judaism acquired in school and Sunday school (an 'eye for an eye', for example). Positively, by the time children leave school they should understand what it means in terms of belief and practice to be a Jew.

Content

The major areas of content with some minor ones included in brackets are contained in the flowchart opposite.

RESOURCES

The teacher of Judaism is particularly fortunate, for so many Jewish writers and agencies exist which have provided readable and educationally sound material. Where Myer Domnitz ably led, others like Rabbi Douglas Charing and Clive Lawton, the compiler of this list, have followed. Attention is also drawn to the Summer 1981 edition of

116

Judaism Flowchart

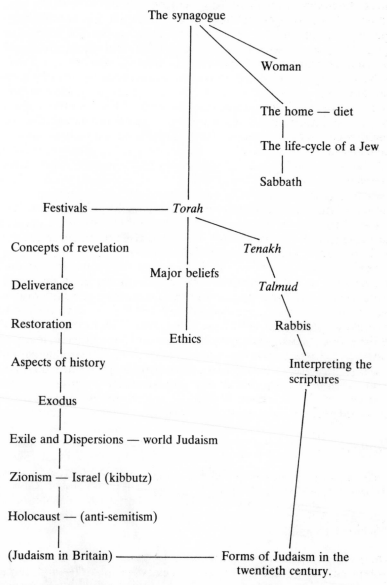

The flowchart indicates possible sequential development and provides checklist of content. It does not imply that the religion should be covered in a single course (see p. 153).

the British *Journal of Religious Education*, which was subtitled, *Teaching Judaism Today*.

Books for the Teacher

This is My God, Herman Wouk, Fontana. This is an excellent personal introduction to the living religion of a contemporary Jew.

Judaism, I. Epstein, Pelican. A good introduction to the study of Judaism.

Jews — Their Religious Beliefs and Practices, Alan Unterman, Routledge and Kegan Paul. An introduction to the rituals and customs of Judaism. Alan Unterman is an Orthodox rabbi and lecturer in comparative religion.

What Does Judaism Say About . . .? Louis Jacobs, Keter. An overview of Jewish teaching on more than a hundred contemporary issues ranging from abortion to Zen Buddhism. A fine introduction to the ethics of Judaism which will balance Unterman's book on the rituals and customs.

The Jewish Festivals, H. Schauss, Schocken. The best of the summaries of the history, practices, customs and teachings surrounding the Jewish festivals.

A History of the Jews, Grayzel, JPS. A straight history of the Jewish people from earliest times up to the modern state of Israel — all in one volume!

The Jewish Catalog, 3 vols, Stassfeld and Stassfeld, JPS. Lively and imaginative modern approach to all the various aspects of Jewish living. Written, and particularly relevant, for the Jewish community in America, there is still more than enough material to make the books valuable in order to gain an insight into Judaism from the inside.

Hitler's War Against the Jews, Lucy Davidowicz, Pelican. Without doubt the most authoritative overview of the Holocaust.

History of The Jewish Experience, Leo Trepp, Behrman. A more interpretive approach to Jewish history than the Grayzel text. Therefore more engaging and thought-provoking, but also more subjective.

A Rabbinic Anthology, Schocken. An excellent anthology of Rabbinic (mainly Talmudic) writings which helps to establish the Pharisees in a fairer light as great ethical teachers. It also gives the flavour of general Talmudic teaching.

118

Books for Pupils

Primary

Jewish Days and Holidays, G. F. Cashman, SBS. An attractively illustrated introduction to Jewish festivals suitable for the middle primary age.

Stories from Our Living Past, Francine Prose, Behram. Several Jewish stories suitable to be read to middle and upper primary schoolchildren. Useful questions for discussion at the end of each story.

The Way of the Jews, Louis Jacobs, Hulton Educational.

All about Jewish Holidays and Customs, Morris Epstein, Ktav, and *Exploring the Jewish Holidays and Customs*, Shirley Stern, Ktav. These are both books that give attractively illustrated and well-structured introductions to Jewish holidays and customs for the upper primary age range. The second is more particularly designed for internal Jewish education and therefore has some Hebrew text as well. This may well be considered a bonus rather than a hindrance.

Our Jewish Friends, Margaret Clark, Denholm House Press.

Understanding Your Jewish Neighbour, Myer Domnitz, Lutterworth. Also recommended for younger secondary pupils.

Secondary

I am a Jew, Moshe Davis, Mowbray. An easy introduction to Jewish life in Britain taken from a series of radio broadcasts. Short chapters dealing with particular aspects of Jewish experience.

The World of Jewish Faith, Myer Domnitz, Longman.

This is my God, Herman Wouk, Fontana. This is an excellent personal introduction to the living religion of a contemporary Jew.

Thinking about Judaism, Myer Domnitz, Lutterworth.

Jewish History Atlas, Martin Gilbert, Wiedenfeld and Nicolson. An excellent visual introduction to Jewish history dealing with different periods and places through a series of maps. Easy to understand, and valuable at all levels.

History of the Jews, 2 vols, Abba Eban, Behrman. Beautifully illustrated and attractively composed summary of the history of the Jewish people. Suitable for the first three years in secondary school.

Final Journey, Martin Gilbert, Allen and Unwin. An excellent text on the Holocaust which, by concentrating on individual stories, makes the mass experience more easy to relate to and understand.

Judaism, Alan Unterman, Ward Lock. An attractive introduction to Judaism through its art and artifacts. Suitable for fourth year upwards.

When a Jew Celebrates, Harry Gersh, Behrman. An easily comprehensible introduction to Jewish practice, both the festivals and the life cycle. Suitable for early secondary pupils.

The Popular Judaica Library Series, Keter. Beautifully illustrated and comprehensive books on the synagogue, marriage, family, passover, *Sukkot*, the high holy days, *Hasidim*, the return to Zion, minor and modern festivals, the Jews of England, etc. Essential books for pupils doing special studies. CSE, 'O' level onwards.

Fiction, Fact and Fun

The Diary of Anne Frank, Pan. Still one of the most telling books for children ever written. Although a true record by a Jewish girl in hiding from the Nazis in Amsterdam, it is also about adolescence everywhere and holds a universal appeal.

The Chosen, Chaim Potok, Penguin. One amongst several of his books that, although fictional, give a fascinating insight into contemporary Jewish life and tensions created by its encounter with the non-Jewish world.

Exodus, Leon Uris, Corgi. One of several books by Leon Uris in the documentary fiction style. Helps to explain something of the experience of the Holocaust and the hopes and aspirations that went towards the founding of the state of Israel.

The Source, James Michener, Corgi. A *tour de force* of historical romance. The whole of Jewish history is surveyed by this exploration through archaeology.

One more River, Lynne Reid-Banks, Puffin. An engaging novel which contains a good introduction to contemporary life in Israel.

Ten and a Kid, B. Weilerstein, JPS. An entertaining selection of short stories for younger children.

The Joys of Yiddish, Leo Rosten, Penguin. A dictionary of Yiddish words, most of which are illustrated with good Jewish jokes.

Sarah and After, Lynne Reid-Banks, Lion. A change from Ms Banks's usual contemporary writing, this is set in earliest biblical times and tells the Bible story from the viewpoint of the women involved. Suitable for top juniors onwards.

Complete International Jewish Cookbook, Evelyn Rose, Pan. An introduction to Jewish cookery with a concise but accurate summary of Jewish dietary laws and the way in which they affect the recipes one might usually encounter.

The Aleph-Bet Story Book, Deborah Pessin, JPS. An entertaining little story book that introduces the letters of the Hebrew alphabet. Junior children often find the challenge of a new alphabet to be a most entertaining one.

Audio-visual Aids

Living Judaism, Council of Christians and Jews. A 25-minute slide/tape presentation on Judaism well supported by notes. Probably the best general introduction to Judaism in audio-visual form.

Jewish Family Events (×2), CJLIC. Two filmstrips on *Brit Milah* and *Bar Mitzvah*, place the events of circumcision and *Bar Mitzvah* in the context of a modern Jewish family living in Britain today. (Filmstrip is supplied with notes and explanatory material.)

16-mm Holocaust Films, Yad Vashem Committee of the UK. A range of four films (short and full-length, black and white and colour) dealing with the Holocaust at different levels from a variety of angles. Yad Vashem Committee, Woburn House, Upper Woburn Place, London WC1.

Shabbat; The Seder, United Synagogue, Woburn House, Upper Woburn Place, London WC1. Two tapes produced primarily to teach Jews the melodies for the celebration of *Shabbat* in the home and the Passover evening *Seder* service. A good source of Jewish home music.

Colour Posters on Judaism, Christian Education Movement. A set of full-size colour posters on both the home and synagogue, together with explanatory notes.

Jewish Year Game, CJLIC. In poster form, it enables children from 9 onwards to play their way around the Jewish festivals and learn their sequence and significance.

The Jewish Festivals, Pictorial Charts, 27 Kirchen Road, London W13. A set of four full-size colour posters portraying the Jewish festivals.

The Synagogue; Jewish Marriage, The Slide Centre. Two slide/tape presentations on the synagogue and a Jewish wedding in a synagogue.

Useful Addresses

Central Jewish Lecture and Information Committee (CJLIC), Woburn House, Upper Woburn Place, London, WC1.

Executive Director: Clive Lawton. The CJLIC provides a full range of booklets, colour pictures, filmstrips and games. Also gives further advice and information. Serves as a centralising agency for all organisations providing information about the Jews to the non-Jewish community. Its personnel undertake teacher training courses, lectures to schools, the Jewish London Tour (for advanced students) and a variety of other activities.

The JNF Education Department, Harold Poster House, Kingsbury Circle, London NW9.

The JNF provides a comprehensive range of teaching materials — catalogue available on request.

Jewish Education Bureau, 8 Westcombe Avenue, Leeds LS8 2BS.
Director: Rabbi Douglas Charing. The JEB provides a comprehensive service to teachers and an extensive catalogue of materials and books, many of which are imported and only available from them. The Director is prepared to undertake teacher training courses and visits to schools. The JEB also produces a periodic journal for subscribers on the teaching of Judaism entitled *insight*.

JMC Bookshop, Woburn House, Upper Woburn Place, London WC1. Many of the books mentioned and many others are not easily available and can only be obtained from Jewish bookshops. There are several commercial Jewish bookshops to be found in areas of sizable Jewish population but the bookshop operated by the Jewish community is the one above, which contains all the books referred to plus a range of artifacts, records, tapes and games for children.

Viscom Ltd, Park Hall Road, Trading Estate, London SE21 8EL.
A very wide range of 16-mm films covering all sorts of aspects of Jewish identity, history, etc. Catalogue available on request.

BIPAC, 126–34 Baker Street, London W1M 1FH.
A source of comprehensive information on contemporary Israel.

CLIVE LAWTON
Education Officer,
Board of Deputies of British Jews

TEACHING BUDDHISM: ISSUES, APPROACHES AND RESOURCES

ISSUES

Next to Christianity, Buddhism seems to be the most popular religion among teachers. This certainly calls into question the criticisms which some people have made that RE is pandering to pressures from minority religions. Not only is the teaching of world religions apparently stronger in schools which claim to be mono-cultural than in those which are multi-cultural, there are also very few schools which have any Buddhist pupils.

Reasons why Buddhism may be a popular religion to teach are probably, first, that it is not represented in the schools so it enjoys a neutral position. No-one is going to be upset by it and embarrassed by questions of personal belief, for neither the teacher nor the pupil is a Buddhist. Second, it appears to share the scorn of the post-religious RE teacher for rituals, priesthood and the supernatural, including God. It is geographically and culturally detached from Christianity though implicitly critical of it, even in its Unitarian and Quaker forms.

The observations made above are subject to qualification. There may well be Buddhists on the staff or in the classroom, but they feel it wise to keep their beliefs a secret. The insensitive teacher might make some derisory comment, 'When are you going to get your head shaved then, Tim?' Or he might say, 'Next week we're going to be into Buddhism. Jack's a Buddhist, he'll be able to tell us all about it — and try to explain why he isn't a Christian'. The English Buddhist might appear to pose a threat to the Christian, as the Indian Christian may to the Hindu. Some Buddhists will remain quiet, of course, not for prudent reasons but because Buddhism is not a demonstrative religion, its adherents do not go out of their way to evangelise.

The non-theistic nature of many expressions of Buddhism is one of the issues which should be explored with older pupils. However, there is a need to avoid the pitfall of regarding Buddhism as a protest against classical Hinduism. Certainly the Buddha rejected the religion of the priests and the popular cults of the village, but what we call Hinduism, including the name, was still emerging towards the form depicted in many books. Perhaps it is best to regard the Buddha as one of the many teachers of the upanishadic period, a person whose analysis of the human condition and solution to it eventually attracted so many followers, and was so different from other forms, that, like Jainism, it became a distinct religion.

Being non-theistic, Buddhism also provokes reappraisals of what we

123

mean by the term 'religion'. Many dictionaries (seldom useful guides to serious students of religion) provide definitions which include phrases like, 'belief in God or gods'. This is a subject to be pursued in secondary school. In primary school it will help the teacher to concentrate on the exemplary nature of the Buddha's life and teachings.

Which Buddhism? This perhaps is the most teasing issue for the teacher. Not Thai or Tibetan, but Eastern or Western. The books are likely to cover Therarada and Mahayana Buddhism but not the Buddhism of English adherents, who may be represented on the school staff or in the classroom. These will be followers of the philosophy and practisers of the ideal as pacifists and vegetarians. This Western form, though authentic, is very different from what one may experience in Sri Lanka or Bangkok.

APPROACHES

With younger children stories from the life of the Buddha might be told and some of the *jataka* tales of the Buddha's former lives. The purpose of these stories is to demonstrate Buddhist virtues such as kindness, selflessness and generosity, or the art of skilful living through being alert to the feelings of others and learning how to respond appropriately to them.

In the middle years the life of the Buddha might be explored more systematically and historically, though always with awareness of the religious context (the course *is* one in the study of religion and not of history). Life in a Buddhist country like Burma or Thailand might be combined with a geographical study of the same area. The story of a *bhikku* from one of these countries can also provide an interesting focus, especially when it is realised that it is often customary for young boys to follow the monastic path for some period of time.

With senior pupils the spread of Buddhism, its disappearance in the land of its birth and its adoption of cultural aspects of the societies into which it moved raises many religious studies issues as does the question of theism already mentioned. The difference between *Theravada* and *Mahayana* need not be regarded as important, but a look at Buddhism in Britain will provide opportunities for asking 'what is Buddhism?'

In any thematic courses on religious teachers and messengers, the religious life and especially on ethics, Buddhism has an important contribution to make. It is perhaps worth making the point here that in Buddhist ethics intention is all-important. In some Indian teachings the action itself has a karmic effect, in Buddhism only well-intentioned or evil-intentioned acts have such a consequence. This concept is worth exploring.

Perhaps the best starting-point in teaching about Buddhism in the life of a *bhikku*, possibly following his story from leaving his own home,

Buddhism Flowchart

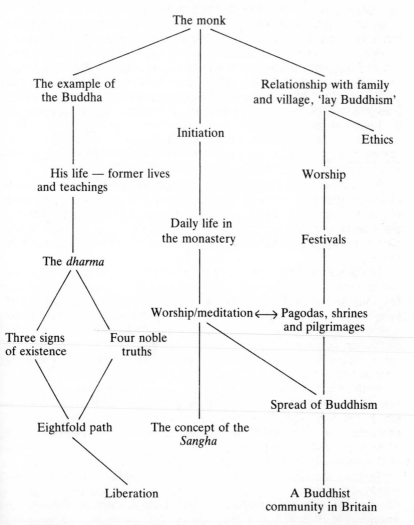

The flowchart indicates possible sequential development and provides checklist of content. It does not imply that the religion should be covered in a single course (see p. 153).

being initiated, and going to the lay community daily for his food (the use of the term 'begging' may be misunderstood), to his arrival and settlement in Britain. Through him the three signs of existence, the four noble truths and the eightfold path can be encountered as living and meaningful as well as being the message of a venerated teacher of long ago. Buddhism may be the most human religion in some respects, but it can be taught in a way which fails to humanise it.

Buddhism could easily appear remote and impersonal, so to begin with a monk and constantly refer back to him might be helpful.

A way of coping with the varieties of Buddhism and making them interesting could be to begin with a monk in a specific country, perhaps Thailand or Sri Lanka, and bring in the differences through the spread of Buddhism or Buddhism in Britain and such a person as the Dalai Lama. This would demonstrate variety, and remove stereotypes. The purpose would not be to do justice to *Therevada* and *Mahayana*, which would not even be mentioned in a general course.

Anatta may take many lives to attain. It is scarcely a doctrine for fifteen-year-olds.

RESOURCES

Books for the Teacher

The Buddha's Way, H. Saddhatissa, Allen and Unwin.
Buddhism: a Modern Perspective, C. S. Prebish (ed.), Pennsylvania State University.
Buddhism, E. Conze, Cassirer.
The Buddhist Religion, (2nd edn) R. H. Robinson and W. L. Johnson, Dickenson.
Buddhist Ethics, H. Saddhatissa, Allen and Unwin.
Buddhism, Zürcher, Routledge and Kegan Paul.
The Buddha, M. Pye, Duckworth.
The Life of the Buddha as Legend and History, E. J. Thomas, Routledge and Kegan Paul.
The Buddha, T. O. Ling, Penguin.
The Life of the Buddha, Bhikki Nanamoli, Buddhist Publication Society, Sri Lanka.
The Buddha's Philosophy of Man, T. O. Ling, Everyman.
Buddhism in Britain, I. P. Oliver, Rider.
What the Buddha Taught, W. Rahula, Gordon Fraser.
Buddhist Scriptures, E. Conze, Penguin.
Jataka Tales, E. Beswick, John Murray.
The Teachings of the Compassionate Buddha, E. A. Burtt (ed.), Mentor Books.

The last four books in this list contain material which can be adapted for telling to children.

Books for the Classroom

These are few.
Buddhism, T. O. Ling, Ward Lock (14–17).
Thinking about Buddhism, D. Naylor, Lutterworth (15–17).
Zen and Modern Japanese Religions, M. Pye, Ward Lock (14–17).
The Perfect Generosity of Prince Vessantara, M. Cone and R. Gombrich, Oxford University Press (the longest and most famous *Jataka* story).
One must add the relevant chapter in
Gods and Men, B. W. Sherratt and D. J. Hawkins, Blackie (14–16).
With hesitation one also lists
The Buddha, F. W. Rawding, Cambridge University Press (13–15), which begins by describing a 'Hinduism' which did not exist when the Buddha lived, or for another 500 years, and contains other inaccuracies.
For use with younger children there is only
Our Buddhist Friends, Joan Ascott, Denholm House Press (9–13).
Buddhism provides a real area of need which publishers might try to fill.

Audio-visual Aids

One must begin with the Argus kit which includes two useful books, which could have been listed above, in their own right. Also two filmstrips and sound cassettes.
Buddhism, Concordia. Surveys the life of a boy in Thailand. Inadequate notes spoil useful material.
Buddhism, Educational Productions. Disappointing but some worthwhile frames on pilgrimage, the rosary, leaf fans and the monk's vessels.
Encounter with Buddhism, BBC Radiovision. An excellent audio-visual study for use with older pupils.
The Life of the Buddha, Hulton Educational. Modern paintings from Thai, Malaysian and Singapore temples.
Ann and Bury Pearless have produced excellent slide sets on a variety of topics. Send for lists. Address in the section on useful addresses.

A very useful essay written by a specialist in Buddhist studies and a comprehensive school teacher, Dave Williams, is to be found in *World Faiths in Education*, W. O. Cole (ed.), Allen and Unwin.
Buddhist Festivals, Pictorial Charts Educational Trust.

TEACHING CHRISTIANITY: ISSUES, APPROACHES AND RESOURCES

It is sometimes said that the coloured members of British society act as a marker dye, indicating areas of need, disadvantage and neglect in our society which have long existed but have been allowed to go unnoticed. It might be pre-schooling or language acquisition in education, the lack of facilities for young people in inner cities or inadequate housing provision. In religious education the presence of Jews or Muslims serves to remind the teacher that the assumptions that everyone in school is a Christian in the making and that syllabuses should be confined to imparting Christian knowledge are false. This has always been the case, but grammar school teachers often upheld Christian values and most of their pupils readily accepted them. It was probably only the secondary modern teacher who was aware of a different world — that which the churches had not lost because they had never won it. Now the reality of a pluralistic, non-Christian society should be plain to all. Stories are told of five-year-olds coming to school who have never heard of Jesus of secondary school pupils who have not a Bible in their home, even of aspirants to public schools who cannot write out the Lord's Prayer when it appears in the common entrance examination! This situation is not new, but it is often the teacher who is faced with ten Muslims, three Jews, five Sikhs and two Hindus who is aware of it rather than the one who is confronted by thirty white, and therefore Christian, faces!

Such a teacher has a number of difficulties to overcome. First, we have never taught Christianity as we teach Judaism or Islam, so there is little guidance to be had and few satisfactory materials. Second, the teacher enjoys a relationship with Christianity which is different from that he has with Islam or Buddhism. He is likely to be a Christian or a lapsed Christian. He will be attached to some form of Christianity or alienated from it. Thus the stories attending the death of Guru Nanak can be told with no misgivings. Muslims and Hindus both claimed him and laid flowers beside him, hoping that theirs would miraculously remain fresh in the dry heat, for he had said that those whose flowers did not wilt could conduct his funeral according to their tradition. Both lots of flowers remained fresh but the body had gone when devotees came to look. The Resurrection or Ascension of Jesus, however, causes acute embarrassment. This goes further. A teacher may happily describe the role of Hindu priests, the use of the rosary in Hinduism, and statues or pictures as aids to worship, but have great difficulty teaching about priests, rosaries and statues in their Roman Catholic context. For these and other reasons the consequence has been, all too often, the elimination of any recognisable study of Christianity from the classroom. The study of the Bible, which seemed sufficient when we could assume that every child participated in the Christian festivals, worship, the observance of the Lord's Day, was baptised, confirmed and initiated into church membership, and shared his parents Christian beliefs and values, is no longer enough. Detached from its total Christian context it presents a distorted picture of Christianity — just as a study of the 'Old Testament' misrepresents Judaism.

Instead of failing to teach Christianity, a solution which is defeatist and deprives children of the right to study the very religion which has been most influential in Britain, ways need to be found of teaching it as we teach Sikhism and Buddhism. To do so, teachers have first to persuade themselves, and their pupils, that the exercise of Christian studies is one of education, not evangelism. If the task can be perceived as one of attempting to understand what it means to be a Christian in terms of practice and belief and the teacher's role can be seen as that of interpreter, then perhaps an attempt to consider content can begin.

ISSUES

There are a number of issues to be considered in planning the syllabus which need to be resolved before we go into the classroom.

(A) The relationship of Christianity to Judaism and Islam. Even if there are no Jewish children in my class, from my own study of religion I am aware of a number of things which I can only ignore if I am prepared to be dishonest.

(1) The New Testament is polemical and not interested in presenting Judaism fairly. The Pharisees in particular are given a hard time, yet the universalism of the Christian message owes much to pharisaic teaching. Without it, Christianity might have been an exclusively Jewish sect. Paul and probably Jesus were pharisaic in their theology.
(2) Jesus views of messiahship stands in strong contrast to that of mainstream Judaism.
(3) The view of the 'Old Testament' as a document pointing inevitably to Jesus, which is found in the New Testament and especially in Matthew's Gospel, is not accepted by Jews.
(4) Jews reject Christian claims for the divinity of Jesus and the necessity of a saviour. In Judaism man is not a fallen being.

With regard to Islam, the virgin birth of Jesus is accepted, as is his messiahship, but the crucifixion is denied and so is Jesus' divinity.

(B) The rich diversity of Christianity — there are probably a dozen forms of it in our own neighbourhood. How can we hope to do justice to it in eleven years?

Possible Solutions

(A) The first group of issues provide areas of interesting and fruitful study in the upper school. They should lead to an appreciation of the distinctiveness of Christianity (something which is unlikely to be noticed when it is studied in isolation). In the lower school they will not be taught, but hopefully they will prevent the teacher from presenting Christianity in a way which distorts Judaism and makes it seem only a parent for its superior offspring. Two matters deserve particular thought. First, the use of 'Old Testament' material under the heading 'Stories Jesus heard'. Personally, I would not associate these with Jesus but call them 'Stories from Judaism', and include them in topics on Judaism. Second, the inclination to present Judaism as legalistic and dead, or a religion of temple and sacrifice. This picture is often conveyed through topics on Palestine in Jesus' day. Somewhere Judaism needs to be presented as a living dynamic faith.

(B) Christianity is nowhere near as old or diverse as Hinduism, but teachers can often cope with that religion in much less than eleven years because they can adopt a detached stance. With Christianity we have to try to do the same. In trying to formulate a syllabus we might begin where we are, rather than in the Palestine of 2,000 years ago and ask:

(1) What do I need to know to understand Christianity as a living faith?
(2) How can I present this to children so that by the time a pupil is sixteen years old he can share this understanding?

By adopting these criteria we might avoid a year-long journey through Luke's Gospel and a similar one through Acts, not to mention a tortuous trek through the history of Israel from Saul to the Exile (something of limited value for understanding Judaism or Christianty as living faiths). Teaching less with more sharpness of purpose is often a way of teaching better.

As Christianity is most obviously the religion which will be taught in school year in and year out, a developmental syllabus is offered in the diagram opposite. In the next chapter I will try to demonstrate how this material can often be tied into one which includes content from other faiths so that the approach can be truly multi-faith, (p. 149).

APPROACHES

Younger Children

It is hoped that the syllabus is self-explanatory but a few comments might be helpful. The starting-point with younger children will be the

Christianity (5–16)	13+	11+	7+	5+
Jesus	Beliefs about Jesus,[a] place of Jesus in Christianity (soteriology and christology)	Ministry of Jesus, rabbinical method, miracles as well as parables as teaching forms, death and resurrection stories, analysis of birth stories	Who was Jesus? What kind of a person?	Fragmentary knowledge of Jesus: birth, home, friends
Issues in the development of Christianity	Presenting Jesus to Jew and Gentile; attitudes to society and Roman state			
The Christian Bible	How and why NT came into existence. Relation of NT to Hebrew Bible	NT material — letters, gospels; types of literature — myths, miracles, etc. How to interpret them. Compilation of NT Translations	Use of Bible in worship, Bible languages, scrolls, codices, illuminated manuscripts. Stories of Peter and Paul. No OT stories.[b]	A book used in church: source for knowing about Jesus and his friends
Christian worship and festivals	Purpose of worship,[a] sacraments, festivals. Their individual meanings	Stories of Christian worship (Christians worshipping), baptism, Lord's Supper, Christian year. Some hymns. Lord's Prayer	What happens in church, Sunday, funerals	Visiting a church. Christenings and weddings. Celebrating Christmas
The worldwide Church	Why mission? Attitudes to other religions.[a] Dialogue	Spread of Christianity.[c] Christianity in other lands, e.g. Christmas in France; a Christian in Pakistan, Africa	How Christianity came to Britain. The local scene	
Authority and Christians living in the world.	Church, Bible, Holy Spirit. Why denominations? How Christians make up their minds, decide attitudes to issues personal and social[d]	Some attitudes of Jesus and early Christians, e.g. Paul and Onesimus. Jesus forgives Peter	Examples of commitment. Jesus and others as decision-makers	
Christianity and the arts	Symbolism of representing Jesus in art and music, literature	Christian symbols.[a] Jesus in art; perhaps in stamps	Stained glass windows	The art of the churches visited

[a] Could benefit from links with other religions.
[b] Better in course on Judaism — but, if any, what criteria? What is religious in David and Goliath, Noah's Ark, Samson?
[c] Not triumphalist (bringing the light of truth to those who live in darkness!)
[d] Must acknowledge pluralism of views — but common basis? Love? Are we afraid of difference? We seem to demand uniformity.

world around them, the locality that they know. For those whose cultural background is Christian this will definitely mean Christmas (though any religious connection may be absent), and possibly the local church and some of its activities. For all children these can be entry points into the study of Christianity. The approach to Christmas will be deferred for inclusion in the section on 'Celebrating Festivals'.

There is no harm in visiting one or a number of local churches so long as parents, through the headmaster, have clearly been informed of the purpose of the exercise. The anxieties of humanists or atheists can be allayed by explaining that it is an educational exercise, part of a study of our town, our high street, the neighbourhood. Muslims or Jews are likely to be acquiescent when they realise that this is one of a number of visits, which will include the mosque and the synagogue. Misgivings are understandable if investigation is restricted to the local Christian church. Some parents (usually Jewish in my experience but also Roman Catholic and evangelical) may be understandably concerned at their young children visiting churches, temples or mosques, because this may lead to them becoming confused. There is a strong Jewish view that children should be made as firm as possible in their own religion before encountering others. Perhaps such parents can be persuaded to see that this is a way in which teachers are trying to encourage material understanding and respect at an early age to help children positively to cope with the pluralistic world which will reach them in the playground or through television anyway. Of course, as always, the answer must begin with keeping the parents informed and involved, perhaps through helping to organise the visit to his place of worship.

Which church may be a problem. There is no need to limit it to one, and with teenagers, of course, there is value in looking at the issues which arise from coupling, say, a visit to a Baptist church with that to the Roman Catholic one. However, with five-to-nine-year-olds my choice would be determined by two factors; the clergyman and the pleasantness of the building. The result of the visit is likely to be affective rather than cognitive. A kind, receptive minister who can interest children, and a light, friendly (warm if possible) building will prove more congenial than one which is dark and damp. The font, the altar or communion table, the organ, the windows — almost anything can be interesting, especially for children who have seldom or never entered a church before. This may lead into some aspects of Christian art symbolism.

Jesus is the key figure of Christianity. That goes without saying. His name, like that of Muhammad or Guru Nanak, will be mentioned from time to time. Some stories, but not many, can be told to younger children. Perhaps Jesus calling his fisherman friends to join him (Mark 1:14–20), or befriending the lonely, rejected Zacchaeus (Luke 19:1–10), but other references can also be made — to Jesus going to a

132

wedding or caring for children (Mark 19:13–14). I would not tell the story of Jesus turning water into wine (John 2), but Jesus seems to have been the kind of person people liked to invite to their weddings. The miracle stories would come later, now would be the time for providing fragmentary information about Jesus as a man. This would lead up to the birth of this person and probably the story of the journey to Bethlehem and 'no room in the inn'. Doubtless the shepherds and wise men would come upon the scene too, if not in the story then in the celebrations.

Something of Jesus' personality would come across through these stories, a kind, friendly, man. What of his appearance? We know he was not white-skinned, blue-eyed and flaxen-haired. If I were using pictures I would want to avoid implanting a stereotype of a white, Anglo-Saxon Jesus in young children's minds. I might already use pictures by African, Chinese or Indian artists, as well as European. I certainly would with junior classes, and would continue to do so in the secondary school.

With infants their introduction to the Bible would be, first, that I would show them one and tell them that my stories about Jesus came from it. Second, I would point it out when we visited a church.

Divisiveness

Allusion has already been made to the fact that there are fundamental differences between Christianity and Judaism. In this respect Christianity, like Buddhism and Sikhism, the Jehovah's Witnesses, Protestant Christian groups and perhaps Islam, is an expression of religion which owes much to its rejection of its parental tradition. Consequently the New Testament, especially John's Gospel, which my Jewish students have often found difficult reading, contains much that is anti-Jewish, and, sadly, the history of Christianity includes many anti-semitic episodes. The teacher needs to be aware of this as a first step to tackling the issue of divisiveness.

With younger children no-one would think of acquainting them with Jewish Christian tension — but like my daughter who came home singing 'Jew, Jew, dirty old Jew' on her first day at school, they may pick it up! Or like the vicar's son who would not visit a Jewish friend because 'the Jews killed Jesus', they may infer it from church, home, Sunday school or day school. We might be spreading anti-semitism by accident in our Christian teaching. Perhaps the ways of avoiding this are by being careful how we teach Christianity, and by introducing children to Judaism as a living, dynamic religion — mainly through its worship, festivals and family life, and by meeting Jews.

In the secondary school differences can become a subject of study through looking at various issues. One might be who were the Pharisees, including their origins, ideas and contributions to Judaism, as well as the New Testament's critique of them — remembering the importance of Pharisaic theology for early Christianity, as was noted earlier. One might also analyse the Jewish concept of Messiah and consider how the Christian one differs from it.

Another topic might examine how the first Christians interpreted their Jewish scriptures — in particular, those many quotations in Matthew's Gospel where it says, 'This was so that the scripture might be fulfilled'.

Finally, attention might be given to Jewish — Christian relations since New Testament times, to ghettoes, missions to the Jews, to the Holocaust and to the Council of Christians and Jews.

The result of these studies may not be a more wholesome attitude on the part of Christian pupils but it may replace prejudiced ignorance with prejudiced informed knowledge, it may cause reflection, and it will have examined a serious religious studies issue, that of the emergence of a religion from its parent culture and tradition.

RESOURCES

Books on Christianity, whether they are intended to be used by teachers or pupils tend to assume belief and basic knowledge. Only recently have writers begun to treat Christianity as they do Judaism or Sikhism, for example. As the meagre list which follows shows much needs to be done, yet publishers still concentrate on church history, the denominations and biblical studies.

Some Books for the Teacher

Priestland's Progress, Gerald Priestland, BBC. Perhaps an idiosyncratic treatment but most of the issues of Christian belief are raised in an interesting manner. Tapes of the BBC programmes may still be obtainable.

Comparative Religions, Blandford. Section on Christianity by W. O. Cole. An attempt to present Christianity as a world religion.

Phenomenon of Christianity, N. Smart, Collins. Not an easy book but it does explore the many dimensions of Christianity and its cultural variety in Europe and beyond.

Christianity, Peter Moore, Ward Lock (*Arts and Practices of Living Religions* series). Much more than a book about art. Explores the whole ethos of the religion.

Some Books for the Classroom

The Chichester Project, based on Bishop Otter College of the West Sussex Institute of Higher Education, is concerned with the presentation of Christianity as a world religion. Its director is John Rankin, to whom enquiries should be addressed. So far it has produced four books for the secondary classroom. They are:

Christian Worship, J. Rankin, Lutterworth.

Christian Communities, A. Brown, Lutterworth.

Christian Experience, C. Erricker, Lutterworth.

Jesus, T. Shannon, Lutterworth.

Christianity, G. Turner, Edward Arnold. Rather brief and too occupied with social concern but does try to present Christianity today with some success.

Visiting a Community Church, G. Palmer, Lutterworth.

Our Christian Friends, A. Nicholls, Denholm House Press (primary and middle).

Audio-visual Aids

The Christian Tradition, Argus, five filmstrips with supporting notes and textbooks, is a serious attempt to do for Christianity what the other kits in the series do for Hinduism, Judaism, Buddhism and Islam. The success may seem to be marred by the American location of four of the filmstrips, but these can be used to demonstrate cultural divergence. The fifth, *Eastern Orthodox* is especially good.

Christians Today, M. Grimmitt and G. Read, Kevin Mayhew. Sets of black and white pictures, written material and a handbook, *How Can I Teach Christianity?*

The Slide Centre Ltd is currently producing a number of sets on different forms of Christian worship, baptism, the eucharist and wedding services, and a funeral.

Christianity in India, Educational Productions. Useful in widening horizons (11–14). Needs to be used carefully in multi-faith schools or the teacher may be thought to be implying that wise Indians have become Christian!

It is through the use of slides and filmstrips, often linked with BBC schools broadcasts (e.g. *Quest*, or the *Coventry Square Mile*) that an open, multi-dimensional approach to Christianity can be undertaken. Hopefully, the books will follow.

derogatory words

TEACHING ISLAM: ISSUES, APPROACHES AND RESOURCES

ISSUES

Islam is present in our schools in two ways, through the media and the world at large and through Muslim pupils in the classroom. Sometimes a third influence is present — the legacy of the Crusades, which misrepresented Muslims as cruel and Muhammad as lecherous and epileptic.

The first two issues are represented by the first form of the Muslim presence. 'Paki' is a general term applied, often abusively or at least in a derogatory manner, to all non-whites. I have heard West Indian children called 'Paki' in the playground and a lady once introduced me to her 'Paki' neighbour, who turned out to be from Africa via Jamaica! Muslim is synonymous with 'Paki', for many pupils who are blissfully unaware that there are Algerian, Iraqi, Nigerian, Indonesian, Russian and even Israeli and English Muslims. If Muslims are not stereotyped as 'Paki', which seems to mean dirty, docile and backward, they are militant and fanatical — that is the other contribution of the world at large, this time of the media, especially television and the tabloid press. More than once when I have been giving a talk on Islam or teaching Islam, teachers have questioned me about Islamic fanaticism. My comments on Christian militancy and fanaticism in Northern Ireland by way of reply have sometimes been seen as in bad taste. The fact is that there is a zeal attached to commitment. Sometimes it emerges in an Iranian revolution, a Crusade, a vast commitment to mission, but this is never the whole truth about any one religion, and is a phenomenon common to many religions and ideologies. It might provide an interesting topic for study in the secondary school, where devotees of pop stars and soccer clubs might be expected to treat the subject with understanding.

It is daunting to teach Islam with Muslims present. I remember talking to some librarians in Huddersfield about Islam. Afterwards I was going to Muslim friend's for tea. He turned up at the lecture — and still gave me tea, which demonstrates the generosity of Muslims! How can the teacher overcome the real or imagined difficulties created by Muslims being in the class?

First, we have to assume that specialists in religious studies may teach it and should. Some Muslims, because of their concern or zeal, their commitment to their religion, have told me that I should not teach it. With some success I have argued with them along the following lines.

If I do not include Islam in the syllabus what will my Muslim pupils

136

Should I teach Islam?

Steping on eggshells

conclude? Either that I do not consider Islam worth studying, or that I am intent on converting them to Christianity. What will this do for Muslim self-esteem and for race relations? If I do not include Islam what will our post-Christian whites conclude (and our Sikhs, Hindus and Jews)? They, too, will think that Islam is not worth knowing about and that the folklore about it stretching back to the Crusades and media presentations must be true. This will only reinforce prejudice.

I then try to explain the revolution in religious education and persuade the Muslims to understand it, accept it, and join me in it. This is not easy. Muslims have been on the receiving end of Christian missions for a long time, and are sometimes suspicious that openness and dialogue, even religious studies, are new names or soft techniques for the same end — evangelism. Partly for this reason, but also because for most people religion has to do with practising it and studying it to be a better believer, the notion of studying or teaching a religion which is not one's own is strange and unintelligible. Sometimes it has been said by Christians, and hinted at by Muslims and Sikhs, that my interest in religions must mean that I lack faith in my own religion. It is not easy to convince people that the open and empathetic study of religion is possible and desirable.

To try to convince Muslims that I am not pretending to be a Muslim but am a teacher of Islam, and that I, a Christian, am not setting myself up as the fount of knowledge, I need to take refuge in resources which are Muslim-written, or Muslim-approved and are educationally sound. Fortunately Muslims, for example, Muhammad Iqbal and Riadh El-Droubie, have concerned themselves with religious education in British schools and have produced materials which meet both criteria.

In addition to textbooks and audio-visual aids there is the potentially most valuable resource of all, the Muslim pupils and their community. If you were asked, as I was in Pakistan during a train journey, 'You are a Christian aren't you? You believe in three gods!' you might find it difficult to defend yourself. In the same way the Muslim child who is told 'We're doing your religion next week Shafiq, you can tell us all about it,' might find the prospect awesome and impossible. Perhaps it is because invitations are expressed in this way that teachers sometimes tell me that they have tried to use their Muslim pupils as resources without success. (Of course, there is the point, too, that as not every child in the class is a Christian so not every Bangladeshi is a Muslim; the pupils we think are Muslim may be as lapsed as any one else. But they celebrate the festivals, you say. Yes, most English people celebrate Christmas, but that does not make them Christian!) Another reason lies in the nature of Islam. It is more a matter of practice than of theological study for most Muslims, but then this is true of most religions at a popular level. However, to receive helpful answers we must always ask helpful questions.

To ask a pupil, or even an adult visitor, to tell the class about Islam is no easier than asking the vicar to explain Christianity in forty minutes. Where does one begin? 'Tell us about prayer in Islam,' might be easier, but 'describe what you do when you pray in the mosque' might be more helpful still (having discovered first that the boy does go to the mosque). For girls the request would be 'Describe what you do when you pray at home'. One of the most interesting and worthwhile sessions that I can remember was one at which a man who had been on the *Hajj* spoke to some students. The first week I explained the place of the Pilgrimage in Islam, the second he talked us through some slides on the *Hajj*, told us what the experience had meant to him and answered questions. He provided a personal experiential element which I could not have conveyed to the same extent. However, if he had been asked to come and talk about the Pilgrimage I doubt whether he would have succeeded in sharing with us his distinctive insights. The teacher, not the pupil or the visitor, is the professional educator. That must not be forgotten, even when using human resources to help a religon come alive.

There are few important theological issues that we must be aware of in teaching Islam. Christianity tends to regard Islam as a daughter-religion; after all, Jesus and Mary as well as many Old Testament personalities feature prominently in it. This is not a Muslim view. Islam teaches that God revealed to Abraham, Moses, Jesus and others the message which was given to Muhammad, but their followers corrupted it. Consequently, the *Qur'an* is a corrective to the Bible, not a distortion of it, as Jews and Christians might claim. The Islamic view of Jesus as a prophet and the Messiah, born of the virgin Mary, but not divine, is the truth. Christians have fallen into the trap of deifying Jesus. Muslims, learning from them, have taken great pains to insist on the humanity of Muhammad. The Christian error has led them to worship three gods; this is how Islam regards the Trinity.

These theological differences between Christianity and Islam are fundamental. Clearly, they cannot be discussed or even mentioned in primary schools or the middle years, but they are essentially items in an upper secondary school treatment of Islam and provide opportunities for interesting study.

APPROACHES

The reluctance of Muslim ladies to socialise with men outside the family circle clearly does not prevent them coming to primary and especially infant schools, where most of the teachers are usually female and the children are below the age of puberty. However, the Muslim mother who may be invited to bring her new baby may also have little English because of her limited contact with English-speaking people. The solution may be to encourage her to demonstrate such things as cookery or embroidery rather than give a talk.

There is a cultural variety in Islam, but if the Muslim children in our infant school come from one country, probably Bangladesh or Pakistan, it is natural to concentrate on that country, though beginning with the community here in, say, Dewsbury, South Shields or Coventry. There is a need for care here. Most of the white population of Batley, in Yorkshire, and some of the teachers, think that their Muslim community is Pakistani. It happens to be predominantly Indian — and the pioneer member who settled in Batley before the Second World War was called 'the Italian' by the locals! *Nahda's Family* plus *Understanding Your Muslim Neighbour* or *The Way of the Muslim* will inform teachers of things that can be explored with infants and juniors, aspects of family life, a visit to Grandma, a sister's wedding, the mosque school (probably less harmful than a night of television-watching, however much the prospect alarms some teachers!). A little later one can alert children to the widespread presence of Islam through topics on Egypt, oil or even Spain, if that is a country that the teachers or some pupils have been able to visit.

The Crusades provide another opportunity, but it is to be hoped that the children acquire information rather than the romantic unrealities associated with Richard the Lionheart. If there are any heroes in the wars, then it is Saladin who has the best claim to the title.

The story of the spread of Islam demands similar thoughtful treatment. The Arab conquest of north Africa and the old Persian Empire as well as the defeat of Byzantium are not synonymous with Islam. Zoroastrians, Jews and Muslims were permitted to keep their faiths. Those who belonged to tribal religions were required to become Muslim as part of the terms of surrender, a condition not unknown in Britain, where defeated Saxons and Danes became converts to Christianity. Both the Crusades and the spread of Islam cry out for co-operation between the history and religious studies departments, and, hopefully, the geography staff as well. They are popular in the middle-year courses, but often inaccurately taught.

Through Islam's contact with the West both before and during the Crusades there was rich interchange in the areas of science, including mathematics and philosophy. Offa's penny, our numerals, algebra, even the word 'alcohol' (though the drinking of it is forbidden among Muslims) came to the West with Islam. This cultural dimension can be explored in the middle years and beyond, though it should always be implicit in courses on Islam.

The stuff of the secondary school syllabus will be studies of Muhammad's place in Islam, the significance of the Five Pillars, Muslim beliefs, and the *Qur'an* as a guide to life and faith, amplified by the *Sunna*. Some attention may be given to the mystical element in Islam, Sufism,

Islam Flowchart

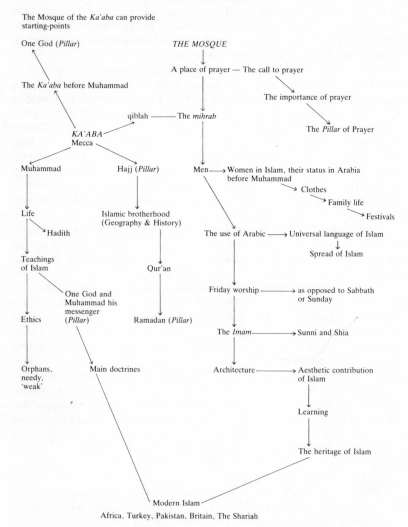

The flowchart indicates possible sequential developments and provides checklist of content. It does not imply that the religion should be covered in a single course (see p. 153).

and to the division into Sunni and Shia, but the purpose should be one of explaining the differences. (Speakers have been heard to mention them with no better intention than that of showing that Islam is really no more a unity than 'Christendom'.) Such topics as woman in Islam, or even the relationship between Judaism, Christianity and Islam, need to be kept in perspective. The inclination to slip into a course on woman's rights or inter-religious dialogue should be avoided. Otherwise the subject will quickly cease to be Islam!

The mosque would seem to be an excellent point from which to begin a study of Islam in the secondary school, whether the approach be thematic (the most practical one in the multi-faith school) or a sharp one-term or one-year burst. Islam in a term may be possible, but what is the pupil going to conclude about its importance vis-à-vis Christianity, and is it going to be taught at such a time that its beliefs as well as its practices can be studied? Islam is an intensely practical religion, the right path, or the straight path, Muslims often call it, but through the practices Muslims imbibe the spiritual essence and their theology, and these the student of Islam must encounter, or the story will merely be one of physical exercises, a great journey, dietary and clothing restrictions, and sublime architecture. Those who know Muslims know that Islam is more than these. The aim should be to know what it means in terms of belief and practice to be a Muslim today in Birmingham, Lahore, Cairo, or Mecca.

RESOURCES

An essential book for any student and teacher of Islam to possess is *Approaches to Islam* by Richard Tames, John Murray, 1982. It might be said to mark a milestone in the study of world religions. Ten years earlier the paucity of material and often trivial level of teaching would have made this 264-page book much slimmer and it might have been regarded as premature. Its timely appearance demonstrates that the willing teacher has now available resources which are ample in quantity and sound in quality. This book, which is first of a series, sets an exacting standard for others to maintain.

Some Books for the Teacher

Islam, H. A. R. Gibb, Oxford University Press. A useful introduction.
The House of Islam, K. Cragg, Dickenson.
What is Islam? W. M. Watt, Edinburgh University.
Muhammad, Prophet and Statesman, W. M. Watt, Oxford University Press.
The World of Islam, E. J. Grube, Hamlyn, is one of many fine books which introduces the rich aesthetic experience of Islam.

141

Islam from the Prophet Muhammad to the Capture of Constantinople,
   B. Lewis (ed.), Vol. 1 *Politics and War*; Vol. 2 *Religion and Society*,
   Harper and Row.
Sufism, R. J. Arberry, Oxford University Press.
The Muslim Guide, M. Y. McDermott and M. M. Ahsan, Islamic
   Foundation, Leicester.
The Qur'an; Basic Teachings, Islamic Foundation, Leicester, is an an-
   thology of Qur'anic passages thematically arranged and thus very
   useful for the teacher.
The Holy Qur'an, Text, Translation and Commentary, A. Yusuf Ali,
   Ashraf Lahore, provides an English rendering and traditional Muslim
   exegesis.
   The Islamic Foundation, 223 London Road, Leicester LE2 1ZE and
the Muslim Information Service, 233 Seven Sisters Road, London N4,
are sources from which books, information, and many forms of assistance can be obtained.

Books for the Classroom

Nahda's Family, M. Blakely, Black. A delightful book about a Muslim
   family growing up in Yorkshire. Colour photographs (9–14).
The Way of the Muslim, M. Iqbal, Hulton Educational (9–14).
Islam, R. El-Droubie, Ward Lock (13–17).
Call from the Minaret, M. Iqbal, Hodder and Stoughton (13–16).
Understanding Your Muslim Neighbour, M. and M. Iqbal (11–15).
Islam, R. El-Droubie and E. Hulmes, Longman (12–14).
These last five books, written wholly, or in part, by Muslims, can be
   used with confidence in schools with Muslim pupils.
Arab Village, R. Dutton and J. B. Free, Black (9–13).
Pakistani Village, A. and A. Scarsbrook, Black (9–13), describes
   aspects of life in two Muslim societies.
Thinking About Islam, J. B. Taylor, Lutterworth (15–17).
Muslim Spain, D. Townson, Cambridge University Press (12–15).
The Muslim World, R. Tames, Macdonald (11–15).
Barbarians, Christians and Muslims, T. Cairns, Cambridge University
   Press. Links the rise of Islam with the contemporary conversion of
   Anglo-Saxon England in an interesting way.
Our Muslim Friends, Anne Farncombe, Denholm House Press (10–13).
   None of the books in this list depicts the Prophets, something which
Muslims find distasteful. All can be regarded as educationally sound.

Audio-visual Aids

One immediately mentions the *Argus* box of books, filmstrips, and
cassettes. To this must be added the Church Missionary Society films-

trip, *The Way of Allah*, produced in careful collaboration with British Muslims. The result of this co-operation is an excellent teaching aid.

Such studies as *Rites of Hajj*, *Muslim Worship* and *A Muslim Marriage Contract Ceremony*, from the Slide Centre as well as Ann and Bury Peerless's *Eid at Fatehpur Sikri* cover particular aspects of the religion. The Gateway Learning Package, *Muslims in Europe* (ESL Bristol Ltd), used in conjunction with *Muslim Spain*, a textbook by Duncan Townson (Cambridge University Press), could introduce pupils to the rich culture which once existed in a country they might visit.

TEACHING SIKHISM:
ISSUES, APPROACHES AND RESOURCES

ISSUES

Like Buddhism, Christianity and Islam, Sikhism may be regarded to some extent as a religion critical of the tradition from whose womb it emerged, in this case Hinduism. Although it has never totally freed itself from Hindu culture, partly because even today there are only some 13 million Sikhs in India compared with over 600 million Hindus, nevertheless its scriptures and the account of Guru Nanak's life contain many criticisms of Hindu rituals, brahmin priests, the inferior and despised status of women and the class–caste system.

From 1605 CE, when the fifth Sikh Guru died in Mughal captivity until the nineteenth-century, relations with their rulers, often regarded as a religious struggle with Islam, were unhappy. During the Partition period of 1947, when many Sikhs in what is now Pakistan had to leave their ancestral lands and many Muslims migrated westwards from that part of the Punjab which remained in India, the bitter memories of three hundred years ago were revived. Muslims who reject the claims of Sikhism to be a distinct revelation on the theological ground that Muhammad was the last Prophet may therefore also share an emotional antipathy to Sikhism if they come from Pakistan. Of course, many settlers in Britain hold the view that the past is gone and Muslim–Sikh friendships are many, but the person who teaches either in the presence of the other does well to be alert to possible tension. Although pictures of British atrocities will be seen on the library walls in *Gurdwaras* no animosity seems to result from this, not for prudential reasons but because Jallianwala Bagh and similar incidents fell outside the seminal period of Sikhism from 1469 to 1708.

The teacher will be presented with a number of views of Sikhism and of the Gurus by Sikhs and Sikh writers. Guru Nanak is often depicted as a religious reformer comparable with the Buddha, or a precursor of Gandhi, seeking to ameliorate the lot of the masses. The religion itself is often presented as an alternative to Hinduism and Islam, containing the best elements of both. Leaving on one side the question of what criterion we use to decide what the 'best' elements of any religion are (presumably those we approve of — the most Christian, humanistic, or woman-affirming?), we are in danger of forgetting something of greater importance. Though all these views may contain some truth, the basis of Sikhism is the belief that God revealed himself directly to Guru Nanak and to his successors. In common with the other religions (how different is the case of Buddhism?), Sikhism does not see itself as a human search or a social response but as the medium of God's message to a world which was straying from the truth.

The religion of Guru Nanak, the first messenger, was anti-ritualistic, yet by the time of the tenth, Guru Gobind Singh, the Sikhs possessed a uniform, the five Ks and the turban, an initiation ceremony and a form of worship. Sikhs do not see any contradiction here, any more than most Christians or Jews do between the presumed simplicity of their religions aeons ago and later elaborations. Though Sikhism does provide the student of religion with an interesting example of the process of institutionalisation it must be remembered that a basic Sikh tenet is that the teaching of all ten Gurus was one and the same, and all held the same principles. Hence no picture of Guru Nanak as a man will show him without a beard or turban, though the formal injunctions relating to these came long after his lifetime.

APPROACHES

In teaching Sikhism all these elements can be explored at an appropriate time in the secondary school if the teacher's professional judgement regards them as proper and possible.

However, with younger children it is the tangible aspects of Sikhism which will be most attractive and intelligible. Perhaps an older brother can show how a turban is tied and turn the sometimes mocking derision ('hope your head gets better soon') into wonder and respect as three metres or more of cloth are deftly, quickly and neatly tied. One always picks a skilled practitioner, of course, and asks for a private performance first. Children can write some words, including their non-Sikh friends' names in the written form of Punjabi, known as *gurmukhi*, which they are learning in the *Gurdwara*. There can also be a visit to a *Gurdwara*, and the visit of a Sikh bride, perhaps with a video of her wedding. There are a number of stories of the Gurus which can be told, especially some of the humorous acted parables of Guru Nanak (like hiding the bowl of the yogi who said he could see into the future but could not find it behind his own back!). Some of these were at the expense of Hindus and Muslims, so care is needed. The festivals of *Baisakhi* and *Diwali* have stories attached to them which can be told when these occasions are celebrated in assembly. Picture storybooks like *Pavan is a Sikh* or the Coventry Minority Support Group's *How a Sikh Prays* (together with *How a Muslim Prays* and *How a Hindu Prays*), can provide a basis for chats about home life and the *Gurdwara*.

In the middle years some of these topics can be developed and explored more deeply, augmented by studies of the Gurus, of the *Gurdwara* and its worship, the place of the *Guru Granth Sahib* in Sikhism and the Sikh initiation rite. Topics could also include the Punjab and the Golden Temple at Amritsar but, as with other religions, the starting-place can be here and should be now, the past and India being used as and when the need arises.

The distinctive aspects of Sikhism can be studied in the upper school. These are the concept of guruship, the place of the Guru Granth Sahib in Sikhism, the Sikh concept of community and, of course, the Sikh path of liberation as well as Sikh ethical teachings. To these could be added the relationship of Sikhism to Hinduism, Islam and other religions in general.

RESOURCES

Some Books for the Teacher

The Sikhs, their Religious Beliefs and Practices, W. O. Cole and P. S. Sambhi, Routledge and Kegan Paul. A comprehensive study to the religion and the Sikh way of life.

History of the Sikhs, Khushwant Singh, Oxford University Press (2 vols).

Evolution of the Sikh Community, W. H. McLeod, Oxford University Press. An analytical study of important aspects of Sikh development.

The Guru in Sikhism, W. O. Cole, Darton, Longman and Todd. An examination of the central concept of Sikhism.

Sikhism and its Indian Context, 1469–1708, W. O. Cole, Darton, Longman and Todd. An attempt to assess the interests and aims of early Sikhism.

Sikhism, W. H. McLeod, Manchester University (*Sources for the Study of Religion* series). A documentary introduction not only to the scriptures but to the other important literary works.

The Sikh Religion, M. A. Macauliffe, Oxford University Press. Six volumes, now reprinted in three, faithfully presenting the Sikh tradition.

Sikh Ceremonies, Sir Joginder Singh, Chandigarh. Often used by *Gurdwaras* as a guide to ritual practices.

Sikhism: its Ideals and Institutions, Teja Singh, Orient Longmans. A brief but informative presentation of the essence of Sikhism.

Sikh Children in Britain, A. C. James, Oxford University Press. Written a decade ago but still of immense value.

The Sacred Writings of the Sikhs, Trilochan Singh and others, Allen and Unwin. An anthology containing some of the main hymns of the Guru Granth Sahib.

Hymns of Guru Nanak, Khushwant Singh, Orient Longmans. Includes many of the main compositions of the first Guru.

Sikhism Flowchart

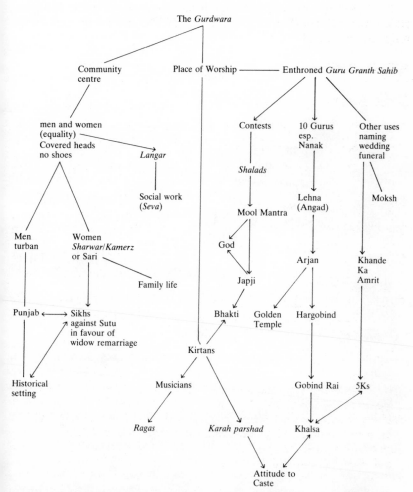

The flowchart indicates possible sequential development and provides checklist of content. It does not imply that the religion should be covered in a single course (see p. 153).

Some Books for the Classroom

Pavan is a Sikh, Sean Lyle, A. & C. Black. A largely pictorial description of a Sikh family in Britain (7–10 years).

Sikhs of the Punjab, W. H. McLeod, Oriel Press (12–15). Really an excellent little essay by a great expert.

Our Sikh Friends, A. Farnecombe, Denholm House Press. A clear, simple presentation, very useful for younger children (9–12).

Sikh Family in Britain, W. O. Cole, Pergamon (11–15). Written to help pupils understand the lives of Sikhs living in this country.

Understanding Your Sikh Neighbour, P. S. Sambhi, Lutterworth (10–15). Written by a Sikh bringing up a family in Britain.

The Way of the Sikhs, W. H. McLeod, Hulton Educational (10–14). Carefully written for younger pupils.

Meeting Sikhism, W. O. Cole and P. S. Sambhi, Longman (10–14). Presents Sikhism in its Punjab context.

Sikhism, W. O. Cole and P. S. Sambhi, Ward Lock (14–17). Has proved a useful introduction for students and teachers as well as an 'O' level textbook, being intended as an accurate, brief account of Sikh beliefs and practices.

Thinking About Sikhism, W. O. Cole, Lutterworth (14–17). Concentrates on Sikh worship and beliefs.

Visiting a Sikh Temple, D. K. Babraa, Lutterworth (11–15). Especially useful for CSE or 'O' level project work, or for the teacher before visiting a *Gurdwara*.

Baisakhi, a resource pack, Multicultural Education Resources Centre, Bristol.

Audio-visual Aids

Sikhism, Educational Productions (9–16 years). A survey of Sikhism in India.

The Sikh Religion, Concordia (9–16). Mainly about Sikhism in the UK.

Sikh Amrit, Educational Productions (9–18), tape study for use with older pupils (15–18). Study of an initiation ceremony performed in Leeds.

Sikh Worship, Slide centre (9–16). Other materials from the Slide Centre, based on Sikhism in Leicester, are in preparation.

Innumerable slide sets are available from Ann and Bury Peerless; send for lists.

Records of hymns used in Sikh worship can be obtained from Asian record shops. If *Sikhism Through the Songs of the Gurus* (Polydor, India 2675–068, 2 discs) can be obtained, teachers will find it useful with older pupils.

A useful address is the Sikh Missionary Society (UK), 10 Featherstone Road, Southall, Middlesex.

THEMATIC AND INTEGRATED APPROACHES

'With ten religions in my class how can I do justice to them all?' That is a frequently heard cry from teachers in multi-faith schools. Sadly, a common answer is simply to study one, Christianity — because as *they* must all know English to live here so they must all know Christianity!

There is a better way. Take a topic or theme and explore it across the religions. An obvious example might be worship. It is a religion-wide activity in one form or another. Everyone can join in and bring his own experience to bear, be he Buddhist, Muslim, Quaker Christian or Mormon. But what about the humanist or, more difficult, the pupil who 'goes' nowhere, and the atheist? There are perhaps two responses which might be made. One is that of discovering what worship is and why those people worship, and trying to discover what those who are not 'religious' do instead. There is no material that I am aware of that I could give to pupils below sixth-form level which deals with this issue, but there may be colleagues who would be prepared to talk about their own responses, and the teenagers may have their own solutions. Members of the local British Humanist Association group may be willing to come to school to answer questions. The second response depends on understanding the purpose of religious studies. What has been suggested in the last two or three sentences is only possible in an open classroom, where all life-stances and all pupils are treated with respect. If the position of the religious studies department is clearly known and understood an agnostic colleague may be persuaded to give up a marking period (if he has one) and enter what might otherwise be a lions' den. So, too, a local humanist. However, a cold letter, from someone unknown who describes himself as 'head of religious studies', is likely to start alarm bells ringing and ensure that the humanist, if he does come, is wearing his whole armour. If you already know him through CND or some anti-pollution campaign, for humanists are usually very socially active, good; if not, a chat over a pint, or at least a phone call, would allay his suspicions. If he has his stereotyped expectation of religious studies teachers (Christian warriors seeking out for destruction the hosts of Midian!), some children may also have similar views of him. Some ground-rules for entertaining visitors to your class may be necessary. He is coming to explain, augment and enrich the course, not to defend and justify his beliefs against Muslim or Christian witnesses to the truth of theism.

The strategy for studying worship when we have ten religions present in the school might be, first, to enable each group to study its own form, or forms, of worship in order to present them to the whole class.

149

Second, to provide sufficient time for each group to report back to the rest of the class so that, besides studying one tradition in depth, every pupil will have learned about the rest. An exhibition of models, photographs, descriptions of acts of worship and artifacts might be displayed in the hall so that other classes could share the topic. It would provide an excellent focus for one or more assemblies.

Worship is also a good example of a topic which can and should be treated in a spiral manner.

WORSHIP WITH YOUNGER PUPILS

The aim might be to discover when, where, and how people worship. Content might include Stonehenge, the Jerusalem Temple or St Peter's, Rome, but it would be likely that most attention would be given to places of day-to-day worship, especially those in the locality. Things noted would be shape, typical layout, orientation (if any) and focal point.

Next, the examination could move to how people worship, what worshipping activities take place in the buildings and what form they take.

Third, the topic might include a study of when worship takes place, daily, or weekly, and why there is a weekly holy day (if there is one). It is surprising how few of my Christian students know why Sunday is the special day of Christian worship when they arrive at College.

THE MIDDLE YEARS

Where, how and when might be explored in greater depth. Movement might be made towards looking at the notion of holy places, holy time — religious calendars and holy days, as well as religious persons.

UPPER SCHOOL

There is a need to tie up the threads by considering the two questions what is worship, and why do (some) people worship? This will involve some recapitulation of what has been done in earlier years. Besides bringing the topic to a tidy conclusion it will provide opportunities to consider fundamental questions about worship.

As the topic outlines, Worship, on the opposite page shows there can be spinoffs of many kinds — calendars, festivals, pilgrimage, the concept of the holy, what is prayer, mysticism and religious experience being some. These must be left to individual teachers or working parties to develop. All that can be done in the rest of this section is to provide some pointers, largely though drawing attention to books where useful information may be found.

In addition to worship, commonplace but necessary topics are messengers of God ('founders' is a risky term as Muslims would say that God, not Muhammad, founded Islam, and in what sense could Jesus be described as the founder of any manifestation of Christianity that exists today?), scriptures, pilgrimages and festivals. Together with worship, these are covered in *Five Religions in the Twentieth Century* (W. O. Cole, Hulton Educational). Festivals, Worship and the two extremely important subjects, Myth and Symbols, are explored in four sets of work cards *'Looking at . . . '*, by John Rankin, (Lutterworth). The Denholm House Press series, *Search for Meaning*, which includes *Something After Death?* by E. G. Parrinder, is also valuable and is intended for use by pupils (probably 14–16-year-olds). Themes are also featured in the Schools Council *Journeys into Religion* booklets. The series is a little like a curate's egg, but *Pilgrimages, Religion in Britain Today, and Signs and Symbols* (intended for 11–12-year-olds). *How others see Life* and *Myth, History and Ritual* (13–14), plus *Why Do Men Suffer?* and *Worship* (15–16) could all be used in multi-faith classrooms. The two teacher's handbooks are essential. Among other things, they provide additional bibliographies. The Schools Council materials are published by Hart-Davis Educational Limited.

Initiation Rites and *Death* are the titles of two books edited by John Prickett and published by Lutterworth. Others on *Marriage* and *Woman* are in preparation. These are teachers' books which are full of the kind of material and information they need for teaching these across-religions topics in the secondary classroom.

To this list of themes must be added three more. First, ethics in the world's religions. The fourth year secondary school diet is often nothing more than an opinion-swapping journey through sex, drugs, race, war and peace, soccer violence, abortion, women, euthanasia and who knows what else! Little knowledge is exchanged, few attitudes are affected. Instead one might look at how ethical attitudes are formed and what the religions have to teach about some of the major issues of life. Such a study might also correct the all-too-common assumption that only (white) Christians care. The second theme is that of salvation. Weddings, initiation rites, acts of worship may be fascinating or quaint, but ultimately what religions do for their followers is make sense of life and transport them into eternity. They claim to answer the upanishadic prayer:

From the unreal lead me to the real,
From darkness lead me to the light,
From death lead me to immortality.

A course which omits a study of human purpose and destiny must be regarded as incomplete. The theme of the Open University Course

AD208, *Man's Religious Quest* was, from what, to what, by what means? That is, from what position does one start out; unenlightened fallen, or what? To what goal does the religion take him; *moksha* eternal life, or something else? How does it help the believer reach that goal? Not all the beliefs of any religion can be covered by the time someone leaves school at the age of sixteen, but through a topic on Human Destiny the essentials can be covered, and non-religious solutions to the human predicament included.

Finally, a religious studies course should presumably end by raising supra-religions questions, issues which transcend religions. What is religion? What do religions claim to do? Why have religions? How can we decide which religion is true? What do we mean by 'God'?

Through these three topics a religious studies course, enriched by the diversity of beliefs present in the school, the locality and the world can be drawn together. Examples of books which might be found helpful are the following. *Themes for Living*, E. G. Parrinder (Hulton Educational); these are four sourcebooks covering Man and God, Right and Wrong, Society and the Goal of Life, with material from such thinkers as Mercius, Marx and Aristotle, as well as the major religions *Education, Work and Death* and *Sex, Marriage and Family Life* by John Elliot and Eric Pain (Lutterworth) again provide discussion material some of it from Andy Capp and Peanuts, some from established religious thinkers. *World Faiths and Modern Problems*, Anthony Denne (Hamish Hamilton) is a book which follows a brief outline of a religion say, Buddhism, with a consideration of some of the issues facing it today, for example, violence. The final examples are *Patterns of Belief* Books 1 and 2 by Eric Carlton (Allen and Unwin) which deals with some of the questions listed above and many others.

The teacher might now look at syllabus material suggested in earlier chapters and see how it might be fitted into some of the topics recommended above.

INTEGRATED APPROACHES

Falling rolls is not the only reason for linking religious studies with history, music or geography. Reality is a better one. A person who is truly whole does not live life in compartments. Perhaps one of the greatest injuries to school religion brought about by the 1870 and 1944 Acts was that of virtually compelling it to be unrelated to other aspects of the curriculum — to stick out like a sore thumb as dull and irrelevant Only now is the situation changing. Instead of a fascinating topic on India having to be set aside in favour of Northumbrian saints or stories Jesus heard, we are beginning to include Indian religion. Sweetness and light does not prevail everywhere, however. Not long ago a student in a middle school was required to teach the Bedouin in geography the Romans in history and the Joseph saga in religious education to the same class. Any of three combinations would have been preferable — the Bedouin, the Arab expansion and Islam; or Joseph, ancient Egypt and the geography of the Nile and north Africa; or the Romans, the Mediterranean and Jesus or Paul in the Roman world.

Some topics that can benefit from integration are India, Africa, oil, the Crusades (I spent nearly a year on the Crusades at university in a history course, but only twenty years later did I begin to learn anything about Islam), man as a migrant, twentieth-century Leeds, London, Britain, our town and Israel.

However, with the integrated approach, especially in secondary schools, one must remember that the company determines the content. Combining with history will always give religious studies an historical bias, with art an aesthetic one. Care needs to be taken to ensure that the distinctive nature of religious studies as a discipline is not lost. Where practical, explicit, interdisciplinary teaching is not possible something can be done by fitting in with other subjects implicitly. For example, if the religious studies teacher hears that the Crusades is done in the first term of the second-year history course he can make sure that he is teaching about Islam at the same time. If India is part of the third-year geography course he can make aspects of Hinduism coincide with it. Religious studies is a flexible subject, and the teacher should take advantage of this. Why take up your own time to teach Indian history or geography, important as they are for a study of Hinduism, if others will do it for you?

Finally, what of the thematic approach where there are only two religions represented in the school, perhaps Christianity and Sikhism, or Christianity and Judaism? It is not appropriate there to teach only Christianity and one other religion — Sikhism or Judaism? I would be inclined to say 'No'. A sound religious studies course will choose good examples to elucidate a topic. For one reason or another they may well be found outside the religions present in the class. In a topic on concepts of God I would certainly want to examine the Hindu view as well as the Jewish and Christian. I would also want to bear in mind the sad fact that not only do Sikhs often have a distorted view of Islam, they have been known to express anti-semitic sentiments, though they have never met a Jew! I would want to argue that pupils leaving British schools should possess a general knowledge of the five religions to be encountered in Britain, and probably Buddhism too. It happens in Indian schools. We must not pretend, as we do with the acquisition of foreign languages, that the task is beyond all but the ablest children. I have taught children of average ability who speak, read and write English and Urdu, who can read Arabic and are coping with French better than I did. Their parents, with little formal education compared with the average school teacher, may well speak Urdu, Punjabi, Hindu and English and be able to read and write in three of them. Perhaps those of us who teach religious studies expect too little or forget that we are turning out people to live in society rather than students of religion.

WORSHIP

Aims of study: (1) To discover information about worship in a variety of religions — where, when and how people worship.
(2) To try to answer the question: What is worship?
(3) To try to answer the question: Why do people worship?

(1) *Where — places of worship*

(a) Begin with possible references to graves, high places, ziggurats, caves, Stonehenge, but quickly pass on to places about which literary information is available, e.g. Jerusalem Temple, St Albans Abbey, the Sanchi Stupa, the Golden Temple at Amritsar. These are cult centres and might form a topic in their own right, perhaps being related to pilgrimages (journeys theme).

(b) *Places of day-to-day-worship*
The synagogue — its important features — the ark, *bima* men and women separate — orientated with the ark towards Jerusalem.
The mosque — *mihrab*, *muezzin*, minaret, ablution fountain, no seats (frequently), the *minbar* and (sometimes) *dikka*.
The Gurdwara — focal point, the Guru Granth Sahib on a *takht* under a *palki* or *chanini*. No seats.
The Hindu temple — focal point, the statue of a deity. The temple not a place of congregational worship but the 'home' of God.
Christian churches — architectural variety. Layout determined by considerations of theology and liturgy. Orientation.

(c) An examination of the main features leading to an analysis of the reasons for their shape and style. Religious belief determines the shape of religious buildings.

(2) *How people worship*

An examination of how members of each faith worship based upon
(a) What happens in the buildings;
(b) Going beyond the building, e.g. Jeremiah's attitude to the Jerusalem Temple (Jeremiah 7, of Solomon's words 1 Kings 827).

(a) *Inside the building* — sacrifice, dance, sacraments, hymn-singing, prayer, meditation. The purpose of these varied activities. (This might develop into a deep study of prayer or sacramentalism.) Those who conduct worship in the various religions and denominations.

(b) *Beyond the building*

    (i)   Festivals and processions in some of the religions, e.g. Corpus Christi, Good Friday or Easter Day processions, the Jagannath festival at *Puri*, *Diwali*, Sikh *gurpurbs*.

    (ii) Worship in the house — Jewish *Kiddush*, *Havdalah*, Passover, Hindu *puja*, Sikh use of a room as a *Gurdwara*.

After finding out where and how people worship discussion can take place on the value and limitation of having special places of worship and on what the phrases 'holy land' or 'holy place' mean.

3. *When people worship*

Holy Days. Festivals. Religious calendars.

  (a) *Basic Information*

      The Jewish Sabbath, the Muslim Friday, the Christian Sunday, obligations laid upon the faithful. The origins of these weekly holy days. (The Sikh in Britain holds *diwan* on Sunday because it is a holiday when he is free to worship, but Hindus, Buddhists and Sikhs do not have a weekly day of worship. The practice is to worship daily, often individually and at home.)

  (b) The religious calendar. Jewish, Muslim, Christian; methods of dating from creation, the *Hijra*, the birth of Jesus.

  (c) The relationship between the cycle of nature and annual religious festivals.

  (d) The development from nature to history. Aetiological myths, salvation history, e.g. the barley harvest becomes Passover; the wheat harvest becomes a reminder of the giving of the Law and for Christians a reminder of the giving of the Holy Spirit. The purpose of holy days. Are all days holy?

4. What is worship?

5. Why do people worship?

These may lead to a study of the being who is worshipped, various concepts of God, and to the religious 'founders' and ideas of revelation.

CHRISTIANITY AND THE RELIGIONS

Religions express and interpret experience and the meaning of life. They enable people to encounter the ultimate reality of life and to grow in relationship with that reality to which many faiths, though not all, give the name God. However, though most religions argue that they were made in heaven (Buddhism is a special case to be discussed later) to help man reach 'heaven', nevertheless they took birth and grew up on earth. They used the language of the people to whom they were revealed, be it Hebrew, Greek, Arabic, Punjabi or some African language; they addressed themselves to particular cultures. In doing so they often commented upon the religions which already existed in the part of the world where they took birth. Consequently the Christian New Testament frequently refers to Judaism either implicitly or explicitly. In the *Qur'an* both Judaism and Christianity are mentioned many times. The Sikh scripture, the *Guru Granth Sahib,* often alludes to Hinduism, Islam and other contemporary Indian religious movements, and the Buddhist scriptures contain information about the Indian religious tradition from which Buddhism emerged which was not yet Hinduism either in name or form. Naturally, Christianity does not feature in the Jewish *Tenakh* or Islam in early Buddhist texts, but then neither Hinduism nor Buddhism occurs in the *Qur'an.* Religions are affected by cultural factors.

In the late twentieth century the religions not only exist cheek by jowl in a global village which is becoming a secular city, their theologians, often prompted by rank and file members of the faiths, are concerned about relationships with and attitudes towards people of other faiths. Jesus is on the agenda of Judaism; not only Judaism and Christianity, but Sikhism, Buddhism, Hinduism and African tribal religions are the cultural neighbours of Islam. Somehow the religions have to search their scriptures or early traditions to extrapolate from the past a response to the religious interaction of today. How each religion goes about this task is a matter for its own members to work out. Though there is a history of dialogue between Jew and Muslim, Buddhist and Brahmin long ago, so that today's discussions are by no means the first, nevertheless there is no blueprint, no universally approved technique for carrying out the exercise. What follows is therefore to be regarded as the response of an individual hopefully, thoughtful, committed and responsible but not an official representative making pontifical statements.

I want to begin my Christian appraisal of the other faiths represented in this book by asserting my belief in the authenticity of the real experience of God possessed by people of other faiths. Having lived among and worked with the people I cannot deny — indeed I would want to affirm — the authenticity of their experience and my own.

There are real issues of disagreement and therefore potential tension, and it is to these that attention must be drawn here. They cannot be glossed over, and I cannot claim to produce solutions. Each religion will be approached independently.

Judaism is the cultural parent of Christianity. Jesus was a Jew. He was regular in his synagogue worship, and the evidence suggests that he went up to Jerusalem for the major pilgrim festivals and either killed his own Passover lamb or at least ate the meal with his friends. Though Christians regard Jesus as more than Messiah, Jesus did not deny that he was the Messiah, and one reason for his crucifixion was clearly the refutation of that claim, which many of his co-religionists regarded as blasphemous. St Paul, before he became a Christian, was convinced of the threat which the followers of Jesus posed to true religion. A theme of St John's Gospel is the failure of Judaism to witness to the truth. Ever since, Jew and Christian have often been seen at loggerheads, though the power to add injury to insult has generally lain with Christians who in York, Lincoln, Spain, Tsarist Russia and Nazi Germany have been willing to use it.

The issues which cannot be disguised are as follows. Judaism does deny the concept of a Messiah who will come to deliver mankind through suffering, from sin. Such a Messiah is unnecessary. Adam's sin has not affected the whole human race. Each man is his own Adam, each woman her own Eve. God will forgive the sinner who rebels against him, if the sinner is sincere in his repentance. Sins committed against one's neighbour only the injured neighbour can forgive. Should a Messiah come, and not all Jews believe in a Messiah, he will be a man — not God — incarnate, and he will come to inaugurate the messianic age (to which all Jews look forward) described in such passages as Isaiah 60. Judaism regards Christianity as tritheistic rather than monotheistic.

It must be acknowledged that the early ill feeling between Judaism and Christianity has never been allowed to die. A collect for Good Friday in the Book of Common Prayer still mentions the hardness of heart, ignorance and 'contempt of thy Word' of Jews who are linked with Turks (Muslims) infidels and heretics! The grasping 'Shylock-image' of folklore is not one of which Christians have always sincerely disapproved and attempted to eradicate. On the contrary, especially at Easter and through many frequently used hymns, enmity is still fostered so that people can still be heard to say 'Hitler had the right idea'.

Although the theological disagreements over the Trinity and messiahship of Jesus must divide Jew and Christian and exercise the minds of theologians it should be possible for members of both faiths to gain a sound knowledge of the other faith, so that they stop wilfully misrepresenting it (for example, Christians often argue that the Jews are searching for God, or that Judaism does not take sin seriously, despite the evidence of the 'Old Testament'). To do this the acquiring of accurate knowledge is a prerequisite. Ultimately this means listening to and learning from a member of that faith.

Islam regards both Jews and Christians as people of the book, that is, as religions revealed by God. However, each of them has corrupted the pure message. Consequently it was necessary for God to reveal Himself again, this time to the Arab people through His Prophet Muhammad, who faithfully transmitted the revelation. Thus the *Qur'an* is a corrective to both *Tenakh* and New Testament. Once the Christian has overcome his annoyance at being told he is wrong, or at best not wholly right, and has freed himself from malicious impressions that Muhammad was a lecherous epileptic and other distortions which have been present in Western society at least since the time of the Crusades, the theological issues are first, that the *Qur'an* asserts that Jesus was human and not divine, and second, that Christians worship three gods. It also contains biographical information about Jesus which conflicts with that of the New Testament, denying that he was crucified, though affirming the virgin birth and ascension and calling Jesus 'Messiah'. The Muslim and Christian revelations cannot both give correct accounts. For Muslims, Jesus is a great Prophet; for Christians he is the Word made flesh. The *Qur'an* also explicitly states that Christians worship three gods. The reconciling of these statements and beliefs may not be possible, but again there is room for a better understanding of one another's faiths to take place. For example, Christians can stop asserting that Muslims worship the Prophet Muhammad and can discover how Muslims regard him, while Muslims can learn about the Christian view of Jesus and grapple with the Christian doctrine of the Trinity.

Hinduism, together with Sikhism, did not encounter Christianity in its formative period. Confrontation coincided with the development of large-scale Christian missionary work in India in the nineteenth century, as a result of which stories about idol worship, widow burning, lazy fatalism and an oppressive caste system reached the West, so that Hinduism became equated with superstition and backwardness. Now we have learned that underlying the Hindu readiness to use statues as aids to worship is a rich and profound concept of Brahman (a neuter name for ultimate reality), and that the ills of Indian society have concerned Indians as much as Christians but, being deeply rooted in the culture, have proved as obstinate as sexist or racial prejudice and class distinction to remove from British life, despite legislation in both countries.

Perhaps the chief difficulty which Hinduism poses for Christians lies in its eclectic nature. When the Hindu is told about Jesus he gladly accepts his divinity and adores and worships him, but sees him as one

159

of many enlighteners sent by God to bring to life a divine spark which is latently present in every human being. Assertions that Jesus is unique and demands exclusive loyalty and worship are strange, incomprehensible and unacceptable. So, too, is the idea of Jesus bearing the sins of mankind. Hindu and Sikh lives of Jesus tend to present him as a guru, an enlightener, and pay little attention to salvation from sin wrought by his death. The Indian religious tradition, which embraces Hindu, Sikh and Buddhist, regards man as being beset by original ignorance rather than as a fallen person in rebellion against God.

On the agenda of Hindu–Christian dialogue must be a discussion of human nature and the concept of God, but this can only take place when Christians, especially Protestants, are willing to disabuse themselves of some of their misunderstandings of Hinduism.

Sikhism for our present purpose might be regarded as a religion which had its origins in Hinduism and is to some extent a reaction against it. The one aspect of this reaction which is relevant here is the Sikh insistence upon the immanence of God, so removing the need for priestly rituals, the use of statues in worship, the belief that God ever manifests himself in animal or human form. This means that Sikhs can regard Jesus as an enlightened teacher, a Guru like their own Gurus, but only a man, and not unique. Like Hindus, they would value the message of Jesus but not regard his death as necessary, though it was a wonderful example of the invincibility of love.

Buddhism presents a distinctive challenge to all the religions mentioned in this book because in its essence it is non-theistic. There may be a God or there may not be, His existence is inconsequential as He cannot help us to acquire peace of mind or eternal bliss. Only a right understanding of the world and proper conduct as a result of that understanding is effective. Again, therefore, Jesus may be an enlightened being, a buddha, but nothing more. Christian dialogue with the Buddhist, as with the Sikh and Hindu, has to do with the nature of man, the reality of the world, but also has much to contribute to helping the Christian sharpen up his understanding of what he means when he rather loosely and thoughtlessly uses the word 'God'.

A few concluding points need to be made. First a distinctive feature of Christianity which emerges from considering it in the context of these other five faiths is its belief in the necessity of Jesus' death as the remedy prescribed by God for overcoming sin and restoring man to the sonship God intended Him to enjoy. The emphasis upon a fallen human nature incapable of obeying God sets Christianity apart.

Second, as a consequence, Jesus is often regarded as an intermediary between man and God. Christian beliefs about his divinity are not understood so that one frequently hears particularly Jews and Muslims saying 'We don't need an intermediary, we can approach God direct'.

Third, despite the differences which exist between the religions covered in this book there are unifying features which it would be wrong to ignore. Some of the most important are:

(1) Each of the religions believes in one ultimate reality and might be described as essentially monotheistic. (Here, of course, Buddhism presents something of a problem.)

(2) Each religion attaches importance to social responsibility and caring for one's neighbour. In matters of ethical principle there is considerable agreement. It cannot honestly be said that only Christians care.

(3) Each religion has within its teaching and traditions somewhere a belief in the love of God (though again, Buddhism is a special case). In the *bhakti* tradition of Hinduism, in the *Sufi* movement of Islam, in the Prophets of Judaism, this is especially strong, and is a general theme of Sikhism. The fatherhood of God, too, is a concept by no means unique to Christianity.

(4) Each religion claims to be revealed (though again, Buddhism raises peculiar problems). Those Christians who wish to say that their religion is revealed but others are searches for the truth must be aware that this is a misrepresentation of Hindu, Jewish, Muslim, Sikh and Buddhist teaching.

(5) Each religion believes in eternal life, an existence of the soul after bodily death.

(6) Each religion, with the exception of Sikhism and Buddhism, believes in an Age to Come. Sikhism and Buddhism, together with some forms of Hinduism so emphasise the inwardness of spiritual experience that they have no need of the concept of a messianic age or Kingdom of God on earth.

DIALOGUE AND RELIGIOUS EDUCATION

The teacher in the multi-faith school is, by definition, working at the place where a number of religions, and probably secular ideologies, meet. These can be ignored. A Jewish headmaster of a first school once said 'We treat them all the same', by which he meant first, and very emphatically, that his was a humane school in which every child was respected. It certainly was. However, culturally, 'same' resulted in every child being treated as white Anglo-Saxon working-class British Christian. The curriculum had not changed in twenty years, though the cultural composition of the school had altered radically.

At the other extreme came the school which celebrates its multi-cultural nature and rejoices in it to the enrichment and benefit of all its pupils. The ordinary everyday life and the festival days of its different members are shared. In secondary schools so are the tensions and griefs caused by sectarian disputes, discrimination or violence in the community where the school is situated. In such schools, especially at secondary level, questions related to which religion is true, if any, are likely to emerge. Even where the religious studies course is open and objective, where no religion has been threatened or discounted as odd, whether it be Rastafarians, Jehovah's Witness, Ahmaddiya or Pentecostal Christian, pupils are bound to be perplexed by the different claims they discover. After all, Jewish, Christian and Muslim views on Jesus cannot all be right, can they? While the differences may not upset me if I am a mature Christian, and may only amuse me if I happen to be an agnostic, the fifteen-year-old Muslim growing up between two cultures and the pressures of secular subcultures may be both perplexed and disturbed. So may be a Roman Catholic or any other youngster who belongs to a faith community.

To avoid the difficulty, some religious leaders and groups advocate no school RE and withdraw their children from it and school assembly, but they are not happy with this solution. It attracts unwelcome attention and emphasises difference and oddity. If schools were totally secular, things might be better, but they recognise that this would only leave pupils open to rumour, prejudice and the hand-me-down distortions which Jews, especially, know to exist in society at large. It would therefore seem healthier to explore differences, similarities and points of agreement openly in an educational atmosphere.

Dialogue, which is the name given to such explorations and exchanges, is a minority interest among adults. As yet it does not appear as a topic in any Agreed Syllabuses or as an examination option. *Northbourne Tales of Belief and Understanding,* by Graham Cleverley and Barbara Phillips (McGraw-Hill, 1975) is not quite a book on dialogue, but it is perhaps the nearest thing to it available for pupils in secondary schools to read. It examines the effect of different beliefs upon relationships and conduct, the human aspects but not the theological. It might be argued that the theological are beyond the understanding of fifteen- and sixteen-year-olds, but if the perplexities exist, if a readiness to take part in Catholic–Protestant street fights or to smash synagogue windows is there, perhaps we should be encouraging a healthier type of dialogue in the classroom. *Why Do Men Suffer?* (Hart-Davies) might be regarded as an attempt at the theological dialogue. It is based on *Problems of Suffering in the World's Religions* by John Bowker. There is also Donald Butler's *Friends and Neighbours* series (Edward Arnold). These are three books of plays exploring life in inter-religions ways. They are based on programmes broadcast by Radio Manchester.

For teachers who are interested, three sources of help already exist. One is the British Council of Churches, 2 Eaton Gate, London SW1W 9BL. It is in touch with all local dialogue and interfaith groups in the UK and could help people wanting to establish contacts or to form new groups. The second is the World Congress of Faiths, 28 Powis Gardens, London W11 1JG. It is dedicated to the development of interfaith understanding. Third, there is The Standing Conference of Interfaith Dialogue in Education (SCIFDE), which might be described as an offspring of WCF and is concerned solely with educational aspects of interfaith relations. Since 1973 it has discussed them at annual conferences which anyone may attend. Enquiries addressed to SCIFDE, c/o World Congress of Faiths will reach the appropriate person.

Undoubtedly, the teacher wishing to explore dialogue in the classroom should do some reading in the subject. Better still, he should join a group which is engaged in it so that he is aware of the intellectual and human concerns, for real dialogue begins with the meeting of people.

Where to begin reading about dialogue is probably a question to be answered awkwardly, with the suggestion to study at least one religion other than your own on its own terms. Until we discover the authenticity, integrity and spirituality of another religion the questions raised in dialogue are unlikely to be very real. Some books are as follows.

With People of Other Faiths in Britain, published by the United Reformed Church, 86 Tavistock Place, London WC1 H9 RT. This is an example of publications which Christian denominations are producing as they become more aware of Britain as a multi-faith society.

Shall We Greet Only our Own Family? Methodist Church.

Christianity and Other Religions, J. Hick and B. Hebblethwaite (eds), Fount paperback. A collection of views.

The Meaning and End of Religion, W. C. Smith, Sheldon Press, is not perhaps a book to start with but certainly one to reach out to.

All Their Splendour, David Brown, Fount, is by a Christian bishop whose life was a dialogue.

Four others which are essential reading in themselves and point to other books are

Guidelines on Dialogue, World Council of Churches.
Relations with People of Other Faiths, British Council of Churches.
Considering Dialogue, K. Cracknell, British Council of Churches.
Christian Community and Cultural Diversity, Barbara Holden and Eric Rolls, National Centre for Christian Communities and Networks, Westhill College, Birmingham.

Sooner rather than later, dialogue must find a place in school religious studies courses, though it does not feature as yet in many university, college of higher education or theological college syllabuses. We are only likely to do something about it as we become aware of harmful misrepresentations such as the words of a preacher who once said 'We should all study the religions in our midst', and went on, before I called for three cheers, 'but we must remember that Christianity is the only true religion. It was revealed by God; the others are human searchers for the truth!' Perhaps the beginning lies in voluntary discussion groups. Later dialogue might be written into courses.

Some areas which might be explored are: (1) the relationship between Judaism, Christianity and Islam; (2) Jesus: how Judaism, Christianity and Islam regard Him; (3) Suffering; (4) The Path to Eternity.

(The editor would be pleased to enter into dialogue with teachers attempting some exploration in their schools.)

VISITING PLACES OF WORSHIP

Such visits can be stimulating, can help the self-esteem of children whose place of worship is visited and may be a means of increasing understanding by developing school and community links. Without exception, those who have made such visits have found the hosts kind and extremely hospitable.

However, there are a number of considerations to be borne in mind by the teacher. There may be language difficulties, and it may not be possible to arrange a visit during school hours. One must make sure that the time does not conflict with a service or festival, unless the intention is to observe this and the community representatives have agreed to this.

Jewish communities are well established, no language problems arise and some member or other of the synagogue is likely to be available during the day to conduct a school party. Hindu, Muslim and Sikh leaders are seldom, as yet, self-employed and able to take time off work. Arrangements should therefore be made well in advance.

As with all school visits, adequate preparation is essential. It is hoped that some of the filmstrips listed in this book will prove helpful but also it may be advisable to prime the children with questionnaires or work-cards telling what to look for; otherwise, if the guide has only a limited command of English the experience may be counterproductive resulting in frustration.

At present many temples, mosques or *Gurdwaras* are still converted houses or churches lacking in aesthetic or architectural merit. The impression received by the children may not be a good one, in consequence. Rather than visit the empty building, it is better to see it with worshippers in it, if this is possible, and it may be if the group is less than twenty.

In many mosques girls will not be admitted, certainly at times of prayer. In the synagogue and *Gurdwara* men and women are seated separately, and this means that somehow provision must be made for both groups to follow the service.

Small groups are always better than large ones to take on educational visits. A few formalities must be remembered:
Synagogue: the head must be covered in the case of men.
Hindu temple: shoes should be removed, the head need not be covered.
Gurdwara: no shoes, covered head.
Mosque: no shoes, covered head.

ARRANGING A VISIT

(1) Contact can often be made through children, their parents or the local community relations officer.

(2) An attempt should be made to visit the building oneself and, if possible, to observe an act of worship before taking the class. As a result of this experience the class will receive better preparation. Otherwise, it has been known for parties to turn up at a *Gurdwara* at 10 a.m. on a Sunday to sit through the rest of the service in Punjabi, which does not have any liturgical form until near the end — which may be at 1 p.m.! If there are separate entrances for men and women a few shocks and anxieties can be caused if the girls are suddenly led away without warning!

(3) Plenty of notice should be given of the desire to visit the place of worship and the hosts should be asked to suggest convenient times and occasions. Weddings, festivals or other community gatherings of which the teacher is unaware may be taking place at the time the teacher would like to make a visit, which may make it impossible for the hosts to give the attention they would like to provide. Also it gives the hosts an opportunity to inform their guests of such things as the prohibition against cigarettes and tobacco being taken into the *Gurdwara*.

(4) If they are going to a service the children should recognise that they are going as observers rather than participants, and are not therefore expected to adopt attitudes of prayer or try to sing hymns but to sit watchfully and reverently, unless requested to do otherwise.

WHAT OF THE GREAT UNCOMMITTED?

Some teachers might like to call the 80 per cent of children in our schools who have no religious beliefs 'the immoral majority'. Not too long ago there was a story circulating of a hospital matron (or number 7) who refused to employ a young lady who described herself as a Humanist in her application form. She said that the work required dedication and love which could only be found in a Christian!

It is not surprising that sometimes Christian religious education is supported by government ministers and employers because they think it will preserve moral standards and traditional values, but teachers should beware of what they are being required to do. In an explicitly multi-cultural school they are being invited to suggest that only Christians care, that Muslims or Jews are lazy, devious and unreliable. In all white schools they are being asked to prejudice their children to believe that any Sikhs or Hindus they may eventually meet are lacking in moral fibre. However, teachers are also being encouraged to revert to the old religious education, which was not a study of religion but an attempt to make children religious, not so much for their own spiritual benefit but in order to reduce crime figures and to be meekly acquiescent of the society in which they live.

Besides being contrary to current developments in religious studies, this approach to religious education promises to make it yet again the sore thumb of the curriculum. While history, geography, English and other subjects adopt a spirit of enquiry, religious education should take an affirmative stance, not questioning but approving values. It also invites the teacher to ignore or conceal the prophetic nature of Christianity, like many other religious questions, rather than endorsing values and standards. However, it also leaves untouched that large majority of pupils referred to at the beginning of this section.

If schools are to involved in affective moral education, that is, in trying to produce — what? People who are socially respectable and acceptable, honest, hard-working, caring? If that is something that society requires teachers to do, then it must first decide what its values are. Then the teacher must attempt to be realistic. To invite youngsters to be schizophrenic is hardly to be realistic, yet that is what we are doing if we attempt to inculcate Christian ethics apart from Christian belief (and the same is also true of other religions). This is also what we are doing if this kind of moral education is left to the religious studies department. If it is to be done, the task is one for the whole school, both staff and pupils. The role of religious studies in this might be to examine the principles upon which the religions base their ethical teachings, and to explore practical responses which they have made to such things as war, social injustice, the place of woman and the whole purpose of living. In doing so it would be contributing to the debate which would be carried out throughout the school, and to the social experiment that this school would be engaged in as well as an analysis of its hidden curriculum.

Perhaps the ultimate aim in any school can only be to produce autonomous human beings. All Christians may agree that we should be honest, but as the horizons of personal honesty extend this can include the question of whether it is honest to buy certain brands of tea or coffee, knowing that they are cheaper because labourers are paid starvation wages. At this point Christians begin to disagree, though not as much as on the Christian attitude to pacifism, abortion or euthanasia. It may seem that the Muslim view on many issues is more uniform, but as we learn more of Islam and other religions, we discover that there are shades and degrees of interpretation on moral issues.

In a pluralistic society the school's aim might be to produce autonomous human beings, using this phrase to include those whose autonomy is found in the company of Jesus, or in obedience to the will of God as taught in the *Qu'ran* and the life of the Muslim community. There will be, and must be, disagreements, but all religious and all secular communities which are wholesome and dynamic desire their members to be personally sensitive and responsible, people who have thought out their attitudes. If schools can set sensitivity, thoughtfulness and responsibility as their targets they may be setting themselves not only a realistic task but one which is worthwhile and beneficial to a radically changing society as well as to maturing individuals. In practice, it will mean schools in which authority is shared not only among senior staff and with parents but also with the pupils.

AN END OR A BEGINNING?

The multi-faith agenda has been by no means exhausted by the contents of this book. The following are only a few of the items which must concern teachers both now and in the years ahead. They are not placed in order of priority. They are all important, but in some schools the urgency may be greater than elsewhere.

THE CHRISTIAN CHILD FROM A CARIBBEAN BACKGROUND

Three issues are represented by this heading. First, the African has been subjected to denigration ever since he was torn from his continent. Here the word 'denigrate' is not used in the *Oxford English Dictionary* sense of 'to blacken' but in the even more serious one of denoting the attempt to deprive him of his negritude, his African-ness, his culture. As students of the history of slavery will know, the aim of the process was to reduce him to the status of an animal. This often entailed forbidding him to be baptised, for that would have been to admit that the slave possessed a soul! Since emancipation, inhabitants of the British Caribbean have been nurtured into the 'British way of life' — cricket, English literature, British history, even the geography of the British Isles rather than that of the islands. West Indians were encouraged to take a pride in the Empire, to regard Britain as the mother-country and to fight for it against Germany. Some were attracted to their 'homeland' by invitations in newspapers asking them to work in its factories, hospitals and transport systems. They came, and were not welcomed. The shock of being made British and converted to Christianity as part of the process, only to be rejected by the inhabitants of Britain, is surely something which any teacher of so-called West Indian children must take into account. If there is such a thing as group resentment this is certainly one reason for it. Black studies or the search for identity in Africa will not remove the underlying causes, which are social. The remedies are political. Perhaps the school can, at best, provide the child with a community in which he is accepted and welcomed — and enabled to compete on equal terms with white adolescents in the job market. (That is what his parents usually want.)

Second, the prize possession of the West Indian has often been his Christianity. He now finds this to be a leisure activity, not taken seriously by many people. He finds that the churches do not always welcome him, and in school his children study Islam! What they ask for is a faith to live by, not the kind of religious education advocated in this book. Indeed, were teachers from the Caribbean to have one criticism to make of this book it would probably be that it is another

169

example of tokenism, some reference to the needs of the child from their background, but not enough, and too little is almost worse than neglect: as much of an affront as reading *Little Black Sambo* in story time! Incidentally, I hope with all my heart that they will regard this book as an attempt to make a positive contribution, but we have a long way to go in working out approaches to religious education in schools where the largest group is black Christian. The difficulty of responding may be made even greater by the introduction of Rastafarianism into the syllabus, something which I would be inclined to do.

Third, the members of our society who have come from the Caribbean look in amazement at the help which is given to those from the Indo–Pakistan subcontinent or Vietnam, and wonder why they have been forgotten by their co-religionists. Dialogue with Jews and Muslims, mother-tongue and ESL language programmes, somehow it all seems out of proportion — and as well as being Christian, they are the largest minority ethnic group in Britain.

More needs to be done in response to the religious education needs of these children in our classroom. Some would say we have not even begun, but the 1982 Supplement to the *Birmingham Handbook*, the Afro–Caribbean material listed elsewhere in this book and some of the articles to be found in it may indicate that we have begun, but not gone very far.

EXAMINATIONS IN RELIGIOUS STUDIES

During discussions about a new examination at 16-plus it has become clear that there are teachers who are eager to use it as an opportunity for removing the study of world religions from the classroom and replace it by Christian education. They appealed to the need to protect Christian studies, implying that they were under attack. There is no one other than those who would get rid of religious education altogether who wishes to threaten Christian studies. Certainly it is not in any danger from what is sometimes called the 'world religions movement'. On the contrary, teachers like myself regard its study as an essential part of religious education, not only because it is the major religion of Britain and the one nearest to hand, but for its own intrinsic worth. Its doctrine of God, its incarnational theology, its teaching about the nature of man and salvation, as well as its worldwide distribution, would cause any course which excluded it to be maimed from birth. Actually the danger to religious education comes from head teachers who believe that any non-specialist can teach it so long as he is devout, and from those who equate religious education with morality and replace it with programmes of social action. The world religions movement demands that religious education should be taken seriously, and that the subject of study should be religion.

170

If opponents to the new religious education replace it with Christian studies their motives are as likely to be as misunderstood as mine, but the consequences will be more severe. First, it will result in the mass withdrawal of Muslim, Jewish, and probably Sikh children, if not Hindus. This would be a pity, just when one hears that the new approach to religious education is resulting in some Jehovah's Witnesses staying in lessons and taking religious studies at 'O' level, and of withdrawal being a thing of the past. Second, it is likely to result in secularist pressure for the removal of religious education from the curriculum. It may be remembered that there was a demand for this in the mid-1960s, but that since religious education became more broadly based and rejected confessional aims, few voices have been raised against it. On the contrary, humanists as well as Jews and Muslims are now working alongside people like myself to develop religious studies into a demanding, and meaningful, as well as enjoyable part of the curriculum. One would hope that commonsense rather than its status as a compulsory element in examinations would ensure the place of Christianity in religious studies. One hopes examinations will respond to reality and not be used to advance the teaching of one religion at the expense of another. Should a teacher wish to teach only Christianity, that is something that I would accept, though I might doubt his professional wisdom. Should he require me to do the same I would strenuously question his right to be so prescriptive.

RELIGIOUS STUDIES IN HIGHER EDUCATION

There is a saying sometimes heard in the north of England, 'If tha knaws nowt tha can't teach owt'. It has a bearing on multi-cultural education in general as well as upon religious education. The universities have always insisted on the academic integrity of their disciplines. They are not in the business of producing clergymen, teachers or museum curators, but theologians or historians. It is up to vocational institutions or such courses as the PGCE to provide specialist training. This view is acceptable to a point, but the PGCE is a professional course, so that if in his degree course the student has not studied Hinduism, he cannot expect to be taught it now. The situation is critical in religious education, where many university students receive a traditional theological training which does not equip them for the schools in which they will teach. In colleges of higher education the real position may not be much happier. The students may study Judaism, Islam or Sikhism, but the emphasis may still be on the pure discipline (after all, their teachers are the products of the universities), rather than those areas of the religions which are likely to be taught in the classroom. One of the greatest negative factors upon curriculum change is probably the student's failure to acquire knowledge during his four-year training which will be applicable in the classroom. He is therefore compelled to fall back on the things he learned in school, the Romans, the Great Fire of London, the miracles and parables of Jesus. Even Joseph's coat still remains many-coloured rather than long-sleeved. Most teachers who are attempting to extend the religious education syllabus are self-taught in world religions, certainly if they have been teaching for more than ten years.

If the academic content of courses taken by intending teachers needs to be radically reappraised the professional area asks for similar scrutiny. Many primary school teachers receive less than fifteen hours of curriculum training in religious education. Most students are given no training in multi-cultural education. Where questions appear in examination papers the opening words are often 'What problems might . . .'! Positive approaches to the prospect of teaching in multi-cultural schools seem rare. In universities especially, multi-cultural education should be taken seriously, for it is from these institutions that most of our HMIs, chief education officers and other education policy-makers, as well as many of our secondary teachers, are recruited.

THE RESPONSE OF ETHNIC MINORITIES

There is a need also to recruit more religious education teachers from religious minorities. If the emphasis is on academic ability and professional competence there is no reason why a Jewish religious studies specialist should not teach Christianity. Such students are only likely to come forward if they are offered courses in world religions, including their own.

The religious communities have an important role to play in religious education. Not only can they encourage young people from their communities to come forward to teach the subject, they can also support those of their number, and there are many, who have a talent for presenting their religion to schoolchildren. There are now at least six writers, some of whom have contributed to this book, following the trial blazed by the remarkable Myer Domnitz years ago. More are needed, but I hear tales of how difficult it is for such writers to catch the eye of a publisher, and sometimes evade the criticisms of their own communities.

If the churches are gradually recognising that the school is not a place where evangelism should take place, it is necessary that other religious groups should share the view. The priest no longer enters school to catch those of his flock who will not go to church, but sometimes the *Imam* seeks to do so. It has to be recognised that the privilege of nurturing children into religion belongs to the home and the community. It is not an aim to be pursued in schools in the maintained sector.

WIDER HORIZONS

There is little point in religious studies alone responding to the multi-cultural world. If mud huts are the stuff of geography and Arab cruelty part of the history diet, religious education cannot do much to give children esteem, either in their own eyes or those of their peers. Similarly, if the churches are paternalistic to Christians who do not happen to be white, there is little chance that the West Indian or Asian in our midst will be considered a person of worth. If homes foster racial hatred and the media encourage the telling of racist jokes, there is little chance of the next generation being more accepting than ours. When all these things happen in a country which makes people from its 'New Commonwealth' feel unwanted, social disaster might seem to be the only possibility. In other words, the schools can do no more than reflect the attitudes and aspirations of society. Teachers cannot establish a multi-cultural Britain any more than the police can create a law-abiding one if they lack the backings of the general public.

It may be in the nature of religions to be visionary, and many religious education teachers are devoted idealists, but the time has come for asking what kind of Britain they are being asked to struggle to produce. There is no need to be defensive and no hope in putting back the clock. The years of Empire have gone, their legacy, a multi-cultural Britain, is here to stay. It can be one in which those things of worth in Britain's heritage are retained and developed, as well as being one in which the riches of our world heritage are recognised and explored for the first time.

EXAMPLES OF WORK DONE IN MULTI-FAITH SCHOOLS

HOMES AND FAMILIES

In a Multi-faith Reception Class

The Infant School in Batley at which the theme 'Homes and Families' was developed has children, in the main, of 'working-class background'. Immigrants, all of Asian background, number approximately 25 out of a total of 90, and the reception class was therefore not quite typical of the school as a whole, having only 4 out of 24, of which 3 were Pakistani and 1 Indian, all Muslims. The headteacher and her staff are friendly, co-operative people who do their utmost to make the school lively, hospitable and in every way a means of enriching the lives of their children.

Background to the Project

The project coincided with the Eid-ul-Adha (27–31 January in 1972), which marks the end of the pilgrimage to the *Ka'aba* at Mecca. It is also associated with Abraham's readiness to sacrifice his son, Ishmael, and therefore celebrated by all Muslims, not only those who have fulfilled the *Hajj*. (This readiness of Abraham and that of pilgrims undertaking the arduous journey to Mecca are regarded as ideal symbols of obedience to God.) This is the one occasion upon which sacrifice (lamb, chicken, etc.) is offered by Muslims and a portion of the meat, one third, is always given to the poor. Children receive something new, perhaps a present, frequently new clothes. It is a festival which corresponds very much in terms of atmosphere, to Christmas. *Eid* cards frequently extremely attractive, are sent. It should be pointed out that the teacher did not, of course, explain the *Eid*, the children could not have understood it. She simply taught it as a time of festival.

Glossary

Islam: 'submission' or 'peace'. The name given to the religion revealed to Muhammad.
Muslim: an adherent of the faith of Islam.
Muhammad: (570–632 CE) the Prophet to whom the teachings of God were revealed.
Qur'an: the sacred scripture of Islam, revealed to Muhammad by the

174

angel Gabriel and written down as a single volume soon after this Prophet's death.

Ka'aba: 'cube', a small building in Mecca which houses the black stone which, according to Muslim tradition, was given to Adam by the Angel Gabriel. Traditionally the *Ka'aba* was built by Abraham. The *Ka'aba* is the focal point of Islam, to which Muslims turn at prayer-time.

Hajj: pilgrimage to the *Ka'aba* at Mecca. Every Muslim should make this journey to Mecca once in his lifetime if health and wealth permit.

Mecca: the Holy City of Islam.

Mosque: Muslim place of prayer. Some Pakistani children may call it 'masdjid'.

Chapatti (or *Roti*): Indian equivalent of scones or Welsh cakes, etc., made of wheat flour and water.

The Religious Education Element in the Project

The aim was to build up an understanding of faiths and cultures between immigrants and non-immigrants, between Muslims and Christians.

Homes, Food, Clothes and Festivals

Linking with the main theme of homes and families, pictures of houses were shown to the children and a general discussion about houses, and the type they lived in followed. I asked them to tell me another name for a house and they told me 'home'. We then discussed what went into making a home and concluded it was people.

This led us to talk about the family and I was told all about each member. Muhammad assured me he had six brothers and many sisters, though I learned later he had three brothers and no sisters. The others, therefore, were part of the extended family of the Pakistani. Activities resulting from this were a cut-out paper collage of members of the family, houses and flats made out of boxes, and people made out of boxes. An enormous wall frieze was started and, as we began to explore the environment around us, we made things to include. We started with houses and flats, the school, the hospital, the park, the church, the mosque. All were suggested by the children, apart from the Mosque, which I eventually mentioned because the Muslim children did not. They smiled and were very happy to make one.

We talked about the food we eat to help build our bodies and make us strong as well as the food we enjoy eating, like sweets, etc. We discovered that not everyone liked the same food and some children had food at home which other children did not. The immigrant children liked many of the things the English children liked in addition to chapattis. Later we talked about the things Mummy bakes at home and made some of these ourselves. I took in some pastry which the children

175

made into tarts, scones, buns, etc. Halima and Hassina made some chapattis. These were then displayed and became the goods sold in a shop. Chapattis were just as popular with English children as with immigrants and I often heard the request for two chapattis and a jam tart.

I asked the children what they were wearing. What were their clothes made of? Did they always wear the same sort of clothes? They were able to tell me that in summer they wore different clothes and why. I asked if people in other countries wore the same clothes. They did not think they did. We concluded that some did, depending upon custom and weather. I asked if people in this country all wore the same. They said, 'No'. We discussed what some Muslim women wear. Lovely baggy silk trousers called 'shalwar', worn with a tunic or dress called a 'kemise'. We talked about the meaning of custom and I went on to say it was the custom for some Indian ladies to wear a sari. I took a real sari and, after practising the art of putting it on, I dressed one of the bigger children in it. She looked beautiful. We also dressed a large rag doll in a sari made from a piece of material. It was noticeable that from then on the old net curtain in the Wendy house, which had previously been used as a bridal veil, was in constant demand as a sari.

The Muslim children were away from school to celebrate the Festival of *Eid*. When they returned they were wearing new clothes which had been bought for the occasion. We talked about the festival and I explained to the class what happened at this special time. The Muslims go to their Mosque to pray. (They had already discovered when we were planning the village that this was their church.) When they return home they have lots of good things to eat but they never forget to share what they have with poor people. They visit friends and relatives, buy new clothes and have a happy time. They also send cards to each other. I asked if they could think of a time when we, Christians, do something like this. 'Yes, Christmas,' they answered.

We then looked at *Eid* cards and saw they were illustrated with pictures of mosques and had greetings written inside. We also looked at Christmas cards and saw they also contained greetings. Some had pictures of churches and some pictures of Mary, Joseph and baby Jesus. The children then drew about some part of their festival they liked best. Unfortunately the Muslim children were not able to communicate very well and they themselves had not been to the mosque, so apart from saying, 'Yes', to everything I said about *Eid*, they added very little to the discussion.

Two points of religious significance emerge from this. First, the immigrant child should not be expected to be the authority; the teacher must provide stimulus and information. Second, though most Muslim children will attend the mosque for religious instruction (especially to learn to read or recite the *Qur'an* in Arabic), Muslims do not go to the mosque as a family (on Friday), as Christians go to church. The father and his teenage sons, or perhaps younger boys, will go to the mosque; mother, daughters and other womenfolk will say their prayers at home.

Evaluation

Half the children in the class had only started school at Christmas, the other half in September. Therefore, their output in the form of written work and even drawings was limited. Much of my work with them was, therefore, oral, visual and practical. A topic of this kind had not been tackled with the children in the school before and two encouraging things happened which made me think it was worthwhile. Other members of the staff were interested in it and in learning more about the Muslim faith, and asked about books they could read to find out. The second happened one day when Muhammad's father came into the classroom. He was curious about the *Eid* cards so I explained that we — the children and I — had been talking about the festival. 'You very good,' he said and to my astonishment pulled a sweet from out of his pocket and gave it to me. He was obviously pleased that we were interested.

Conclusion

The stories, the dressing-up and the acting all have value in themselves and the emphasis for the younger children will be on enjoyment. Older children may observe that there are common themes running through the various festivals. As well as enjoying the festivities the children are reminded at *Ramadhan* and *Baisakhi*, for example, that discipline is required of them as committing themselves to the faith of their community. Also the stories told at *Hanukkah* and *Diwali* show that good will in the end triumph over evil and that light will shine in the darkness.

This could lead into a fresh look at the Christian festivals of Christmas (light shining in the darkness); Easter (good overcoming evil) and Whitsun (the call to baptism and allegiance to a new community which is led by the Holy Spirit). Compare, for example, Peter's call to the people in Acts 2:37–41 at the founding of the church with that of Guru Gobind Singh at the founding of the Sikh *Khalsa*.

MARJORIE GEE
*Alverthorpe Church of
England School, Wakefield*

DIWALI IN THE INFANT SCHOOL

It was early November, at *Diwali* time, that we put a number of small lamps — some were night lights which we stood in jam jars surrounded by coloured tissue paper — on the tables and window-ledges in the school hall. It was a dark morning and the children came quietly and wide-eyed into the hall for assembly while Indian classical music was being played. We sang one of our well-known hymns, 'Teach me to love, teach me to pray', which ends with the words 'Guard me when Mother turns out the light', and then we talked about fear of the dark, how glad we are to have light, how we burn candles at Christmas and at birthday parties when we are happy. In India, in October, the summer rains are over, and people are happy because the skies are clear and they can see the stars at night and the rice harvest is gathered in. The festival of lights, called *Diwali* is held then, and the story of Prince Rama is remembered. I told the story at assembly:

Long ago, in India, a king who had several wives felt that he was getting old and that he should choose the wisest of his sons to rule in his place. He chose Prince Rama and his wife, Sita, who, because of their courage and gentleness, were loved by all the people. But another of the king's wives was very angry because her son had not been chosen, and, by a wicked trick, she ordered the old king to banish both Rama and Sita to the forest for fourteen years. The old king was heartbroken and soon died, whereupon Rama's brothers went to the forest to beg him to return. Rama refused to go back until the fourteen years were completed, but one of his brothers took his golden sandals and put them on the throne, saying that he would not sit upon the throne but would govern until Rama returned to claim both the throne and the sandals.

Now, the people and the animals that lived in the forest were glad to have the kindly prince living amongst them. He protected them from giants and demons, and when the wicked demon king took away Sita, his wife, the birds brought news about her and a great tribe of monkeys helped to rescue her. At last the fourteen years were over; Rama's brothers went to fetch him, and people came out of their homes with little earthen lamps to light their way through the dark forest. When Rama's friends who had been in the forest with him returned to their homes and families, there was great rejoicing and feasting; fireworks were lit, and presents were exchanged. And so it is in India at *Diwali* nowadays: when the summer harvest has been gathered in, the children return to their homes and families and exchange presents; lamps are lit and put in the windows for all to see, and light and happiness return once more after a period of rain and darkness.

At the end of the story we all joined in saying the following prayer: 'Dear God, thank you for the joy of light and candles and twinkling stars. Help us not to be afraid when it is dark, but to be brave and helpful to all your creatures as Prince Rama was.' We then sang the hymn 'All things bright and beautiful', and afterwards the Asian children, each holding a candle stood in the middle of the hall while we wished them 'A happy *Diwali*'.

In the classroom we made a collage of Prince Rama in the forest with a border of lamps; we made earthen lamps of plasticine or plaster. During a free activity period in the hall, we acted the banishment of Rama, overcoming demons in the forest, the animals helping Rama and the happy homecoming when we played Indian music and the citizens came to offer gifts, kneeling and touching his feet in the Indian custom.

ELIZABETH WILSON
Huddersfield

INTERDEPENDENCE

Introduction

This work was done in a primary school opened in 1965 which draws from an area of mainly semi-detached houses of pre-war design. The children are well cared for and are provided with a stimulating environment in their homes.

The proportion of immigrant children in the school is large, but in an area like this there can sometimes be a deep-seated parochialism, which is what led us to think of 'Interdependence' as a Harvest theme.

The children work an integrated day. They arrange their own work and where they will do it. All through the day children move about, often working in other classrooms, and not always with their own age groups. When working in groups, children of different abilities work happily together.

For assemblies the school is divided into three groups, upper junior, middle junior and infant, so that whatever theme has been chosen can be presented at the appropriate age level. Once the assembly theme has been selected, children will often work on it, and present their own ideas in assembly. Other times, teacher and children may work together, pooling ideas. Assembly preparation can sometimes take a long time, depending on the amount of classwork done.

A harvest theme

Aim: to show our interdependence one upon another.
Age: 5–11 years.
Infants: Each teacher decided upon one aspect of the theme and then developed it with stories, visual aids and visits. Since the children were

already familiar with the local shops, some of them looked at those which sold goods from abroad. Others were interested in some of the ways in which goods are brought from other parts of the world. Public services were looked at to find out how we depend on other people's work in our everyday lives.

Middle juniors: We have several children from other countries in our school, so we started by asking them to tell us about such things as customs and food. Their parents gave a good deal of help with this. We went on to find out all we could about their countries, and about the ways in which people who come from abroad to live in this country, bring with them their own customs, including different foods, sometimes very beautiful clothes, exciting music and traditional stories which enrich our own lives.

In one of our assemblies a Chinese meal was eaten as an example of people of very different ways using chopsticks instead of knives and forks, and having rice instead of bread as a staple food.

We had our own pan and the school cook entered into the spirit of the thing and lent us a large frying-pan for the crispy noodles. The children cooked and stirred and kept an eye on proceedings. I fried the noodles because they tend to spit. When finished, the meal was carried triumphantly into assembly and divided up into four proper Chinese bowls, to be eaten with chopsticks — and some difficulty!

The assembly ended with a hymn sung to a Chinese tune.

Upper juniors: These children studied local industries which rely on imported raw materials, and export the finished goods. There were visits to local factories, and visits to the school by people from the factories who talked to the children about their work.

This work was used to show how imports and exports benefit both the people in the countries which sell the raw materials and the people from whom the finished goods are bought, as well as the buyers.

Every class produced a chart or frieze connected with their particular aspect of Interdependence, and also an assembly for the other children of the same age groups, explaining their work, and how they came by the information, listening to stories and music from other countries.

After six weeks all this work was gathered together and arranged in one large display in the hall, with interesting things from abroad, kindly loaned by parents. A tape was made of the children singing hymns and songs which they had learned for Interdependence, and parents were invited to come and see the display and listen to the singing.

At this point we received a telephone call from a local old people's home asking if we were going to have our usual 'Tin Harvest'. They said they had come to depend on the tins for Christmas, so we asked the children to bring some, and explained to them about the dependence of these old folk upon us. The children brought some tins, and visiting parents brought many more which were incorporated into our display.

Conclusion

This particular piece of work was not done in a multi-cultural school but as Britain is becoming a country of many faiths and cultures, teachers have to think about helping children to live in it. Learning about one another makes a good beginning. When they grow up, children in school today may well find themselves involved with people of different faiths. The living Islamic and Indian, as well as Christian cultures, could come to have considerable significance in their everyday lives.

SERVICE: A RELIGIOUS LIFE-THEME IN A JUNIOR SCHOOL

The theme of Service was developed with a class of chronologically streamed 8–9 year olds. The class was made up of 17 boys, 17 girls, which included two immigrant Pakistani girls, both very Westernized. There were a number of other Pakistani children in the school.

The theme was decided upon to encourage the children to find examples of service freely given in contemporary life, to challenge the children to see the need for service and perhaps realise why people help others.

I decided to start with the child's own experience and deal with service given within the community, following on with nationwide service, and finally extending the child to world wide service.

The theme was introduced with a discussion of what is meant by the word 'service'. A frieze was made of 'people who serve', which ranged from the school-crossing patrol to soldiers serving in the army.

1. Service within the Community

This took the form of looking closely at service which is generally taken so much for granted by children, for example, the services of the postman, policeman, fireman and nurse.

A visit was arranged to the local fire station where the children spent a very profitable afternoon examining the fire station as a working unit, and discussing with the firemen the nature of their jobs. This led to the usual letter of thanks.

The historical development of the Post Office service was examined, and then the children were allowed to develop folders on any aspect of community service. The children worked easily in pairs for this work, and most seemed to organise themselves into working units of one child writing, one drawing and vice versa. The class now arranged their own assembly on this work, choosing the story of Gladys Aylward (Service for God) and writing their own prayers and choosing the hymn.

2. Nationwide Service

The Lifeboat Service was decided upon as a suitable nationwide service. The children listened to the story of Grace Darling and to real-life accounts of lifeboat rescues. Then the children wrote their own imaginative stories of a brave rescue.

3. Service to the World

The class had recently seen a schools' television programme on 'Eskimos', and it was an easy task interesting the children in the work of the Wilfred Grenfell Missions of Labrador. The mission provides a medical service for the fishermen, the Indians and the Eskimos who live along the coast of Labrador. The children listened with interest to the story of Wilfred Grenfell arriving in Labrador and finding that the people living there had no-one to care for them. Then the children saw 35 mm slides of the up-to-date mission hospitals and Flying Doctor service.

It was decided to look at the services of Oxfam, Save the Children Fund and War on Want, in connection with work particularly in Africa and India. We talked about the message of hunger from 'War on Want' 'So many hands in the hungry half of the world reach out for aid. And many hands stretched out in generous giving can do much to meet their need'. Examples of the staple diet (sweet potato and maize) of many African villages were taken into the classroom. At this point some of the children made menu charts to compare their diets with that of the African child. Work was done on Oxfam's Thabo charts.

(1) What makes Thabo grow.
(2) What makes Thabo's village grow.
(3) What makes Thabo's country grow.

Oxfam photo sets of 'Home in Africa' proved to be very useful (the children would have gained a lot more from these pictures had they been in colour!).

It has been said that Lesotho's most valuable export is her soil, swept by rain and blown away in the dry season by the wind. How, then, can the African farmer grow plenty of nutritious food? Various types of experiments were done on soil to find out what soil is made up of, how soil varies from district to district, etc. Up-to-date work of the leper colonies were looked at, especially that of David Burgess, a

Wakefield man, who has devoted his life to helping the lepers of Ethiopia (the story of Father Damien was also read at this point to highlight the needs of the leper colonies). Two stories about the Caliph Umar were told. First, helping a Bedouin woman who was having a baby, second, feeding hungry children at Medina. These showed service in Islam and related to the Pillar of Islam, charity.

We looked at India through the problem of water, starting with Project B.41 of War on Want 'Stop a Desert Campaign' in Anantapur. This led on to the two problems of the Indian farmer:

(1) Water he cannot get (subterranean).
(2) Water he cannot keep (monsoons).

Work was done on the development of dams, wells and irrigation.

India is a country of villages, and a visit must be made to one to see how the ordinary Indian family lives. This was done through a set of 35 mm slides and Oxfam's 'Home in India' photosets. The children were shown how to wear a sari and appreciated the texture of the material and the richness of colour.

Stories from the *Mahabharata* and *Rama and Sita* were told to the children. Both were enjoyed and the children seemed to grasp the basic ideas behind the stories that those who act in an evil way will always suffer the consequences and that good is ultimately victorious.

The caste system was looked at but some of the children found difficulty in grasping the concept which was behind the system.

India's most sacred river, the Ganges, was looked at in geography. The story of Ganga and Vishnu was told to the class. The children were now ready to understand Project B.15 of 'War on Want', the making of Boys' Town at Madurai for destitute boys, comparable with Dr Barnardo's in this country, but the boys grow their own crops and support themselves.

The class once more arranged their own assembly, this time basing it on service to the world, concentrating on the need for food and water. The story of the little Rhino was told (Joseph and his tractor), a two-way dialogue between an Indian child and English child was arranged on the problems of water (in England one cannot always go out to play for the rain, an Indian has a desperate need for it to grow crops).

PAT LORD
*Kirklees Education
Committee (Youth Service)*

THE CRUCIFIXION OF JESUS: WITH A CLASS OF FOURTEEN-YEAR-OLD BOYS FROM JEWISH AND CHRISTIAN BACKGROUNDS (Selective Grammar School)

Aim: To explore a variety of interpretations of the meaning of the death of Jesus.

Lesson 1:   *How did Jesus die? What reasons can be suggested for killing him or allowing him to be killed?*

Background knowledge: An awareness of Palestine as an occupied country: of various Jewish groups, especially Sadducees and Zealots.

Without being gruesome, a beginning was made by considering the 'Haas' view that Jesus was probably nailed to the cross half-sitting on a rough ledge, arms outstretched and pierced above the wrist, legs bent and forced together by a single nail smashed through both heel bones. (An opinion based upon archaeological remains of a man crucified in the first century CE and found in 1968.) This was compared with the traditional representation found in churches.

'This is interesting but does it matter'? was asked. It did matter, to find out what really happened, to know that there is archaeological evidence that people were crucified is important.

But were there questions as important or more important than factual accuracy? Why didn't anybody stop them? Why did they want to do it to such a kind man? Why didn't Jesus fight? Perhaps he hoped to be rescued? Why did God let it happen?

At this point the lesson could have become the mere expression of uninformed opinions. We tried hard to find evidence for solutions to questions. The main groups were listed. The Jews, the Romans and the disciples of Jesus. The attitude of the disciples: they ran away, Peter denied Jesus. Why? A discussion of part of Mark 14 resulted in conclusions of fear, cowardice and bewilderment.

The attitude of the Romans: some prompting was needed. Turning to Mark 15, the significance of 'King of the Jews' was considered. A Jewish boy referred to the tension in Jerusalem at Passover time, there was always the danger of a rising. Pilate could not afford to take risks.

Lesson 2: Jewish and Christian attitudes to the death of Jesus: The Attitude of the Jews

Very quickly, Jewish boys pointed out that this should be 'the attitude of some Jews'. Most Jews would have no say, no influence, would not know what it was all about. To suggest that the Jews (i.e. all were

184

implicated) killed Jesus was inaccurate. The terms of this discussion were reformulated. Which groups of Jews might have wanted Jesus out of the way and why?

The Zealots were the first to be identified. If Jesus' followers were claiming that he was the Messiah they would be looking to him for leadership. He failed to initiate the insurrection they hoped for. Disappointed, they may have betrayed him or at least refused to help him. (The Jewish boys arrived at this conclusion apparently unaware of recent books which have much similar suggestions.)

That the religious leaders may have wished for the removal of Jesus was a suggestion which the teacher had to make, as also was reference to the Herodians. They were supported by examining John 11:45–50, and Matthew 22:16, and John 19:12–16, a passage in which again the Jews are all lumped together as is common in the anti-Judaic polemic.

Finally, the class looked at Christian attitudes. The views expressed in the hymn, 'There is a Green Hill Far Away', were quoted accurately by a few students. It was linked with Mark 10:45, and also, as pointed out by the teacher, with Romans 5:6–8.

What was the Christian claim? That this man's death had meaning for everyone.

How could this be? Christians claimed he was the Christ (The Messiah), that he was divine. They claim that he is unique and that therefore his death has a unique significance.

Here the Jewish students interposed to say how, from a Jewish point of view, the claims made for Jesus were completely unacceptable. In no respect did he come up to Jewish Messianic expectations; in fact it would be difficult to imagine anyone less like the promised Messiah. Second, to describe a man as divine or call him 'Son of God' (whatever was meant by the expression) was to depart from all Jewish teaching and to speak blasphemy.

The study ended by reaching the conclusion that the meaning of the death of Jesus depends, in the last resort, upon who he was, or upon who people today believe him to be — the Son of God, a madman, a good man struggling against evil, a false prophet, a true prophet but nevertheless a man.

Evaluation

(1) General benefit from examining the issue systematically rather than having a lively discussion in which opinions are aired based upon ignorance rather than knowledge.

(2) Students from Jewish and Christian backgrounds were able to discuss a divisive subject without heat, and to appreciate one another's points of view.

(3) In discussing it as objectively as possible a certain care was acquired

in using words in attempting to conduct the exercise in this way. For example, to call Jesus 'Christ' or 'Our Lord', to write the pronoun 'he' with a capital 'H' when referring to him (Jesus) were all seen to be expressions of commitment.

Endpiece

With this class this was the end of the topic for the time being. It could be picked up again at a later time by considering the Muslim attitude to Jesus, by looking at what Jewish scholars at various periods have said about him, by discussing some humanist views or by examining a variety of interpretations of the person and work of Jesus.

A *DIWALI* PROJECT
by David Baldwin

A note-form outline of content

Ram Lila
Traditional dramatisation of the story of Ram and Sita: English versions in the classroom/school.

The Ramayana
Serial presentation by the teacher of the epic story of Ram and Sita.

School assembly
A *Diwali* assembly, items from: story, dance, songs, drama, colour slides, film.

Songs and dances
Traditional Indian songs and dances, esp. Punjab and Gujerat. Performances by Indian children and multi-racial groups. Records and tapes of music and song from the sub-continent.

Diwali festivities
Diwali puja explained and described with Hindu children bringing puja vessels, pictures, etc. *Lakshmi puja* described. Singing devotional songs (*bhajans*). *Aarti* ceremony on record or tape. Readings from poems/prayers, etc.

Art/Craft
Props for drama — Shiva's bow, Hanuman's mace, Ram's shoes, crowns and regalia. Masks for Ravanna and the demons/ogres; also masks for Hanuman and the monkeys. Puppets for a puppet version of a *Ram Lila*. Effigies of Ravanna, like the ones made in India at Dussehra, to be made. Series of paintings and collages depicting the *Ramavana* story — displayed with reading cards or compositions. *Alpana* patterns — festive designs on the floor.

Project on Diwali in the Punjab
E.g. life in the Punjab, *Diwali* fairs, Golden Temple, Amritsar

186

illuminations, seasons in India, family life, etc.

Preparation of a tape
Class to put together a recorded programme of dialogues, music, songs, talks, interviews, stories. Or a dramatisation of the *Ramayana* story highlights, e.g. marriage of Ram and Sita, death of Ravanna, return to Ayodhaya.

Cooking
Children to prepare festive sweetmeats, e.g. *ladoos* and *binfi* for distribution. Cook an Indian meal for a meeting of friends, parents or teachers. Demonstration by Indian children or parents at a parents' evening.

A *DIWALI (DEEPAVALI)* PROJECT IN THE SCHOOL OR CLASSROOM

Cross-cultural work
English and world festivals, e.g. universal symbol of light, songs and family celebrations. Stories from other mythologies good versus evil (cf. Ram v Ravanna).

Dasera
Ram defeats Ravanna and the *rakshasas*. Traditional burning of effigies of Ravanna and his brothers — here made by children at school. (cf. UK 5 November).

School magazine
Special *Diwali* issue with descriptions of *Diwali* celebrations, *Ramayana* stories, drawings and decorations on *Diwali* theme. Indian cooking. Possibly several items in Punjabi or Hindi for Indian parents or by Indian parents and teachers.

Diwali in Ealing
Visiting homes of Indian friends exchanging sweets, *Diwali* entertainment programme (e.g. Hindu cultural society), decorating house with candles/lights, fireworks and sparklers, *puja* in Hindu homes or *mandir* (temple) or visit to the *gurdwara* (Sikh temple) in Southall.

Diwali cards and letters
Greetings and letters to be written and sent to children and friends in England and India.

Class/school entertainment
Items from: storytelling, songs, dialogues, sharing food/sweets, decorations; *divas* and decorations to be made by the children for teachers and friends in the school.

A PROJECT FOR GURU NANAK'S BIRTHDAY

Guru Nanak's journeys — map-work and related stories.

Social studies — the Sikhs today — achievements and homes all over the world and in India.

Art: paintings and collages of the Sikh Gurus, similarly of the chief *Gurdwaras* — model of the typical Sikh temple including notable features such as the communal kitchen.

Life in the Punjab — towns, cities and villages. Farming and industry.

Pictures and collages illustrating Guru Nanak's life — displayed with reading cards and compositions.

School assembly: putting together a programme on Guru Nanak and the Sikhs and their life in the Punjab — cultural appreciation.

Local visits to the *Gurdwara* and meetings with Sikh friends. Interviews and reports to be written — including drawings and photographs. Attending a service and sharing a *langar* meal.

A PROJECT MARKING GURU NANAK'S BIRTHDAY IN THE CLASSROOM

The Sikh Gurus after Nanak; esp. Guru Arjan and Guru Gobind Singh. The *Khalsa*; its foundation and importance.

Entertainment programme of storytelling, songs, Indian dances (esp. *Bhangra* and *Gidda*) and music.
Note: Guru Nanak should not be dramatically impersonated in any way as this is strictly forbidden by Sikh leaders.

Visit to the cinema to see an appropriate film, e.g., *Nanak Nam Jahaz Hai, Nanak Dhukia Sub Sansar*. Indian children to host school friends.

Children to prepare and share typical Punjabi festive foods.

Guru Nanak's life and teaching. Biographical stories and traditional material.

Preparation of a tape by the class including background material, interviews, relating of stories, music and songs.

Sikh devotional and folk music. Singing and listening, collecting recordings of shabads, etc.

Making an anthology from Japji, Sikh morning prayer, in English and Punjabi.

Best *handwriting in English and Gurmukhi* script of the opening passages from *Japji*.

USEFUL TEACHING MATERIAL

The Sikh Religion. Colour filmstrip, concerned with the Sikh community in Leeds. Good notes supplied from Concordia; tape available.

The Sikhs of the Punjab. Set of twelve superb colour slides from Bury Peerless, 22 King's Avenue, Minnis Bay, Birchington, Kent.

Booklet *The Sikhs of the Punjab* by W. H. Mcleod, Oriel Press. Very well-written survey which could be used by secondary pupils.

Guru Nanak by Pam Wylam, Children's Book Trust, New Delhi. A helpful book in English with traditional stories for Sikh children.

A package of material can be obtained from the Sikh Cultural Society, 88 Mollison Way, Edgware, Middlesex.

LP record *Guru Nanak Shabads* ECLP 2440 EMI (India) Sikh devotional songs, from The Indian Record Shop, 70 South Rd., Southall, Mddx.

A PROJECT FOR *Eid-ul-Fitr*

Eid-ul-Fitr, the celebrations in Islamic countries and *Eid* in England. What a Muslim family does at *Eid* — family get together, special foods, new clothes, visiting friends, etc. Research on local Muslim community.

Project: life in a Muslim country Work on homes, occupations, towns and country, oil, industries and commerce, Islamic society and customs, crafts, architecture, history and development, contemporary problems, children growing up, education, diet, etc.

Model of mosque to be made by children. Special attention to the important features such as: Minaret, *mihrab* (niche), *minbar* (pulpit), courtyard, ablution place, etc.

Ramadhan its significance for Muslims and the purpose of fasting — a starting-point for work on the *Five Pillars of Faith*. What

Muslims believe and what Muslims observe — daily life. Written up for the school magazine.

An assembly to mark *Eid-ul-Fitr*: film or slides on life and worship in an Islamic country. The significance of *Ramadhan* brought out in reference to the Muslim way of life. A Muslim boy to intone from the *Qu'ran* or a recording played. Children to describe celebration of *Eid*. Project work displayed.

Stories of the Caliphs and from Arab history. Islamic stories from the Moghul period in India, e.g. stories of Akbar's chief minister, Birbal, Nasrud-ud-din Hodja, etc. *The Arabian Nights*.

The life of the Prophet Muhammad and early Islam.

Note: All Muslims dislike the representation of Muhammad in drawings or in drama.

A PROJECT TO MARK *Eid-ul-Fitr*

Projects on Islamic culture.
Topics for research to cover: architecture, art and crafts, astronomy, navigation, maths, science, medicine, literature, textiles. *Exhibition arranged.*

Museum visits, e.g. to the Islamic sections of the Victoria and Albert Museum, British Museum.

Islamic decoration designing elaborate patterns and decorations inspired by Islamic decorative art and calligraphy, display in school.

Visit to a mosque in the UK. A group to meet the *Imam* and local Muslims. It is possible to attend congregational prayers in the mosque on the occasion of Eid.

Film show: relevant films on Islam and life in an Islamic country. The cultural heritage of Islam.

Calligraphy: a senior pupil, teacher or visitor to demonstrate calligraphy and the Arabic script. Fine examples and photographs to be displayed.

Basic reference material for pupils

Mohammed, Prophet of the Religion of Islam, E. Royston Pike, Pathfinder Biographies. Weidenfeld and Nicolson, 1968.
Islam, 1. Muhammad and Islam; 2. Islam in the Middle Ages; 3. The Achievements of Islam, P. W. Crittenden. Macmillan (*The Making of World History* Series).

DAVID BALDWIN

PART 3: SCHOOL WORSHIP AND ASSEMBLY

MEETING RELIGIOUS NEEDS

Christians, as well as Hindus, Muslims, Bahais and other teachers and pupils, have religious beliefs which, because of the tradition of school worship in British schools, they will want to express. Had schools been wholly secular, this issue might not have arisen — but they are not.

The 1944 Education Act requires the school day to begin with a collective act of worship by the whole school. If everyone cannot assemble in one place, there should legally be several, presumably simultaneous, acts of worship.

Traditionally the act of worship has been Christian, though undenominational and non-secretarian, because the only religion represented in most schools before the 1950s was Christianity. Where there were Jews, they withdrew, as did Roman Catholic children and teachers.

It was possible to regard many schools as Christian communities. Probably most teachers, and many pupils, were regular worshippers at their local churches. Now it is unusual to find a school where more than a third of the staff and a similar proportion of the children attend church, even occasionally. The question therefore has to be put: Is compulsory worship something we can regard as a proper and appropriate collective school activity? It must present problems of conscience for many teachers and for older pupils. The solution is often a communal act which is an educationally worthwhile and justifiable assembly but it is not an act of worship in any recognisable sense.

In the typical, non-denominational-maintained school situation the non-worshipping assembly may be the only viable answer. However, at the moment such assemblies are often negative responses to a problem, and, strictly speaking, they are illegal. Perhaps the time has come to relieve schools of anxiety by officially positively endorsing and encouraging such assemblies.

There are, of course, three other possibilities, or combinations of them. One is to have no assemblies at all, except for those at which notices are given out and other aspects of school administration dealt with. Probably no-one wants this solution. It would deprive the school of opportunities to explore and express its corporateness.

The second is to hold occasional religious assemblies with the consent of the school. 'What shall we do at Christmas?' is a question which everyone should consider, not one to be put by the headmaster to his music and religious studies teachers. The answer is likely to be a demand for a carol service. I would consider it proper to meet such a request rather than awkwardly ask; Why at Christmas but not weekly or daily? If the decision has been taken thoughtfully and deliberately made by the community that is enough, but attendance should be voluntary and minority views should be respected, not just tolerated in the worst sense of the word.

Third, a regular act of worship might be held as a voluntary extra-curricular activity in schools where a group of Christians wish to hold one. It might occur once or twice a week, though it could be held daily. It could be time-tabled if this was the decision of the school and administratively possible.

THE MULTI-FAITH SCHOOL

So far, the school envisaged has been a typical all-white school in somewhere like Horsham, Bognor Regis or Hexham. One such that I know has about 1,400 pupils and a large proportion of Christians — some two hundred regular churchgoers: not at all bad for many urban secondary schools.

Now we must turn to the multi-faith school and immediately state that corporate activities like singing hymns together or saying the Lord's Prayer are not possible. Schools have devised collections of theistic, non-trinitarian hymns, but this is not a response to the many Muslims who disapprove of the religious use of music, regarding it as something secular. What is possible is the reading of a passage from the *Qur'an*, Bible or other scripture and an invitation to the school to reflect on it, aided, perhaps, by a prayer from the same tradition — but not with the injunction 'Let us pray'. Members of a faith, be it Christian or Bahai, might explain their festivals, as they come around, to the rest of the school and share their significance. Whatever is done of a corporate, interfaith, religious nature, all participants and the communities they come from need to be aware of the ground-rules. This especially includes vicars or *Imams* who might be invited, otherwise the sharing of the meaning of Christmas, the Prophet's Birthday or Guru Nanak's Birthday might be used as opportunities for evangelism or abuse.

More regularly the various religions may want to hold their own act of worship. This would be especially true of Muslims on Friday afternoons. It might be a time when its faith can hold its assembly for twenty minutes, those who belong to none remaining in classrooms or having a non-religious assembly. It might be extra-curricular or time-tabled. Such occasions need not emulate the builders of Babel or provide times for criticising those of other faiths or none. However, it·must be acknowledged that we always tend to uphold our own political party, nation or religion in two ways; the one is admirable, by praising its virtues, the other is despicable, that of portraying the 'others' as insincere, superstitious liars and less than human. This approach should have no place in the multi-faith school.

There will be rumour. It is therefore as well that once a term or so the Muslims tell the rest of the school what they do when they gather for prayers, and so also the other groups. This would be the kind of sharing which would also take place at festival times.

Many corporate assemblies would be non-religious, though in the multi-faith school each culture and faith would enrich the activity with its own insights. Such assemblies might have such aims as:

(1) The awakening of aesthetic awareness;
(2) Reflection upon experience;
(3) Awareness of human issues and possible responses to them;
(4) The realisation that the school is a community and the exploration of what this means;
(5) The examination of these four aims in a wider way than is possible in the classroom.

Assembly in the multi-faith school can be a rich activity in which diversity and unity are openly celebrated, accepted and explored, or it can be a place where some lowest common denominator is sought and the pupils and staff find nothing of worth. Between the two comes one which may be worse, that which demonstrates the authority of a mainly white staff to a largely 'non-white' school, and uses the Christian religion in justification.

In practice, the best assemblies are often held weekly rather than daily, attended by two or three years of age-range at most, and conducted by pupils and teachers instead of being imposed from the top. They should not be regarded as one of the tasks of the religious studies department, but of everyone.

CELEBRATING FESTIVALS

Festivals exist to be celebrated and enjoyed rather than studied, so before considering how to teach them let us consider how they might be observed by the school community.

Some years ago, I visited a particular centre which had a 100 per cent Muslim intake. The date was mid-January, in that year the time when the Festival of Sacrifice, *Eid-ul-Adha*, was being celebrated. The classrooms were decked out with Christmas scenes and decorations but not one of the teachers knew that it was *Eid*. They did not particularly care, either. 'In England the great festival is Christmas, and we wanted them to enjoy it.'

This story represents a common attitude; a concern that the children should enjoy the fun of Christmas, a genuine desire for their well-being — and the teachers had worked hard to produce a Happy Christmas. But also there was a lack of awareness that the children might possess any culture, any worthwhile beliefs, any festivals of their own. There was also the view that the sole task, and a difficult enough one at that, was to make those Muslim children competent in English. The argument that their linguistic achievements might be enhanced if the content of lessons was linked with their own culture was listened to but not accepted.

At the other extreme is a school which celebrates one of the two *Eids* with a party and a special assembly, and *Diwali* and Christmas in the same way. They also observe Chinese New Year, though there are now no Chinese children in the school. Such is memory and popular demand.

Of course, there are practical considerations to be taken into account if a school wants to respect and demonstrate the worth of everyone's festivals. It is easy to forget dietary requirements, for example. Jelly is often the staple diet of parties, but gelatine comes from cows, and so is not acceptable to many Hindus and some Sikhs. 'Food fads', as some insensitive people need to describe them, have proved far less irksome and difficult than teachers once thought. With a little care and co-operation with parents everyone can be satisfied.

Muslim and Jewish festivals must be observed on the date specified and are marked by special acts of worship at the mosque or synagogue and in the home. This means that Muslim and Jewish children and members of staff will be absent from school for one or sometimes two days. Hopefully, this will not be an excuse for the passing of intolerant remarks, usually audible to the children, matching those which accompanied Roman Catholic holy days of obligation when I was a boy — 'Another Saint's day, no wonder there are no clever Catholics.' A pleasant and acceptable approach would be to tell pupils in assembly

194

that the Jews or Muslims will be absent on the next day, to explain why and to wish them the appropriate greeting, such as 'Eid Mubarak', a Happy *Eid*. On their return the party can be held, a feature of which could be sweet foods normally eaten at this time, or at least belonging to the culture whose festival is being celebrated.

One benefit that I would welcome as a result of celebrating a few festivals would be the giving of less time to Christmas. If it could be confined to the last ten days of term many teachers, and not a few children, would rejoice. By the time the celebration does arrive lengthy preparations have frayed the teachers' nerves, shortened their tempers to the point where spouses and pupils risk physical injury and rendered the children heartily bored. Respect for Christmas does not depend on the time given to it.

Hindus and Sikhs both celebrate *Diwali* but for different reasons. Sometimes both stories are explored at one assembly, probably a good idea if parents are being invited, and, of couse, festivals provide excellent opportunities for developing parental contact with the school if the time chosen is convenient. However, the same cannot usually be done with *Hannukah* and Christmas, and certainly not with Passover and Easter in schools with Jewish and Christian children. In such a situation Easter has to be handled with great care.

Should a Muslim girl be invited to take the part of Mary in a Christmas tableau or Nativity play? After all, Mary is shown great respect in the *Qur'an* and Muslim tradition, and so is Jesus. The heart may find nothing wrong with such casting, but the head realises that some Christian parents may be offended, that some Muslims are not in favour of drama and that many more have severe reservations about religious people such as Mary, Jesus or Muhammad appearing as characters in plays. My inclination would be to ask only Christians to participate in the worshipping part of the Christmas celebration and to assure the rest that their turn will come when their festivals are celebrated in assembly (but more of this in the section on assemblies, (page 200)).

Once again we are left with small minorities who apparently have no *Eids* or *Diwalis*. They often have a national day or a saint's day when, especially in primary school, they can wear national costume and assembly can be used to inform the rest of the school (and perhaps themselves) of their culture. Harvest time might provide another occasion when diversity can be represented by national dress and unity explored through a theme of interdependence.

To demonstrate unity and the richness which lies just below the surface in many parts of our drab inner cities, many schools now hold annual cultural evenings. The best that I have experienced was also the saddest. An Indian girl danced beautifully, so did a group of Latvians, the West Indians provided reggae as well as some American–Caribbean folk songs and Christmas songs, it being late November. There was the school orchestra, mainly white, and a choir which was richly multi-ethnic. Its contribution spanned Europe and reached to America. A dance drama of the conflict between good (in white costumes) and evil (in black) was a little thoughtless, but it apparently raised no hackles. In fact, everyone seemed to go home happy after a lively evening of high-quality entertainment. Unfortunately, the headmaster was approached by a number of white parents who felt that coloured children should be seen only when it could not be avoided, and never heard. Not being a very strong man, he decided to revert to holding the traditional Christmas service in the local church as the only end-of-term activity. The concert which had complemented it so well was his first and last multi-coloured venture. The steel-band grudgingly survived, but no white children were allowed to play in it, only the least able West Indians, and it was never permitted to perform publicly in that school until the headmaster had retired. Perhaps he should linger in our minds as a reminder that teachers are often faced by unacceptable pressures. In his mid-fifties he suddenly found that his three-form entry grammar school had become a nine-form entry comprehensive school. No-one told him how to respond to that situation or to the strong cultural mix which accompanied it, replacing the Jewish and Asian high-fliers whose cultures had always been ignored, though their intellects were welcomed.

TEACHING FESTIVALS

Let festivals be enjoyed, but, hopefully, they can also be taught enjoyably in the classroom. The main obstacle to this is repetition, and the danger is greater with Christmas. There is no sure safeguard against boredom, it is, after all, an attitude of mind. There are bored children, and perhaps boring teachers, but no boring activities. Some people find enjoyment in almost everything under the sun, even going to church, playing golf, washing up dishes, weeding a garden or marking essays.

Repetition may be overcome by adopting a spiral approach to festivals — as to other aspects of the syllabus. This will also go some way towards creating a course which will match step by step the interests and understanding of children.

Every festival has three principal ingredients, a story, significance and celebration. Obviously, these are interrelated, but to prepare lessons they must be separated and then put together again. The story may be complex; for younger children it will be simplified. If we take Christmas as our example, the story will probably be that of the journey to Bethlehem and the birth in a stable, followed by the visit of the shepherds and wise men.

A little later, in junior school, some background might be added, the census, the wise men's mistake in going to Herod's palace in Jerusalem, the flight to Egypt. In the middle years the Roman and Jewish backgrounds might be extended to include the Annunciation and Presentation in the Temple in the story.

Finally, with older pupils the focus might shift from the Gospels of Matthew and Luke to John, and the way in which his story puts theirs into a cosmic framework.

The significance may be implicit in the story but has often to be made explicit by the thematic context into which it is put, especially with younger children. Families, birthdays, caring are topics which will bring out some of the inner meaning with younger children. Refugees, light, new birth, the last two related to exploring Christmas customs, can make other aspects explicit to children in the middle years. Links can also be forged with *Diwali* and *Hannukah*. At an older stage Christmas hymns and carols, art and poetry can be explored to see what men and women through the centuries have made of the event of Christmas, and pupils now, as at any stage, might be encouraged to put their own reflections into music, words or pictures.

The celebration might bring together the story and the significance, without imposing a kill-joy moralism upon it, and without staging something which is so elaborate that only the clever and reliable children may participate, and the staff are in too high a state of tension, lest words are forgotten or a crown slips, to enjoy it. Once Christmas has been replaced by an elitist production its meaning has been lost beyond redemption.

In this section Christmas has been used as the example becuse of its familiarity. Shorthand phrases such as 'no room in the inn' can be used where, in a description of some aspect of *Diwali*, a whole paragraph of explanation would be necessary. Should this book go into another edition, hopefully the stories of other religions would be well enough known for simple allusions to them to suffice. Hindu, Sikh, Muslim and Jewish teachers usually know the Christian stories well enough for them to flesh out the briefest allusions.

Further Reading

Supplement Number 1 (April 1981) of the new Hertfordshire Agreed Syllabus has a very useful and detailed section on festivals (pp. 19–51). This covers Christmas, *Diwali*, *Hannukah* and Easter. It can be obtained from County Hall, Hertford SG13 8DF.

AIDS FOR ASSEMBLY

'Bring your sacred book to school to show us', might well be the innocent invitation extended by a teacher. What confusion it might cause!

In the Muslim home the *Qur'an* is wrapped up in a piece of cloth and reverently placed on a shelf reserved for it and no other book. It is opened and closed with a prayer. Because it contains the word of God it is handled with a veneration which almost becomes worship. The idea of bringing it into an English school would be greeted with horror.

Many Sikh homes have small books containing about seven of the main hymns because of the elaborate ceremony involved in installing a copy of the *Guru Granth Sahib* and in reading from it day by day. It should be properly housed in a room reserved for it alone. To bring it to school might involve a full-scale procession! A fascinating prospect! No objection would be raised to bringing the small book of *shabads*.

The Hebrew Bible, too, is accorded respect so that many Jewish children would prefer not to bring the copy they use (or even an English version) to school. It is well known that old torn copies of the scriptures are not burnt but buried, though they may often lie about on a shelf for some time. One of these a child might bring.

A Hindu home is more likely to possess a booklet of *mantras* (prayers or sayings used to aid meditation) than a copy of the *Vedas* or even the *Gita*. These may be written in Sanskrit or sometimes in the vernacular of the worshipper (perhaps Gujerati or Hindi). Once again, however, its place would be on the family shrine and parents would not view the possibility of its being taken to school with pleasure.

What emerges is the fact that the four faiths we have been discussing respect not only the teachings enshrined in their sacred books but also the books themselves as physical objects. This is something which seems to belong to the past as far as Christianity in this country is concerned, for good or ill! Occasionally, for example, when the New Testament is solemnly carried into the nave of the church during the communion service, or when, as in at least one free church, the congregation stand as it is carried into the pulpit before the service begins, one is reminded that the Bible has been regarded as an object of respect. One cannot help wondering what effect its day-to-day use as a textbook has been and with what surprise people of other faiths regard this!

ACCEPTABLE VERSIONS OF THE SCRIPTURES IN ENGLISH

The Jewish Scriptures: The Pentateuch, J. H. Hertz (ed.), (Soncino). The Soncino books of the Bible (Soncino) or, for the Apocrypha, the Revised Standard Version.

The *Qur'an*. To translate its poetry and convey its meaning other than in Arabic is regarded as impossible by the Muslims. However, one English interpretation is regarded as acceptable, *The Meaning of the Glorious Qur'an* by Mohammed Marmaduke Pickthall. Mentor.

The *Guru Granth Sahib*. An English version is available from Luzacs. A satisfactory collection of some of the hymns or sections from them is published by Allen and Unwin under the title *The Sacred Writings of the Sikhs*, translated by Trilochan Singh and others.

The Hindu Scriptures. The book of that name by R. C. Zaehner (Dent/ Everyman) is probably the best translation academically, but the spirit of Hinduism is missing from it. For this reason teachers may prefer such publications as those in the Penguin classics, which are often disliked by the scholars.

Better known than the Vedas by many Hindus are the verses and writings of such men as Chaitanya, Tulsi Das, Rabindranath Togore or Gandhi. Writings of these men and others can be found in *An Anthology of Indian Literature* by J. B. Alphonso/Karkala (Pelican).

With One Voice by Sid G. Hedges (REP) is a good anthology of prayers and thoughts from world religions. *A Year of Grace* by Victor Gollancz confines itself to the Judaeo–Christian tradition.

Many Lights, Donald Butler, Chapman. A wide ranging anthology produced by a headteacher who is a religious studies specialist.

Note: Few books offer anything to the black Christian.

EXAMPLES OF ASSEMBLIES IN MULTI-FAITH SCHOOLS

ASSEMBLY: INFANTS: FAVOURITE THINGS

Two of the infant classes had been finding out what favourite things they, and other children in the school had and why. They had asked about colours and pets and produced graphs. One little girl who had been abroad questioned others about their favourite countries and the fact that few of them had been outside England did not prevent them putting forward France, Austria or Canada! Favourite foods, flowers, and sweets were also listed.

The idea of 'favourite things' was brought into the assembly. Pictures, photographs, graphs were displayed in the hall, and, with the teacher acting as compere, or link-woman, the assembly began, naturally enough with the song from *The Sound of Music* which had given the topic its name.

Some children explained their research into favourite colours and pets and analysed the results. Others held up their favourite toys — mostly guns. A tape was played of other children interviewing classmates to discover their favourite types of holiday.

The seasons of the year provided an opportunity for giving some attention to aesthetic sensitivity and awareness. Not surprisingly, the assembly taking place in May, the emphasis was upon the colours, scents and sound of spring, through one child read a poem about autumn.

The assembly lasted for about ten minutes and ended as it had begun with 'Favourite Things'. It had been a very simple shared experience through which, one hopes, children had become aware of the variety of likes which people have, recognising that we differ very much one from another, but that differences are to be accepted.

ASSEMBLY: INTERDEPENDENCE

A Harvest Theme in a Junior School

Background: Children throughout the school had been preparing for a harvest festival, some by work based upon the foods we eat, others upon the clothes we wear and older children upon manufactured projects, especially Concorde (a detailed description can be found in the CEM Primary Association Scheme mailing of summer 1972).
Aim: To help the children to become aware of the ways in which we depend on one another.

200

Age: First-and-second-year juniors (7-plus, 8-plus).

The teacher began the assembly by describing what some of the classes had been doing — finding out where the foods we eat and the materials we wear come from.

One of the older junior children, whose father was a butcher, had joined the younger ones for the occasion. Dressed in his father's apron, very tall for a ten-year-old, John told the assembly in a very firm voice what it meant to be a butcher. His father rose very early in the morning, when most people were still asleep, and went to the meat market. His mother rose equally early to clean the shop. John helped sometimes. The meat came from Yorkshire but also from Scotland, Wales, Australia and New Zealand. If his father didn't begin work at about six o'clock no-one would be able to have meat for dinner.

Three children whose parents had come to England from Eastern Europe were wearing national costume. They stood in front of the class whilst the teacher pointed out the embroidery, delicate stitching and other features of their clothes. They talked about some of the dairy produce which comes to Britain from Poland and they sang a song which they had learned at Polish school. From interdependence the emphasis had shifted a little to an awareness of other people, languages and customs in our midst, especially when the assembly heard of these children going to Polish school on Saturday!

ASSEMBLY: JOURNEYS: TOP JUNIOR

Background: A fourth-year junior class had been expanding its horizons through a topic on journeys which the teacher had also used to try to help the children begin to use an atlas and have some sense of the past. Journeys had taken place to the moon, with Concorde to the Middle East and Japan, to ancient Egypt (the story behind Tutankhamen exhibition at the British Museum) and from Pakistan and the Caribbean to Britain.

The Assembly: Close your eyes, listen to the music and the commentary, imagine yourself as a member of an Apollo team going to the moon. That was the instruction given to the school by a fourth-year boy. They listened to a tape-recording of a BBC television broadcast of a 'blast-off' at the beginning of a moon flight.

The maps, photographs and paintings which were on the wall as well as an exhibition of books about explorers were brought to the attention of the school and their significance explained. Children were invited to look at them during break.

Daily bus journeys to school, the annual school outing were other experiences referred to but the highlight was four children from the Caribbean and two boys and a girl from Pakistan describing their journey to Britain and giving their impression of arriving here as far as they could remember it. They indicated the home areas from which they had come (from three different West Indian Islands, each hundreds of miles from the other) and pointed out the route on the map. Food, language and weather difficulties were indicated.

The assembly ended with the children being asked to think of the dangers of travelling and the loneliness of people in strange countries, and with a prayer for travellers.

West Indian steel band music played as the children left the hall.

A SIKH ASSEMBLY

The founding of the Khalsa (Juniors)

There are many Sikh children at the Leeds Primary School at which this assembly took place.

Therefore, it was decided that as soon as possible after the Easter holiday some of them should tell the rest of the school about the most famous event connected with their festival of *Baisakhi*, celebrated annually on 13 April.

The participating children, all Sikhs, were aged between 9 and 11 years.

The amrit bowl, *Khanda*, and other things used in this assembly and put on exhibition after it were lent to other schools by the Sikh community who showed considerable interest and pleasure in what was done.

Preparations: A 'tent' was erected in a central position at one end of the hall. To the side of it were arranged a table and three chairs for the use of the reporters and the narrator. On the other side was a screen upon which, as the assembly proceeded pictures of Guru Nanak and Guru Gobind Singh were pinned and then drawings of the 5 K's. Other pictures, some of them painted by Sikh children, others brought from home, were displayed on the walls at the side of the hall.

The assembly was introduced by the head teacher who referred to the *Baisakhi* festival and the kindness of the Sikh community before handing over the conduct of the assembly to the children and one of their teachers, Mr Barry Swain.

Narrator
The Sikh religion started about 500 years ago. It was a man called Nanak who was responsible for its foundation, and he became the first Guru. That means leader or teacher. There were many people who did

202

not like this new religion, and, as the years passed, they made it as hard as they could for the Sikhs to practise it.

Things came to a head when Guru Arjan — the 5th Guru — was tortured to death because of his beliefs. The next Guru was his son Har Gobind, and he decided that the time had come for the Sikhs to learn to defend themselves and their religion. So he trained them to become first-class soldiers. In the years that followed the Sikhs had many battles but it was not until the reign of the 9th Guru that another Guru was put to death for what he believed.

The Emperor made an order that either the Guru changed his religion or he had his head cut off. The Guru refused to change and so in 1675 he was beheaded, leaving Gobind Rai, his nine-year-old son, to be the leader of the Sikhs. Even though he was so young, he knew that he had a very hard job, and so he set about learning how to become a great leader.

It is part of the story of this man that we are going to tell you today.

We are using our imagination to travel back through time and distance.

Our reporters are Habarjan Singh, Billy Gill, Stinder Kalsi. (Billy Gill is a Sikh! Gill is a Sikh surname but Billy — is another story.)

(i) Since arriving here we have asked one or two people where we are and when it is. It seems that it is the year 1699 and that somehow we have become involved in *Baisakhi* — the Sikhs' spring festival. We are at a place called Anandpur, which is in the country that we know as Pakistan.

(ii) There is a vast crowd of people here and at the moment they all seem to be praying or something. They are led by a young man who is standing on a platform at the front. Let us listen for a minute and see if we can hear what he is saying.

Tape

(i) I didn't understand a word of that so we had better use our interpreter so that we won't miss anything. I think that we can be sure though that that was a prayer. At the moment the man seems to be waiting for quiet.

(ii) Look he is taking his sword out of his belt. What is he going to do now?

Guru: I want the head of any of my true Sikhs.

(i) Did I hear what I think I heard?

(ii) I think so, but the crowd don't seem able to believe their ears either. At least no one is going forward.

Guru: I want the head of my true Sikhs.
 (i) He must mean it. I think he must be mad.
(ii) So does the crowd. I cannot see anyone doing a thing like that.

Guru: I want the head of any of my true Sikhs.
 (i) I think that I must be seeing things but — no — look, there is a man who is coming out!
(ii) No, what's happening? The Guru seems to be taking the other man into his tent. I think that I heard him say something like 'There can be no greater gain than to die under your sword'. There is hardly a sound.

 (Sound of thud from tent)
 (i) Did you hear that thud?
(ii) Look, the Guru is coming out again on his own. Just look at his sword. That looks like blood all over it to me.

Guru: I want the head of any of my true Sikhs.
 (i) Oh no. It looks as though he isn't satisfied with one head — he wants two. The man must have gone mad.
(ii) Look, some of the crowd are getting up and going away. I can't say that I blame them. (*A number of Sikh children from the body of the hall get up and go out as the reporter is speaking.*)
 (i) There is one man though who is not going away. Look, he is coming up to where the Guru is standing.
(ii) Again the Guru is taking this man into his tent and it looks as if the result is going to be the same. I don't want to watch this. (*A further thud.*)

Narrator
Sure enough, the Guru returned alone — blood on his sword and then went through the procedure again, and again and again until five men had gone into his tent. By this time the crowd was becoming very worried and many people had left the gathering. Let us return to our reporters and see what is happening now.

 (i) It seems incredible to me that a religious leader should slaughter five of his followers. I just don't understand it and I'm sure that most of the people left here don't either.
(ii) The tent door is opening once again and the Guru is coming out. Just a minute though, he is not alone this time. I do believe — yes — it is, the five men who we had believed killed are following the Guru on to the platform.
 (i) The Guru is now stirring water in a bowl with a double-edged sword.

(ii) His wife is now coming on to the platform carrying what look like sweets and she is putting them into the water.

(i) Each of the five is now having a drink of the Amrit.

(ii) Quiet — the Guru is holding up his hand — he is going to say something.

Guru: These five men have shown their willingness to follow their Guru and even give their lives for their religion. They have shown that they are fit to form the core of the new organised brotherhood and I am going to baptise them as the first members of the *Khalsa*.

Narrator

The Guru then told them that the foundations of the brotherhood had been formed. In future they would consider themselves to be members of one family and the men would take the family name of Singh — which means lion — and the women would take the name Kaur meaning princess. He then gave instructions that members of the *Khalsa* were to be distinguished by distinct features of dress, the five 'Ks'.

(i) The first of the K's is the *Kesh* — long uncut hair (including the beard).

(ii) The second K is the *Kangha* — a comb.

(i) The third K is the *Kirpan* — a sword.

(ii) The fourth K is the *Kacha* — a pair of shorts worn by men to give mobility when in battle.

(i) The fifth K is the *Kara* — a steel bracelet to be worn on the right wrist.

(*As each of the five K's is mentioned a card is displayed with the word on it and a large drawing of the object. On the card with the hair (kesh) a boy with his 'top knot' came forward.*)

The teacher concluded the assembly by mentioning the turban which Guru Gobind Singh had worn and which all male Sikhs who were members of the *Khalsa* brotherhood should wear to show that they were following his example and teaching. There were no human Gurus now, he said, but the Sikhs had a book, the *Guru Granth Sahib*, in which their teachings were collected. In the *Gurdwara* these teachings, in the form of hymns, were sung. As the children went to their classrooms they would hear a recording made in the Temple.

(*Exit to tape recording of one of the hymns of Guru Nanak.*)

Postscript

Two frames from the filmstrip *East Comes West*, produced for the Yorkshire committee of Community relations by Educational Productions, Wakefield (September 1972), show scenes from this assembly. The filmstrip describes the social and religious life of Asians now living in Yorkshire. Many of the frames are of children.

BARRY SWAIN
Leeds

GANDHI

Event: a recent television showing of the film *9 Hours to Rama* and the anniversary of Gandhi's death (30 January 1948).
Materials: indicated in the script.
The assembly: The fifth- and sixth-formers sitting in semi-circular rows. The teacher stood to one side of with the two Indian readers in white costumes either side of a large portrait of Gandhi. A table at one side, on it are items to be referred to in the assembly and a tape recorder. A record player was out of view on the platform.

Page references are to *All Men Are Brothers*, life and thoughts of Mahatma Gandhi as told in his own words, Centennial Reprint UNESCO, HMSO.

Also useful for children *The Story of Gandhi* by Rajkumar Shanker, 1969, Children's Book Trust, New Delhi, from Oxfam Enterprises Ltd.

BBC Radio material *The Story of Gandhi* in the BBC Schools' series 'Man' (may be purchased at 3¾ ips from Stagesound (London) Ltd, 11 King Street, London WC2E 8HT. Order on school headed paper. An adaptation of this was made for a middle school (3rd/4th year) assembly covering the followng material:

Death of Kennedy — death of Gandhi and *9 Hours to Rama*.
Legend in India and the worlds — Mahatma explained — Father of Modern India.
Born in Gujerat — Gujerati stick dance by girls of the school.
Simplicity in life style.
Colour slides of Porbandar, schools, temples, towns, villages and children presented as a background for Gandhi's ideals of service and social reform and non-violence.
His death.
Recording of a Hindu bhajan played from LP record *Songs of Devotion*, ECLP-2278, HMV (India).

On 22 November 1963 shots rang out in the crowded streets of Dallas, Texas, and John F. Kennedy slumped dead in his open car.

206

Some of you may remember how the wave of disbelief and horror swept round the world on that occasion. Most people, at least of my age, can remember exactly where they were when the news broke — in my case it was late in the evening in a library, where the silence was broken by someone bursting in and announcing the awful news.

Well, just over twenty years ago, on 30 January 1948, then, too, gunshots had rung round the world and a similar shock wave brought news of an assassination. This time the world mourned the death of Mohandas Karamchand Gandhi, the great Indian leader and teacher. Those of you who saw the film on television of *9 hours to Rama* will know that Gandhi, a Hindu, was murdered by a fanatic who hated Gandhi's work at that time to save the Muslims in India from further killings and persecution. These terrible killings and mob violence had followed the division of British India into two — Pakistan for the Muslim separatist party and modern India.

There have been many great men and women in this century but one of the greatest was Mahatma Gandhi. Probably no other statesman of this century has left behind him so much love and respect all over the world. He is a legend in India and his greatness is recognised all over the world. In 1969 there were celebrations in every country of the world to mark the centenary of his birth. In Britain this stamp (Gandhi centenary stamp on an envelope held up) was issued and it was the first time the head of someone other than the king or queen had appeared on a British stamp. Gandhi was one of the great social reformers of the world. He was also a very saintly and remarkable man — one of those very rare men who really do practise what they preach. Many years go by before the world sees a great teacher like this, someone we recognise by what he does and how he lives.

(*Large portrait by a boy in the school displayed.*)

The name 'Mahatma' is the Hindi for 'great soul' (*large flash cards*) and although Gandhi himself disliked this title, the more you learn about him, the more you realise how well 'Mahatma' describes him. But more often in India he is simply referred to as 'Bapu', which means 'Father' — and in a very real sense he is the Father of modern India — and this gives us some idea of the respect in which he is held there. These coins (*Gandhi centenary coins held up*) from India have Bapu's head on them.

(*Gandhi's voice — few opening words from side 1 LP BBC RESR 4 'Gandhi, Man on Trial'.*)

That is the recorded voice of Mahatma Gandhi, but to give us a clearer idea of what Gandhi stood for, we are going to listen to some readings from his writings and speeches. . . . (a girl) and . . . (a boy) are going to read for us. You will be listening to his own words. (*Reference made to plain white colour sari of the girl and khadi kurta and pyjamas of the boy.*) As you see, they are dressed in the simple

white costume of Gandhi's followers in the Indian independence movement. Gandhi and the people close to him led lives of complete simplicity in regard to food, dress, travel and most other things. This white
cloth is 'khaddar' and is entirely handspun cotton. Handspinning and
handicrafts were greatly encouraged by Gandhi and they provided valuable employment for the villagers of rural India. But everyone, from
the highest to the lowest in society, was expected by Gandhi to spend
time spinning and in other manual work as an act of dedication and
humility, and, importantly, because it helped to make India less de-
pendent on the textile mills of industrial England. (*Skein of handspun
threads held up.*) These threads were spun by the headmaster of a big
school in India. And Gandhi himself, although a highly educated lawyer, trained in London, for most of his life dressed like this (*large photo
poster displayed*). He dressed and lived like a villager. He usually wore
a handspun loincloth and home-made sandals.

Boy: I am a poor mendicant. My earthly possessions consist of six
spinning wheels, prison dishes, a can of goat's milk, six homespun
loincloths and towels, and my reputation, which cannot be worth much.
(132 page 44).

Gandhi was not just interested in seeing an end to foreign British
rule in India. He saw this as only a part of his work for his country. In
this he tried to completely identify himself with the very poorest and
weakest members of Indian society who did the most menial tasks —
these were the 'untouchables', the lowest of the low in the caste system,
people who had no place in the caste system Gandhi did his best to
destroy. He renamed these people the 'Harijans', which means the
'people of God'. He, himself, performed the lowliest tasks to show his
concern for the people who usually did them. He taught that no-one
was too high and mighty for manual work and he often stayed with the
outcasts as he walked from place to place.

Boy: Why should I, who have no need to work, spin? — may be the
question asked. Because I am eating what does not belong to me. I am
living on the spoliation of my countrymen. Trace the course of every
(cent) that finds its way into your pocket, and you will realise the truth
of what I write . . .
    I must refuse to insult the naked by giving them clothes they do not
need, instead of giving them work which they sorely need. I will not
commit the sin of becoming their patron, but on learning that I had
assisted in impoverishing them, I would give them neither crumbs nor
cast-off clothing, but the best of my food and clothes and associate
myself with them in work . . .

God created man to work for his food and said that those who ate without work are thieves. (11 page 133).

As you know, India has at present a woman Prime Minister and such a thing would have been unthinkable without Gandhi having championed the women of India and given them full responsibilities in his work — previously the women of India had largely been subservient to the men.

Girl: To call woman the weaker sex is a libel, it is man's injustice to woman. If by strength is meant brute strength, then, indeed, is woman less brute than man. If by strength is meant moral power, then woman is immeasurably man's superior. Has she not greater intuition, is she not more self-sacrificing, has she not greater powers of endurance, has she not greater courage? Without her man could not be. If non-violence is the law of our being, the future is with woman . . . who can make a more effective appeal to the heart than woman. (10 page 162).

As this was bound up with Gandhi's religious ideals and values (*large flash cards displayed SATYA/TRUTH and AHIMSA/NON-VIOLENCE*). He regarded his whole life as a search for Truth and Non-violence. This was a self-search by trial and error and he called this book, the story of his early life (*book displayed*), *My Experiments with Truth*. *Satya* and *Ahimsa* were Gandhi's two great principles.

Girl: Mine is not a religion of the prison-house. It has room for the least among God's creation. But it is proof against insolence, pride of race, religion or colour (104 page 78).

Boy: To see the univeral and all-pervading Spirit of Truth face to face one must be able to love the meanest of creation as oneself. And a man who aspires after that cannot afford to keep out of any field of life. That is why my devotion to truth has drawn me into the field of politics; and I can say without the slightest hesitation, and yet in all humility, that those who say that religion has nothing to do with politics do not know what religion means. (11 page 58).

Gandhi was a great internationalist and certainly has a message for today's world. He had a real sympathy and appreciation for all cultures and religions.

Girl: I do not want my house to be walled in on all sides and my windows to be stuffed. I want the cultures of all lands to be blown about my house as freely as possible. But I refuse to be blown off my feet by any. (6 page 156).

Gandhi was a patriot and a national leader with fine ideals; he wanted freedom for his country so that India could be free to make her rightful contribution to the life of the world.

He did not hate England, and his struggle for independence was based on non-violence. He developed strictly disciplined fasting and civil disobedience (what he called 'satyagraha' or 'truth force') as powerful weapons for his revolution by which he hoped to bring out the best in the foreign rulers of India.

Boy: For me patriotism is the same as humanity. I am patriotic because I am human and humane. It is not exclusive, I will not hurt England . . . to serve India. (15 page 121).

Girl: We want freedom for our country, but not at the expense or exploitation of others, not so as to degrade other countries. I do not want freedom of India if it means the extinction of England or the disappearance of Englishmen I want the freedom of my country, so that the resources of my country might be utilised for the benefit of mankind. (12 page 121).

And Gandhi remained non-violent even in the face of ferocious baton charges and gunfire by police. On one terrible occasion (Amritsar, Jallianwalla Bagh) which was never repeated, several hundred people were killed and more than a thousand wounded — after that Gandhi was still able to say 'I say do not return madness with madness, but return madness with sanity'.

Sometimes as many at 60,000 people were arrested in one operation throughout India. These were ideals which Gandhi put into practice. Now when many people are disillusioned with politicians and politics, it is interesting to listen to what Gandhi said about the high principles he stuck to in politics — often in very adverse circumstances; he himself spent many years of his life in prison standing up for these principles.

Girl: My notion of democracy is that under it the weakest should have the same opportunity as the strongest. That can never happen except through non-violence. (1 page 138).

Boy: Let those who are ambitious to serve democracy qualify themselves by satisfying first this acid test of democracy . . . a democrat must be utterly selfless. He must think and dream not in terms of self or party but only of democracy. Only then does he acquire the right of civil disobedience. (18 page 142).

On the day of festivities when India achieved independence, Gandhi fasted and took no part in the proceedings and he began his last and greatest work. This was when Lord Mountbatten described him as a 'one-man army' when he brought peace to one area of the country (Bengal) where over 50,000 troops had failed to stop Hindu and Muslim mobs killing and molesting each other at the time India was divided.

Some time before his death at the hands of that fanatical Hindu extremist, Gandhi wrote these prophetic words in his diary.

Boy: I do not want to die (in later life) of a creeping paralysis of my faculties — a defeated man. An assassin's bullet may put an end to my life. I would welcome it. But I would love above all, to fade out doing my duty with my last breath. (158 page 55). I believe in the message of truth delivered by all the religious teachers of the world. And it is my constant prayer that I may never have a feeling of anger against my traducers, that even if I fall a victim to an assassin's bullet, I may deliver up my soul with the remembrance of God upon my lips. I shall be content to be written down an imposter if my lips utter a word of anger or abuse against my assailant at the last moment. (156 page 54).

Gandhi at the age of 78 was shot three times at point-blank range as he was walking to prayers. As he fell, the crowd heard him say the words 'Rama, Rama' — the name of God. And that is how Mahatma Gandhi died twenty-four years ago.

Listen (*recording of an Indian eye witness account from a BBC radio programme 'Gandhi — the last phase' broadcast January 1968 on Radio 4*).

Now will you join in listening to this prayer of freedom written by Gandhi's contemporary, the Bengali poet Rabindranath Tagore:

Where the mind is without fear and the head held high;
Where knowledge is free;
Where the world has not been broken up into fragments by narrow
    domestic walls;
Where words come out from the depth of truth;
Where tireless striving stretches its arm towards perfection:
Where the clear stream of reason has not lost its way into the dreary
    desert sand of dead habit;
Where the mind is led forward by thee into ever-widening thought
    and action —
Into that heaven of freedom, my Father, let my country awake.

(page 29, *Gitanjali*, Macmillan, 1962).
DAVID BALDWIN

EVENT: GURU NANAK'S BIRTHDAY (*GURPURB*)

Materials: LP record *Guru Nanak Shabads*, ECLP-2440 (HMV) India) — from The Indian Record House, 70 South Road, Southall, Middlesex. Tel.: 01 571–1306.

Portrait of Guru Nanak by Sobha Singh for 500th birth anniversary.

Portraits of Guru Nanak by Sikh children.

Large flash cards: GURU
                                     NANAK
                                     SAT SRI AKAL

Colour slides of Golden Temple, Amritsar, *Gurdwara*, schools and towns in the Punjab.

The assembly: (duration — about 20 minutes)

India — a land of travellers great and small, today and in the past — 1500 years ago Guru Nanak was travelling with his friends Mardanna and Bala.

With reference to flash cards and permits, Guru Nanak introduced — first Guru of the Sikhs (10 million out of 550 million in India; some with us in Britain).

Often on the move, Nanak composing and singing hymns and telling people, Hindus and Muslims, about God at a time when many people were forgetting what was really important in their religion — imagine him being greeted at each village as he walked from place to place.

DANCE — Punjabi girls in costume sign and dance in a typical Punjabi dance. Guru Nanak would have seen dances like these.

Colour slides (about 24) showing children at school in the Punjab, children's games, *Gurdwaras* and fairs at Anandpur Sahib, and the Golden Temple at Amritsar thronged with worshippers at the 500th birthday celebrations — important features of Sikh life and teaching referred to when illustrated in a slide, e.g. Guru *ka langar* (common kitchen).

Guru Nanak — first in a line of gurus — reference to Sikhs in England. Children taught the Sikh greeting SAT SRI AKAL — repeated several times from flash cards.

Closing music — a *shabad* from the record played on a gramophone.

'Now let's listen to these words taken from the prayers which are always said at the end of the service in the *Gurdwara*':

They are translated into English for us:

'O true King, O loved Father, we have sung Thy sweet hymns, heard Thy life-giving Word, and have discoursed on Thy manifold blessings. May these things find a loving place in our hearts and serve to draw our souls towards Thee.'

DAVID BALDWIN

EVENT: *DIWALI*

Material: Large collages made by children of Lakshmi and the Golden Temple lit up at *Diwali*.

Children's pictures illustrating episodes in the *Ramayana* and masks used in classroom drama.

Puja items set out before Hindu prints of Lakshmi, Ram and Sita. Colour slides of Hindu temples, festivals and daily life.

Record of the Aarti ceremony *Jai Jagdish* Odeon (India), EMOE–2136 from the popular Hindi film *Purab aur Pacham* and *Songs of Devotion*, by Juthika Roy, ECLP–2278, HMV (India).

Arrangement of the Hall: Pupils sitting in semi-circular rows leaving a half circle at the front. The collage of Lakshmi displayed. At the front in the centre, to one side of this the *puja* items laid out on the platform and to the other items of children's work ready to be held up. In one corner at an angle facing the children the screen.

The assembly: 25 minutes to a group of fifth- and sixth-formers.

Indian music playing quietly as pupils assemble.

The other day in Southall — *Diwali* in Southall described — festival of lights, fireworks, candles and brightly lit shops selling wide range of sweets — reference to the Hindu calendar.

Diva = a lamp — *Diwali* in India described — unites India, celebrated in millions of homes, north and south, villages and towns. Reference to clay lamps.

Its meaning and significance — a joyful occasion. Light as a symbol. Link with the story of *Ramayana* — thz story of Ram and Sita outlined with reference to pictures of important episodes and props made for classroom drama. *Diwali* follows the festival of *Dussehra* (victory of Lord Ram over Ravanna, the demon king). At *Dussehra* — effigy of Ravanna burnt to celebrate Ram's victory and at *Diwali* the lamps light Ram's and Sita's triumphant return to his kingdom. *Ayodhaya*.

A time for celebrating — a joyful dance by Indian girls in costumes and singing an accompanying Punjabi song.

Hindu New Year — presided over by the Goddess Lakshmi who visits lighted homes. *Puja* — Hindu ritual worship referred to and compared to homage to a monarch. Lakshmi is invoked for the welfare and prosperity of the family. A *family-puja* in the home, giving of sweets, card-playing, new clothes, new account books for businessmen, etc.

Diwali fairs in India. Sikhs visit *Gurdwaras*.

Hindu girls help the teacher describe *puja* and show how the different utensils and offerings, would be used in a Hindu home. Teacher explained *Aarti* ceremony in the temple.

Lights out and a series of slides showing temples, festivals, and everyday life shown in quick succession on the screen as the recording of *Jai Jagdish* is played after the teacher has asked the pupils to try to think of India with all its diversity united in worship and celebration.

A poem from *Gitanjali* by Rabindrandth Tagore read:

'In one salutation to thee, my God let all my senses spread out and
touch this world at thy feet.
Like a rain-cloud of July hung low with its burden of unshed showers
let all my mind bend down at thy door in one salutation to thee.
Let all my songs gather together their diverse strains into a single
current and flow to a sea of silence in one solution to thee.
Like a flock of homesick cranes flying night and day back to their
mountain nests let all my life take its voyage to its eternal home in
one salutation to thee.'

Closing music: a *kabir bhajan* sung by Juthika Roy on the LP record
Songs of Devotion.

DAVID BALDWIN

EVENT: Eid-ul-Fitr

Materials: A long low table spread with a woven rug with a typical
geometric pattern — at one end a large copy of the Holy *Qu'ran* on a
carved wooden book rest and at the other end a large framed copy of
an illuminated manuscript on which the *Qu'ran* has been meticulously
inscribed in full. Behind this, a large simple *mihrab* painted by children
on card and to one side of this a large cut-out of a minaret drawn and
painted by children in the Immigrant Reception Class.

Outside the hall, a display of children's work, visual aids, etc.,
illustrating life and culture in the Islamic world.

Other items to refer to during the assembly: Flash cards *Eid-ul-Fitr*,
a woven prayer carpet, a white prayer cap from Mecca, a copy of the
Holy *Qu'ran* with Arabic and English in columns, picture of a crescent
moon and star over a mosque.

Record *mubarak mahina hai ramzan ka* EMI Angel (India) TAE
1559 from The Indian Record House, 70 South Road, Southall, Middlesex. (Another useful record from the same supplier: *The Gloriou.
Qu'ran — Recitation from the Holy Qu'ran*, Qari Mohammed Islam
EMI Angel (India) 3AEX–5322).

The assembly: (duration about 25 minutes, celebrated several days afte.
Eid).

Our assemblies often mark festivals and events in the Christian
calendar — today another festival *Eid-ul-Fitr (flash cards)* in the Mus
lim calendar.

Eid-ul-Fitr — a happy occasion marks the end of *Ramadhan* — ；
long and difficult month of fasting and prayer. Reference to visua
aid — the crescent moon of Islam — the lunar calendar. *Eid* begin
when the new moon is sighted, the following day the fast is broken an·

the festival celebrated. The Holy *Qu'ran* and its revelation to the Prophet Muhammad especially remembered in this month.

Ramadhan explained and described briefly — fast from dawn to dusk (*reference to difficulties in a hot country and boys in our school*): Muslims believe this brings them closer to God — learing self-control, patience, the meaning of suffering; while fasting trying extra hard to avoid anger and malice and to do good deeds.

Eid in London — teacher described his visit to London mosque and time spent with a Muslim family — especially greeting '*Id-mubarak*' — Happy *Eid* — embrace, etc.

The miracle of the *Qu'ran* — dictated over a period of about 20 years, etc. Meaning of the word 'prophet' — a man through whom God speaks. Most Muslim children learn to recite the 114 chapters of the *Qu'ran*.

A Muslim boy takes his place sitting cross-legged on the table and intones several of the opening sections of the *Qu'ran* reading from the open book. (*No translation was given.*)

Brief reference to the *Five Pillars of Islam* as illustrated by the visual items in the assembly, e.g. *mihrab*, minaret, prayer carpet, prayer cap, etc.

Call to prayer (*Azan*) on record (Supreme Council for Islamic Affairs, UAR available from Islamic Cultural Centre, London).

Children invited to listen to a reading of one of the Prophet's prayers said before going to the mosque (*in translation*):

'O my Lord put light in my heart and put light on my tongue, and put light in my hearing, and put light in my sight, and put light behind me and in front of me and make it all light in what is above me and make it all light in what is below me. O my Lord, grant me light all around.'

After explaining that music has no part in Muslim worship the closing music is played after giving the meaning in English of the song *mubarak mahina hai ramzan ka* — '*Ramadhan* is the most blessed month'.

DAVID BALDWIN

MEDITATION

Aim: A senior assembly aiming to present a few ideas about the Asian approach to meditation.

Materials: George Harrison record *My Sweet Lord*.

Assembly: duration about 15 minutes. Teacher sits on a chair close to the pupils not on the platform.

My Sweet Lord played.

East is East, West is West?

Search for novelty — digging shallow wells, we must dig deep.

Wisdom of the East?

Distinction between Hatha Yoga and meditation.

Hinduism and Yoga are not the same thing.

Meditation practised in different forms in Asia.

Hindu Yoga aims at much more than physical fitness.

For some coming closer to God; for others finding out about their real self. Why do people meditate? Look at the words of the song 'I really want to see you . . . but it takes so long, my lord'.

The four yogas — ways to God of Hinduism;

Bhaktiyoga — the way of devotion

Jnanayoga — the way of knowledge and discrimination

Karmayoga — the way of action

Rajayoga — the way of mind control and self search.

Mind control — symbols to help us understand — the most common is the lotus flower, then the lake:

The bottom of a lake we cannot see, because its surface is covered with ripples. It is only possible for us to catch a glimpse of the bottom, when the ripples have subsided, and the water is calm. If the water is muddy or agitated all the time, the bottom will not be seen. If it is clear and there are no waves we shall see the bottom. The bottom of the lake is our own true Self; the lake is the (mind) and the waves (all the activity and thoughts in our minds). (See p. 126 *Raja-Yoga*, Swami Vivekananda Advaita Ashrama, 13th impress, 1966.)

Many have found lasting benefits from meditation, some have glimpsed what they were searching for, and a few have found what they were seeking, but all could benefit from more time for quiet reflection.

Children asked to sit upright with eyes closed for a few moments of quiet, trying to direct their mind towards an image free of associations — suggesting perhaps a colour or a diminishing light (see p. 175, *Hinduism* — teaching Hindusim in secondary schools — eds. John Hinnells and Eric Sharpe, Oriel Press, 1972).

Closing words — a poem from Rabindranath Tagore's *Gitanjali* (Macmillan, 1962, p. 28):

'This is my prayer to thee, my lord —

Strike, strike at the root of penury in my heart

Give me the strength lightly to hear my joys and sorrows

Give me the strength to make my love fruitful in service.

Give me the strength never to disown the poor or bend my knees before insolent might.

Give me the strength to raise my mind high above daily trifles

And give me the strength to surrender my strength to thy will with love.'

DAVID BALDWIN

DIWALI IN A FIRST SCHOOL

Narrator. Long, long time ago in India, there was a great king called Dasharatha. He ruled over the city of Ayodhya in India. He had made the city happy and safe and the people loved him.

King Dasharatha had three wives. In those days a king could have more than one wife. His first wife had a son called Rama. His second wife had a son called Bharat and his third wife had two sons, Lakshmana and Shatrughna. One day, king Dasharatha called his people together in front of his palace and said:

Dasharatha. Once I was young and strong, but I have now grown old. It is time for me to rest. I want to pass my crown to my eldest son Rama. I have chosen Prince Rama to be your new king.

Narrator. All the people in Ayodhya were very happy that Prince Rama would rule and Sita will be his queen.

When the second queen heard about the king's plan, she decided to stop Rama becoming king. Now it so happened that this queen had saved the life of the king in a war many years ago and the king had granted her two wishes. The queen went to ask for them and said:

Queen. I have come to ask you for the two favours which you promised me a long time ago. First of all, I want my own son, Prince Bharat, to become king, and secondly I want you to banish Rama from this kingdom for fourteen years.

Narrator. King Dasharatha was very upset, but he could not break his promise. He called Rama and explained the situation.

Rama. I will leave Ayodhya today. Give me your blessing, father. I must take leave of Sita and say goodbye to her. Sita, I am not going to be the king. I am leaving Ayodhya to live in the jungle for fourteen years.

Sita. Rama, I am coming with you. I can't stay here without you. I am your wife, if you are banished, I am banished. I will come.

Rama. No.

Sita. I will come.

Rama and Lakshmana. I will come with you, too.

Narrator. Rama, Sita and Lakshamana went to live in the forest. Soon after they left, King Dasharatha died from grief.

In the forest, Rama, Sita and Lakshamana lived happily for several years. They protected birds and animals from the giants and demons.

One day Sita saw a golden deer:

Sita. Rama, look, isn't that lovely? Can you catch it for me Rama? I want it for a pet, please.

Rama. It's a deer. I can't catch it.

Sita. Please, Rama.

Rama. Stay here, Lakshamana, and don't leave Sita alone for a minute.

Narrator. Rama went to get the deer with his bow and arrows and chased the deer deep into the forest.

Now, at the same time, on an island called Lanka, there lived a wicked demon called Ravana. He was a fierce and powerful demon. It was his wicked trick to send the golden deer into the jungle so that Sita would be left alone. You see, Sita was very beautiful and this wicked demon Ravana wanted to marry her. He used this cunning trick. He copied Rama's voice and shouted out.

Rama. Help, Lakshamana! Come and save me! Help!

Narrator. Lakshamana did not realize this was a trick. Quickly he drew a magic circle around Sita.

Lakshamana. Do not step out of this magic ring or you will not be safe.

Narrator. Then he ran off into the forest to help Rama.

When Sita was alone, Ravana disguised himself as a holy man and came to Sita's hut.

Ravana. Please help me. I am an old man. I have no friends and no food.

Sita. Poor old man. I must help him.

Narrator. So gathering some food, she stepped outside the magic circle to give it to him. Immediately the holy man seized Sita and took her to his kingdom. When Rama and Lakshamana came back to their hut, they could not find Sita. They looked everywhere for her. Then, they met monkey God Hanuman.

Hanuman. I am Hanuman, the monkey God. I will help you.

Narrator. Hanuman could fly, and it was he who found Sita imprisoned on the island of Lanka.

Hanuman. If we can build a bridge across the ocean we can kill Ravana and rescue Sita.

Narrator. So they built a bridge across the sea to the island. A fierce battle took place between Rama and Ravana. The battle lasted for ten long days and in the end evil Ravana was killed with an arrow. Rama rescued Sita. Now, at last, fourteen years of banishment were over. Rama's brothers and people of Ayodhya went to fetch Rama, Sita and Lakshamana from the forest. Everybody was happy to see them. They sang songs and lit fireworks to welcome them. All the roads to the palace were lined with little lights called *divas*. Rama was crowned as the king and he ruled for many years.

Now we are going to sing a song called 'Diwali avi'. First, we will sing it in Gujarati and then we will sing it in English.

The day after *Diwali* is our Hindu New Year's Day. We wish you all a very Happy, Prosperous and Peaceful New Year.

NILA PANCHOLI

218

HARVEST FESTIVAL SERVICE

The following text of a service at Ash Brow Infants School, Hudders-field, has been supplied by Elizabeth Wilson, who wishes to thank the school staff for their permission. With its mixture of hymns and secular songs from or about many parts of the world it may hopefully provide teachers with ideas which they can develop to suit the needs of the children they teach. *(Editor)*

This year, for our Harvest Service, we have been thinking about the harvest of the earth everywhere in the world. You can see in the Hall the pictures we have painted about them.

We are going to start by singing a hymn about our lovely world, 'O Father, the Maker of beautiful things'.

Whole School: 'O Father, the Maker of beautiful things.' In order to grow things well we need the right kind of weather — warm sun, gentle breezes and soft rain. The Nursery class will sing for us 'I love the Sun'.

Nursery: 'I love the sun'.

You can see here the picture of our own harvest in England. Listen to this poem about it.

Group: 'Farmer, is the harvest ready?'

Class 2 will sing a song about the fruit which grows wild in our countryside — the blackberry.

Class 2: 'We are picking berries for our tea.'

Do you like sweets and chocolate? Do you like cakes and puddings? All these have sugar in them, and over there is a picture of sugar cane growing in the West Indies.

Here is a song with a lovely rhythm about the harvesting of the sugar cane.

Class 7: 'Island in the sun'.

In our country we grow and eat many cereals such as corn, maize, oats and barley, but in countries like China, India and Pakistan the main food is rice. Sometimes the rice harvest is ruined because of the heavy rain which floods the rice fields and life is hard for the people in these countries.

Listen to this song that Class 5 is going to sing about rice planting in China.

Class 5: 'Planting rice is never fun'.

When we talk about the harvest we usually think of food, but, the earth gives us other things besides, which we use but do not eat — things like coal, oil, gas, rubber, cotton and wood. Without the harvest of the forests we would have no tables, no chairs, no books to read and no paper to write and draw on. All these things are made from the wood of tree-trunks. Look at our picture of lumberjacks in Canada. Class 4 will tell us what they do.

219

Class 4: We are woodmen chopping trees.

Did you know that we get cotton from a plant? It grows in warm countries like the United States of America. The white fluff which covers the seeds of the cotton plant is picked off, cleaned, combed and twisted, and made into cloth. Our handkerchiefs, tablecloths, curtains, sheets and clothes are often made out of cotton.

Class 3 will sing a song about the cotton-pickers in the fields.

Class 3: 'Oh Lordy, pick a bale of cotton'.

Our picture over there on the wall shows us coconuts, pineapples and bananas growing in the tropical forests of the Fiji Islands, a very long way from England. Here is a coconut and this is a little dish made from half of a coconut husk when the milk and flesh have been taken out.

One of our favourite fruits which class 6 is going to sing about is the banana, and the song is called 'Banana Boat Song'.

Class 6: 'Banana boat song'.

And now, listen to our Harvest Prayer. Hands together. Eyes closed.

Dear Father God, our school looks beautiful to-day with these Harvest gifts from all over the world. People in many countries have worked hard to produce this food and we ask you to bless them all and help them in their daily lives.

We thank you that we in this country have enough to eat but we remember those who are hungry.

Make us willing to share with them the rich harvest of our earth. Amen.

Whole school: 'Thank you, God, for sunny days'.

ELIZABETH WILSON

INTRODUCING THE *QUR'AN* TO CHILDREN IN A CHURCH OF ENGLAND CONTROLLED SCHOOL

St Matthew's CE School, Bolton, is an inner urban primary school situated three quarters of a mile from the town centre. It is a one-form entry school with an approximate 15 per cent intake of children of immigrant parentage.

Daily morning assemblies are Christian-based but the format of these services varies. The head teacher or deputy head teacher leads the assemblies generally. However, they are sometimes taken by the vicar of St Matthew's Church, who attends an assembly once a week, or by the children themselves who are trained to do so from an early age by the class teachers. The school tries to foster a caring attitude and emphasises the importance of tolerance and respect towards others, irrespective of creed or colour.

At the suggestion of the fourth year junior teacher the head teacher agreed that eight Muslim children from the third- and fourth-year junior age group should plan a service for a morning assembly when they would have the opportunity to relate and explain their own beliefs and practices. The children concerned were very keen to co-operate and immediately began the task of preparing and planning. They asked if they could bring items to school which they thought would be of interest to everyone. Mohammed, whose father is the *Imam* at the local mosque, reported that his father would permit him to bring along the *Qur'an* on condition that it was treated with due respect. Mohammed was given the assurance.

Two weeks later the service was ready and it was arranged for the following Wednesday when the vicar would be present. On the day in question the boys arrived at school early and made their way to the hall. The head teacher, who was also the school pianist, asked the boys what hymns had been decided upon. She was met with a horrified expression from the contingent of eight as one of them explained: 'But no-one can sing in the presence of the *Qur'an*.' With a smile, the head teacher accepted the explanation. A few minutes later the boys disappeared. The head teacher, rather perturbed about this, went to investigate. She found them in the cloakroom washing their hands. This ritual is known as *Wazu,* which must take place before the *Qur'an* is handled. The boys soon returned to the hall and waited for the full school, both infants and juniors, to assemble.

The head teacher first addressed the school, explaining that the assembly service that day was to be presented by eight Muslim children and explained the reason for the omission of hymns. She then introduced the boys and sat down with the other staff at the side of the hall. The talk the boys presented proved most interesting, as they related their beliefs and traditions, describing the mosque and the worship which took place there. The boys stressed the importance of male domination in their society and their system of separating the sexes for worship.

Mohammed presented the *Qur'an* and very briefly related its content, reading some of the text, in Arabic, of course. By now the audience was captive. Everyone was very interested to see the mosque caps and garments the children had brought along. The head teacher suggested that Riaz (who was wearing the clothes) should stand on a chair to give everyone a better view. At this suggestion Mohammed (who was holding the *Qur'an*), immediately scrambled onto another chair, holding the *Qur'an* above his head. The head teacher looked questioningly at Mohammed, who explained 'No one must stand above the *Qur'an*' and he continued to hold the book aloft until Riaz stepped down from his chair.

At the conclusion of the service questions were invited from the assembled throng and both children and teachers took advantage of the opportunity. Many thoughtful questions were asked and many interesting answers given. The head teacher than thanked the boys for their efforts and congratulated them on such an interesting half-hour.

When the school had returned to their classes Mohammed asked if the *Qur'an* could be left in a safe place until he went home. The head teacher suggested that it should be left in her room. On arrival in the room, Mohammed glanced round the room and put it on the filing cabinet opposite to the head teacher's desk, saying 'I think this is the best place for it as there you will not turn your back on it'.

It had been a most enlightening morning.

(Reprinted from SHAP mailing 1982 with permission of the editor.)

PART 4: RESOURCES LIST

GENERAL BOOKS ON THE WORLD'S RELIGIONS

FOR THE TEACHER

Reference Works

Concise Encyclopaedia of Living Faiths, R. C. Zaehner (ed.), Hutchinson
Man and his Gods, E. G. Parrinder, Hamlyn
A Dictionary of Comparative Religion, S. G. F. Brandon (ed.), Weidenfeld and Nicolson
Illustrated Dictionary of World Religions, A. A. Jones, Religious Education Press
Penguin Handbook of World Religions, J. R. Hinnells (ed.), Penguin
Penguin Dictionary of World Religions, J. R. Hinnells (ed.), Penguin

Books surveying a number of religions

Man's Religions, J. B. Noss, Collier-Macmillan
Religions, M. Langley, Lion
Religious Experience of Mankind, N. Smart, Collins
A History of Religion East and West, T. O. Ling, Macmillan
A Taste of Heaven, L. Blue and J. Rose, Darton, Longman and Todd. This is a fascinating book about food in religion. It has inspired many teachers to explore the theme in their religious education courses.
Festivals, W. O. Cole (ed.), Longman. This is the provisional title of a book scheduled to appear in 1983. It will cover the major religious festivals of the world.

FOR THE CLASSROOM

These are most appropriate for secondary school, though the first book on the list has been used successfully with eleven-year-olds.
A Book of World Religions, E. G. Parrinder, Hulton Educational
Gods and Men, B. W. Sherratt and D. J. Hawkins, Blackie
Five Religions in the Twentieth Century, W. O. Cole, Hulton Educational

The Many Faces of Religion, S. Dicks, P. Mennill and D. Santor, Ginn *Friends and Neighbours* series, D. Butler, Edward Arnold. A series of short plays with participants from the major religions to be found in the UK.

Comparative Religions, D. Charing, W. O. Cole, R. El-Droubie, N. Pancholi and P. S. Sambhi, Blandford Press. Suitable also as an introduction for teachers, students and social workers.

The Argus Communications kits have been mentioned frequently in this book. They deserve to be included here also.

Looking at . . ., J. Rankin, Lutterworth. Four sets of work cards covering myth, festivals, symbols and worship.

Attention is also drawn to the many useful books which comprise the basic reading material for the Open University course, Man's Religious Quest, AD 208. The course is open to teachers wishing to enrol as associate students.

For further bibliographies see *World Religions: A Handbook for Teachers,* W. O. Cole (ed.), available from the Commission for Racial Equality.

AFRO–CARIBBEAN RELIGIONS

Black identity is often sought in Africa and fed by knowledge of that continent and its indigenous religions. However, this heritage is one which the white Christian has often been led to regard as primitive or savage. This view of the African persists among children whose working class parents never read *Little Black Sambo* (an odd Afro–Indian mix) and were not influenced by the paternalism of Albert Schweitzer. Black studies can benefit all students but needs to be incorporated into religious studies with care.

SOME BOOKS FOR THE TEACHER

Afro–Caribbean Religions, B. Gates, Ward Lock. Part one is an introduction to religion in the Caribbean, influenced by both Africa and Christianity. Part two relates this information to the primary and secondary school. If one book is to be chosen, this is it.
African Civilisations in the New World, R. Bastide and C. Hurst. An analysis of African survivals in the New World. Fine descriptions of religions beliefs or practices.
Living Tribal Relibions, H. W. Turner, Ward Lock. A brief, illustrated, study.
African Tribal Religions, E. G. Parrinder, Sheldon Press.
The Primal Vision, J. V. Taylor, SCM. Though written as recently as 1963, this was one of the first books to educate British Christians into an awareness of the spirituality of African religion.
Gods Many and Lords Many, J. Ferguson, Lutterworth. A study of concepts rather than a survey of religions. Not confined to Africa.
Roots, A. Haley, Picador. Fictional, but as, those who saw the television series will remember, it helps the white reader to understand the American negro.
The Rastafarians, L. E. Barratt, Heinemann.
Two smaller books are:
The Rastafarians, K. M. Williams, Ward Lock, which can be used by secondary school pupils, and
Movement of Jah People, J. Plummer, Press Gang.

FOR THE CLASSROOM

The Story of Anasi, P. Appiah, Evans. A fascinating collection of tales for younger children.
Also useful is:
West Indian Folk Tales, P. M. Sherlock, Oxford University Press.

Factual books are:

The People who Came, E, Braithwaite, 3 vols, Longman. A historical and cultural survey published for Caribbean schools (10–14 years).

The Making of the West Indies, F. R. Augier and S. C. Gordon, Longman.

Benin, K. Elliott, Cambridge University Press, describes one rich African culture (13–16).

African Heroes, N. Mitchison, The Bodley Head, (10–14) is about eleven figures of the period 1300 to 1900.

Black Settlers in Britain, 1955–1958, N. File and C. Rower, Heinemann, (10–14) will surprise many readers who regard the negro as a newcomer. Battersea had a black mayor in 1913.

The Heinemann *African Historical Biographies* written for use in Africa provide a rich vein for teachers to exploit. They include Menelik of Ethiopia, Khama and Obaseki of Benin. Colonialison and missionary enterprise are subjected to some criticism. Some teachers will find their views on African history challenged. (See the section on 'Black Heroes in the Primary School', pp. 320–24.)

AFRICAN WRITERS IN ENGLISH

(*Note:* AWS = paperback edition in Heinemann's African Writers Series)

AFRICAN BOOKS SUITABLE FOR 'UPPER PRIMARY' AND 'MIDDLE' SCHOOLCHILDREN, OR FOR ADAPTATION BY THEIR TEACHERS

O. Equiano, *Equiano's Travels,* edited by P. Edwards, Heinemann (AWS), London, 1967. Fascinating true adventures of a West African of the Igbo tribe who was caught, sold into slavery as a youth, transported across the Atlantic and eventually freed. The book, written by himself, was first published in 1789.

B. Gbadamosi and U. Beier, *Not Even God Is Ripe Enough: Yoruba Myths.* Heinemann (AWS), London, 1968. Translation into English of some myths of the Yoruba people of Western Nigeria, which give insight into traditional West African customs and religious beliefs.

Barbara Kimenye, *Kalasanda* and *Kalasanda Revisited,* Oxford University Press (Three Crowns Series), London, 1905 and 1966. Both these books consist of sketches of village life in Buganda, East Africa.

Camara Laye, *The African Child,* translated from the French by James Kirkup (London, 1955), Fontana Books, London, 1959. A lyrical account of an African childhood in a village in French Guinea before the Second World War.

Wole Soyinka, *Aké: The Years of Childhood,* Rex Collings, London, 1981. This account, by the most versatile of the West African authors, of his childhood in Yorubaland, Nigeria, presents a 'world in which spirits and wood daemons were as real . . . as catechists, traders, kings, educators, missionaries . . .'

ADULT BOOKS BY AFRICAN WRITERS SUITABLE FOR SECONDARY SCHOOL PUPILS

Chinua Achebe, *Things Fall Apart,* Heinemann (AWS), London, 1958. A very fine novel about the effects of Christian missionaries and European colonial officials upon the culture and beliefs of Igbo villagers in Eastern Nigeria.

Chinua Achebe, *No Longer at Ease,* Heinemann (AWS), London, 1960. A kind of sequel to the above, two generations later; a semi-satirical novel about a young Igbo graduate of London University and his inner moral conflicts on his return to Lagos in the late 1950s.

Chinua Achebe, *Arrow of God,* Heinemann (AWS), London, 1964. A novel about political tensions within an Igbo village at the time of the earliest contact with European colonial officials; a delicate evocation of old African culture and religion, and the tragedy of an African priest's misuse of his ritual power.

Chinua Achebe, *A Man of the People,* Heinemann (AWS), London, 1966. A searingly satirical treatment of African politicians and public corruption in a fictional West African state, until a military *coup* takes place.

T. M. Aluko *One Man, One Wife* (Lagos, 1959), Heinemann (AWS), London, 1967. A comic novel that presents amusedly, with delight in the absurd, the dilemmas of Nigerians caught between their traditional ways of life and the *mores* of Western Christian and commercial culture.

T. M. Aluko, *One Man, One Matchet,* Heinemann (AWS), London, 1964. A comic novel about an outrageous political demagogue in rural Nigeria, with a more serious undercurrent about the public responsibilities of the first local officials taking over from British colonial administrators.

T. M. Aluko, *Kinsman and Foreman,* Heinemann (AWS), London, 1966. A comic novel about a Nigerian engineer trained in Europe and now stationed in the area of his birth trying to do his job honestly without improper influence upon him from his kinsmen and fellow-villagers.

T. M. Aluko, *Chief the Honourable Minister,* Heinemann (AWS), London, 1970. A very satirical novel about the corruption and dishonesty of civilian West African politicians until their corrupt regime is overthrown by a military *coup.*

Elechi Amadi, *The Concubine,* Heinemann (AWS), London, 1966. A novel of delicate relationships, involving a beautiful young woman believed to be the 'wife' of a water god in a pre-colonial Ikwere village in Eastern Nigeria; it gives a penetrating insight into relationships between traditional African villagers and their deities.

Elechi Amadi, *The Great Ponds,* Heinemann (AWS), London, 1969. A tautly written and structured novel about a disastrous conflict between two pre-colonial Ikwere villages at about the time of the First World War. It is particularly valuable for its evocation of traditional African culture in part of Eastern Nigeria.

Ayi Kewi Armah, *The Beautyful Ones Are Not Yet Born,* Heinemann (AWS), London, 1968. A deeply sombre novel about a railway signalman in Ghana (representative of ordinary people) who tries to retain his personal integrity while surrounded, even in his own family, by disease-like corruption in a dictatorial state drawn from Nkrumah's Ghana.

228

John Pepper Clark, *Three Plays*, Oxford University Press (Three Crowns Series), London, 1964. These three plays, set in Nigeria, are firmly based in the traditional culture of the Ijaw people.

John Pepper Clark, *Ozidi*, Oxford University Press (Three Crowns Series), London, 1966. This is a dramatic, compressed adaptation of the traditional seven-day Ijaw epic performance of the myth of Ozidi (translated in full by Clark as *The Ozidi Saga*, Ibadan, Nigeria). Ozidi's humanity is destroyed by his being trained up to avenge his warrior-father, treacherously murdered.

Cyprian Ekwensi, *People of the City* (London, 1954), Heinemann (AWS), London, 1963. A morally ambivalent novel about the dangers and delights of modern urban life in West Africa, with the author responding very much as his characters do to what allures as well as endangers.

Cyprian Ekwensi, *Jagua Nana* (London, 1961), Heinemann (AWS), London, 1975. About a Lagos prostitute, this is a novel not unlike Defoe's *Moll Flanders* in theme and moral outlook, though in a very different setting, and much more concerned with the prostitute's attempts to find respectability than with her trade.

D. O. Fagunwa, *The Forest of a Thousand Daemons*, translated from the Yoruba by Wole Soyinka, Nelson, London, 1968. Fantastic adventures drawn from Yoruba folk-tales (see also Amos Tutuola, below).

Charles L. Mungoshi, *Waiting for the Rain*, Heinemann (AWS), London, 1975. This work by a very find young Zimbabwean writer sensitively explores the impact of 'learning the Western world' on traditional African beliefs and values in Zimbabwe.

John Munonye, *Oil Man of Obange*, Heinemann (AWS), London, 1971. A moving novel about a petty trader in palm oil pitting all his strength against fate, accident and malice to raise money for his children's schooling. A stark account of the everyday hardships for most people in the Third World.

Gabriel Okara, *The Voice* (London, 1964), Heinemann (AWS), London, 1970. A most unusual novel in the form of a political parable about the role of the artist in a demagogic or dictatorial African society. Okara uses a most unusual kind of English, often very successfully, which follows the word-order sometimes of his native Ijaw speech.

Christopher Okigbo, *Labyrinths*, Heinemann (AWS), London, 1971. The collected poems of a writer who was killed in action on the Biafran side in the Nigerian Civil War in 1967. Okigbo is a very sophisticated poet deeply read in English poetry, who uses African mythology and imagery extensively.

229

Okot p'Bitek, *Hare and Hornbill,* Heinemann (AWS), London, 1978. A collection of thirty-two African folk-tales retold very vividly by the Ugandan poet, Okot p'Bitek.

Poems of Black Africa, Wole Soyinka (ed.), Heinemann (AWS), London, 1975. Probably the fullest and most far-ranging anthology of African verse available. It draws upon all parts of Africa, and, though most of the poems were originally written in English, there are also translations from Swahili, Yoruba, French and Portuguese.

Wole Soyinka, *Five Plays,* Oxford University Press (Three Crowns Series), London, 1964. Contains, in addition to *A Dance in the Forest,* four shorter plays that deal with modern Nigerian life but draw upon the rich repository of Yoruba beliefs and legends.

Wole Soyinka, *The Road,* Oxford University Press (Three Crowns Series), London, 1965. A play about Nigerian lorry drivers and the chief character's attempts to find out the mystery of death, with the aid of Yoruba belief about life and death.

Wole Soyinka, *Kongi's Harvest,* Oxford University Press (Three Crowns Series), London, 1967. A satirical play about the conflict between traditional, hereditary chiefs and the modern demagogue politicians in a 'Westminister-type' African state.

Wole Soyinka, *Collected Plays,* 2 vols, Oxford University Press, London, 1973 and 1974. This collected edition includes the plays in the preceding three items.

Wole Soyinka, *The Interpreters* (London, 1965), Heinemann (AWS), 1970. An angrily satirical novel about the dilemmas, personal and cultural, of Nigerian intellectuals, who believe they ought to be interpreting the modern world to their people, but are full of uncertainities themselves.

Efua T. Sutherland, *The Marriage of Anansewa,* Longman, London, 1975. A skilful adaptation of one of the comic, wryly philosophical Ananse stories as an English play, incorporating singing, ritual, fluid staging and other conventions of popular Akan theatre in Ghana.

Amos Tutuola, *The Palm-Wine Drinkard* (London, 1952), Faber Paperback, London, 1962. An extraordinary 'novel' in highly idiosyncratic English by a man who draws on traditional Yoruba folk-tales, but reshapes them, and, instead of telling them orally in the village in the traditional manner, writes them down in the best English he can muster. It gives a penetrating insight into the West African imagination.

Amos Tutola, *My Life in the Bush of Ghosts* (London, 1954), Faber Paperback, London, 1965. Another, more consciously structured tale based upon folk-talkes, about a purgatorial, nightmare-like series of fabulous experiences among the spirits of the dead.

Ngugi wa Thiong'o (formerly James Ngugi), *Weep Not, Child*, Heine-mann (AWS), London, 1964. A novel about a young boy's sufferings when his whole world is overturned violently during the Mau Mau Rebellion in Kenya in the 1950s. Told from an African point of view, it is a very healthy antidote to Ruark's pro-white-settler novel, *Something of Value*.

ARTHUR RAVENSCROFT
School of English,
University of Leeds

INDIAN WRITERS IN ENGLISH

K. A. Abbas, *Inquilab,* Jaico Publishing House, Bombay, 1955; Himalayan Pocket Books, New Delhi, 1976. Set in Delhi and Aligarh, this is the story of a boy of unknown parentage growing up in a Muslim family. By following the picaresque mode, but avoiding personal involvement in the narrative, Abbas exploits the life of Anwar as a means of focusing light on the impact of some of the major political events, including the Jallianwala Bagh massacre, during the years 1919–32.

Mulk Raj Anand, *Untouchable,* Lawrence and Wishart, London, 1935; The Bodley Head, London, 1970; Hind Pocket Books, Delhi, 1973 (paperback). This novel about the Indian caste system clearly shows the influence of Gandhi's teachings upon Anand, and was in fact written during the author's stay in Gandhi's *ashram* in 1932. The hero is Bakha, an eighteen-year-old untouchable, who is a sweeper employed to clean out latrines, and the theme is Bakha's spiritual crisis, which, because the novel is a deeply committed piece of social writing, seems to involve the whole of India. E. M. Forster said of it: 'Avoiding rhetoric and circumlocution, it has gone straight to the heart of its subject and purified it.'

Mulk Raj Anand, *Coolie,* Lawrence and Wishart, London, 1936; The Bodley Head, London, 1972; Hind Pocket Books, Delhi, 1974 (paperback). The story of Munco, a young hillboy who deserts his homelands for the cities of the plains, full of the joyful expectations of earning his own living and gaining wider vistas. But the only kinds of work he can find consist of degrading drudgery that denies the human spirit. He goes from one job to another, each bringing worse suffering and degradation than the one before. Himself warm-hearted, comradely and full of curiosity and the joy of living, he is battered and pounded and exploited by a cash-conscious society, until he dies of tuberculosis.

Zulfikar Ghose, *Confessions of a Native-Alien,* Routledge and Kegan Paul, London, 1965. Ghose is not a Bengali (his 'Ghose' is a corruption of his father's name 'Ghaus' but 'emphasises the feeling of not belonging'). This well-written autobiography is free of political bias, has sustained human interest and is particularly noteworthy for the delineation of the author's childhood and the recapitulation of his feelings about the Partition of India in 1947.

Anita Desai, *Bye-Bye, Blackbird,* Hind Pocket Books, Delhi, 1971. This novel is about the experiences of Indian immigrants in Britain; Sen, comfortably settled and married to an Englishwoman, returns on a visit to India, while Dev, full of enthusiasm for India, arrives in England for the first time. This reversal of situations enables the novelist to explore the two characters' relationships with India's rich past and seemingly maze-like present, as well as with British attitudes to immigrants.

Ruth Prawer Jhabvala, *An Experience of India,* John Murray, London, 1971. A collection of short stories which deal with the cultural differences between Europeans and Indians. These differences point to different attitudes to life, and seem to reflect the Polish-born, Europe-educated Mrs Jhabvala's difficulties in adjusting to India. She is tolerant but alienated; though her involvement in Indian life is not emphatic, it is genuine and convincing, with a shrewd insight into the more obvious aspects of life in India. The Introduction, 'Myself in India', gives the novelist's views about her adopted land.

Kamala Markandaya, *The Nowhere Man,* Allen Lane, London, 1973; Orient Longman, New Delhi, 1976 (paperback). Like Anita Desai's *Bye-Bye, Blackbird* (above) and Timeri Murari's *The Marriage* (below), *The Nowhere Man* scrutinises the position of Indian immigrants in Britain. The central character, Srinivas, has been long settled in England and the story is about his attempts to cope with steadily increasing white prejudice and violence against coloured immigrants.

Ved Mehta, *Face to Face: An Autobiography,* Little, Brown, Boston, USA 1957; Weidenfeld and Nicholson, London, 1970. Mehta is a non-Sikh Punjabi and has been blind since the age of three. *Face to Face* is a recollection of his life from childhood until he went to a school for the blind in the United States: it is particularly valuable as an accurate portrayal of the Punjabi family, with a lively account of a Punjabi wedding, and of the struggle of a disabled child to adjust himself to a world which he could not see.

Ved Mehta, *Daddyji,* Secker and Warburg, London, 1972. '. . . The first of a series of books I hope to write exploring my own history' outlined in *Face to Face,* it is written not 'from the fragments of my memory', as the former is, but 'from the testimony of all the witnesses I could find to talk to'. Mehta's relaxed and limpid style is admirably suited to such an engaging account of Indian family life in the progression from peasantry to the professions. *Mamaji,* the second volume in the series, was published in 1979.

Timeri Murari, *The Marriage,* Macmillan, Delhi, 1973. A grimly realistic novel about the exploitation of immigrant labour in the Midlands, with some of the immigrants choosing for the sake of gain to align themselves with the exploiters. Murari deals ably with the cultural tensions among the immigrant population, who try very hard to maintain rigid Indian conventions in family life while unable to do so at school or work.

Chaman Mahal, *Azadi,* Arnold Heinemann, New Delhi, 1975; André Deutsch, London, 1977. A novel that tells the straightforward story of a Hindu family that has long lived peacefully and comfortably among its Muslim neighbours in the Punjab, until the Partition of India in 1947. Their plight is vividly and movingly presented as they flee from home during the disturbances and then try to make a new life in India.

R. K. Narayan, *Swami and Friends,* (London, 1935); Indian Thought Publications, Mysore, 1944 (paperback). This is a simple story about a boy, Swami, and his adventures with his friends, set in the fictional town of Malgudi, which figures in most of Marayan's novels and gives an extraordinarily authentic portrayal of a South Indian town. Professor K. R. S. Iyengar describes the plan of the novel as consisting of 'a flight, an uprooting, a disturbance of order — followed by a return, a renewal, a restoration of normalcy', during which the boy-hero grows emotionally and comes to terms with his own weaknesses and virtues.

R. K. Narayan, *The Guide,* Indian Thought Publications, Mysore, 1958; The Bodley Head, London, 1970. One of the finest of Narayan's novels, it is about Raju, who begins his career as a news-stall holder on Malgudi station and gradually sets himself up as a guide to tourists, conducting them about the area and telling them what they like to hear. He becomes a full-time impressario to a woman dancer, misappropriates some of her funds and goes to jail. On his release a peasant mistakes him for a holy man, and because the error brings Raju offerings of food, etc., from the local populace, he plays along with it, until, quite imperceptibly, he fulfils genuinely the role he has simply been acting at. He sacrifices his life like a saint, and one is left wondering just where the confidence-trickster merged into the holy man. The book is full of subtle echoes of the life of Indian spirituality, but simultaneously ironic and down to earth.

R. M. Narayan, *Gods, Demons and Others,* Heinemann, London, 1965; Hind Pocket Books, Delhi, 1979 (paperback). Unlike Narayan's other books, this collection of short stories is not concerned with modern life, but gathers together Narayan's own re-tellings of classical myths and legends from the *Ramayana* and the *Mahabharata.* Narayan has himself claimed that all imaginative writing in India has its origin in these two Sanskrit classics, which continue to serve as models both for traditional story-telling in the villages and for urban and urbane written literature.

R. K. Narayan, *A Horse and Two Goats,* The Bodley Head, London, 1970; Hind Pocket Books, Delhi, 1977 (paperback). Short stories, not retellings of legends, but original creations which reflect much of the ethos of the classical Indian myths. Beneath the surface of modern life, Narayan's subdued and at times very subtle irony suggests the exploration of the relationship between human beings and their gods. It conveys superbly the feel of the South Indian countryside and the ordinary country folk, with all their foolishnesses and their shrewdnesses.

Raja Rao, *Kanthapura,* Allen and Unwin, London, 1938; Hind Pocket Books, Delhi, 1971 (paperback). This novel deals with the powerful influence of Gandhi and his ideas on a simple village near Bombay in the 1930s. Raja Rao is concerned not so much with the sociological aspect, though it is implicit, as with the way in which the villagers' simple minds transform a political movement into a myth. He successfully re-creates in English the Indian mode of telling a folktale — repetitive and seemingly interminable.

Kushwant Singh, *Train to Pakistan,* Chatto and Windus, London, 1956; India Book House, Bombay, 1977 (paperback). A somewhat documentary, but very readable, account of the human atrocities that followed the Partition of India in 1947, it centres upon the ill-fated love between a Sikh youth and a young Muslim woman. His selfless sacrifice of his own life saves a train-load of Muslim refugees from slaughter and contrasts with the complacency of officialdom and the ease with which ordinary villagers allow themselves to be influenced by zealots.

Kushwant Singh, *I shall not Hear the Nightingale,* John Calder, London, 1959. Particularly interesting for its depiction of a Sikh household and for the effective translation of the earthy flavour of the rhythms and idioms of colloquial Punjabi speech into English (e.g. 'Sardar Sahib, you are a big man and we are but small radishes from an unknown garden').

ARTHUR RAVENSCROFT
School of English,
University of Leeds;
and
DEVINDRA KOHLI
Department of English,
Ramjas College,
Delhi

BOOKS IN ENGLISH WITH PAKISTANI AND SIKH SETTINGS

Twilight in Delhi, Ahmed Ali, Hogarth Press, London, 1940; Sterling, New Delhi, 1973. This novel by a writer and scholar who became one of the first of Pakistan's ambassadors abroad is a recording, and elegaic celebration, of the fast-fading Muslim culture of Old Delhi early in the twentieth century. The private concerns of Muslim families are presented against a rich background of life within the old city walls, later demolished by the British.

The next two titles provide vivid fictional encounters with Muslim culture as rooted in, and expressed by, the ways of life of the ordinary people of what is now Pakistan:

Folktales of Pakistan, Masudul Hasan, Ferozsons, Lahore, 1978.

Stories from Rumi, Maulana Rumi, Ferozsons, Lahore, 1976; 100 stories translated from the Persian by Masudal Hasan.

WEST INDIAN WRITERS IN ENGLISH

STORIES BY WEST INDIAN WRITERS INTENDED OR SUITABLE FOR YOUNGER SCHOOLCHILDREN

Andrew Salkey, *Hurricane*, Oxford University Press 1964; *Earthquake*, Oxford University Press, 1965; *Drought*, Oxford University Press, 1966; *Riot*, Oxford University Press, 1967; *The Shark Hunters*, Nelson, 1966; *Jonah Simpson*, Oxford University Press, 1969. Each of these titles is a novel specially written for children; in each of the first four, children are placed in the exciting and alarming situation suggested by its title and are convincingly shown to cope with the difficulties. Salkey won the German Children's Book Prize in 1967, but he is also a distinguished writer of adult novels, a poet and an anthologist of West Indian writing.

P.M. Sherlock, *West Indian Folktales*, Oxford University Press, 1965. A collection of folktales from the West Indies, some of which are suitable for reading aloud or retelling to younger schoolchildren.

Michael Anthony, *The Year in San Fernando*, André Deutsch, London, 1965; Heinamann, London, 1970 (paperback). A simply told story about a young Trinidadian boy from the country who goes to live in the big town of San Fernando, and how he develops under the impact of many new experiences. Interesting for children as a story, and for adults as a delicate and perceptive understanding of a child's mind.

George Lamming, *In the Castle of My Skin*, Michael Joseph, London, 1963; Longman, London, 1970 (paperback). A very fine, semi-autobiographical novel about a young schoolboy's life in Barbados, as he grows up during the Second World War and begins to understand the relationship between employers and employees and between white plantation owners and black workers on the island. It gives an intimate insight into the kind of childhood in the West Indies that many of the immigrants into Britain of the 1950s experienced.

ADULT BOOKS BY WEST INDIAN WRITERS SUITABLE FOR SECONDARY SCHOOL PUPILS

Michael Anthony, *Green Days By the River*, André Deutsch, London, 1967; Heinemann, London, 1973 (paperback). An adult novel presented through the consciousness of a boy-narrator, which unfolds his learning how to accommodate himself to the difficulties of adult life, and his first experiences of the conflicts between passion and responsibility in a Caribbean setting.

237

E. R. Braithwhite, *To Sir, with Love*, The Bodley Head, London, 1959; New English Library, London, 1968 (paperback). This book about a West Indian immigrant teacher in a tough comprehensive school in London hardly needs any introduction. It is probably the most widely known West Indian novel in Britain, because of the film based upon it, though its popularity owes a good deal to a sentimentalising of the immigrant position less likely to occur in other novels on this list.

E. R. Braithwaite, *A Choice of Straws*, The Bodley Head, London, 1965; Pan Books, London, 1968 (paperback). A humane and rational novel about an inhuman and irrational subject. A pair of East London lads, twins, attack and kill a West Indian, and in escaping from the scene one of them (the actual murderer) is killed in a car crash. The story is about the survivor learning how complicated the whole matter of white–black relationship is.

Wilson Harris, *Palace of the Peacock*, Faber, London, 1960: Faber Paperback, London, 1968. The first novel by this very unconventional novelist, it is set in Guyana and is the 'story' of the trip up a great Guyanese river by a group of men representing the various racial origins of the people of Guyana. Harris deliberately confuses the 'normal' conventions of novel writing, and the crew are both twentieth-century characters and members of an historical seventeenth-century expedition. Their identities and personalities interplay and merge, while the journey comes to assume the symbolism of a spiritual quest. The Guyanese landscape is described with great vividness and power.

R. A. K. Heath, *A Man Come Home*, Longman, London, 1974. K. Ramchand describes this novel as 'Heath's attempt to combine a realistic story of Georgetown [Guyana] lower-class life with a well-known piece of Guyanese folklore (the "fair maid" who loves a human being, wins him with riches and then destroys him because he wants to return to his human love)'.

Ismit Khan, *The Obeah Man*, Hutchinson, London, 1964. A novel about a West Indian obeah man who practises 'magic', and his realisation that the success of his magic depends not on the supernatural but upon his own dedication to the task of understanding his clients' psychological make-up as well as his own. The story gives the reader some understanding of West African respect for 'magic' and the supernatural.

Edgar Mittelholzer, *My Bones and My Flute* (London, 1955); New English Library, London, 1974 (paperback). Although this novel shows such typical Mittelholzer preoccupations as Guyanese social history and landscapes as well as the supernatural, it is chiefly an unprentious ghost yarn likely to titillate readers of all ages swing to its skilful handling of atmosphere and racy narratives.

V. S. Naipaul, *Miguel Street*, André Deutsch, London, 1959; Penguin,

London, 1973 (paperback). A collection of connected sketches, mostly humorous, sometimes satirical, about life in the poorer quarter of Port of Spain, Trinidad, seen through the eyes of a group of youthful friends. It gives a vivid impression of growing up in a West Indian urban setting.

V. S. Naipaul, *The Mystic Massuer*, André Deutsch, London, 1957; Heinemann, London, 1971 (paperback). Ganesh the chief character in this amusingly satirical novel, exploits the hunger of his fellow-Trinidadians of East Indian origin for assurances that things Indian have not entirely disappeared from the Caribbean, first by setting himself up as a holy man, but later as a political leader — who steadily becomes anglicised and ends up as Ganesh Ramsumair, MBE.

V. S. Naipaul, *A House for Mr Biswas*, André Deutsch, London, 1961; Penguin, London, 1969 (paperback). A long novel about a Trinidadian of East Indian origin who pits himself against society in general and the restrictions of a dying East Indian culture in Trinidad, to cut out for himself an individual life of his own, symbolised in his efforts to build a separate house for himself and his immediate family. It is both a satirical presentation of deracination caused by imperialism in the past and a celebration of freedom from ways of life that have become irrelevant in the present.

Andrew Salkey, *Come Home, Malcolm Heartland*, Hutchinson, London, 1976. An extremely sober novel about a middle-aged lawyer from the West Indies deciding to return to his island just when he sees that the young British blacks of Brixton are finding a new identity and aggressive solidarity for themselves. A novel eminently suitable for discussion because, although Malcom is sympathetic to 'the knife thrust of Black consciousness', he questions its outcome, and the novelist himself seems unresolved on the central issue.

Sam Selvon, *The Lonely Londoners*, Wingate, London, 1956; Longman, London, 1972 (paperback). This is the classic novel about the first decade or so of West Indian immigrant experience of London. It gives comically, but with a sharp, underlying pathos, a very vivid impression of the bewilderment of the first immigrants in the search for jobs and homes in the 1950s, their nostalgia for the tropical Caribbean, their loneliness is an unfriendly city. The dialogue consists of skilfully modified Trinidardian dialect, which can be readily understood by non-West Indian readers. A companion piece to this book, in much the same mode, is Selvon's *The Housing Lark*, MacGibbon and Kee, London, 1965.

Sam Selvon, *Moses Ascending*, Davis-Poynter, London, 1975. Another treatment of the immigrant experience of Britain, but after twenty years of it the comparative geniality of *The Lonely Londoners* and *The Housing Lark* is replaced by a grimmer mood. The West Indian

Moses has materially 'made good' in a small way, by aping the shoddy methods of English landlords and even acquiring a white servant. The book is full of such ironic reversals; the satire, whether of 'liberal' whites or of Black Power groups, is very pungent indeed.

Derek Walcott, *Another Life*, Jonathan Cape, London, 1974. This, a full-length autobiographical poem, is one of the finest works of the creative imagination to have come out of the West Indies. It describes the physical, mental, emotional and intellectual growth of the poet from boyhood and youth to maturity, as he works out for himself a genuine West Indian identity.

Derek Walcott, *Dream on Monkey Mountain and Other Plays*, Jonathan Cape, London, 1972. This volume contains, in addition to the title play, *Ti-Jean and His Brothers, Malcochon* and *The Sea at Dauphin*, in which Walcott has evolved a distinctive drama based upon such indigenous West Indian folk activities as singing, story-telling, and dancing: an emphasis, thus, on bodily expression reacting with richly metaphoric dialogue that draws discriminately upon colloquial West Indian speech.

ARTHUR RAVENSCROFT

School of English,
University of Leeds

INDIAN STORIES IN ENGLISH FOR CHILDREN

A mixture of folktales, stories of Indian life and religious tales, many of them in the Indian idiom.

J. E. G. Gray, *Indian Tales and Legends*, Oxford University Press. An attractively presented collection of stories in the epic of Rama and Sita.

A. W. E. Crown, *Folk Tales of the World – India*, E. J. Arnold. Eight attractively presented stories including that of Rama, Sita and Hanuman.

R. Thapar, *Indian Tales*, Bell.

M. Frere, *Hindu Fairy Tales,* Dover. An interesting collection of folk tales made in the mid-nineteenth century.

C. Turnbull, *Indian Fairy Tales,* Muller.

R. K. Wilson, *Fairy Tales of India,* Cassell.

B. L. Picard, *Story of the Pandavas*, Harrap. Some of the important stories well told.

R. Mehta, *Ramu: A Story of India,* Angus & Watson. Ramu, an Indian boy looks forward to *Diwali* with some anxiety. Will the goddess Lakshmi visit his home or not?

Sister Nivedita, *Cradle Tales of Hinduism*, Advaita Ashrama. Many of the best known tales told to Indian children.

B. L. Picard, *The Story of Rama and Sita,* Harrap.

I. Macfarlane, *Tales and Legends from India,* Chatto.

D. G. Mukerji, *Gayneck,* Angus & Waton. The adventures of a pigeon above its native city of Calcutta but also in the Himalayas and in Flanders in 1914.

R. Mehta, *The Life of Keshav,* Angus & Watson. Keshav, a poor village boy who gets the chance of an education.

J. C. Jain, *A Treasury of Tales,* Echo Books. Ancient Indian stories retold.

Anjali Pal, *Tales of Humour from Bengal,* Echo Books. Tales of the commonplace and magical in the Indian tradition.

S. Keshar, *Tales The Ramayana Tells,* Echo Books. A few of the many stories: retold by an Indian.

K. Chaitanya, *Shakuntala and Damayanti,* Echo Books. Two of the famous epics of India.

H. Chatto-Padhyaya, *The Queen's Parrot and the King's Ape,* Echo Books. A collection of poems for young children.

E. de Souza, *All About Birbal,* Echo Books. Fifteen stories about a friend of the Emperor Akbar.

S. Gangoli, *Kidnappers at Nandipur,* Echo Books. A collection of adventure stories in which youngsters outwit a variety of criminals.

(Echo Books are available from the Independent Publishing Co., 38 Kennington Lane, London, SE11.

The following books published by the New Dehli Children's Book Trust of India are available from Oxfam, 274 Banbury Road, Oxford, OX2 7DZ. Mostly for young primary school children.

Bommaka. The story of a courageous buffalo.

The Elephants and the Mice. An Indian fable illustrating the need for great and small to live in harmony.

Mahagiri. The story of a courageous elephant.

Mother is Mother. A small boy learns that a squirrel's place is with its mother.

Swarup's Returns. Monsoons and floods and poor villagers who eventually manage to make ends meet.

Four Brothers. Jealousy divides them, a wise father reunites them.

Hari and Other Elephants. Stories of how elephants feel, think and behave.

Tiger Tales. Six sensitive stories about tigers — what they feel, how they think and behave.

Life with Grandfather. Indian background, temples, caste and crocodiles.

USING THE RESOURCES

The subject of this section is the use of resources (mainly books) for multi-faith schools or for teaching about world religions other than Christianity. The material available is assessed critically for the benefit of teachers trying to find a way through this subject.

BOOKS AS CULTURAL BACKGROUND

There is a difference, which must influence our teaching, between the multi-faith school and the school which is uni-cultural whose pupils have a Christian background. With adherents of other faiths, Jews, Hindus, Muslims and Sikhs usually present in the classroom, it is essential from the outset to recognise their presence and refer to their cultures sooner and in a more detailed way than one might in a uni-cultural school.

Therefore, one would find on the teacher's shelf or in the class library some of the books published by India Book House (which I obtained from W. H. Smith). Some titles are *Tales the Ramayana Tells*, *Shakuntala and Damayanti*, *Indian Fables and Fairy Tales*, *Princess Vasavadatta* and an anthology of poems, *The Queen's Parrot and the King's Ape*. These books are not well produced but they are authentically Indian and this is their value. By failing to include Indian or Afro–Caribbean tales in the stories we tell in the multi-cultural classroom we are, by implication, expressing the view that they have no stories worth telling. In rejecting the culture we are rejecting the children. Other Indian books can be obtained from 'Oxfam'. These are published by the Children's Book Trust, New Delhi.

Perhaps it had better be pointed out that many of these stories are not obviously or explicitly religious and contain no moral, they are simply Indian stories.

PITFALLS IN RELIGIOUS TEXTS

In using religious material two words of warning need to be uttered. First, as we move away from indiscriminatingly telling the miracle stories of Jesus to primary school children, we should not begin to tell the Buddhist or Sikh equivalents, for example, the story of Guru Nanak healing the leper of Depalpur, or the story of Guru Amar Das and the leper Prema whose lost limbs were restored as he confessed his new Sikh faith. These are extremely significant narratives, as the Christian miracle stories are. They make the point that, like Jesus, the Gurus received and did not shun lepers. They must not be devalued by being relegated to the level of pious stories of magic for telling to six-year-olds.

This is the great problem which one has with regard to Mrs C. M. Kay's book *Story of Stories*. It is an interesting and enjoyable collection of material from eleven religious traditions, but the birth stories of Abraham and Moses, the gazelle which talked to Muhammad, the blood which came from the bread which Malik Bhago gave to Guru Nanak, these are not stories for young children.

The other word of warning is with regard to myth, a term here used in its technical religious sense and not as a derogatory term! Hinduism, in particular, is rich in myth. Many of them are included in *Indian Tales and Legends* by J. E. B. Gray, or, with some explanation, in *Myths and Legends of India* by J. N. Macfie, T. & T. Clark. With younger children these can be told simply as fascinating stories, but the teacher needs to remember that they are more than fairy tales (some anthologies quite wrongly describe them in this way). With children in the middle years, somewhere between twelve and fourteen, it is vital that the teacher should return to these stories as well as to those of the Judaeo–Christian tradition, and help them discover how to understand myths together with legends, epics, parable and miracle stories. Such a book as *Beginnings* by Fahr and Spoerl (Beacon Press) may help here. So long as this is done there seems to be no reason why the Ramayana, for example, should not be told.

If this teacher reads *Gods, Demons and Others* by Narayan (Heinemann) the flavour of Indian storytelling will be obtained — and also the realisation that Indians like their stories as they like their curries, not necessarily hot, but with a rich variety which can be savoured with relish! Often the teacher needs to simplify complex Indian stories for the benefit of English listeners.

BACKGROUND FOR TEACHERS

The teacher in a multi-faith school needs to know something of the beliefs and way of life of children. *Comparative Religions*, edited by W. O. Cole (Blandford) is of value in this respect and may be supplemented by the *Scope* Handbook I, the chapter on 'The Ethics and Customs of the Main Immigrant Peoples' by Professor G. Parrinder in *Comparative Religion in Education*, edited by J. Hinnells, or by *The Background of Immigrant Children* by Ivor Morrish (Allen & Unwin). C.E.M.'s own *Probe* No. 14, *Community Relations*, though written for secondary pupils, is a convenient summary of five religious cultures. The book by Ivor Morrish quoted above goes some way to helping the English teacher to understand the concepts of schools and religion which the child and his parents are likely to have. This is of particular importance for understanding Muslim children from Pakistan. If they have had a previous experience of education, it is likely to have been in a school dedicated to the fostering of Islamic faiths and cultures. They therefore expect the English educational system to be devoted to the promotion of Christianity!

IT'S A SMALL WORLD

Where teachers have no Muslims or Sikhs in their primary school classes, they seem to fall into two groups, those who argue that the absence of immigrants means that there is no need to mention other faiths and cultures, and those who, because of their interest in the Orient in particular, include material about Hinduism or Buddhism in what they teach. *Britain is a multi-cultural society*. The East is with us and one hopes teachers in Ripon or Wells may prepare their children for the Sikhs or West Indians they will see when they do their Christmas shopping in Leeds or Bristol. Besides *Religions Round the World* by L. and C. Wolcott or the *Bodhi Tree* by Greta James, it is hoped *Ramu* by R. Mehta, *Gayneck* by D. C. Mukerji (both Angus & Watson) which describe life in India, will find a place in the classroom and also Peter Bridger's *Hindu Family in Britain* (Religious Education Press), and other titles in this series as they become available.

Both *Hindu Family in Britain* and *Sikh Family in Britain* have been written by Englishmen though, of course, with considerable Hindu and Sikh help. To persuade the new settlers to produce books about their beliefs and cultures for use in school is not easy, but one hopes that as they settle into British society and know more about our schools, they will feel freer to make their contribution. Meanwhile, we must beware of misrepresenting their beliefs and suggesting that Hinduism, Sikhism, Islam or (and this is, of course, a real problem) Judaism, are merely preparatory to the Gospel. *The Developing World* series of Longmans, their history books as well as those on religion, accept a progressive evolutionary view of man; this is disastrous for the books on religion, for though their presentation is attractive and they are the result of much hard work, they imply that *the* religion is Christianity. In the *Bodhi Tree* by Greta James, one cannot help asking why, on the final page, she tells this story. 'Before he died the Buddha foretold that 500 years later there would be born on earth another Buddha, another Enlightened One, and men would call him the Teacher of Brotherly Love, and he would be the Christ and Saviour of the Western peoples. And so it was, for Jesus was born 500 years afterwards and he became the great teacher for men in the western world — Europe, Britain and America.'

SOME GAPS

One book written by an Indian is *The Story of Gandhi*, by Rajkumari Shanker (available through Oxfam). The teacher will find it interesting to compare this version with *Gandhi*, by Taya Zinkin, and so might some able 13–14 year olds if they are asked to compare, say, the treatments of Gandhi's journey from Durban to Pretoria (Zinkin. pp. 53–8, Shanker, pp. 26–8), the Salt Marsh (Zinkin, pp. 150–56, Shanker, pp. 95–101f.). Rather than think in terms of which biography we prefer, we should perhaps be asking what each writer is attempting to convey. All too soon students, teachers and tutors begin asking for the one book which in the minimum time can produce all the answers. It does not seem desirable to encourage this approach to learning among our children.

Generally speaking, one must be on one's guard against books which try to cover ten or so religions in a sweep. If one looks at the treatment given to Christianity in such books one can begin to assess the adequacy of the section on, say, Islam. E. G. Parrinder in *A Book of World Religions* was the first person to attempt this with the classroom in mind and the only one to succeed. One is better advised to buy the relevant Ward Lock books (intended for 14–16 year olds), or the REP books mentioned above, or the Lutterworth 'Understanding' and 'Thinking About' series.

In the same way caution must be exercised with regard to radio programmes and filmstrips. If they are used carefully the filmstrips on Hinduism, Islam and Sikhism produced by Concordia and Educational Productions and that on 'Judaism' by Concordia can be very helpful and are suitable for use with 9–13 year olds, but no sensitive teacher would think of 'doing' a religion in 30 minutes in this way!

It is time now for broadcasters and the makers of filmstrips to turn from attempts to put a whole religion into a package of 20 minutes or 50 slides and to concentrate instead on one particular aspect — as 'Quest' did for example, in its programme on the Passover, though Barmitzvah and Kiddush had to be added as fillers spoiling the unity of an otherwise very interesting programme. The Slide Centre and Ann and Bury Peerless are doing precisely this.

The booklists indicate what is available. This section has commented upon the use of some of the material; in closing perhaps one may indicate needs.

First — pictures. As yet there appear to be few apart from some on Judaism. The teacher must manufacture her own using Air India or Islamic Book Centre calendars and the like.

In the record libraries of big cities it may be possible to obtain readings from the *Qur'an*, or the Muslim call to prayer. Argo Stereo ZFB-54 Religions of the Middle East includes both of these, and by

245

combining them with some frames taken from the available filmstrips on Islam, the teacher can produce his own 'radio vision' lesson on a visit to the mosque or 'Muslims at Worship'. This will have to do until some firm markets a package for him to use.

(Pictorial Charts Educational Trust, 27 Kirchen Road, W. Ealing London W13 0UD, are now moving into the religious studies poster market.)

SOME USEFUL ADDRESSES

Many others are given in *World Religions: A Handbook for Teachers*. The purpose of this list is to direct the reader to those agencies which are particularly interested in religious education in a multi-cultural society.

The Shap Working Party on World Religions in Education, c/o Bishop Otter College, West Sussex Institute of Higher Education, College Lane, Chichester PO19 4PE. Publishes the annual *Shap Mailing*.

The Committee for Relations with People of Other Faiths, British Council of Churches, 2 Eaton Gate, London SW1 9BL.

The Christian Education Movement, 2 Chester House, Pages Lane, London N10 1PR. It is the publisher of the *British Journal of Religious Education*.

The Commission for Racial Equality, Elliot House, 10/12 Allington Street, London SW1E 5EH.

The Commonwealth Institute, Kensington High Street, London W8 6NQ.

The National Association for Multicultural Education, c/o Doles Lane, Findern, Derby DE6 6AX. Publishes the journal *Multiracial Education*.

Independent Publishing Company, Soma Books, 38 Kennington Lane, London SE11. A bookshop geared to the needs of teachers in multi-cultural schools.

Ann and Bury Peerless, 22 King's Avenue, Minnis Bay, Birchington, Kent, CT7 9QL. Publishers of slide sets on most major world religions.

Argus Communications, Edinburgh Way, Harlow, Essex, CM20 2HL. Publishers of audio-visual studies on the major world religions.

Extramural Division, School of Oriental and African Studies, Malet Street, London WC1 7HP. Organises many courses on world religions for teachers.

PART 5: STORIES

INTRODUCTION

The thematic approach to religious education is an extremely popular one, especially in the primary school. It is a way of exploring abstract concepts through concrete, real-life situations. For example, a theme on courage might be by asking children what was the most courageous thing they had ever done. 'Jumping off a wall', 'Going to the dentist,' 'Saying I was sorry', might be some of the answers, immediately showing that there are a number of sorts of courage. This might be pursued further. One might then look at famous examples which catch the children's imagination, but being careful not to make courage so remote from their lives that they regard it as the preserve of astronauts, explorers and princes, and beyond the possibilities of ordinary man and woman.

Hitherto these people, listed in Agreed Syllabuses have all been white Christians; integrity demands that we recognise that courage is not a peculiarly Christian virtue. (England has had its Bradlaughs Huxleys and Russells). In a multi-cultural society it must be acknoweldged, in the curriculum, that it is not confined to white people.

The following stories and booklists are intended to help the teacher correct the balance. Much work remains to be done in this direction and this is merely a beginning. The stories themselves should be regarded as raw material and the compilers of this book recognise that they are inflicting something of a burden (not too great, it is hoped) upon the teacher to supply the background information and pictures which are necessary if these stories are to live for the children who hear them. They are, let it be said, authentic. That is, the Sikh and Muslim stories were collected by Sikh and Muslims and are stories told to children of those faiths.

The Hindu examples fall into the same category but are fewer in number because collections of stories, folk tales and myths exist in fair abundance and can easily be obtained. It is hoped that before long members of the Muslim or Sikh communities of Britain will meet what is now an urgent need and that '*Ramu*' and '*The life of Keshav*', or the '*Sweet Vendor*' might have its equally enjoyable Pakistani or Sikh counterpart.

One would like to assure the Christian teacher that in using this material she is not in consequence undermining the Christian faith. In

Christianity is true and dedicated to the truth it cannot be harmed by the fair presentation of other faiths. Sufficient inter-faith contact has now been established for us to know that Muhammad preached and demonstrated brotherly love and the Muslim practises hospitality, that the third Sikh Guru, Amar Das, established a leprosarium and that Sikhs have often cared for the sick and protected the oppressed. In the past the truth of one faith has sometimes been proclaimed by mispresenting others. We now humbly recognise this. So that a true dialogue may be established one hopes the teacher will use these stories to prevent children obtaining such false beliefs as the one that only Christians care. It is after all in the realm of belief and doctrine rather than ethics that particular religions claim to be unique, though in Hinduism, Sikhism and in Islam it is possible to find the statement that God is love.

Whoever uses this raw material is asked to remember the dictum of Canon Max Warren.

Our first task in approaching another people, another culture, another religion, is to take off our shoes, for the place we are approaching is holy. Else we may find ourselves treading on men's dreams. (Introduction to the *Christian Presence* seriés. SCM Press)

HINDU STORIES

INTRODUCTION

A Western visitor once complained about the dearth of children's stories in India. Hardly could a reality be more misperceived and a judgement more mistaken. India seems to have an almost inexhaustible fund of stories, accumulated over many centuries and little known in the West. Even today the oral tradition is still alive in India. As the sacred scriptures were handed down through verbal recitation before they found their fixed written form, so also were the stories which often form part of the scriptures, transmited from one generation to the next by word of mouth. The various stories have their written form but it is less through reading than through hearing that Indians learn about them. Even today the stories are largely known through being retold by grandmothers and mothers, through being recited by bards and professional storytellers, or through being dramatised by a wandering theatre-troupe.

If we look at the wealth of Hindu mythology, it may often appear rather like a jungle in which we get lost than a treasure from which we might benefit. However, this may be more due to our lack of familiarity with the setting and background of the stories than to an intrinsic quality of the related material. Yet it is a fact that the mythological stories neither follow a strict logical sequence nor is their content precisely fixed. They form a rather loose series with fluid boundaries. Thus there is no 'authorised version' of a story in the strict sense of the word; each storyteller may adapt and shape the actual form of his story according to the needs of his audience.

There seems to be a story to fit any occasion and to illustrate any facet of life. In a culture where the religious and secular have been so closely interwoven, it would be artificial and anachronic to separate 'religious stories' from the rest. As the stories reflect the whole spectrum of man's life, it is taken for granted that the religious dimension is an integral part of this. All stories are meant to teach something; they have a 'moral' which may consist in showing the merits and demeritsof a particular attitude or action, or in reflecting man's pattern of life, his joys and his struggles, his duties as well as his rewards. The stories may be about kings or ordinary people, about gods and goddesses, about man's love and hatred, or about man's search beyond himself.

The major sources of Indian stories are found in the epics, the *Ramayana* and in particular the *Mahabharata*, and in the later religious writings called *Puranas*. The collection of stories most easily understandable for the English reader is perhaps Sister Nivedita's *Cradle*

Tales of Hinduism, although the background of the individual stories is not explained. (The book is available from the Ramakrishna Vedanta Centre, Unity House, Blind Alley East, Bourne End, Bucks SL8 59L.)

Given the great wealth of Indian story-material, the choice of the two following stories must of necessity be arbitrary. In order to give a more representative sample of Indian mythological stories, it woud have been appropriate to have at least one story from each of the epics, one story about each of the two major gods Siva and Vishnu, and another story about each of their consorts or some other goddesses. Unfortunately, this has not been possible in the present collection.

The two stories have been chosen not only because they are widely known (which would be true of a great many other stories) but also because they can be understood without knowing too much about their background. The stories have been simplified in order to avoid too many unknown names and they are presented in such a way that the religious message can be conveyed to a child. The first story is a village tale and the second is one of the many stories from the *Mahabharata*. The first story is easier to understand because it is less complex than the second one. Both stories may be found in a more elaborate form in *Cradle Tales of Hinduism*, which is equally useful as a source-book for other stories.

1 THE STORY OF GOPALA

Gopala was a little Indian boy who had very kind and good parents. His father and mother were poor but they put all their trust in the divine child Krishna. They loved Krishna so much that they named their son 'Gopala', which means 'cowherd' — for Krishna had once lived in this world as a simple cowherd.

Gopala's mother prayed to Krishna every day. She also burnt incense before his picture and decorated it with flowers and garlands. And she taught her little boy many songs and stories about the divine child.

One day, the time had come for Gopala to start school. As his mother had much work to do and the way to school was not very far, she sent Gopala off on his own. But he had to go through some woods, and Gopala was a little frightened to be all by himself. On coming home, he said to his mother that he did not want to go to school again. So his mother told him a little story. She said: 'You know, I have another son called Gopala. He looks after the cows near the wood. So next time when you go to school and you are frightened again, you only need to call him: "O brother cowherd, come with me to school" and he will come and take care of you.'

Gopala believed his mother. The next time when he went to school and felt frightened, Gopala called out for the cowherd as his mother had told him. He was filled with wonder when he suddenly saw a big boy appear who wore a little golden crown with a peacock's feather in it. The boy played with little Gopala and made all his fear disappear. He left him at the entrance of the school and asked Gopala to call out for him again on his way back home.

This Gopala did, and he told his mother what had happened, she was not in the least surprised that the child Krishna, whom she worshipped and loved so much, should take care of her son. Gopala now met the cowherd every day and grew fonder and fonder of his companion, who was always full of fun and at the same time so kind and gentle.

When one day the school was having a party and everybody had to bring a present. Gopala asked his cowherd friend to help him as his own mother was too poor to give him something. The cowherd had nothing but a little pot of sour milk — some curds which people always like because they make a refreshing drink. But, of course, it was only a small gift for a party.

Gopala took the pot of curd to school. But when the teacher poured the curd from the little pot into a larger vessel, he was surprised to see the little pot filling up again. He emptied it a second time, and again the pot was full. It happened again and again, and everybody asked with surprise where the curd had come from. Gopala replied that it came from his brother, the cowherd in the forest, and for the first time he began to realise that this cowherd was Krishna himself who had come to help him.

The teacher was curious to see this wonderful cowherd. But when Gopala took him to the woods and called out for his friend, nobody appeared. He called out once more and a voice replied from far: "Oh Gopala, I cannot come any more. My face remains hidden from all those who do not believe and trust me as your mother and you do.'

Commentary to 1

The story of Gopala comes from a village background. As there are thousands of villages in India, many well-known stories of gods, heroes and saints gets adapted to the local village situation and become at the same time further elaborated. Thus each region and language-group of the Indian subcontinent has its own tradition of stories.

As a rural and agricultural setting is the dominant background of most of India's inhabitants, it is not surprising that the cycle of legends woven around the figure of Krishna, the cowherd, have always enjoyed great popularity. Krishna is the human embodiment of the great god Vishnu who regularly comes into the world to help men in need. Krishna is also at the centre of a fervent cult of religious devotion, the *Bhakti* path (different from, but not opposed to the path of works and the path of knowledge which traditional Hinduism teaches as the three possible ways of man's union with the divine). The birth of the divine child Krishna is annually celebrated all over India (the feast *Janam Ashtami* in August) but especially at his place of birth in Vrindaban near Agra. The joy and religious impact of this festival are vividly described in K. Klostermaier's book *Hindu and Christian in Vrindaban* (SCM, 1970). There are innumerable stories about Krishna's childhood and youth, and about his love for the *gopis*, the milkmaids, especially for Radha. The cycle of Krishna legends has been an incessant inspiration for Indian painting, literature, music and dance through the ages. It is only with a certain knowledge of these stories and their message that one may hope to gain access to an understanding of the arts of India.

The story of Gopala should have an immediate appeal to children because it is so close to their own experience: going to school, having fear, not wanting to go to school again, a school party where everybody contributes something. But Gopala's mother has taught the child more than that. She has a fervent devotion to the divine child Krishna and performs daily *puja* to him (an explanation of this form of worship with the help of slides may be useful here). Through her example the little boy has learnt from early on to have an intense love for the divine child and a complete trust in his protection.

The story relates a legendary tale which stresses the wonderful and miraculous. But by doing so, it emphasises the love and trust which Gopala has learnt from his mother to set in a divine helper. This divine figure does not appear as a father figure but as a *companion* to the child, somebody commensurate to his own experience — an elder brother with whom Gopala can play and have fun, somebody who takes away the fear of the unknown, and yet who one day reveals himself as greater than a mere brother.

The golden crown and peacock feather are traditional attributes of the Krishna figure. Their mention here is a first indication of the fact that Gopala's companion is no ordinary cowherd, although the little boy does not realise this yet. The cowherd's hidden greatness is revealed to Gopala and his classmates only through the miraculous refilling of the pot of curds which one cannot explain in the terms of ordinary experience. Gopala, however, because of his faith in Krishna, understands what has happened and who the cowherd really is. In contrast to the believing child stands the doubtful teacher who is merely curious to find out but whose curiosity is not going to be satisfied. The divine child and helper has withdrawn and does not show himself to the incredulous, to those who do not believe or worship him.

This village tale which originated in and belongs to a completely different cultural context, may remind some readers of possible Christian comparisons (for example, the importance of the nativity festival;

the devotion to the child Jesus; the miracle of the multiplication of the loaves). The Hindu story of Gopala may perform a similar function in teaching a child the love of God, a deep devotion and trust in God's help, God's nearness and closeness to man as well as the complete gratuity of his giving — he cannot be forced into making himself available on request. This similarity may be enhanced by the quotation of another very short story:

The Lord Krishna and the Broken Pot
Now, the Lord Krishna was bidden by a certain rich man to a feast. And they set before Him many dishes. But His eye took note of a cup that by chance was blemished, and first this imperfect one He drew to Himself, and out of it began to eat. Which when the rich man saw, he fell at His feet and said, "Oh Lord, dealest Thou even thus with men? Choosest Thou always the broken vessel first?"
(Quoted from Sister Nivedita, *Cradle Tales of Hinduism*, p. 221.)

For other Krishna stories, see Sister Nivedita's book, or Veronica Ions, *Indian Mythology* (Paul Hamlyn, 1967) which contains several illustrations from paintings and sculpture.

2 KING YUDHISHTHIRA'S ASCENT TO HEAVEN

The great king Yudhishthira was always known as the king of justice and righteousness. In his old age he decided to leave his royal court and to practise the life of renunciation in the high Himalayas. There, amidst the great forests and the snow-peaked mountains, man can look back at his entire life, renounce all his desires and be freed from bondage. There, he can meditate in silence and gain deep inner peace.

On leaving the world, king Yudhishthira left everything behind except for his faithful dog. One day, he was wandering in the mountains when suddenly, in a cloud of light, Indra, the god of heaven, appeared before him in his chariot. Indra invited the great and just king to enter the chariot so that he might ascend to heaven with him. But Yudhishthira first wanted to know whether he would find his queen and brothers there. When the god Indra assured him of their presence in heaven, Yudhishthira was willing to come but only on condition that he could bring his faithful dog too. Now Indra argued with him that there was no place for a dog in heaven and that Yudhishthira had to leave him behind. But the king refused to separate himself from someone who had shown him such loyalty and devotion and who was too weak a creature to be left by himself.

When he was thus fervently pleading for the fate of the animal, the dog suddenly vanished and in his place stood the radiant Dharma the god of righteousness, who exclaimed: 'Praise to you, Yudhishthira, you have renounced the chariot of heaven on behalf of a dog. Happiness will be yours for ever.'

Yudhishthira then took a seat in the chariot and ascended to heaven. On arriving there he was surprised not to find his friends. He could only see his former enemies. The gods explained to him not to resent their presence, as in heaven all feuds come to an end. Yudhishthira could understand this but if those he had fought were in heaven, where were those he had loved?

When he pleaded to see them, a messenger led him away from the heavenly regions to a place of terror and darkness, a gloomy region where many souls suffer and long for light. Yudhishthira was shown all the terrors of hell but he had every right to return back to heaven. However, he heard the sighing of voices which implored him to stay. On listening more carefully, he recognised their familiar sound: they were the voices of his long lost brothers and queen. Was he awake or did he dream? Those he had hoped to find in heaven, he encountered in hell, whilst his former enemies were enjoying heavenly bliss. What injustice! Yudhishthira now refused to return back to heaven on his own. He was going to stay for ever with those he loved — he was going to share their misfortune and lighten their suffering through his presence.

When Yudhishthira had decided to remain with his people, he was suddenly surrounded by a blaze of light in which the gods appeared: 'You have seen the terrors of hell but the vision of your kinsmen is an illusion. Shed your mortal form and take your place in heaven where your brothers and friends already dwell. There, before Indra's throne, you will be united and enjoy never-ending glory.'

Commentary to 2

This is a well-known story from the vast source book of the *Mahabharata*, the great Indian epic. The latter is such a treasurehouse of stories that it is hardly surprising to see Sister Nivedita's *Cradle Tales of Hinduism* dedicated 'To all those souls who have grown to greatness by their children's love of the *Mahabharata*. The stories of the epic are told over and over again to an always untiring audience, which takes great delight in hearing about its favourite heroes.

Children and adults alike take in the stories and absorb them. Any message contained in the stories, whether specifically religious or not, is always implicit; it is usually not spelled out or articulated — like in a play on the stage (and many stories are meant to be played) or in a novel, it is up to the beholder or reader to work out the message and application of the story for himself.

The religious message of Hindu stories may not always be easy to detect for us. It is not only found in stories about gods or goddesses. On the contrary, a religious message may often be embedded in stories about particular men by describing their actions or attitudes to others.

The story about king Yudhishthira's ascent marks a certain dramatic climax: it is the end of the life of a very great king. But after the glorious battles and the many activities of the king's life, the story begins on a contrasting note. The king has chosen to withdraw and renounce the world completely. This is the theme of the great renunciation so familiar from Indian sources (cf. Buddha's renunciation) and it is also the traditional fourth stage in Hindu life which is thought to be a suitable preparation for one's end of life. It is interpreted as a deep search for inner unity and sometimes union with the divine. The ideal place to practise this renunciation are the Himalayas, a completely different setting to the wide and hot plains of India. It is there, where nature is both grander and more benign, where everything is on a vaster scale, that the gods live on the highest and most hidden peak and that the mind of man can be appeased.

Yudhishthira's behaviour underlines the king's duty of being righteous and just unto the last. This is illustrated by the way in which the king pleads for the fate of his faithful dog. It is part of the duty of a king to give protection to all, particularly to the weak and needy and to someone who has been such a faithful servant as his dog. Thus the story brings out the theme of *dharma*, the duty of a particular man in a particular situation—in this instance the duty of a king. The story further shows how Yudhishthira practises the love of all living beings by not abandoning an animal.

It is interesting to note the descriptions of heaven and hell which certainly evoke comparisons. The heaven of the gods is seen as a place of blessedness and glory where all battles and enmities, cease whilst hell is a place of exile and darkness. The more elaborate versions of the story describe Yudhishthira's visit to hell in terms which remind one of Dante's description of his wanderings in inferno, guided by a messenger as king Yudhishthira was.

The visit reveals itself to be a visionary experience meant to test for the last time the king's worthiness and goodness. This greatest challenge before the ascent to heaven proves the king's love for his kinsmen, the complete surrender of his own happiness for the sake of others whose sufferings he wants to share. Having passed this greatest test, king Yudhishthira is finally recompensed and admitted to full glory.

The story deals with a great and extraordinary individual. But his unswerving fulfilment of duty, love, devotion, and compassion are set us as an example to be emulated by others. 'King Yudhishthira's Ascent to Heaven' also implies the notion of divine reward or punishment for men's deeds and the possibility of a life of blessedness which, however, man cannot gain easily without being put to the test.

URSULA KING
*Department of Theology,
Leeds University.*

A GIFT OF LOVE IS NEVER LITTLE

Long ago in India, there lived a greater teacher — we call him Buddha now — who was wonderfully loving, wise and good. Millions of people in Asia love and honour him still as God. In China there are great temples and in them stand images of gold and silver and bronze of Buddha, the wise teacher who knew and taught so much above love and gentleness.

One of these images stands in a very old temple in a town called Lin-Hsien in China. It is a very tall figure of bronze, nearly ten feet high and on its breast is a copper coin. The coin is not valuable, for sixty such coins make about one-half a new penny. So you see, it is worth very little indeed. But there is a story about it which Buddha himself would have loved to tell.

There was once a little slave-girl named Ya-teo who lived in the house of the rich merchant Liu-Teh-Jong. She worked as a slave because her father and mother were poor. She worked all day as she was told. She had food to eat, clothes to wear and a mat to sleep on. Many people had hardly any of these things, so Ya-teo did not think she had anything to be sorry for. Nobody loved her or kissed her or played with her; nobody told her stories at night or gave her money to buy sweets and toys. Little Ya-teo had nothing of her own in all the world.

But one day she found something she could really keep as her own. It rolled away when she was sweeping the yard. Ya-teo ran and picked it up as if it were a gold coin. It was only a copper coin. Someone had dropped it in crossing the yard and perhaps had not even cared to look for it; it was worth so little. But it seemed like a whole fortune to Ya-teo, who had never had anything of her own before. She rubbed it as clean as she could on her blue cotton jacket. It seems very little to us but it was a great deal to Ya-teo.

One day, all the household of Liu-Teh-Jong was called together to listen to a young priest from the great temple of Lin-Hsien. All came — Liu-Teh-Jong and his sons, the ladies of the house, the servants, even the little slave girl — all gathered together to hear what the young priest had to say. He talked to them of Buddha, the beloved.

Everyone listened gladly, for all knew of Buddha, of his gentleness, his wisdom and his goodness. Then the priest told them that a grand statue of the great teacher was to be set up in the temple of Lin-Hsien.

257

He asked for their gifts and everyone gave willingly. The ladies of the household gave gold and silver ornaments, rings, combs and bracelets. The master of the house gave precious vessels and gold and silver money; the servants gave silver and copper coins, and Ya-teo said happily to herself, 'I can give too!' She held out her precious coin to the priest and said, 'It is mine to give. I found it when I swept the yard'.

Instead of taking it, the young priest shook his head as if he disliked it. 'Should I put a dirty copper coin with that for the image of Lord Buddha?' he said pointing to the shining heap of treasure that lay before him. And he gathered it up and went away to the temple of Lin-Hsien without another word to Ya-teo.

The young priest went proudly back with his precious load. Other priests came also, bringing more and more treasure and soon all that was needed had been gathered together. Then the metal for the statue was melted and poured into the mould and set to cool, but when the mould was taken away, it was seen that the statue was marked with ugly lines and patches. 'The metal is badly mixed,' said the priests and they melted it again, more carefully still. Once more it was poured into the mould but this time too it was spoiled.

Then the head priest called the priests together and asked about the gifts they had brought. 'Was all done in love and kindness?' he asked. 'For only love must go to the making of the image of him who taught us of love.'

When it came to the turn of the young priest, he confessed how he had refused the dirty coin offered by the little slave-girl.

'My son,' said the priest, 'that was not well done. She loved and gave all she had; none could do more. There can be no greater gift. Now do as I tell you. Return and humbly accept it, for there is need of Ya-teo's gift.' So the young priest went back to the house of Liu-Teh-Jong and to Ya-teo's great surprise, she was sent for and told that he had come to ask humbly for the treasure which she had offered and which he had refused. She gave it joyfully.

The priest returned and once more the metal was melted and poured into the mould and last of all the coin was dropped in also. When the mould was taken away, there stood the great statue — fair, smiling and perfect. On its breast, just over the heart, was the copper coin, Ya-teo's gift, no longer dull and dirty but fair and smiling too!

Ya-teo was very glad to know this and after that many people were kind to her. She was not a lonely little slave-girl any more.

N.P.

SHRI KRISHNA

Most of you celebrate your birthdays. Do you know that many children in India still celebrate the birthday of a boy who was born nearly 5,000 years ago? He was born in a prison in Mathura.

His uncle Kaunsa was the king of Mathura. His mother's name was Devki. It was said by the wise men that Kaunsa would be killed by a child of his sister Devki. Kaunsa was afaid of this; he kept his sister and her husband Vasudeva in the prison. This cruel king then killed, one by one, seven children of Devki and Vasudeva. When the eighth child was born at midnight, there was a miracle. The guards slept, and Vasudeva put his new-born son in a basket. He crossed the Yamuna river and came to the village named Gokul.

Vasudeva left his son with his friend Nanda and his wife Jashoda. These faithful friends gave their own new-born daughter to Vasudeva, who returned with her to the prison.

When king Kaunsa heard of the child's birth in prison, he killed the baby, but Devki's son was safe at Gokula. This was Krishna.

Everyone in Gokul loved Krishna very much. As he grew up, he played with cowherds and teased the milkmaids. He ate away their curds and broke their pots. They complained to Jashoda, yet they loved him. He played the flute and its sweet music made them forget everything else.

Even as a boy Krishna was very brave. He fought against the deadly snake called Kali, who troubled the people of the village.

News of this brave young boy reached his cruel uncle Kaunsa. He felt sure that this lad was his own nephew. He feared that Krishna would one day kill him. He made many plans to kill Krishna, but without success.

At last, Kaunsa invited Krishna to attend a grand feast at Mathura. His plan was to kill Krishna but it was Krishna who killed Kaunsa. The words of the wise men came true. Cruel Kaunsa met his death at the hands of Devki's son. Krishna then set his parents free from the prison.

It is his birthday that is still celebrated by millions of Hindus wherever they are. This day is known as *Krishna Janmashtami* or *Gokul Ashtami*.

N.P.

THE BOWL OF MILK

Thousands of years ago men lived as hunters. Slowly they began to tame animals like sheep and goats and became shepherds.

A group of such shepherds living in Central Asia travelled in search of pasture lands and came to India. They were known as the Aryans. Another group of these shepherds travelled to Persia and were known as Persians or Iranians. Some of these Persians left the shores of Iran in small boats and after a very long journey came to Sanjan in Gujarat.

The ruler of Sanjan was a Rana. He was a wise and kind ruler. The leader of the Persians sent a message to him saying, 'We have left our home and suffered many hardships. Please allow us to settle down in your country'. In reply, the Rana sent a bowl of milk which was filled to the brim. He wanted to tell the newcomers that there was no room for them in his kingdom.

The leader was also wise and clever. He took some sugar and put it in the bowl of milk. The milk did not overflow, on the contrary, it became sweet.

The leader of the Iranians wished to convey that just as sugar mixes with milk and sweetens it, so will they become one with the people of Gujarat and help them to make the country a better place. The Rana was very happy at the wisdom of the leader. He gave them shelter and allowed them to live in his country.

These newcomers are the Parsees, who live in India. They have kept the promise they made and have lived in India as Indians.

(Many Parsees have become famous poets, writers, industrialists and patriots. Khabardar, Dadabhai Naoroji, Jamshedji Tata, Phirozesha Mehta and others are great names in the history of India.)

N.P.

DADABHAI NAOROJI

One such Parsee was Dadabhai Naoroji. He was born at Navasari. When he was hardly four years old, his father died. His mother then brought him up with love and care. Dadabhai's mother went through a very hard time and suffered many hardships to bring up her son.

After passing the School Leaving Examination, he joined a college at Bombay. He was such a brilliant student that after graduating, he was selected as the Professor of the college. This was a rare honour because in those days Indians were rarely given high posts in government colleges.

Later, he joined a firm as a partner and went to England. The firm was making a lot of profit in its wine and opium trade. Dadabhai felt that it was wrong to do business in things which harmed people. So he gave up his partnership in that firm.

Dadabhai Naoroji lived in England and became so popular that he was elected to the English Parliament. After some years when Dadabhai came back to India, he was welcomed warmly by the people. When the Indian National Congress started its work, he was elected as its President three times. It was he who gave people the idea of 'Swadeshi'. Like Gandhi, he believed that the only way to end the British rule in India was to use Indian goods.

When he honoured he said, 'I owe everything to my mother'. He remembered how his mother had suffered to bring him up. He started schools for girls because he believed that a nation will be great only if its women are educated.

He died at the age of 93 and is loved and honoured even today as the Grand Old Man of India.

N.P.

NARSINHA MEHTA

Most of you would have heard Gandhi's favourite *bhajan* 'Vaishnav Jan'. The writer of this popular *bhajan* was Narsinha Mehta.

Narsinha Mehta was a Brahmin and lived at Junagadh in Saurashtra. He was a great devotee of Lord Krishna. He used to compose *bhajans* or hymns and sing them all day long.

In those days, the lower caste, the Harijans, were very badly treated. People of the other castes did not mix with them nor would they touch them. But to Narsinha Mehta all were God's children. He started going to the homes of these low-caste people. He sang *bhajans* with them and became their friend.

Such behaviour was unheard of. People began to talk about his 'evil ways'. They even complained to the king of Junagadh. The king ordered Narsinha Mehta to be put in prison. Mehta had to suffer a lot in prison but he did not give up his ideas or his *bhajans*. The king was astonished at his great faith in God and released him from the prison.

Mehta spent his entire life composing and singing *bhajans*. It is said that many a time God helped him in his difficulties. Today, in India, the Harijans have the same rights as other citizens, but it was Narsinha Mehta who first had the courage to mix with them and treat them as equals even in those days.

Gandhi perhaps learnt much from the life of Narsinha Mehta.

N.P.

LORD BUDDHA — A BUDDHIST STORY

There was a river, on either bank of which there was a village. The people of both the villages used the water of the river for their fields. Once the rain was scarce and there was very little water in the river; and the villagers on either side accused each other of using too much of it.

The quarrel became acute. The people of both the villages took their bows and arrows and prepared for a fight, but a Mahatma arrived on the scene and appealed to them: 'Friends, is water more precious than human blood? Should differences be settled by fighting or compromise? The rain will come in due course. Why sow the seeds of bitterness? Why are you prepared to shed blood unnecessarily over a matter which can be settled with love and peace and wisdom and seflessness?'

Both the excited parties were pacified by the words of the Mahatma. They laid down their arms and came to a peaceful settlement. The Mahatma was Lord Buddha.

The real name of Lord Buddha was Siddarth. As Buddha belonged to the Gautama lineage, he was also called Gautama. His father's name was Shuddhodan and his mother was called Gautama. Shuddhodan was the ruler of Kapilavastu, which is situated at the foot of the Himalayas in Nepal. The people of the Shakya tribe lived there. Theirs was a democratic state and as such they had no ruler, but a chief — though his position was like that of a ruler. A son was born in his family after a long time and, as the wish of the royal family for a child was fulfilled, they named their son Siddarth.

At the birth of Siddarth, astrologers predicted that he would be either a great king or a great saint. The king was farsighted and, therefore, arranged things in such a way that Siddarth might not see the miseries of life which might lead him to give up the world.

When he reached the right age, Siddarth was married to a princess called Yashodhara. Though the king built palaces with beautiful gardens for them, the prince did finally see the miseries of the world. Once he saw a wrinkled old man with a humped back who could hardly hobble along with the help of a stick. At another time he saw someone suffering the agonies of a bad disease. Next, he saw some people carrying a dead body to the burning place. All this made him realise that life was full of miseries such as old age, disease and death. He wondered if there was any escape from them.

While he was thinking of renouncing the world and becoming a *sadhu,* Yashodhara gave birth to a son. Siddarth exclaimed, 'Rahul', which means bondage. The child was a new bondage to keep him tied to a worldly life and so he was named Rahul.

Those who have the well-being of the world at heart cannot be tied down by worldly pleasures. Siddarth decided that he should not be a slave to pleasure. One night he woke up and, looking through the window, saw stars twinkling in the sky. They seemed to be inviting him and saying, 'How long will you be tied down by illusions while the world is waiting for you? If you sleep, how will you find out the cure for worldly unhappiness? Wake up, Siddarth!' And leaving behind all pleasures and illusions with firm determination, Siddarth left the palace in search of Truth. It seemed as if Nature was singing in the dark peaceful night, expecting the Light — True Knowledge.

Siddarth went to a forest to meditate. His handsome body became very weak because of his severe penance and was reduced to a skeleton. In this manner, he meditated for six years. Once, when he fainted and collapsed, a shepherdess called Sujata gave him some milk to drink.

When he regained consciousness, he realised that True Knowledge could be gained neither from worldly pleasures nor by making one's body undergo great suffering. He decided to avoid both these extremes and to find out the middle way. He started taking regular meals. His weak body soon regained its strength and he restarted meditation.

One day while meditating under a pipal tree, all of a sudden he felt that he saw a light. It was the light of True Knowledge, which he explained to the ignorant people and became the Buddha — the Enlightened One. It was after that, that he came to be known as Gautama Buddha — and he preached to the people for the rest of his life.

Buddha offered the masses a religious law easy to understand and follow. He preached not in Sanskrit but in Pali, the language of the people, who came in thousands to hear him. It was as if they had found their saviour. Rich and poor and people from all sections of society became his followers. Even his father, wife and son became his disciples.

He spent the rest of his life preaching and attained Nirvana at the age of eighty, at Kushinara. Today Buddhism is followed in many parts of Asia.

NILA PANCHOLI

IDOL WORSHIP

Western critics always harp on the note that the Indian's whole outlook is otherwordly. But everything a Hindu is called upon to do in life is intricately interwoven with religion, behind every act is dedication, perhaps imperceptible, to the Lord of all action. The spiritual tendency of the Hindus does not shoot upwards only to the abstract, the hidden and the intangible. It also casts its rays downwards and outwards to embrace the multiplicities of thought and the richness of worldly life. The criticism has also been levelled that there is no Hindu religion but only a social system and a bundle of inconsistent religious beliefs and institutions. To the Hindu mind the religious spirit matters, not the dogma. This story relates to the criticism about 'idol worship' and polytheism, the belief that there was thirty million gods.

Long ago, a king considered idol worship to be ridiculous. He expressed these thoughts to the saint. The saint kept quiet, but slowly advanced to the picture hanging on the wall in the king's parlour. The king asked politely: 'Maharaj [great man], what are you looking for?' The saint did not reply but put down the picture on the floor. The king was amazed and did not understand the peculiar behaviour of the saint. Slowly, the saint stamped his foot on the picture. The king could no longer control his temper and forgot who he was talking to. He shouted: 'What do you mean by stamping your foot on my dear father? It is ridiculous and shameful.'

The saint was unmoved. He smiled, and when he realised that the king was overpowered with anger, he calmly said: 'Are you out of your mind? What did you say? Is this your father? I can see only a piece of canvas. Your father died long back.' 'But it is the picture of my father,' said the king. 'It gives me immense pleasure to look at it and remember him.' 'Oh!' exclaimed the saint. Then alone the king realised that he was wrong in denouncing idol worship. Everyone who worships photographs, pictures or stone or metal images as deities should remember that they are not really God but a reminder of him. God is one and He is omnipotent, omnipresent and omniscient. He is OM. He has no shape, no size, is neither male nor female. As everyone is not able to grasp the abstract concept of God, so one uses the symbol of one's own choice — the form which one wishes to see and worship. Hinduism grants this freedom of choice.

VIMAL KHADE
The Walsingham School,
St Paul's Cray,
Orpington, Kent

WHY THE INDIAN SQUIRREL HAS THREE WHITE STRIPES ON HIS BACK

Long, long ago, the Demon King of Lanka had stolen Lord Rama's faithful wife, Sita, and taken her to his palace at Lanka — ancient Ceylon. While Lord Rama's monkey-allies were helping him build a bridge between Lanka and India, a small squirrel was bringing pebbles in its mouth to the workers saying, 'These pebbles are for the bridge so that our Lord Rama may bring back the blessed Sita. I must do my share of the work.' 'You are doing what?' cried a monkey, in disbelief. 'I am helping to build the bridge, sir,' replied the squirrel. 'These pebbles, together with your rocks, will help build the bridge.'

The monkey burst out into laughter. He cried to the rest of the monkeys, 'Did you hear that? The squirrel says she's helping to build the bridge with her pebbles! Ha! ha! Have you heard anything as funny as that?'

The other monkeys burst out laughing, saying to the squirrel, 'Little one, do you think Lord Rama, who commands the largest army in the Seven Worlds, is in need of your pebbles? For him we carry whole mountains of granite and rock. What use are your little pebbles?'

The squirrel replied, 'God has only given me the strength and ability to carry pebbles. I cannot carry mountains or rocks but what I am able to do I will do, as my heart weeps in sorrow for my Lord.'

The monkeys said, 'That's enough foolishness, little creature. Go back home and stop wasting our time.'

But the squirrel would not go, returning with more pebbles each time the monkeys put her out of their way. Eventually the monkeys lost their temper and threatened to throw her into the sea. Still the squirrel insisted. Then an angry monkey flung her away. But she, crying the name of Rama, fell into his hands, where he had been standing.

Lord Rama held the squirrel close and said to the monkeys, 'Despise not the weak and the small, for according to each man's strength will he serve. And to me what matters is not how great the strength and service is, but how great the love and devotion is. This little squirrel with her pebbles has love in her heart that would move the earth and the heavens by its strength and power.'

In this way, he lessened their pride. To the squirrel, however, he said, 'Little one, your devotion has touched my heart. Be blessed then, by me, whom you have loved and served.' As he put her down, he stroked her back and all saw upon her brown fur the three white lines that were the marks of Rama's fingers.

And ever since then the Indian squirrel has carried the three white stripes on its back.

E.W.

REAL LOVE

Krishna had two sisters, Subhadra, his real sister, and an adopted sister, Draupadi. Subhadra was jealous of her adopted sister because she thought Krishna loved Draupadi more, and she grumbled to Krishna about it. Krishna agreed that he did love Draupadi and thought she loved him more than Subhadra did. 'Nonsense, that's not true,' said Subhadra angrily. Some time later Krishna cut his hand very badly and went to Subhadra to ask her to bind it up. 'O dear I've nothing here to bind it,' I'll go and see if I can find a bandage for you,' she said and went hurrying off. Krishna waited some time and still she did not return and the hand was bleeding heavily, so he want to Draupadi. On seeing his hand, Draupadi at once tore a strip off the end of her sari and bound up his hand to stop the bleeding. Who do you think loved Krishna the most?

E.W.

SHIVA'S MILK

One day the king thought he would pay extra respect to the god Shiva in the temple, so instead of taking the usual amount of milk, honey for the bathing of the god, he thought that on Monday he would take sufficient milk to cover the god that stands in a deep wide bowl. So everybody was commanded to take all their milk to the palace early Monday morning where the people would be paid as they came. The day arrived, the calves were mooing and the babies crying as they were hungry, the children and the grown-ups had no milk, but they had other things to eat. All the milk was then taken to the temple, but, however much the king poured, he could not fill the bowl. After a time the king went back sadly to his palace, leaving some of his attendants near the shrine to watch in case any more milk was brought. An old woman who lived some way away in the jungle disobeyed the king's order; she fed her calf and grandchildren and then took the small bowl of milk she had left to the temple and poured it over the god as she said her prayers. Immediately the bowl became full to over-flowing. Amazed, the attendants took the old woman to the king and told him what had happened. 'Why did you not give all your milk to me?' asked the king. 'My lord, it is my duty to feed my animals and children first and then give what is left freely to Shiva,' said the woman trembling, thinking she would be punished for disobeying the order.

Old people are given respect in India, so for a while the king sat quiet thinking, then said, '*Agi* (grandmother), go in peace. The Lord Shiva is more pleased with you who have cared for your family than with me who have left the calves and babies crying for food.'

E.W.

THE STORY OF DHRUVA THE POLE STAR

King Uttanapad had two wives and two sons. One was called Suruchi, whom he loved very much, the other Suniti, the mother of Dhruva, of whom he was not so fond. Now Suruchi, the favourite wife, was jealous when she saw the two sons playing with their father and that the son of the other wife, Dhruva, was sitting on his father's knee, so she came up angrily and pushed the child away. The child, who did not like being treated roughly so, ran away crying to his mother, who asked him why he was crying. 'Where can I go where there is a safe place and no-one can be angry with me?' 'If you pray to God he may tell you of a safe place, there is nowhere here in the palace'. 'Where can I find God?' 'You may find God after much praying in a quiet place such as the temple or the jungle'. The boy made up his mind to go to the jungle to find god. His mother tried to dissuade him and told him of the wild animals and dangers there. The king offered to give him anything he asked, but the boy said he wished to go to the jungle to find God. At last the king thought he should let his son go on the way. Dhruva met Narad Muni (a mischief-maker), who told him a prayer to repeat, saying that if he said this earnestly he would see God. So Dhruva stayed and prayed and prayed for weeks and months. It is customary to bring food to those who are praying and are without food in India. At last, God appeared and asked him what he wanted. 'I want a safe place of my own where there is no anger and I cannot be pushed away from.'

In the twinkling of an eye God made a place for him and he became the Pole star around which all the other stars revolve.

E.W.

SUDAMA AND KRISHNA

To protect the baby Krishna from his wicked uncle who was king, Krishna was taken to some farmers in the country who brought him up as his own son. So Krishna grew up looking after the cattle, milking them and playing with all the village boys and girls. There was one boy, Sudhama, who was not as strong as the others, but whom Krishna specially loved. They often went out together and Krishna, who was strong, was able to help his friend. When they grew up and the wicked king had died, Krishna became king, left the country to live in the palace, married and seldom saw his old friend. Sudhama married as well, but as he was not strong and could not work hard, they were very poor. One day his wife said to him, 'You have a friend who is now king, and is very rich, go and see him and ask for help'. Sudhama wanted to see his friend, but he did not want to go begging for help, but his wife kept urging him, and at last, because he wanted to see his friend, he gave in. Whenever you go to visit a friend in India it is the custom to take a small present, just a little loving gift of sweets or a few flowers, but Sudhama looked everywhere but could find nothing, only a few grains of *poha,* what we call rice crispies. At first, the servants at the door of the king's palace could not believe that so poor a man was the friend of the king and refused to let him in, but Krishna, who was sitting on the throne in the audience room, looked down the hall. Perhaps he had heard his friend's voice; he recognised his friend, left his throne and walked across the hall to the door to welcome him. Overjoyed to meet again, the friends sat side by side on the wide thrones and talked of all the happy times they remembered when they were young. Sudhama gave Krishna his little gift as he was leaving at the end of the day but never thought of asking for his help. He returned to his wife after a very happy day but worried lest she would be angry with him for not asking Krishna for help. But when he returned to his village he could not find his little cottage but saw his smiling wife standing on the steps of the verandah of a well-built house that had store-rooms filled with grain, spices and vegetables and all that he needed. With thankfulness and joy Sudhama knew that a real friend knew of his needs without having to ask.

E.W.

SERVANA

Servana's parents were poor and blind and old, which is not uncommon in India, nor is it uncommon for the children to look after their old parents with great care. Servana looked after them well and even carried them in a *bangi,* a kind of basket hanging from a yoke on his shoulder, to the temple when there was a special festival. As he was carrying them one day in the country, his parents felt thirsty, so he put down his heavy load and went with his little brass water pot to the river. As he was filling it with water, king Dashradta, who was hunting nearby, heard the noise and, thinking it was an animal drinking water, shot an arrow in that direction. The arrow struck Servana, who called out in grief 'Hé Ram' as he was dying. Hearing this and realising it was a human voice, the king hurried to the river and, finding out what he had done, was very grieved, and asked the dying boy if there was anything he could do for him. Servana told him that his parents were thirsty and asked the king to take them some water and to look after them. The king humbly took water to the parents but was too overcome with grief to speak. The parents asked why Servana had taken so long and why he did not speak. At last the king told them what had happened and said he would care for them. The parents were heartbroken and asked the king if he had any sons. Then he would understand how they felt, and that they now no longer wished to live.

E.W.

A FAITHFUL WIFE

One day, when Savitri was walking in the jungle, she got to know a boy called Satiwan who lived there and who looked after his blind mother and father with great kindness. She told her father she wished to marry Satiwan, so her father consulted with the family and the astrologers to see if it was a suitable match and, if so, to find the best day for the wedding. The astrologers warned them that Satiwan was going to die within a year, but Savitri would not be deterred, and the wedding took place, but Satiwan had to promise to take her wherever he went. At the end of the year the husband was bitten by a snake, Savitri sat down beside him and took his head in her lap and he died. Yama, god of death, sent his messengers to take away the life, but they could not do so while she was touching him so they asked her to lay him on the ground. She did so then followed them and refused to go back. She followed them over mountains, rivers, over seas and through fire and tempest. As she still would not return to her home the god, Yama, came to persuade her, but she still refused to part with her husband. The Lord Yama said, 'I will grant you three wishes if you return tonight'. Savitri then said, 'My mother and father in law are blind; please give them back their sight. They were once a king and queen; let them have their kingdom back. Let me be the mother of seven children'. 'Your wishes are granted. Now you can return.' But Savitri still followed him and Lord Yama asked why. 'How can my last wish be granted when you have taken my husband'. (Widows do not remarry in India.) Lord Yama said, 'You win, I lose'. Savitri returned and life came back into the body of Satiwan, who awoke and thought he had just had a long sleep, and the wishes were granted.

Other stories such as 'Bakasa', 'Hanuman', and 'Bhima' appear in *Tales from the Indian Classics,* Books, 1, 2 and 3, *Stories from the Panchatantra* and other books published by the Delhi Children's Book Trust and available from Oxfam, 274 Banbury Road, Oxford.

The stories can be used as a basis for discussion, comprehension exercises with the older children, for dramatic work or picture-making with younger children. The themes of loyalty and friendship, of caring for the old or the young or the ill may be followed up on the classroom or school, or maybe an occasion in the school may lead to the telling of one of these stories, which can provide a background for further study on housing, clothes, temples and festivals.

E.W.

GANDHI AND A CHINESE YOUTH

Some time in 1925 a young Chinese student came to India. He had heard of Tagore and Gandhi. He was himself a poet and writer of promise. He joined Tagore's Visva Bharati at Shantiniketan and soon became popular there. However, after some time he was suspected of being a spy. This upset him so much that he decided to leave the place. He did not know where he could go in a strange country. He wrote to Gandhi and explained what had happened. Gandhi was then in Calcutta. The young Chinese got a reply from Mahadeo Desai, Gandhi's secretary, asking him to come up to Calcutta and meet Gandhi. Since the youth was anxious to keep the appointment, he wasted no time and was soon standing in the presence of Gandhi.

Gandhi looked at him straight in the eye. There was great kindness in his voice as he said, 'The people at Shantiniketan are my good friends. They always welcome people of other nations. Why did they suspect you? Are you a spy?'

The young Chinese answered, 'They are good people. they must have been misled about me. I am deeply hurt by their suspicions. I am not a spy; I am only a student anxious to study India'.

Gandhi listened carefully to what the young Chinese said. 'I accept what you say,' he said. 'Shall I give you a guarantee for you and send you back to Shantiniketan?'

The young Chinese was deeply moved by Gandhi's kindness and his eyes were filled with tears. 'Please let me stay with you,' he begged of Gandhi. 'Let me enter your *ashram* so that I can stay with you'.

'But,' said Gandhi with his usual smile, 'My *ashram* is a harder place than Shantiniketan. You will have to do hard physical work in addition to your studies.'

'The Chinese are hard workers and they are not afraid of work,' he replied.

Gandhi allowed him to stay in his *ashram*. As he could not easily pronounce the youth's Chinese name, he offered him the choice of two Indian names for use in the *ashram*. The youth chose 'Shanti', and during all the years of his stay in India he was known as Shanti. Shanti joined the Sabarmati Ashram and, as earlier at Shantiniketan, he soon became a favourite with everyone. He had the heart of a child and was full of fun. Little children were particularly fond of him, for he could make wonderful toys for them almost out of nothing.

Shanti's main task in the *ashram* was to fetch water for the kitchen and wash clothes. He picked up spinning in no time. He also studied Gandhi's writings carefully. Then one day he sat down to write. He wrote page after page and when he had finished he put the pages in order and marched into Gandhi's room.

What he said to Gandhi is very interesting. 'I have set down briefly here the story of my life. Before I came to India I lived a wild and wicked life in Singapore, like hundreds of other young Chinese. I have felt an urge to open my mind to you. Do please read this manuscript. Permit me to fast for ten days so that I may purify myself. At the end of the fast I want to take certain vows, with you as my witness.'

Gandhi was greatly surprised. He knew that Shanti was trying to give up his bad ways and he said, 'Your manuscript is very long but I shall find time to read it. Don't start your fast until I have studied what you have written. Let me first find out what you need and what you seek'.

Gandhi found time to read the manuscript and was moved by the frank confessions of the young Chinese whom the *ashram* life had changed completely. He sent for Shanti and talked to him kindly. He permitted the fast and Shanti lived only on water for ten days. Gandhi visited him every day and spent fifteen minutes talking with him. What exactly passed between them during these daily conversations is not known to anyone, but Shanti looked very happy. At the end of the ten days' fast, Shanti did take certain vows. The vows were written down on paper and signed by Shanti. Gandhi signed as a witness. Shanti always said afterwards that he felt like a man who had left a heavy burden behind.

Later Shanti went back to China and started a newspaper there. A editor he always signed himself 'Shanti'. The chief aim of his life was to carry Gandhi's message of love and truth to the Chinese people.

N.P.

A STORY OF COURAGE: THE SALT OF FREEDOM

This is a story based on the biography of Mahatma Gandhi by Louis Fischer. It is one of the many stories about Gandhi.

Gandhi was one of the world's greatest men, the prime mover of India's struggle for independence, and a spiritual leader whose simple life has influenced millions throughout the world.

In 1928 India seethed with labour and nationalist unrest. India wanted to be free. Gandhi also wanted to see his country free, but he did not want to fight the British with guns, but with a special sort of weapon which he called non-violent disobedience.

In December 1928 the annual Congress session was to be held in Calcutta and Gandhi travelled there by train. When the train stopped at Nagpur some of his friends met him there and asked him: 'What would your attitude be towards a political war of independence?' Gandhi replied 'I would not take part in it. Today I am teaching the people how to meet a national crisis by non-violent means'.

The young men at the Congress session wanted immediate action. Gandhi wanted them to wait and see if the British would grant them their freedom. Finally they agreed to wait one year. Unfortunately, at the end of that period the British still refused to give India her freedom. Then Gandhi announced publicly: 'I must declare myself an independence wallah!'

Gandhi felt that it was his responsibility to show the way to gain for India her independence. What could he do? One small man against the military power of the British on the one hand, and on the other hand the wish of his younger friends to fight the British with guns.

He thought about this for six weeks, and then he found a way. He now knew what he had to do.

Before putting his plan into operation he wrote to the Viceroy, explaining what he intended to do. In his letter to the Viceroy he explained that, while he disliked British rule, he had no intention of hurting any English person. He also explained why he disliked British rule. The whole system, he said, seemed to be designed to crush the life out of the peasant. Even the salt which he must use to live was so heavily taxed and in such a way as to make the burden fall heaviest on him. The salt tax showed itself to be really cruel when one considered the poor person. Salt was the only thing that the poor person had to flavour his meagre diet of rice and dahl. He could not afford the spices which others used. In addition to this, the peasant used more salt than the rich because he perspired more while working in the fields under the tropical sun of India.

Gandhi wanted to convert the British people through non-violence, and thus make them see the wrong they had done to India.

Finally Gandhi told the Viceroy that if he did not get a favourable answer by 11 March then he and some of his followers would break the salt laws. The British salt laws made it a punishable crime to possess salt not purchased from the government salt monopoly.

As 11 March approached, the whole country bubbled with excitement. Scores of foreign and Indian newspapermen dogged Gandhi's footsteps in the *ashram*. What would this strange little man do? Gandhi received telegrams from all over the world encouraging him and wishing him well.

On 11 March, prayers having been said, Mahatma Gandhi, with seventy-eight male members of his *ashram* left the village on foot. 'We are marching in the name of God,' said Gandhi. They walked two hundred and forty-one miles in twenty-four days. Gandhi could have gone by train, bus or car, or even on a bullock cart, but he preferred to walk like the poorest of his countrymen. At this time Gandhi was sixty-one. Some of his company soon became fatigued and footsore but not Gandhi!

Gandhi and his company followed the winding dirt roads from village to village. They visited more than three hundred villages.

On 5 April they reached the sea at Dandi, and by this time his small band of eighty-seven had grown into a non-violent army of several thousand strong. They rested for the rest of the day and the following morning went down and bathed in the sea. Then when he returned to the beach he picked up some salt left by the waves.

Gandhi thus deliberately broke the British law which made it a punishable crime to possess salt not purchased from the government monopoly. He himself had not used salt for six years.

This simple act was like a signal to the Indian nation. If one man could defy the mighty British Raj then could not a whole nation do the same? On 4 May, less than a month after he had become a salt criminal, Gandhi was arrested in the night while he was sleeping in a tent a few miles from the scene of his crime.

The salt march and its aftermath did two things. It gave the Indians the conviction that they could lift the foreign yoke from their shoulders, and it made the British aware that they were subjugating India. It was inevitable after 1930 that India would some day be free, and, more important, that England would some day refuse to rule.

When men like Gandhi allowed themselves to be imprisoned without resentment or hatred, they showed that Britain was now powerless and India invincible.

Reprinted by permission of EWART THOMAS

DACOITS FOR DANGER

When India became independent in 1947 many followers of Gandhi who had joined the Congress party wished to join the government and be active in politics. Others took up work in the villages where Gandhi urged that the training for democracy and a better quality of life must be developed. Thereupon Damodardas, a friend of Gandhi, and some others went to work in a very backward tribal area in the Satpuda mountains north of Bombay. The area is often cut off for six months during the monsoon, making the rivers impassable. The tribal people have cut down much of the forest where they only hunted and the soil is being washed away from the hillsides. The tribal people are hungry and angry that the government will not let them cut down more trees as they have no work. Here, then, was an opportunity to teach these hunters to become farmers, to look after cattle, grow grain, terrace hillsides, to start schools, clinics and co-operative stores where a fair price is charged in time of scarcity and a man can borrow until the next harvest without going to a moneylender, who often charges 150 per cent on loans.

However, some of the tribal people had become desperate and did not only hunt wild animals that were becoming scarce, but became what are called *dacoits,* who plunder and steal from other villages or travellers.

As Villabhai, one of the Gandhian workers, was travelling on foot down the fifty miles of mountain track with some gifts for his old parents that live in the plains, he was set upon by *dacoits*. His gifts and clothes were taken, he was clubbed and left for dead. As he recovered he realised he did not want to be eaten by wild animals, so, slowly and painfully, he made his way back to the *ashram* at Dhadgaon, where he told Damodardas what had happened. A week later, as he was recovering, tribesmen who came to the co-operative shop brought news of the *dacoits* and where they lived. A few days later, alone and unarmed, Damodardas and Villabhai set out to find the village where the *dacoits* lived, but they, fearing that the police would also be coming, fled to the jungle. The two Gandhian workers said they would wait until the *dacoits* returned. So they waited and waited, and talked to people about their clinics, schools and co-operative stores. After two days, seeing that the strangers had not brought the police, the *dacoits* crept back to the village and joined the village council that was discussing with the visitors ways of helping the village. A party of the villagers, including the *dacoits*, accompanied the two workers back to Dhadgaon, saw the work that was being done there and were given hospitality for the night. This is how one village became friends and happier, healthier and better cultivated.

ELIZABETH WILSON

FACING FEAR

Many people loved and revered Gandhi in India, and when he told young men that colleges were teaching a lot of useless book knowledge and that true knowledge came with serving people, many young men left their colleges and came to work with Gandhi. One such young man was Baba Amte, whose job was to work with the sweepers who collect the night soil from houses and take it in baskets on their heads to a dump. Only the lowest castes of people will do such dirty and unpleasant work, but the best way of getting to know such people and their problems is to work with them. So for some time Baba Amte persevered in this unpleasant work.

One day, as he dumped his load of excrement, he saw amongst it an apparently dead leper; he gazed in horror and then slowly the eyes opened and looked at him. Leprosy is greatly feared in India, as it causes such disfigurement and was believed to be highly infectious. It is only in the last few years that an effective treatment has been found to arrest the disease. Baba was revolted, his deep-rooted fear and disgust of leprosy, the smell and the horror were too much. He fled and was violently sick. He decided that this was too much, he would give up and return to college. Having made his decision, he began to ponder; perhaps this was where real service began when one saw a need and had to equip oneself to meet that need.

With renewed dedication and courage, he went back to the refuse heap. The leper was still there and still alive, so he got him out of the refuse, fetched water and washed him and, as he told me, 'Having made my decision, suddenly all my fear of leprosy fell away'. He took the man to a home for lepers and went to a medical school in Calcutta for two years to learn all he could about leprosy. He then returned to Warora, near Nagpur, where he started his first leprosy clinic, started a farm and workshops for lepers who were homeless, and who could each do what they were capable of, earning their living and running their little community. Now they are building their own agricultural college and the head of the college is a leper. A number of clinics are held in surrounding villages so that lepers can live at home and come for treatment early before they are disfigured and before the disease has spread to other members of the family.

Baba Amte is now over seventy, but he continues his work with the support of many friends and he is revered like Kamalbai Hospet throughout the whole of Maharasthra.

ELIZABETH WILSON

VINOBA BHAVE: A MAN OF COURAGE

The India in which Vinoba Bhave lived and worked was completely different from the country which had once dazzled the world with its wealth and splendour. It was now faced with the burden of the poverty and land hunger of the majority of its people.

During the time of India's glory there seemed to have been no problem about the ownership of land or the unequal distribution of wealth. Long before Christian Europe was taught that 'the earth is the Lord's' the Indian people had been taught: 'The land is my mother.' By this they understood that they had a right to be fed from the earth's produce.

As time went on, things changed and the land no longer belonged to the people but became the property of a very small minority, and the peasant began to suffer want. As the population increased, his plight became worse. The land was no longer his mother.

Although industry on the Western pattern is being developed in India, seventy-five per cent of the population still depend upon agriculture for a livelihood. The majority of these are tenant farmers, but unfortunately their farms are usually small and unprofitable. Alongside these tenant farmers are the landless labourers.

When India became independent her leaders realised that the future of India lay in her agriculture, but as long as the present division of land remained unchanged there was really little hope. No-one seemed to have an answer. All realised that there had to be land reform, but who had the courage to make such reforms? The majority of the people had not enough land to maintain a fair standard of living, while vast areas were owned by a small number of landowners. The majority lived in poverty while the few lived in luxury.

It was Vinoba Bhave's courage which offered the Indian people a possible answer and a ray of hope for the future. The following story shows how he began to do this.

After Independence Day, 15 August 1947, while the Nizam, the ruler of the Hyderabad State, manoeuvred to preserve the independence of his state, armed bands of Communists entered the Telenga villages which were remote from the capital and mostly situated in arid forest and scrublands. Often these people were not Communists in the Western sense of the word, but men driven to despair by the existing social conditions and saw violence as the only answer. Ordering the villagers to gather round, the Communists explained that henceforth all land would belong to the people. No rent was to be paid to the landlords and all debts were to be cancelled. The landless were entitled to seize the property of the rich, and they should resist all attempts to re-establish the old order. In over a thousand villages the landlords and agents of the Nizam were brutally attacked, and there were over five hundred murders in the first few months. At the height of this rural trouble the Indian army crossed the Hyderabad border and the Nizam yielded to its demand that his state should become part of the Indian Union. Then the army switched its attack from Nizam to the Communists in Telegana, who at once mobilised guerrilla warfare in country ideally suited to it. The village of Panchampalli was one of their strongholds. Into this dangerous situation went Vinoba Bhave, with no army or police to help him, only his own courage and his love of the peasant.

Vinoba Bhave believed that this ugly situation had been caused by the greed of the rich, and neither the Indian police nor the Communists could cure this sickness. He decided that he had to try and do something himself.

He left his *ashram* at Shivarampalli before dawn on 15 April 1948, and made his way towards Panchampalli, the notorious Communist stronghold. He arrived there on the 18th. Little did Vinoba realise that his mission to Hyderabad would be the beginning of an amazing movement which would bring hope at last to the exhausted workers of the land.

Hyderabad was a grim example of the inequalities which Vinoba abhorred. The Nizam himself owned five million acres of land, and barely a thousand families controlled almost the entire wealth of the state. Conditions in the poorest districts were as pitiful as those round the wealthy estates. In one village of six hundred and ninety families he found that the cultivable land was only three hundred acres, and this land was owned by only ninety families, and the remaining six hundred families were landless. This was a typical example of the conditions which Vinoba Bhave found.

When Vinoba arrived at Panchampalli he made his customary tour of the village, and in the untouchable quarter he went into a hut and played with a tiny baby which he found lying on the mat. The mother was extravagantly grateful that a holy man should hold her child. When he came out of the hut a crowd of untouchables had gathered; they began in their practised whine the usual melancholy tale of poverty. Vinoba asked them to see him in the afternoon, and by 1 p.m., the hottest hour of the sweltering day, a large crowd had gathered at his camp. The whole history of individual miseries began again. '*Maharaj*' — the great king — 'there can be no peace in this village while so many cannot eat. If only we had land for cultivation, our sorrows would be lightened'. 'How much land do you want?' asked Vinoba. After a prolonged whispering among the old men, someone said, 'Eighty acres'. Vinoba did not speak at first, he was looking at the dusty earth in meditation. Then he raised his eyes and asked whether among the good people sitting round him there were any owners of land. A few moved their heads in acknowledgement. 'Brothers,' asked Vinoba, 'are there some among you who will give land to your brothers so that they may not die of starvation? They need only eighty acres.'

Once more silence, this time anxious and intense. Then a landowner stood up and came to the front of the crowd. He spoke gently, unboastingly: 'I offer one hundred acres of land as a gift.' This was India, where to millions ownership of land was the sole earthly ambition. The landowner was called Sir V. R. Reddy. Vinoba looked at him and asked him to repeat what he had said. He answered firmly: 'I will give away one hundred acres. If people here do not believe what I say, I will make a written declaration here and now,' Vinoba could hardly believe his ears, and it was not until the next day, when the landowner, still good-humoured, produced a written deed, that he believed that this 'miracle' had happened.

This first land gift, 18 April 1948, initiated *Bhoodan* — the land gift movement. Vinoba Bhave's courage may have found the answer to India's rural problem. Neither the existing social unrest nor the deep-rooted attitude to the ownership of land could daunt him. He faced both, and showed his people a new way of life by which all could share with others, and so re-establish the belief that 'the earth was really their mother'. (Vinoba died in 1982).

(The above story is adapted from the book entitled *The Five Gifts*, by R. P. Masani).

Reprinted by permission of EWART THOMAS

A STORY OF COURAGE:
THE DALAI LAMA OF TIBET

Ever since Europeans first penetrated Tibet, the Dalai Lamas have been regarded as a mystery, and even today few Westerners have entered the forbidden City of Lhasa. In 1959 the whole world was roused by the Dalai Lama's dramatic escape into India. This story of his escape is based on his own account of the event.

The Dalai Lama is a man of great intelligence, humility and ideals which do not permit him to hate his enemies. These qualities did not permit him at the time of his escape to hate the Chinese, who were destroying his country and killing and torturing his people.

After the Chinese had invaded his country the Dalai Lama was faced with a serious question: should he or should he not try to escape from the Chinese? His government officials advised him to try to escape, but he knew that the final decision rested with him.

He felt then, as he still does, that he was only a mortal being like all his countrymen, but his people thought and believed differently. To his people, including all his government officials, he, the Dalai Lama, represented Tibet and the Tibetan way of life. They were convinced that if he was killed or taken prisoner by the Chinese, that would be the end of Tibet. He finally decided that the only thing he could do was to escape, but was it possible? The Chinese had told him that he would never be allowed to leave Tibet. Still, he was now convinced that if he was to try to save his people then he had to escape. But where could he go?

When he announced his decision to escape all his family and those close to him wanted to go with him. It was finally decided that the closest members of his family, four members of his cabinet, his tutors and his personal officials should attempt to escape with him.

The attempt had to be a secret not only from the Chinese, but also from the mass of the people who during this critical time were more or less living right outside the palace.

If he was to escape then it would have to be almost immediately. There was no time or the means of taking anything that was not strictly essential. All the important government papers and the treasure of the palace had to be left behind.

They decided to leave in small parties. The first essential was to cross the river which stood between them and their escape to freedom. The Chinese camp was close to the northern bank, and so it was only on the southern bank that there was a chance of finding a safe crossing.

An official of one of the monastries was sent off immediately to cross the river and arrange for sufficient horses and an escort for the party. The commander (Doji Dadul) of the second battalion of the Tibetan army went with about a hundred men to guard a place on the southern bank where it would be possible to cross. The whole plan was almost wrecked because on the way, about a mile from the crossing-place, the soldiers sighted a Chinese patrol. However, the soldiers immediately opened fire, and the Chinese, thinking that they were a band of Tibetan freedom-fighters retreated to the safety of their camp. Now we take up the story in the Dalai Lama's own words.

'When it was my turn to leave I took off my monk's clothing and put on a soldier's uniform and a fur cap. I had already arranged for these to be left in my private apartment. Then I went to my private prayer room, and in a short time I was ready to leave.

'At the inner door of my house there was a single soldier waiting for me and another at the outer door. I took a rifle from one of them and slung it to my shoulder to complete the disguise. The soldiers followed me and I walked down through the dark garden, leaving behind everything I had known and loved.

'My friends met me outside and we made our way to the southern bank of the river. Although it was pitch dark I took off my glasses to try to make my disguise complete. Nobody recognised me, even when one of my friends stopped to chat with some people we met on the way. At last we reached the river bank just above the crossing-place, and then we had to walk down a sort of white sandbank which was covered with clumps of bushes. Was there an enemy hiding behind one of the bushes? We couldn't turn back now and arrived at the crossing safely.

'On the other bank I met the members of my family, and my ministers were there also. They had escaped out of the city by hiding under a tarpaulin in a truck. The monastery official who I had sent on ahead had collected enough ponies for all of us but was not able to get any good saddles. After a hurried farewell to the friends we were leaving behind, we mounted and rode off without delay. The first few miles were likely to be the most dangerous.

'There was no road, only a narrow stony track which skirted across a hill above the river. The clink of the horse-shoes on the stones seemed very loud. We were afraid that some Chinese patrol might hear us, but we had to take the risk because no time was to be lost. We lost our way once, and some of our party got separated from us, but we all met again about three miles downstream.

'We continued on our way, and for a long time saw no sign of life, but about three in the morning we heard a dog bark. We soon came upon a solitary house belonging to a simple kindly man. He had already been warned by an advance escort of mine to expect a very important guest. This was the first of many humble Tibetan houses whose owners sheltered me without any thought of the risk, some knowing and some not knowing who I was.

'Although I had escaped from Lhasa I still hoped that I would be able to stay somewhere in Tibet. We headed south and south-east from Lhasa. In that direction there was a vast area of mountainous country, without any roads, which the Chinese army would find very difficult to penetrate in any strength, so there we would be fairly safe. Before we could reach that sanctuary we would have to cross the Brahmaputra (Tsang-po) and between us and the river there was a high mountain pass called Che-la — the sandy pass.

'We reached the foot of Che-la about eight the following morning, and stopped there to have some tea. The sun was just rising above the peaks to the east when we began the long steep climb towards the pass. The way was rough and difficult, and it took us well above the snow-line. Some of the ponies and mules began to lag behind. But our spirits were raised by an old man called Tashi Norbu, who joined us while we were climbing. He offered me a graceful white horse. I accepted it gratefully, and all my party was now happier, because Tibetans look on such a gift as a very propitious sign.

'At last we crossed the pass, and beyond the summit we found long steep slopes of sand down which we could run, leaving our ponies to follow the winding track. When we reached the valley below we were almost blinded by a sandstorm, but it was comforting to know that if the Chinese were anywhere near they also would be blinded.

'There were no human habitations on the other side of the pass but ten miles to the east we came across a village called Kyeshong (Happy Valley). After enjoying a very warm welcome we set off once more. Now we need not fear a Chinese attack, but still had a long way to go.

'About this time a messenger brought me a letter from Lhasa which described how the Chinese had bombarded the palace in the hope of killing me. I now knew that I had to leave Tibet, so we trudged on. The going was slow and hard. As I neared the Indian border I became very ill, but I had to carry on for my only hope, and the hope of my people, lay in my finding a refuge in India. I couldn't ride my horse, so my friends helped me on the broad back of a *dzo*, a cross between a yak and a cow, which is a docile animal with an easy gait, and on that primeval Tibetan animal I left my country.'

Reprinted by permission of EWART THOMAS

STREE SEVA MANDIR: WOMEN'S LIB. IN INDIA

One of the most valuable assets any community has is the person who can discern and develop other people's latent skills and the joy in using them, and enrich the community in which they live. Such a one is Mrs Krishna Rao, a Hindu lady of Brahmin family, the founder of the Stree Seva Mandir in Madras. She is a woman in her middle fifties, once involved as a representative in the state government, but, at the time of the re-organisation of the state boundaries, she decided she could make a more useful contribution by concentrating her energies on raising the status and economic condition of women in Madras. With little capital except her own skill, the respect of her own community and support of many friends, she has trained many women and now currently trains and employs about one hundred and seventy, many of whom were destitute and with small children. The small rented room where she first started has now spread to two extensive buildings rented from the Ramakrishna Mission. Living is simple and the food adequate, the homeless mothers and children spread their mats out on the workshop floor to sleep at night and a nursery is provided for the young children in the daytime.

It is not just a question of employment, it is watching out for and developing the skills of each woman who comes seeking help, and the happy and relaxed atmosphere one notices in the workrooms that give Stree Seva Mandir a happy family feeling. At first the women are given simple work, maybe putting coloured powder into boxes for a local firm, dyeing odd bits of cloth for making dolls' clothes, varnishing toys with a spray gun. Gradually the women are hived off according to their aptitudes into a suitable class, taking courses in tailoring, secretarial work and book-keeping, making dolls, performing the various crafts of India, and educational toys, batik work, book-binding, composing printing in four languages, light engineering and electronics! Some of the courses take two years, but the women finance themselves by working part-time, making saleable goods, and spending the rest of the time attending classes run by the institution.

The state government buys some of the educational toys, Oxfam has bought some simple but well-made trains, publishers get her to print their books. Most of the equipment has been acquired slowly from businessmen and friends in Madras and the six lathes are on loan from the government until it needs them for its own technical training scheme. The Ramakrishna Mission now wants the use of its property, so Mrs Krishna Rao has acquired by gift and purchase a site on the outskirts of Madras, where she has been able to put up a two-storey building for a school, nursery and a few classrooms which will also provide simple hostel accommodation. The kitchen is being built, so for the time being mothers and children already living here eat at the local clinic she has set up and which the local Lions have furnished. A German agency has now given a workshop and two lathes and Oxfam is giving another building on the same site, but it is still not enough to house all the activities carried on in the rented buildings.

Mrs Krishna Rao is fully occupied! She lives quietly in a small rented house with her husband who has now retired and acts as her scientific advisor in many ways, including stocking the first-rate library and laboratories in a school for girls of high ability, also founded and financed by Stree Seva Mandir. It is a joy to visit Mrs Rao, to meet a woman of great compassion combined with extraordinary business ability which has enabled so many women and girls of such varying abilities to become self-supporting and self-respecting citizens.

I have met a number of girls who are now well qualified and find it easy to get a good husband without having to pay a dowry.

E.W.

DIWAKAR AGASHE

Founder of the Youth League Recreation Centre

Diwakar Agashe's parents were teachers, the mother a headmistress of a girls' school, the father a headmaster. When they retired they started a small training school for delinquent boys financed out of their own very small pensions. Diwakar, a younger son of this Hindu Brahmin family, had therefore been brought up in a home dedicated to voluntary service for the community. He took a degree at the university and then began teaching in a secondary school in Baldana, Mahrasthra, where he soon began organising voluntary service projects with the girls and boys, such as hospital visiting, play groups in slum areas and even

281

clearing waste barren land, where they planted trees and shrubs and made a public park and garden, very unusual in a small town. As the young teacher became more active and took boys and girls on expeditions, some parents began to feel uneasy and the school feared that the pupils would not be giving enough time to school work. Parents and friends who were delighted with this practical approach to education offered to support him with a small salary if he would become a youth leader. Still the school objected to their pupils attending the youth club, so finally, at the suggestion of parents and pupils, they themselves built their own school, a simple one-storey building with a verandah. Like-minded teachers came to help him as the school grew.

As there is no secondary education in the villages where most of the 'backward' classes live, the Youth League Recreation Centre, as it was now called, built a hostel and started to take boarders from those 'backward' villages. The Indian government gives a small grant for the education of children who were deprived, as they once belonged to the 'outcastes', now called 'backward' classes. Sometimes the boys can bring a bag of grain from home at the beginning of the term towards their food. The school helps when it can, but in times of drought and rising prices and when there is no work on nearby farms to earn a few extra rupees, the boys have had to be sent home.

The school has now 450 pupils, of which 60 are girls and 80 come from the 'backward' groups. They have a small farm, so they can grow some of their food requirements, if there is not a drought. Pupil boarders do their own washing, help with the garden and sweep and clean the school. All pupils pay according to their ability, so the fees are very low. They visit the hospital patients, help with nursery schools set up by the Y.L.R.C. in the slum areas, and discuss with village elders the needs of the village. They have cleaned out and reconstructed wells, made new village latrines, made a road down to a well wide enough for a bullock cart, whereas previously all water had to be carried up to the village by women walking up a narrow track. Sometimes they give concerts and organise special celebrations and dramas as they did during Gandhi Centenary Year. The Y.L.R.C. tries to raise some money so that it can send one or two poor but very able students to the university each year, and be able to organise work camps further afield during the holidays.

Now after 18 years of incredible struggle, the school is well established and the many young men trained there in social service are in positions of responsibility all over Maharasthra. More youth groups are being formed by them linked with the Y.L.R.C. and are performing valuable services in spite of the handicap of poverty in food, clothing, transport, in conditions that would make us feel helpless to help others. The service of Baba Amte, Villabhai, Mrs Hospet, Mrs Rao, and Diwakar Agashe shows what Indians are doing to help their own people and are examples where the spirit and dedication have overcome material limitations.

ELIZABETH WILSON

AN INDIAN FLORENCE NIGHTINGALE

In India it is usual for families to arrange marriages for their children; a great deal of care is taken by the family to find a partner that is suitable as regards caste, horoscope, education, family background and character. However, although a young girl is married she does not go to live with her extended family of grandparents, brothers, aunts, uncles and parents-in-law until she is thirteen or fourteen years old. As sixty years ago child mortality was very high, it often happened that a girl became a widow before she had even left her own family. Custom did not allow her to remarry and, so there was little education for women, the child widow led a very sad and restricted life.

Kamalbai Hospet was a child widow at thirteen. She came from a well-to-do-family, was reasonably educated for that time and was expected to help in the family home with her three brothers, but as there were plenty of servants she began to look for other ways of being useful; seeing the appalling poverty and lack of care for mothers and babies in the slums of Nagpur, she saw their need and knew what she should do. Her family was aghast when she said she wanted to train as a nurse, it was unheard of in good families as only the poorest and low-caste and ill-educated women became nurses. It took a long time to win the consent of the extended family that all lived together in the large house, grandparents as well as parents had to give consent. At last, Kamalbai Hospet was allowed to train as a nurse, and in 1909 opened her first clinic in the slums of Nagpur in a four-roomed house containing seven maternity beds. At first the women were shy to come, then the word spread of the help given, crowds came and the little house was much too small. Kamalbai's family came to see her work and other child widows trained as nurses and joined her. The poor could pay little if anything for treatment, but her brothers and wealthy friends were stirred to help and raised money to build a bigger hospital.

Today the biggest hospital is in Nagpur, and there are twenty others in surrounding areas founded by Kamalbai Hospet, who received a decoration from Nehru when he was prime minister. Other women have taken over the detailed running of these hospitals and the founder, who is about eighty, lives quietly in a little one-roomed house on a compound where others of her child widow nurses live and act as loving grandparents to their home for orphans.

ELIZABETH WILSON

A member of Y.C.C.R., met and visited her hospitals and home in November 1971 and again in 1978

GLOSSARY TO INDIAN STORIES

ashram Settlement of people around a leader (e.g. Gandhi's *ashram* at Ahmedabad) or, after his death, to perpetuate his teaching and ideals.

Buddha Enlightened One. Name given to prince Gautama, born c. 566 BCE.

dharma Duty or custom, cosmic order.

Mahabharata and Ramayana Two great Indian epics composed some centuries BCE and containing many of the stories which form the basis of a child's literary and religious education as well as the themes for drama and dance.

Krishna One of the most popular deities of Hinduism. An avatar or descent of Vishnu; i.e. an earthly form taken by Vishnu in order to restore the balance when evil seems to be getting the upper hand.

Shanti Sanskrit word meaning 'peace'.

Siva Popular Hindu deity of many aspects. His dance creates life or can destroy. His consort has many names — Durga, Kali, Uma, etc. — which may show the way in which a major Indian tradition has absorbed many minor ones. It also shows that Hinduism regards the concepts of God as a rich one, including both male and female. As God is in all life and all life exists in God, the Hindu sees nothing surprising in representing the Divine as a monkey (Hanuman) or elephant (Ganesha). However, the main idea must be remembered. 'That which is One men call by many names'.

SIKH STORIES

by MEWA SINGH BASSAN AND PIARA SINGH SAMBHI

CARING FOR LEPERS

Leprosy is a terrible skin disease. Today it can be cured, but not very long ago there was no treatment for it, so healthy people were afraid to go near lepers for fear of catching the disease. Sometimes they made lepers live in separate villages by themselves. In England, long ago, lepers had to carry a bell with them wherever they walked in the streets. If they saw someone coming they had to shout, 'Unclean, unclean' and ring the bell so that healthy people could avoid them.

In the time of Guru Nanak there were no leper hospitals in India.

One day Guru Nanak arrived at a village called Dipalpur, on the edge of the Punjab. He was looking for somewhere to rest, and a villager directed him to a house. He knocked on the hut door and it was answered by a man who Guru Nanak saw to be a leper.

'I have been directed to your house,' said Guru Nanak. 'May I stay here?'

'Someone in the village has been using you to play a joke on me,' replied the leper whose name was Nuri. 'They are always doing things like this. They drive me from the street, they will not let me take water from the well. No-one will speak to me. I am shunned and despised. Yet I have never harmed anyone and I do not hate those who are cruel to me.'

'The sufferings of your body have not harmed your soul. In spite of cruelty you have remained kind and your love for God has kept growing,' replied Nanak. 'You shall be healed. Your body will become as clean and pure as your mind and soul.'

At that moment Nuri recovered. He lived for many years and was well known as the finest person in the village of Dipalpur.

A similar story is told by Guru Amar Das (Guru 1552–74 CE).

A leper named Preema had heard of the kindness of Guru Amar Das and decided that he must see him. The disease was in a very advanced stage. Preema could no longer walk and had to crawl the many miles to Goindwal. He stopped a little way from the Guru's house but near enough to hear the hymns which he and his followers sang. Some of the Sikhs living nearby fed Preema and looked after him. At last Guru Amar Das heard of the leper who was camping in the village and asked the Sikhs to carry Preema to his home. Guru Amar Das bathed him and he was cured of his leprosy. Instead of having to crawl he was now able to walk from village to village preaching the goodness of the Sikh faith.

(Some people say that miracles do not happen. One can argue about this far into the night and into the day beyond. What, at very least, these stories say is that Guru Nanak and Guru Amar Das included lepers in their love. The fifth Guru Arjan built a leprosarium at Taran Taran, which still exists.

In 1969 the Sikhs of Bombay built a hospital and medical school to commemmorate the 500th anniversary of the birth of Guru Nanak. Another foundation of a similar sort which might be noted is a family resettlement centre in Bengal, where many refugees are helped. It is called Nanak Niketan. — *Editor*.)

GURU NANAK AND AND THE TEMPLE OF BREAD

Guru Nanak had always been a kind person, right from the time when he was still a boy. Sometimes his parents found his kindess difficult to bear, as on the occasion when he gave away his mother's wedding ring to a poor beggar who came to the house. When he was a little older his father decided to turn him into a businessman and sent him to town with some money. His instructions were to buy some goods cheaply and sell them at a profit — 'Use your money well, get a good return for it' said his father.

Nanak and his friend Bala, who Nanak's father entrusted with the money, set out on foot. They had gone about fifteen miles and were passing through a forest when they came upon a group of poor, very badly dressed holy men. Nanak, always curious and eager to ask questions, stopped to talk to them. He discovered that they had no money and depended upon kind people for their food. They were not beggars, they said. They never asked for food, they would starve rather than do that.

What better return for my money than to see these poor men well fed, thought Nanak. My father will be pleased. He asked his friend Bala for the 25 rupees. Bala was not sure that this was the way Nanak's father wanted the money to be used, but he gave Nanak the money. Nanak bought food and took it to the holy men. They were overjoyed and Nanak returned home pleased with his day's work.

Needless to say, his father, Mehta Kalu, did not think that he had got a good return for his money and was very angry.

Throughout his life Guru Nanak helped the poor whenever he could. After he became famous, people would give him presents of clothes, food or money. He, in turn, gave them away to poor people, widows and the sick.

Guru Nanak travelled to many places, but as he grew older he decided to settle down with his family at a place called Kartarpur, in the Punjab. Many of his friends joined him and the village became a place where everyone shared whatever he had with everyone else and where a special house was built where the poor and hungry could find food and shelter.

This house was called a *Langar* or Temple of Bread.

Guru Nanak told his followers that they should earn their bread by honest labour and share their earnings with others.

GURU NANAK AND THE GIFT OF DAUD THE WEAVER

Gifts are ways of showing love and friendship. A follower of Guru Nanak, Daud, a weaver, decided that he would make a small carpet to give to Guru Nanak. He was a good weaver, but this was the finest carpet he had ever made. He took it to the Guru and said 'Honour me, Master, by sitting on this carpet and always use it to sit on'. (In Guru Nanak's time people in India sat cross-legged on the floor, as they do very often today, rather than sitting on chairs.) The Guru thanked Daud for his kindness and accepted the gift but then said, 'This fragrant earth and nature's carpet of grass is the only carpet I wish to use. I accept your gift but I would like you to put it to use for me. Over there is a dog with her puppies. They are dying of cold. Spread the carpet over them and then fetch some food and milk. I shall be happy if you can save them from dying of cold and hunger.'

The weaver obeyed and shared the Guru's happiness.

THE REFORMED BANDIT

Guru Nanak was travelling in Assam in East India. He came to a village ruled by the Bhuyan of Nowgong and looked for somewhere to rest. None of the villagers would help him. 'You must go to the Bhuyan,' they said, 'he cares for all travellers who pass this way and he will not allow anyone else to do it.'

The Bhuyan did care for travellers. He fed them well and gave them a room for the night. But he also made them his prisoners and anyone who would not part with his wealth was beaten, tortured and sometimes murdered.

Guru Nanak and his companions went to the house of the Bhuyan and, during an excellent meal, Guru Nanak said, 'Tell me, how is it you can feed us so well? You are so kind to travellers. It must cost you much money and yet instead of growing poorer you become richer. What is your secret?'

The Bhuyan of Nowgong was not sure how to reply. He could tell a lie, but somehow Guru Nanak seemed to be a man who could detect a lie. His eyes seemed to see right into the Bhuyan's wicked heart. He decided to tell the truth — after all, what could Guru Nanak do about it, a kind holy man with no sword or dagger?

'I steal and rob,' he said, 'all the Maharajas, Rajahs and Nawabs do it. I steal from my guests.'

Guru Nanak was pleased that the Bhuyan had told the truth, but he went on to warn him that his kindness in feeding guests could not wipe out his evil in robbing them. One day he would have to pay for his wickedness. He should mend his ways while there was yet time.

'Bad habits are not easily overcome,' said the Bhuyan.

'True,' said Guru Nanak, 'but if you have the will to give up the habits you have made you can make them. Remember three things. First, always tell the truth, second, don't steal if you eat anyone's salt, don't cheat him and don't do any evil in his house; third, don't let anyone who has done nothing wrong be harmed on your account.'

The Bhuyan tried hard to mend his ways but, after a time, seeing his pile of riches grow smaller, he decided to rob a prince who lived nearby.

Late one afternoon he went to the Rajah's palace and hid in a room. There was some food in the room and the thief became hungry. He took some savoury things, some sweets and some fruit. In the middle of the night he broke into the Rajah's treasury and began to take his jewels.

Then he remembered the Guru's words, 'You must not steal if you have eaten anyone's salt, do not commit any evil in his house.' The food he had eaten seemed to choke him. He was ashamed of himself and went home, leaving the valuables behind him.

Next day the Rajah discovered that a thief had been in his house. Although nothing had been taken, he wanted the thief caught and his police went arresting villagers and torturing them. The Bhuyan of Nowgong remembered some of the other words spoken by Guru Nanak. 'Don't let anyone who has done nothing wrong be punished on your account'. He went to the Rajah and confessed that he was the thief. The other words of Guru Nanak came to mind. 'Always tell the truth'. He felt pleased that he had done something right at last.

The innocent villagers were set free and when he had heard the whole story the Rajah forgave the Bhuyan. The Bhuyan became well known for his honesty and kindness and among Sikhs is known as Bhai Bhumia. Bhai means brother and is a title given only to the finest Sikhs who are faithful followers of the Guru.

GURU NANAK THE CAPTIVE

Guru Nanak was about fifty years old when, with his friend Mardana, he was taken prisoner by soldiers of Babur, the Mogul prince who was conquering northern India. With many other Indians he was forced to march to a camp where they were made to grind corn and carry heavy loads.

Many lost heart. Guru Nanak, however, remained cheerful and sang hymns in praise of God. No matter how hard the work or rough the treatment, the Guru never ceased to be happy. News of this remarkable man reached Babur, who came to see him. Instead of being afraid of the Emperor, Guru Nanak reproved him for imprisoning innocent people and treating them cruelly. Ashamed, the Emperor gave them back their belongings, which the soldiers had taken, and ordered their release.

GURU NANAK'S UNWORTHY SONS

In his old age Guru Nanak settled at a village called Kartarpur. Many disciples (*Sikhs*) gathered around him and made their homes near his. One problem troubled him. When he died, who would lead and teach these people? He had two sons, both of them fine men, but were they the ones for the job? He decided to put them to the test.

One night a winter storm damaged the Guru's house. He called upon his sons to repair it. They refused. 'It is the middle of the night. It is dark and cold. Anyway the Guru's sons shouldn't repair walls like common workmen. Wait until the morning, we will call masons and labourers to do it.'

Another disciple, Lehna, got up and rebuilt the wall, but it was not good enough for the Guru. 'Pull it down and do it again,' he said. This Lehna did two or three times. The Guru's sons said he was foolish. 'You'll never please our father, you may as well give up,' they said. But Lehna replied. 'A servant must do his master's work. It is for the master to choose what that work shall be.'

On another occasion a water pot fell into a dirty ditch. Guru Nanak asked his sons to retrieve it but they felt they were too good to do such work. It was Lehna who pulled out the pot, cleaned it and filled it with fresh water.

It was Lehna whom Guru Nanak chose to be his successor shortly before his death — for only a man who could serve his master so humbly was fit to be leader of the Sikhs.

GANGU SHAH AND GURU AMAR DAS

Gangu Shah was a rich merchant who lived in Lahore at the time of Guru Amar Das. His business failed and his friends and relations deserted him. He had heard that the Guru was everyone's friend and therefore decided to visit him in his village of Goindwal. Everyone, rich or poor had to share a meal in the Guru's kitchen. This he did although he considered himself better than many of the people he ate with. Still, he must see the Guru.

He met the Guru and falling at his knees told him of his plight. 'I have come to you for shelter and friendship,' he said.

The Guru advised him to go to Delhi when he had rested, and begin his business again. But when he was rich again he must remember the Guru's teaching — he must worship God, be honest and always be prepared to assist the poor.

Gangu Shah went to Delhi, worked hard and became rich again.

One day, a poor Brahmin came to the Guru. He had a daughter who wished to marry but the Brahmin could not afford a dowry. The Guru had no money of his own so he sent the Brahmin with a letter to Gangu. 'This poor man needs help. Please give him what he needs.'

Gangu wondered what he should do. If he helped the Brahmin, Guru Amar Das might send others for help. But if he gave no help, the Guru would not trouble him again. He decided to send the Brahmin away empty-handed.

Some time later, Gangu Shah's business failed again. 'It is because I have been selfish and not obeyed the Guru's teaching,' he said. He resolved to return to Goindwal and ask for forgiveness. However, back in Goindwal he had not the courage to face the Guru. Instead, he worked in his kitchen cutting wood, fetching water, feeding the poor. The Guru heard of him and summoned him to him. He forgave him, and provided him with a new white tunic.

'Go and live as I told you,' he said, 'worship God, be honest, help the poor — so be a true Sikh,' Gangu Shah did not forget the teaching a second time.

MUSLIM GENEROSITY TOWARDS GURU ARJAN

Guru Arjan, the fifth Guru of the Sikhs, used to travel around north India visiting his Sikhs. He came to a place now known as Tarn Taran. Then it was not even a village, though many Sikhs lived in the neighbourhood. He decided that a large pool should be built and a *Gurdwara* next to it. Such tanks are common in India, especially near temples and serve many purposes.

The Guru found a suitable site and one of his wealthy followers agreed to purchase the land from the landowners, who were Muslims. He paid a good price and the Muslims returned to their village pleased. Their wives saw the money and asked how it had been obtained.

When they discovered that a Sikh had bought the land they became angry with their husbands. 'He has not bought it for his private use or for his family,' they said. 'He has bought it to build a temple like the one at Amritsar. We should not accept money for land which is going to be used for such a purpose. Return it to the Sikhs.'

The Muslims asked the Sikh to take back his money, but he refused; he had paid a fair price. They went to the Guru but he said the money had never been his, how could he take back what he had never given!

At last it was agreed that the men digging the tank should be given the money.

Muslims and Sikhs have not always lived in brotherhood but the *Gurdwara* at Tarn Taran is a continual reminder of one such occasion and that friendship has continued down the years.

GURU AMAR DAS AND THE MOGUL EMPEROR, AKBAR

The third, Guru, Amar Das, was leader of the Sikhs from 1552 to 1574 CE. He was kind and humble and became Guru at the age of 73 years. He only owned two changes of clothing, everything else he gave away.

He lived at Goindwal and, like Guru Nanak, kept a Temple of Bread or free kitchen (Sikhs call it the *Guru-ka-Langar*) where the poor and needy were fed.

However, he asked everyone, rich or poor, who came to visit him to share a meal in the *Guru-ka-Langar*. He wanted to teach people that all, rich and poor, men and women, are equal.

So it happened that one day the great Emperor of India. Akbar, came to visit the Guru. He also had to sit cross-legged on the floor of the *Langar* and eat the simple food which the Sikhs had prepared. Then he came to the Guru, bowed and touched his feet.

The two men sat and talked. When the Emperor rose to leave the Guru he offered him a large piece of land for the service of the Temple of Bread. 'Thank you,' replied the Guru, 'but we have already more than enough to meet our needs.'

'Then may I give it to your daughter, for I regard all your children as my own?' he asked.

'You may, if you wish. The money from the estate will be used for the widows and orphans. My daughter, Bibi Bhani, will look after it.'

This is the estate upon which Bibi Bhani's husband, the father of Guru Ram Das, built the town of Amritsar.

THE GREAT DELIVERER

The sixth Guru, Hargobind, lived in the reign of Jehangir, the Mogul Emperor suspicious of his Sikh and Hindu subjects though a friend of the Guru.

The Emperor became ill, and when his doctors had failed to cure him it was asked whether anyone else might be able to help, or whether perhaps some enemy of the Emperor's had put a curse upon him. One of Jehangir's courtiers, Chandu, saw an opportunity to be rid of Guru Hargobind. His plot had a double edge. He told Jehangir that Hargobind was a man whose prayers could save his life. He should be sent to Gwalior fort to pray. On the other hand, he gave orders that when the Guru came to the fort he should be put to death as the cause of the Emperor's sufferings. Friends prevented this order being carried out but he was held prisoner.

When at last the Emperor recovered, the Guru was forgotten, even though it was in obedience to the Emperor's wishes that he had risked his life by going to the fort. It was not until Mian Mir, the Muslim who had laid the foundation-stone of the Golden Temple approached the Emperor that Hargobind's release was secured. The Guru, instead of returning immediately to his family, drew attention to the plight of fifty-two Indian princes, also prisoners. He refused to be set free until they were given their liberty.

For this act of courage he was given the name Bandi Chhor, Great Deliverer.

GURU GOBIND SINGH AND BHAI GHANAVA

During a battle between Muslims and Sikhs, a Sikh water-carrier called Ghanaya was seen giving water to wounded Muslim soldiers as they lay suffering from thirst under the hot sun. He was brought to Guru Gobind Singh and accused of being a traitor. The Guru heard the charges and asked Ghanaya to answer them. 'When I walked through the battle-fields I saw no Muslims and no Sikhs, only your face in every man,' said Ghanaya. 'You are a true Sikh,' replied the Guru. 'Continue the work; and here is some ointment to put on the wounds. You shall be known as Bhai Ghanaya from now on!' *Bhai* means brother, it is a term of honour among Sikhs, reserved for the best of men.

HOSPITALITY COMES FROM THE HEART

The tenth Guru, Gobind Singh, lived at Anandpur. He instructed every Sikh to keep a free kitchen of his own so that pilgrims and travellers could be fed. No-one should be sent away hungry.

One morning he decided to see if his instructions had been carried out. He rose early and, disguised as a pilgrim, went through the town asking for something to eat. Everywhere his request met with the same reply. 'We are still getting the food ready. We are not ready to receive guests. You will have to wait.'

The Master went from door to door until he came to the *langar* of

Bhai Nandlal. Here the Sikh welcomed the stranger with a beaming smile and invited him into the room. Everything in the *langar* was put before him — butter, half-kneaded flour, half-cooked pulses and other vegetables.

'This is ready and is for you,' said Bhai Nandlal. 'You may eat now or wait until the food is properly prepared.'

Next morning, Guru Gobind Singh told his followers that there was only one *langar* in Anandpur and that it belonged to Bhai Nandlal.

THE GOLDEN TEMPLE AT AMRITSAR

When Guru Arjan decided to build the Golden Temple in the centre of a great artificial lake there were many people who expected him to plan a building which would tower high into the sky, so that it could be seen for miles. This would show the magnificence of Sikhism. To their surprise the Guru replied 'No. The humble will be exalted. The more a tree is laden with fruit the more its branches stoop towards the earth.' He therefore commanded that the Temple should be a low building and that worshippers entering it should descend eight or more steps. Only the humble prepared to become even more meek could worship God.

He also ordered that it should have four doors to show that God is everywhere and that it should be open to men of all four castes, that is, open to everyone. Its foundation-stone was laid by a Muslim friend of the Guru, Mian Mir.

Finally, he had the sacred book of the Sikhs, the *Guru Granth Sahib*, placed in the centre of the Temple, the most important place, to prevent it being occupied by anyone else.

On one ocasion the Emperor Akbar came to the Temple and asked permission to make a contribution towards its maintenance. Guru Arjan refused, pointing out it was well supported by the people. When the Emperor insisted the Guru replied. 'The country is suffering from a severe famine. It would be best if your visit were marked by remitting this year's rent and taxes to the poor farmers.' The Emperor ordered this to be done.

BHAGAT PURAN SINGH (MERCY)

In this world of ours there are scientists who discover new medicines and drugs. There is technology to help the disabled and the crippled. Hospitals and orphanages are everywhere. The aged and the infirm are well looked after in homes and institutions especially built for them. Such benefits and facilities which we take for granted in this country are, however, not available to the poor in India. The welfare services run by the government lag far behind the needs of the people. To alleviate the sufferings of the poor and the unattached, private institutions like Bhagat Puran Singh's Pingalwara (House for the Crippled) at Amritsar have come into existence. The expenses for the treatment and care of the sick in such institutions are met with the voluntary contributions made by public at large.

Bhagat Puran Singh was still in his teens when his father's banking business collapsed and he moved to Lahore — the capital city of the state — in search of a job. He stayed there in the famous *Gurdwara* of Guru Arjan Dev, where he got free food and lodging. He spent most of his time in serving food to the poor and the disabled from the *Gurdwara's* free kitchen. In his spare time he would take the sick to a nearby hospital or a dispensary for treatment. Years rolled by in such humanitarian work, when a small incident changed his whole life. A four-year-old crippled child was left by someone in the precincts of the *Gurdwara*. He took charge of him and made up his mind to dedicate his life to serve afflicted humanity.

In 1947 he shifted his activities to Amritsar — the city of the Golden Temple. His reputation as a social worker had now been established. With the help of a few philanthropists of the city, Puran Singh acquired some tents and pitched them near the Civil Hospital in an open field. As the hospital could not admit all the patients, Puran Singh himself volunteered to look after them in the tents and to ferry them to the hospital for examination and treatment. Soon the donations of cash and clothes, food and fruit started pouring in. As his tenement expanded, doctors and nurses from the city and hospitals came forward to provide medical aid to his patients in his tents. There was no dearth of hands for other social and ancillary work. Eventually in 1950 he was able to provide a permanent home known as Pingalwara. Puran Singh, now about eighty years old, still finds pleasure in keeping the roads clear of banana peels, brick bats, metal and glass pieces to ensure safety and convenience of the public. People lovingly call him *Bhagat* — a saint.

MAHARAJA RANJIT SINGH *(SEWA)*

Voluntary social work is very highly regarded by the Sikh community. In Sikh parlance, the social service is called *Sewa*. A place in God's Court can only be attained if we do service to others in the world, said Guru Nanak. Apart from any other considerations, it is the religious duty of every Sikh, rich or poor, to render some physical act of service to a fellow human being whenever and wherever an opportunity may present itself for such a selfless service.

Maharaja Ranjit Singh — the ruler of the Punjab — would often go round incognito to see if everything were well in his kingdom. There were many small kingdoms in India ruled by Rajahs and Nawabs before 1947 when India attained independence from the British. Personal supervision of this nature was an effective deterrent for checking political corruption and misuse of powers by the state officials. On one such a walkabout the Maharaja saw an old man with a young child by his side looking for help. They had purchased some foodstuff from the market and the load seemed too heavy for them to carry home. Their house was at a distance and it was getting dark. They were wondering what to do. The Maharajah, who had disguised himself as a rustic, offered to carry the sack of food grain for them. They thanked him heartily for this timely help. No sooner had the Maharajah turned back after saying goodbye to them, than he was recognised by a night watchman patrolling the street. In a surprised voice he greeted him with the 'Our gracious king'. The Maharajah brushed him aside and hurried away, leaving the old man dazed but full of praise for him.

MAHARAJA RANJIT SINGH (JUSTICE)

India, like England, is a multi-racial and multi-religious country. The people live in villages and towns in mixed settlements without any serious difficulties. The religious practices and the social customs of the people, however, vary from community to community. It is no wonder that there are sometimes misunderstandings among them.

In a certain village near Lahore during an election to the village council, tension arose between the Muslims and the Sikhs in connection with the appointment of a returning officer for the election. The situation was further aggravated by the local politicians, who took sides instead of affecting a compromise of some sort. The Sikhs outnumbered the Muslims in the village and took advantage of their numerical strength to tease them. They stopped the Muslim priest called the Mullah from saying *Azan,* the Muslim call to prayer. Five times a day, beginning with a prayer early in the morning and ending with one late in the evening, Muslims are reminded to pray to God with an *Azan* by their Mullah. The Mullah, standing at an elevated place in the mosque, cries aloud to make himself heard to the people in their homes and working in the fields around. The Sikhs accused him of making an unnecessary noise and disturbing them. The Muslims had to yield to this high-handedness of the Sikhs just to avoid a violent clash in the village.

Once Maharajah Ranjit Singh was touring through the countryside on horseback, and he happened to stop in that village. The Maharajah was very popular and known for justice and fair play. The Muslims thought it prudent to bring their complaint to his notice. The Maharajah ordered both the parties to appear before him in the village hall. He addressed the gathering by saying: 'It is the foremost duty of everyone to meditate and pray to God. But it is also a potent fact that people worship God according to the traditions inherited by them from their forefathers. Some say their prayers quietly while others sing and dance in praise of God. Hindus, Muslims, Sikhs and Christians, all are dear to me as my loyal subjects. The suppression of the freedom of worship of the Muslims will therefore be tantamount to denying them the equal rights and opportunities in my kingdom. As such it is incumbent upon me to see that no injustice is perpetuated on any community or religious grounds whatsoever.'

P. S. SAMBHI

APPENDIX TO SIKH STORIES

The Sikh Gurus

The full list of the Sikh Gurus reads as follows:

Guru Nanak	1469–1539
Guru Angad	1504–1552
Guru Amar Das	1479–1574
Guru Ram Das	1534–1581
Guru Arjan	1563–1606
Guru Hargobind	1595–1645
Guru Har Rai	1630–1661
Guru Har Krishen	1656–1664
Guru Tegh Bahadur	1621–1675
Guru Gobind Singh	1666–1708

The Sikh Gurus

The kinship of the last eight is as outlined:

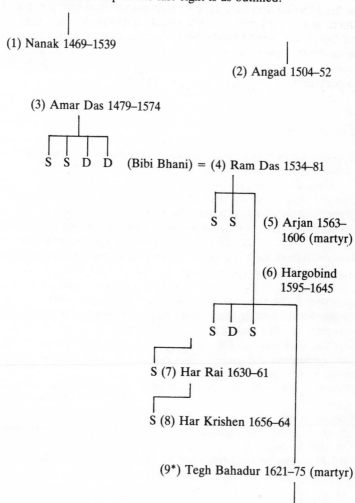

(1) Nanak 1469–1539

(2) Angad 1504–52

(3) Amar Das 1479–1574

S   S   D   D   (Bibi Bhani) = (4) Ram Das 1534–81

S   S   (5) Arjan 1563–1606 (martyr)

(6) Hargobind 1595–1645

S   D   S

S (7) Har Rai 1630–61

S (8) Har Krishen 1656–64

(9*) Tegh Bahadur 1621–75 (martyr)

(10) Gobind Rai 1666–1708

* Tegh Bahadur was the son of Guru Hargobind by a second marriage.

GLOSSARY TO SIKH STORIES

Amritsar 'The city of nectar' or 'The eternal city', Sikh pilgrimage city in the Punjab built by the fourth Guru. Site of the Golden Temple which in its present form is the work of Maharaja Ranjit Singh (died 1839 CE). Original builder Guru Arjan.

Babur Muslim invader and conqueror of Northern India in the sixteenth century CE. Founder of the Mogul Emperor. Descendant of Tamurlane the Great.

Bala Close friend and constant companion of Guru Nanak. Hindu.

Bhai Brother. Honorific title in Sikhism.

Bibi Sister. Honorific title in Sikhism.

Bhuyan A local governor or government official.

Brahmin The priestly caste of Hindus. All priests are brahmins, but not all brahmins become priests, nor are all brahmins rich.

Gurdwara Literally, the door of the Guru, i.e. the home of the Guru. Sikh place of worship, but also a community centre, equipped with kitchen, library and accommodation for guests.

Guru Indian religious teacher and spiritual guide whose experience of God is direct, not second-hand from books and who has been commissioned by God to communicate the revelation to others. In Sikhism a technical term applied only to their leaders and spiritual masters, and to their scripture, the *Guru Granth,* a collection (*Granth* = collection) upon which the last Guru conferred the guruship.

Langar Kitchen or Temple of Bread. Commensiality, as a practical way of rejecting caste and stressing brotherhood, is an essential feature of Sikhism. Full name *Guru-ka-Langar,* the Guru's kitchen.

Lehna Name of the disciple of Guru Nanak who became his successor and is better known as Guru Angad.

Mardana Close friend and constant companion of Guru Nanak. Musician.

Punjab Fertile province in Northern India. Strongly under Muslim influence in the fifteenth century CE when the Sikh faith originated. The Sikh homeland.

Sikh Probably derived from the Sanskrit *sishya,* 'disciple' or 'learner'. Specifically used of the followers of the ten Gurus.

MUSLIM STORIES
Compiled by
Dr Muhammad Iqbal

MUHAMMAD: FRIEND OF ANIMALS

The message which the Prophet Muhammad preached was that there was only one God and that men should be kind to one another, especially to orphans, widows and animals.

One day when he went into his house he saw his cat sleeping with her kittens on the cloak which he wanted to wear. Rather than disturb it Muhammad cut off the end of the cloak on which the cat was sleeping and wrapped what remained around his own shoulders.

Another time he was walking along one of the narrow streets of his town when a camel came running. People were panicking and rushing into doorways to escape its large hoofs and strong teeth. Muhammad was used to camels; before he became a prophet he had been a camel driver. He stopped the camel. The breathless owner came up to him, thanked him and was about to give the animal a beating.

'Why don't you feed this camel properly? He is complaining that he is hungry. Camels don't run away if they are properly treated.' The man was rather shocked, but he admitted that he had been wrong. He realised that the camel was not only there to be his servant, it was also an animal which had to be cared for.

MUHAMMAD OVERCOMES HATRED WITH KINDNESS

A Muslim likes to pray to God. He may pray to God anywhere, and will do so five times a day. A mosque is a special place where Muslims go to pray. The Prophet Muhammad often went to the mosque to pray. He found it a cool and peaceful place to worship the one God. The quiet of the mosque reminded him of the pleasant evenings in the desert, so different from the bustling noisy town.

At the beginning a lot of people disliked Muhammad for his dislike of idols. He told them it was wrong to be unkind, cheats and liars. Many people found it easier to be unkind than to be good and generous.

One woman, who did not like Muhammad, used to sweep her dust and rubbish over him as he passed her house on his way to the mosque. The Prophet always turned his head, and smiling would say to her in the way he would greet a friend, 'Assalam-o-Alaikum'. Perhaps you greet your friends in this way. This lady never replied in the way your friends do. She just swept more dust over him.

One day, as Muhammad came near the woman's house, she was nowhere to be seen. He immediately asked the neighbours where the lady was. The neighbours were very surprised because they knew that she did not like Muhammad and swept the dust and rubbish over him whenever he passed. However, they told him that she was living alone and was very ill. At once Muhammad went to her house. There he set to work, cooking a meal, fetching water from the well[1] and sweeping away the dust and rubbish. The lady was amazed to see someone helping her and even more so when she realised who it was. She was very sorry for her bad deeds and became a good Muslim, following his example of kindness and truthfulness.

1. A well for the poor: The story is told of a young man whose mother had recently died. He went to Muhammad and said that he wished to build a monument in memory of her. The Prophet replied, 'Dig a well for the poor people. Whenever they draw water from it they will remember your mother and bless her name'.

VICTORY OF MECCA

When Muhammad entered Mecca with 10,000 men (630 CE) he asked the conquered people, 'What do you think I will do to you?' They answered, 'You are a kind brother and the son of a kind brother'. The Prophet was happy to hear this. 'Go, you are freed,' he replied. On that day he forgave the Quraish and their bad thoughts and wicked deeds. The Muslims took over the city peacefully and quietly. There was no robbing or looting. No woman was harmed.

One thing alone was destroyed. Going to the *Ka-aba*, the House of God, the Prophet pointed at the three hundred and sixty idols with his staff, saying, 'Truth is come and the falsehood is fled away'. At these words his followers smashed them to pieces. Some people, including Abu Sufyan, a warrior of great skill, said only a Prophet of God could act in this way with so much confidence.

It is reported that not a single person employed to look after the sanctuary was sacked. Even the keeper of the sanctuary was kept.

A MASTER'S RESPONSIBILITY

Muhammad had a friend called Abu Dhar. One day another friend saw him in the street. Abu Dhar was walking with his servant but it was difficult to tell the one from the other because they were both dressed in the same sort of clothes — the rich man and the poor man.

'Why are you wearing the same garments, Abu Dhar, you a rich man and he your servant?'

Abu Dhar replied, 'Once I heard Muhammad, the Messenger of Allah, say, "Your servants are your brothers: Allah has put them under your care. You must feed your servant with what you eat and dress him with what you wear. You mustn't give him too much work to do, but if you do overburden him you must help him to do it". '

DON'T JUDGE BY APPEARANCES
from Sura 80 of the Qur'an

Muhammad, the Messenger of God, was talking to an important man when a poor blind man came to him and asked Muhammad to tell him about God. Muhammad was angry, he frowned and turned away from the blind man who had interrupted him. Then in his heart he felt that God was speaking to him and saying 'the chief you are talking to is a proud man, he will never listen to the teaching, but the blind man is humble you will not bother to teach about me. Yet he will listen and believe'.

Muhammad was sorry and so he warned his followers not to judge people by outward appearances. Later Allah's warning was written down in the *Qur'an*: *Sura 80 vi-10*

'In the Name of God, The Merciful, the Compassionate. He frowned and turned away when the blind came to him. How could you tell? He might have come to grow in grace. He might have come so that he could heed Our warning. But you attended to the self-sufficient man, though it is no concern of yours if he does not pay attention. You failed to heed to the one who came eager and ready to listen.'

KINDNESS ON THE BATTLEFIELD

In the early days of Islam many a battle was fought. The Arabs did not like the teachings of the Prophet Muhammad. They oppressed those who accepted and followed him. One of these battles was fought at Yarmuk in Saudia Arabia.

Human kindness and heroic sacrifice are often tested in terrible conditions. Abu-Jahim-bin-Huzaifah, a companion of the Prophet, told a story about the great kindness and unselfishness of two wounded and dying Muslims.

'During the battle of Yarmuk I went out in search of my cousin, who was on the battlefront. I took some water with me, knowing it would do him good. I found him in the very thick of the fighting. Alas, he was dying. I ran forward to give the little water I had. But, as I did so, another badly wounded soldier beside gave a sigh, and my cousin turned his face and pointed to take the water to the other man first. I took the water to the other person whom I recognised as Hisham-bin-Abilas. But I had hardly reached him when we heard another groaning person nearby. Hisham also pointed to the man, that I should give the water to him instead. However, before I arrived, this third man had died. Hastily I ran back to Hisham but he was also dead. Hurriedly I made my way over to my cousin. Alas, he too had passed away. *Innalillahe wa Innailaihe rajeun.*[1] (All of us came from Allah and we will all return to Allah.)'

1. This is the Arabic formula which a Muslim recites instantaneously on seeing or hearing of a death.

THE WOULD-BE MURDERER IS FORGIVEN

Once, the Prophet Muhammad was travelling to a far-off place. It was the middle of the day and the sun was at its highest. It gave out a burning heat. The prophet stopped for a short while to rest. All his companions got off their camels and rested. The Prophet lay down under the shade of a tree. He was so tired that he went to sleep as soon as his head touched the ground.

Among the travellers was a man who did not like Muhammad's teaching about one God. The man himself, like many of the people of the time, prayed to idols and believed in many different kinds of gods. This man, seeing that the Prophet, who was some distance away from his fellow-travellers, had fallen asleep, thought to himself, 'Now is the time to get rid of this man who tells us that we must pray to the one God and not to our many gods'. He quickly ran over to Muhammad. As he did so, he took out a sword. Just as he was about to be killed, the Prophet woke up. The man said, 'Muhammad, who can save you from me now?' The Prophet did not seem to be worried at all. 'Allah, the one Almighty God will save me,' the Prophet answered. The man was very surprised and began to wonder what kind of man was this who was not afraid of being killed. The sword fell out of his hands.

Quickly, the Prophet got up, picked up the sword with one hand and grabbed his attacker with the other, and said, 'Tell me now, who will save you from me?' The man did not know what to do. He was frightened because he knew he would be killed. He started to tremble and asked the Prophet to be kind to him. 'No-one but you can save me.'

The Prophet let him go and the man followed the teachings of Muhammad for the rest of his life.

THE PRINCE WHO LOVED GOD

As a young boy, Abbas, one of the sons of Haroon-al-Rashid[1] liked to talk and listen to good religious people. He would visit graveyards and talk to the dead. He cared nothing for the way he dressed.

Once, when his father was talking with his ministers and officers, the boy came up to them wearing only two pieces of cloth, one round his waist and the other on his head. The men looked at him. They did not like to see a prince dressed this way. They thought it was not right for a king's son to dress in such a poor manner. 'This boy is very bad, he upsets his father. He should dress properly so that the king may be proud of him when other kings come to see him,' they said. When the king asked his son to dress in rich clothes the boy did not answer but, seeing a bird a long way off, he called it to his side. The bird flew onto the child's hand. He then told the bird to fly away, and it did so.

Having shown everyone what he was able to do because he loved God more than anything else, he turned to his father and told him that he wore shabby clothes because, if he loved God, such earthly things were not important and that he was sad because he loved God more than his father.[2]

Soon, the boy knew it was time to leave his father's court and serve only God. He took with him a copy of the Holy *Qur'an* and a costly ring which his mother gave him to make use of if ever he needed any money.

When the prince reached Basra, he worked as a labourer for one day in the week and took only enough money to last him a week. At this time, Abu Amar Basri[3] was looking for a builder to mend a wall which had fallen down. Suddenly, he saw a handsome youth busy reciting words from the Holy *Qur'an*. He asked the boy if he would do the job. The boy said, 'I will do the job but I want only a small sum of money to last a week and I must stop working at the times of prayer'. Abu Amar agreed to this and the youth started to work. By the end of the day Abu Amar noticed that the boy had done as much work as ten men. He paid him his wages. To his surprise, the boy did not come the next day. As he was so pleased with his work Abu Amar set out to look for him, but could not find him until the next week at the same time and in the same place that he had seen him before. The boy again asked for the same small sum of money and time off for prayers, and carried on building the wall.

At the end of the day, Abu Amar gave the boy more money than he had asked for, but the boy would not take more than would last him a week. Abu Amar waited until the next week for the youth to come for work. He did not come and was nowhere to be found. Abu Amar looked all over for him. He told the story in this way, 'I asked all and sundry. At last a man told me that the boy had been ill and lay unconscious in the forest. I paid a man to take me to him. When I reached the place, the boy was lying on the ground, resting his head on a stone. I spoke to him but he did not answer. I greeted him again and this time he opened his eyes. He knew me at once. I lifted his head and put it in my lap. He raised his head and spoke some holy verses reminding everyone about death and warned against people who were greedy for wordly goods. He asked me to bathe him and bury him in one of his garments, to give the other piece of cloth and his *Lota*[4] to the man who would dig his grave, to take the Holy *Qur'an* and the ring to Haroon-al-Rashid personally and to tell him, 'These are your things. They belonged to your son. Make sure you do as God wishes'. With that, the boy died. Only then did I realise that the boy was the prince. I buried him there as he had asked and took the ring to the king in Baghdad. I stood on a high mound near the palace and saw a troop of horsemen riding out from the palace. Nine more battalions followed. The king himself rode with the tenth troop. When I saw him, I shouted at the top of my voice. The king stopped and I showed him the things that his son had left. He recognised them and me and so I was able to tell him all I could about his son. Tears rolled down his cheeks as I spoke. He ordered one of his guards to look after me until he returned from his royal visit. When I saw the king again he was very sad indeed. He asked me how I came to know his son. He was very shocked to hear that his son, a prince, should wish to work as a labourer and for only enough money to last him one week. I said that I had not known that he was the king's son, the relative of the Prophet Muhammad.[5] The king asked me if I had bathed his son with my own hands. I told him that I had and he took my hands and pressed them to his heart as he said some verses which showed his great sadness. He also visited the grave and said more verses which told of the fact that death must come to everyone.'

Later, Abu Amar Basri dreamt of the departed soul of this boy which told him of his great joy in the after life where he found happiness beyond the realms of human thought or knowledge.

1. Haroon-al-Rashid was the Abbasid Caliph (*d.* 809 CE) who ruled the Muslim empire from Baghdad. He was an extremely just ruler of the time. His stories of wandering in disguise at night to find out what was happening to the poor, are well known to people in the West through the *Tales of the Arabian Nights*. He thanked Allah by praying one hundred units of prayers of thanks *(Nafal)* every night. He made a pilgrimage to Mecca along with one hundred learned men every alternate year.
2. This is known as *Tawakkal* — contentment — in Islam.
3. Abu Amar Basri was a learned friend of the king and a Muslim mystic of repute.
4. Cup for taking ablutions.
5. Generally the descendants of the Prophet Muhammad are revered and looked up to for spiritual guidance.

The teacher of a mixed class of Asian and European children may not wish to use all or any of this story. However, the full Muslim account is given here. *(Editor)*.

FAZIL-BIN-AYAZ'S[1] REPENTANCE

Fazil-bin-Ayaz was the leader of a band of robbers. Although he did bad things and stole from other people, he used to pray every day and especially on Festival days. Sometimes he would go without food and water and he always fasted during the month of *Ramadhan*. He wore very poor clothes and looked like a holy man.

Once Fazil's gang set upon a camel caravan. Fazil did not go with his men. Instead, he sat a little way off and watched. A merchant, the leader of the caravan saw Fazil. He thought, 'Here is a good man. He dresses like a Holy man. I will let him look after my money. Then when the robbers have gone, I will get my money back.' So he gave his purse full of *Ashrafis* to Fazil the robber and sat beside him.

Soon, the thieves started to bring the stolen goods over to Fazil. The merchant was very surprised. He started to worry about this man whom he had thought to be a good, holy man. What had he done! Given all his money to a robber! Suddenly he saw Fazil looking at him. 'What now?' he thought. He became very frightened. But the robber spoke softly: 'Don't worry. I'm not going to keep your money. You have trusted me as if I were a holy man.'

At that moment, a man came riding by on a camel. He was saying some verses from the Holy *Qur'an*. They told of the fact that bad men still had time to change their ways and repent of their sins.[2] As he listened, Fazil went into a trance. When he came to his senses, he found that he wanted only to be good. He called all his companions to him and told them to go their own ways saying, 'From today onwards I am not going to rob people or take any interest in earthly things. I wish I had not done all the bad things that I have done. I repent. I will never do wrong again.'

As the robbers left him, Fazil asked them to forgive him. A Jew amongst them would not forgive him. He felt his repentance was a shame. First, he asked Fazil to do two things. Could he move one mound of sand to another place? It is said, that just at that time a sudden gust of wind blew and in no time at all the mound of sand had been blown away.

Then the Jew put some clay in a rough hessian sack and asked Fazil to bring the sack to him, but it must be full of gold. This Fazil did. When they opened the sack, there before them lay the gold. At once the Jew fell at Fazil's feet and said, 'Now there is no doubt. Truly you have repented. I have read the Holy *Torah* [Old Testament]. If a person really is sorry for his misdeeds, his truth can be judged by two things. First, he will be able to order mountains to move. Second, he can turn clay into gold. I had, therefore, to ask you to do these two jobs for me to test your repentance. Now I am sure of it. You are a good man.'

1. Fazil-bin-Ayaz was one of the early mystics of Islam. Haroon-al-Rashid, the Abbasid Caliph and Ahmad-bin-Hanbal, the founder of the Hanbalic School of Islamic Law, often visited him for spiritual guidance, Imam Abu Hanifah, the founder of the Hanifi School of Islamic Law, was Fazil's religious mentor.
2. Chapter Hadid of the Holy *Qur'an*.

ZAID-BIN-HARTHA

When he was a young boy, Zaid-bin-Hartha set off with his mother to visit his grandparents. On the way they were set upon by thieves who robbed his mother and ran off with the boy. His mother cried all the way home, and told Zaid's father that their goods had been stolen and Zaid had been kidnapped. When he heard this, the father was very upset. He looked all over for his son but could not find him. He was so sad he began to go out of his mind. He took to the hills and spoke to the river. 'Oh, water of the river, tell me where my son is hidden, for he was everything to me.' His eyes were sore and tired with crying but he had no success.

The father began to ask his friends for news of the child. It was not long before some travellers from Mecca told Zaid's father that they had seen a boy who fitted Zaid's description in Mecca. His father grew extremely happy and, helped by this stroke of good luck, set off with his brother as soon as possible. After some hours of searching, the two men came to the Prophet Muhammad's house. 'Is there a boy called Zaid here?' they asked. Muhammad called out, 'Come here Zaid'. As the boy came towards them the Prophet asked him, 'Do you know who these men are?' The boy replied, 'Yes, this is my father and that is my uncle'. 'You must go home with them,' Muhammad told the boy. Slowly the tears rolled down Zaid's cheeks as the child realised that he must leave his Prophet. 'O, Muhammad! I cannot leave you. You have loved me as your own son, I will not leave you now, not even to return to my own home and family.'

A WOMAN AND A DOG

A bad woman went out one day. She saw a dog dying of thirst. She took pity on the poor animal. But there was no water to be seen. After a long search, she found a well a little further along the road. 'Oh dear,' she thought, 'there is neither rope nor bucket to get the water out of the well. What shall I do?' Suddenly, she took off one of her shoes and fastened it to the scarf she had been wearing round her neck. Slowly, she lowered the shoe into the well and collected some water in it. She pulled it up carefully so that she would not spill a drop.

By the time the woman reached the dog it was nearly dead. Gently she poured the water into the dog's mouth. Soon, the dog began to lick her feet and eventually he was able to stand up and walk. At the sight of the good that she had done, the lady felt a happiness which she knew she had never felt before. She asked Allah to forgive her past evil ways for indeed, she had not lived a good life before. She became a loving kind and thoughtful lady for the rest of her life.

The Prophet Muhammad said, 'I saw that woman in Heaven'.

A KIND HUNTER

Nasir-ud-Din was a servant of a king. He was fond of hunting. One day, when he was out hunting, he saw a very pretty baby deer. He thought it would make a lovely pet for his children who would love and take care of it. He caught the animal,[1] put it over his horse and rode on. The mother deer soon discovered that her baby had been taken away. It was a great shock to her. She was very unhappy but she could not get it back. She began to follow the hunter.

Meanwhile, Nasir-ud-Din kept looking at the baby deer and thought to himself what a good catch he had made. He knew that his children would love it.

After a little while, he realised that something was following him and he turned to see the mother deer. He could see the great sadness in her eyes. She seemed to be saying to him, 'You have caught my baby, so what do I care if you kill me? There is no life for me without my baby'.

Nasir-ud-Din took pity on the mother and let the little deer free. The mother licked her baby and they both jumped happily away into the forest. They disappeared from sight but not without the mother first turning to look back as if to say, 'Thank you'.

When the good man went to bed that night, he dreamed of the Prophet Muhammad who said to him, 'Nasir-ud-Din, Allah has put your name on the list of rulers and you are to become a king. But take care! This kingdom will also be a test for you. Just as you took pity on the deer, so you must also show kindness to Allah's human creatures. Beware you don't forget them![2]

1. The Prophet Muhammad (p.b.u.h.) has said, 'Take pity on the earth's creatures, Allah in Heaven will take pity on you'.
2. Nasir-ud-Din's dream did come true. He later became the king of Ghazni (Afghanistan) and ruled under the name of Amir Nasir-ud-Din Subaktgin. There are many stories of Subaktgin's just rule.

A TRUTHFUL BOY[1]

Long ago there lived a youth who was fond of reading and writing. Unfortunately, there was no large school of learning where he lived. His father had died and the boy lived with his mother. One day he asked his mother if he could travel to Baghdad (Iraq) and seek knowledge there.

Baghdad was a very big city. There were many famous schools and colleges where great Sufis and people who were very close to Allah stayed. The youth said to his mother, 'My dear mother let me learn as much as possible because an unread person is called ignorant and useless. He is not respected. He is like a blind person who does not know what is happening in the world around and in the life hereafter. Ignorance is death on earth and leads to gloom and despair. To know many things brings light into a person's life. A knowledgeable person is well known and well liked amongst those who are Allah's chosen ones. Without knowledge, one doesn't even know how to pray.'

The mother was a good lady. She worshipped Allah day and night. Recitation of the Holy *Qur'an* was her hobby. She was delighted to hear that her son wished for learning. She thanked Allah that her son had no bad habits.

This pious lady had only managed to save forty *Ashrafis*[2] but these she gladly gave to her son. She prepared some food for him to eat during his journey and sewed the money into the lining of his coat under the armpit, thus hiding it away.

When everything was ready, she said to her son, 'I must tell you one thing. Listen to it carefully, remember it always and do it. Whenever you speak, speak only the truth. Remember that the Prophet Muhammad (may peace be upon him) said, "Truth is Salvation". You can save yourself from great worry by telling the truth. Truth will save your life'.[3]

In those days there were no motors, buses or trains and the only means of travel was by camel, horse or on foot. It was often very dangerous because travellers were attacked by robbers. So they travelled together in large groups called 'caravans'.

Luckily, there was a caravan going to Baghdad. The youth went with them. They travelled for some time until one day a band of robbers came down from the hills. The robbers began to steal all they could. One of the robbers took everything away from the youth and asked him roughly if he had anything else. The boy calmly answered, 'Yes, I have forty *Ashrafis*'. The robber said, 'You must be joking!' The youth replied, 'No, I am not'. Indeed, had his mother not told him to speak the truth! The robber stared at him as the boy carried on speaking: 'I am travelling for a good cause. Those who go out to look for learning are walking towards Heaven. The angels will help them on their journey. I am going to be a learned man. I am a descendent of the Prophet Muhammad (may Allah bless and preserve him). Telling lies does not befit me. What are forty *Ashrafis* that I should tell a lie in order to keep them? Not even if I were to be killed would I do this. A Muslim[4] does not tell a lie but speaks the truth even in the face of fear and danger.'

While the youth was talking, another robber came up to him. He pushed him and said, 'What have you got?' The boy replied, 'Forty *Ashrafis*'. This prompt reply made the robber stop and think. Everyone except the boy, who remained completely unmoved, seemed to be lost in amazement or terror-stricken. Indeed he must *not* be joking. Puzzled, the robbers took him to their leader.

'What is your name and town?' the leader asked.

'My name is Abdul Qadir[5] and I come from Jilan,' the boy said.

'And where are you going?'

'Baghdad.'

'What will you do in Baghdad?'

'I am going to be educated.'

'Well, well! Have you any money?'

'Yes sir, I have forty *Ashrafis*. Haven't I already said so?'

'Where are they?' enquired the leader. He looked closely at the boy.

'Here, under my armpit,' the boy answered as he pointed to the lining in his sleeve. 'My mother sewed them inside my coat.' The leader laughed, 'You must be very simple. You don't tell people such things'.

'Muslims don't tell lies,' the youth replied. The leader raised his eyebrows. 'The boy is not so simple after all,' he thought. 'What great faith in Islam has this young lad! Without it he would not have told the truth. We make our children into clever liars, we tell lies ourselves day and night and destroy Allah's creatures by making them hide the truth. This life is not worth living. This boy knows more of Allah's wisdom than I, a grown man.'

He bent his head in shame. Tears rolled down his cheeks. He stood up, embraced the youth and asked his forgiveness.

Greatly surprised, the youth exclaimed, 'Pray to Allah for forgiveness, for He expects His creatures to ask Him alone for His mercy'.

There, before him, the leader and his companions repented all their sins and promised to live the lives of noble people, their first good action being that of returning all the stolen loot to the travellers.

. The basic Islamic principle about truth is derived from the Qur'anic injunction, 'O, believers! Fear God at all times and speak the truth'.

. *Ashrafi* was the name of a Persian coin, the unit of the highest value.

. Hadith.

. The Prophet Muhammad (p.b.u.h.) said, 'A Muslim may be anything, but not a liar'. *Mishkat-Sharif-Shahban-ul-Ieman.*

. Syed Abdul Qadir Jilani (*d.* 1166 CE) grew up to be a pious man and the greatest mentor of the Muslim mystics. He was a great doctor, jurist and educationist. He was well known as Mohiy-ud-Din, the revivor of the religion of Islam. See *The Saint of Jilan* by S. A. Salik, An Ashraf Publication, Lahore (Pakistan).

KINDNESS BRINGS ITS OWN REWARD

During the Caliphate of Suleman-bin-Abdul Malik (715–17 CE.) there lived a man named Khazima. He had been a very rich man but later in life he became poor. His relatives helped him for some time, but not for long. When he knew they would not help him anymore he shut himself inside his house and waited for death to come.

In those days the man in charge of that district was Akrama Fiyyaz.

One day the courtiers were talking about Khazima. Akrama aske
about him. They told him that Khazima, now a poor man, had give
up his worldly life. Akrama became very upset. In the middle of th
night he took four thousand dinars from home and knocked at Khaz
ma's door. When the man came out Akrama said to him, 'Here is
purse with dinars in it. Use this money to help yourself'. Taking th
money Khazima asked who had given the money, but Akrama woul
not tell him. But Khazima kept asking him. Finally Akrama said, '
find the cure for those who have no money. I give mine away'. Thu
saying, he went on his way.

When Akrama returned home his wife wanted to know where h
had been at that time of night. Akrama just said that he had som
urgent job which none but Allah should know about. However, whe
she insisted he told her all about the events of the night, cautioning he
not to tell anybody else.

As he had been told, Khazima did use the money well, and becam
rich once more. He at last, went to the Caliph who wanted to kno
why he had been away from court for so long. Khazima told him th
whole story. The Caliph was very sad that the name of such a kin
person was not known. He would have rewarded him for his goo
deeds.

Now the Caliph made Khazima governor of the district over whic
Akrama ruled, and Akrama was imprisoned because he owed a lot c
money to the public treasury. The poor man became very ill. His wif
could stand it no longer and sent her servant to the governor to te
him that this was no way to treat a man whose cure for those who ha
no money was to give his own away. When the governor heard this h
realised who had helped him. He went over to see Akrama in th
prison and asked his forgiveness. He ordered the handcuffs to be take
off him and put round his own hands instead. Akrama said, 'What ar
you doing?' Khazima answered, 'I want to bear all the troubles tha
you have received in the prison because of me'. Akrama would hav
none of this, but asked only that Khazima should take him home an
treat him with respect. After this they both went to the Caliph, wh
was naturally surprised to see them both together.

The Caliph asked if all was well. Khazima answered, 'Amir-al-Mc
menine [King of the Muslims]. I am very well. I am here to tell yo
that I have found the man who gave money to me when I was poor.
want you to meet him. His name is Akrama Fiyyaz'. The Caliph allowe
him to come in and welcomed him happily. He gave Akrama mone
and appointed him governor of another province, saying, 'Is it you
wish that Khazima remains governor here?' Akrama replied, 'Ami
al-Momenine. You reinstate him governor with all honour and dignity

NOTHING TOO LOW FOR THE MOST HIGH

You may have seen some people who after having achieved some worldly honour do not feel like doing a manual job. The high rank the Prophet Muhammad enjoyed is difficult even to understand. He was not only the leader of the people but also very near to God. In spite of all this he never thought he was too good to do household jobs. And not only for himself, but also he helped willingly and happily those whom he found in trouble and distress.[1]

Once Muhammad saw a slave[2] grinding some grains on a grinding mill driven by hand. As he ground the grains he was crying. On seeing this the Prophet became anxious. He asked the slave the reason why he was weeping. The slave said, 'I am sick. I cannot grind the grain. My master is very cruel and he will beat me if I cannot finish my job'. At this the Prophet stepped forward and ground the rest of the grain, saying, 'Always call me if you have any grain to grind. I will do it for you'.

1. Once the Prophet Muhammad (p.b.u.h.) saw an old man walking and trembling under the weight of water which he carried in a leather jacket. The old man walked a few steps and rested a bit. Seeing this, the Prophet took the load and carried it to his place.
2. Once a man came along to Salman, a good and kind mystic of Persia, who was mixing flour and water. On inquiring why the slave was not doing it, Salman said,'The slave was doing another job and I thought he should not be doing even this'.

A MERCIFUL HOST

During the Abbaside Caliphate there lived a man who had many enemies. He looked for a hiding place in Kufa (Iraq). He wore a disguise so that no-one would recognise him. He was wandering about when he saw a big house with a large courtyard and a gate, wide open. He went inside. The owner of the house saw him and asked him, 'Who are you and what are you doing here?' He replied, 'My life is in danger and I am looking for shelter'.

The landlord showed the man to a room in the house. He lived there in great comfort. But one thing troubled him. He did not understand why his host went out on his horse every day. He seemed to be looking for something. One day he could bear it no more and asked him where he was going and what he was doing.

The landlord said, 'I am searching for the murderer of my father'. He also told him the name of the murderer. Hearing his own name the man became frightened; he wondered whether or not to tell his host that he was in fact his father's murderer.

At long last he said with a heavy heart, 'I am going to make your job easy. Because you have been very kind to me I feel I should help you. In truth I am the murderer of your father'.

The landlord was very surprised to hear the man and thought he did not love his own life. He became very angry. After a short while he said, 'I am so very cross that I do not want to spare your life. However, I will forgive you providing you leave my house at once before I change my mind'.

At this the man left, spared by the host who practised the Quranic verses: 'The reward of an ill-deed is an ill the like thereof. But whosoever pardoneth and amendeth, his wage is the affair of Allah. Lo! He loveth not wrong-doers'. (Q-42 : 40) (Q-26 : 126).[1]

1. 'There is in Islam neither the one extreme of tooth for a tooth and an eye for an eye, nor the opposite one of turning the left cheek when the right is smitten or giving away the cloak to one who has already wrongfully taken the cloak of his brother.' *The Holy Qur'an*, by Muhammad Ali. p.939, Note 2232.

UMAR FEEDS THE HUNGRY CHILDREN

Once, whilst he was wandering, Umar reached a place outside Medina (Saudi Arabia). He saw a woman who had a cooking pan on the fire. Around her were some children who were all crying. Umar went up to them and asked the lady what was wrong. The woman, not knowing who he was, said, 'O brother. The children are crying because of hunger. I have got only water in the pan to keep them quiet'.

On hearing this the Caliph went back to Medina, took some flour and butter from the public treasury and returned to the woman and children. His servant saw him and said, 'O Amir-al-Momeneen. Why do you carry such a heavy load? Let me carry it for you'. The Caliph replied, 'Will you carry my load at the Day of Resurrection?' Soon Umar, carrying the food, arrived at the place where the children still sat weeping. There he lit the fire, cooked the meal and fed the children himself. When they had eaten as much as they could the woman turned to Umar and remarked happily: 'May Allah bless you. You, not Umar, deserve to be Amir-al-Momeneen!'

UMAR AND THE BEDOUIN

Once the Caliph Umar saw a Bedouin outside his tent. He looked very worried. Umar asked the man what was the matter. He replied that his wife was having a baby at that very moment and was in great pain, but there was no-one to nurse her. Umar went back home at once and brought his wife to the tent. He spoke to the Bedouin and sent his wife inside the tent. After a short while the lady gave birth to a son. Umar's wife came out and shouted, 'O, *Amir-al-Momeneen* (King of the Muslims). Give your blessings and greetings to your friend'.

On hearing the words Amir-al-Momeneen the Bedouin grew puzzled and amazed. Umar said, 'O, brother. Don't worry. Come to me tomorrow. I will fix a stipend for the baby'.[1]

1. During the Caliph Umar's rule a certain amount of money was given to every child until his or her adulthood. It can be taken to be equivalent to the present family allowance in Britain.

NO TASK TOO MEAN FOR A KING

Suleman (may Allah be pleased with him) was one of the very humble companions of the Prophet Muhammad. He ruled the province of Medina in Saudia Arabia. He led such a simple way of life that nobody would have thought that he was a ruler.

Once a man, not knowing who he was, grabbed Suleman and took him to do some rough work for him. He gave him a bale of grass and made him carry it back to the man's home. Suleman carried the bale and walked on without a word. Another man came along the road and said to Suleman, '*Assalam-o-Alaikum*[1] (peace be on you)'. Suleman greeted him back, '*Wa Alaikum salam*[2] (and peace be on you)'. This third man then addressed the first man, 'The man you have forced to carry your load is Suleman, the ruler of the province'. On hearing this, the man said he was sorry and asked Suleman to put the bale down.

But Suleman only replied, 'I will take the bale off my shoulders when I reach your place and not before'.

1. This is the Arabic formula which one Muslim says to the other. It is a general greeting.
2. This is the reply to the first person's greeting.

A RULER FOR THE CHILDREN

Once, having appointed a gentleman governor of a province, Umar, the second Caliph of Islam, went outside with him to say goodbye. He saw a little boy playing about, picked him up and hugged and kissed the child. The governor was unable to stop the Caliph. He thought it was not the right thing for a king to do. He said, 'This playful behaviour with the boy does not befit your rank and honour. I do not love my child as you love this whom you do not even know'.

Umar was surprised, 'O dear! This is your attitude towards children. A man without a tender and kind heart will certainly not treat the parents of those children kindly. They are the public you will govern'.

It is said that there and then Umar told the man that he could not have the job of governor.

A SUFI CRITICISES THE KING

When Haroon-al-Rashid became the Caliph of the Muslim Empire, learned men from all over came to his court and congratulated him.

The Caliph gave them many riches. Sufyan Sori, a great learned man of the time, did not come. The Caliph sent him a message, 'All the learned men of the empire have come to congratulate me and have received presents from me. If you had come I would have been most thankful. Did we not spend our childhood together? Surely you could have been pleased for me. I am the Caliph. It is a great honour. This is why I expect you to come'.

It took the messenger some time before at last he found Sufyan Sori, who was busy teaching his pupils. When he finished teaching the messenger gave him the Caliph's letter. He read it and threw it away. The messenger was very upset to see him do this. He waited for an answer, but there was none. He begged Sufyan Sori to let him have some message for the Caliph. Finally, Sufyan picked up the letter and wrote on the back of it. 'In your letter you have said that you have given people presents. This must mean that you have misused[1] the public money, of which you are the guardian. You cannot be trusted and I do not like your actions. Therefore I cannot come to your court. Don't write to me about this matter again'.

1. Honesty in handling public money and dealing in the merchandise is very much stressed in Islam. Abu Hanaifa, a great Muslim jurist, was a merchant by trade. Once he sent someone to sell some bundles of cloth. He asked the man to warn the customers about a certain defect in some of the cloth. The man sold the cloth and when he came back told Abu Hanaifa that he had forgotten to tell the customers about the defect. Abu Hanaifa was sad but gave away all the money to the poor.

ABU BAKR, THE PIOUS

Abu Bakr, the first Caliph of Islam, was a pious happy man, who lived a simple life. His family received flour from the public treasury because Abu Bakr had to give up his business when he became the Caliph of the Muslim Empire.

Once, his wife managed to save some flour from the daily ration. She thought she would make a pudding with this flour. When Abu Bakr came to know of it he returned this flour to the treasury, and, not only that, he made sure that his family were given as much flour as they needed for the day.

JUNAID BAGHDADI HELPS THE ROBBER

In Baghdad (Iraq) lived a famous and cruel robber whose robberies always brought him great riches. Nobody could make him stop his wicked life. He would stop at nothing to get whatever he wanted.

One night he broke into a house. He thought that he would grab as many things as he could. But when he got inside the house he could not find anything of value. All he could find were many bundles of cloth. He thought that he was too clever a robber to leave with nothing. So he began collecting up the bundles. After a time, he felt tired and stopped working. He was falling asleep when suddenly he heard someone coming in. He looked up to see an old man with a light in his hand entering the house. At first the robber became frightened but when the stranger talked to him in a very friendly way and offered to help him take the bundles of cloth he didn't worry anymore.

The stranger said, 'This is not one man's job. Tie all the bundles into two large bundles. We will carry one each.'

The robber thought that as he was the first to steal the cloth he should have more than the stranger. So he said to the stranger, 'I will take you with me only if you agree to take the smaller bundle'. 'Alright,' the stranger replied and they both went off together. They had not been walking along before the poor stranger began to tire of his heavy load. He walked very slowly. The robber called to him angrily 'Hurry up. We must reach safety before sunrise. Otherwise we will be caught'. The stranger answered in a weak voice. But the robber did not wait to listen. He hurried on. Once the old man collapsed. But he managed to plod on until at last they came to the robber's hideout.

Now the robber said, 'Right, take your bundle and get out of here quickly'. The stranger turned to him and said, 'I don't want them. The house you visited was my home. I saw that you must be poor to take my bundles of cloth and knew it was my duty to make sure that you had as much comfort as I could give you. All that we have brought is yours. And now that you know where I live you are welcome to come to me for help whenever you need it'.

Saying this, the stranger left. The robber stood staring in amazement at the old man. How could anyone be so good and kind. He thought to himself, 'O God. Can it be possible that there are still people who can give away everything they own? This man has helped me to rob his own house, listened to my angry words, carried one of my bundles to my hideout, and even now he invites me to his house whenever I need anything more'. He could not believe it at all.

He set off at once for the stranger's house. There he met a woodcutter working outside. 'O brother. Do you know who lives here?' he asked. The woodcutter was very surprised, 'You must be a stranger in this city. Even the children of this city know that Junaid (may Allah be pleased with him), the mystic, lives here,' he said.

The robber had heard of this man. He felt very sorry for the terrible thing he had done. Quickly he went inside and saw a man dressed in simple clothes but looking like a king. Now this robber's heart had already begun to change. He put his head on Junaid's knees and cried many tears. Then he asked him to forgive him his wicked deeds. Junaid treated him with love and the robber became a better man.

SALADIN (SALAH-UD-DIN) THE GREAT

Another great man in Muslim history was Saladin, a man who always kept his promise. As a master he was gentle and kind. As a warrior and judge he showed mercy. His enemies found him well mannered and generous. During the Crusades, one of his greatest enemies, the English king, Richard Coeur de Lion, was ill. He sent him pears and peaches to eat and snow from the mountains to cool his drinks.

Vincent de Beauvais tells this story of Saladin before his death. 'He sent for his standard bearer. The young man was ordered to put a piece of white cloth on his spear. When this was done he told the lad to run round and round the city of Damascus shouting to everyone that even the King of all the East could take nothing to the grave with him but this simple shroud.' At his death in 1193 CE the Qadhi of Damascus recited the *Qur'an*. At the words, 'there is no deity but He (Allah); in Him do I trust' Saladin opened his eyes, smiled and died.

A WONDERFUL HAJJ (PILGRIMAGE)

In Isfahan in Persia lived a man who had saved for many years to go on the *Hajj* at Mecca. One day he saw a poor man cooking a chicken which had just died.[1] He was sorry for him and gave him more food and money. But now he had not enough money for travelling to Mecca.

He told his friends that he was ill and would follow when he was better. Of course, he did not go. When his friends returned they congratulated him on his *Hajj*. The man replied, 'I never went'. 'O, but we saw you several times,' said his friends smiling, 'We had a vision in which Allah told us that you had made a most wonderful pilgrimage'.

1. A Muslim is forbidden to eat unritually killed animals but only when there is a danger that death might occur because of hunger. *Quran* 26:115, Pickthall.

DO UNTO OTHERS AS YOU WOULD BE DONE BY

One morning, Muhammad-ibn-al-Munkadir had to go out. While he was away his servant sold a Bedouin Arab some goods for twice as much as they were worth. When he returned and found out what the servant had done, the master went out looking for the man. It took all day. When he found him, Muhammad said, 'The boy made a mistake, he sold you for ten dirhams what is only worth five'. 'But I am quite happy,' replied the surprised Bedouin. 'Ah, but even if you were satisfied, we want you to be satisfied with that which pleases us,' Muhammad answered, as he gave the five dirhams back.

1. The Prophet Muhammad said, 'Truly, none of you believes in Islam until he wishes for his brother what he wishes for himself'.

316

A SHAMED HOST

An Arab engaged a servant on the understanding that he would do everything exactly as he was told by his master. The servant agreed and worked well for a master who was always just and who tried to follow the teachings of Allah. One day the master saw in the distance a number of travellers approaching — he knew there were many, as their donkeys and camels made so much dust. It is customary in the desert where oases are far apart and water scarce for travellers to be well looked after, and the *Qur'an* reminds them of this duty.

'Go quickly and kill the finest of my camels and prepare a meal for my guests. Get water and towels so that they can wash and see there is plenty of cool drink ready!' The servant hastened to the herd of camels that was grazing some distance away, but as he went he thought, 'Who are these people? If I kill the finest camel, what a loss it will be to my master. There is an old one nobody would miss, so I'll kill that'. After the guests had washed and shared their news the meal was served, but the meat was tough and strong flavoured, and the master was ashamed as he saw his guests trying to eat it. When they left he called his servant aside and asked if his best camel had been killed, and the servant had to admit that he had not done so but had killed an old one. Then you have disobeyed me and when I took you on you promised to obey. I have been fair and just with you but you have shamed me before my guests. Leave my tent. I can no longer employ you as my servant'. God, or as Muslims say, Allah, expects the best in work, service and gifts, but too often we only offer our second best.

REFERENCES, READING LIST AND GLOSSARY OF MUSLIM TERMS USED IN THE STORIES

All references to the Holy *Qur'an* can be made to the *Glorious Qur'an*, a translation by Muhammad Marmaduke Pickthall, Allen and Unwin. It is an excellent translation easily available for quick reference to the *Qur'an. East Meets West* — a publication of the Commission for Racial Equality, London — gives a comprehensive resumé of three major regions of the East, Hinduism, Islam and Sikhism, *The Benefactor*, Lion Art Press, Karachi respectfully outlines the life history of the Prophet Muhammad and the first four Caliphs of Islam *The History of Saracens*, by Syed Amir Ali, is a wonderful and unbiased exposition of the history of the followers of Islam.

The Spirit of Islam University Paperbacks, Methuen, describes Islam in depth, its duties and rituals, *Stories of Sahabah* (the Prophet's Companions) obtainable from Pakistani shopkeepers — reveals the true Muslim characteristics *A Muslim Community in Britain* — The Church Information Office surveys the influence of industry on the Muslim community in Bradford. *The Reconstruction of Religious Thought in Islam*, obtainable from Pakistani shops, rationalises and philosophies the principles of islam.

Some of the Arabic/Urdu theological terms which a reader may come across in the suggested books and these stories are translated below for easy reading.

Abbasid, Ummayed, Rashidin, and Ottoman: These are the names of the Muslim Caliphate in a chronoligical order beginning in 632 CE with Rashidin and ending with Ottoman in 1932.

Allah: The personal name for Muslim God.

Amir-al-Momeneen: The Commander of the Faithful (King of the Muslims).

Ashrafi: name of a gold coin used in Iraq.

Assalam-o-Alaikum: peace be on you (a common greeting).

Bet-al-Maqqadis: The old name of Al-Aqsa Mosque in Jerusalem.

Bet-allahm: The Arabic name for Bethlehem.

Bin: son of, e.g. Zaid-bin-Hartha means Zaid, son of Hartha.

Caliphate: sucession/rule.

Caliph/Khalifa in Arabic: successor/leader.

Dirhom: name of a gold coin used in Persia.

Hadith: a tradition or saying — the collection of the sayings of the Prophet Muhammad.

Hajj: effort — one of the fundamentals of Islam, pilgrimage to Mecca, if one can afford to save enough money.

Islam: Islam, the religion of about 750,000,000 Muslims all over the world has two literal meanings, 'submission to the Will of Allah' and 'peace'.

Imam: a leader, a guide, an example, a model of the Muslims in a mosque, town or country any devout Muslim slave or callow youth.

Innalillahe wa Inna-Alaihe rajeune: means all of us came from Allah and we will all return to Allah. A Muslim recites it instantaneously at the sight of a funeral.

Bismillah-irrakhman-irrahim: In the name of Allah, the Merciful, the Compassionate. Every Muslim remembers this Arabic formula by heart and utters it at the beginning of all work.

Ka-aba: a cube-shaped building which is situated in Mecca (Saudi Arabia) and a place of pilgrimage for Muslims.

Lota (Urdu word): a round earthen or metallic vessel of 3-4 pints capacity.

Maryam: The Arabic name for Mary, the mother of Jesus. This is a common name amongst Muslim ladies all over the world.

Muhammad (Sallallaho alaihi Wasallam): The Prophet Muhammad — may Allah bless and preserve him.

Muslim: the one who submits to the Will of Allah — the follower of Islam.

318

Mosque: The place of worship for Muslims.

Qur'an: a recitation — the religious Holy Book of the Muslims.

Sura: Chapter.

Sufi: one who wears clothes made of *suf* (wool), usually pious people.

Tawakkal: contentment with one's lot.

Ramadhan: the name of the lunar month of fasting.

Quraish: a noble Meccan Arab tribe to which the Prophet Muhammad belonged.

Wa Alaikum salam: and peace be on you — an answer to the greeting *Assalam-o-Alaikum*.

The invaluable help given by an Arab or Asian Muslim in pronouncing the terms cannot be overstressed. Some terms have long explanations because of lack of a one-word English equivalent, just as some English words have no one-word equivalent in Arabic. The stories are arranged in a chronological order with those concerning the Prophet Muhammad (570-632 CE) at the beginning and followed by his successors' Abu Bakr, Umar, Uthman, Ali and others to the present time.

MUHAMMAD IQBAL

BLACK HEROES IN THE PRIMARY SCHOOL

(*With special reference to black heroes in fiction*)
by *Geoff Fenwick and Vida Barnet*,
City of Liverpool College of Higher Education

The religious quest in the primary school follows two paths, one exploring the religious dimension of life in terms of prayer, pilgrimage, rites of passage, sacred books, religious leaders, messengers, believers etc., the other exploring caring, responsible decision-making, justice, equality, what it means to be human.

Our understanding of the hero and heroism also takes different forms. We admire those who achieve great things in the arts, sciences, politics, sport and the world of entertainment. We admire those who suffer and sometimes die for what they believe to be right, often because of religious beliefs. The primary child's hero, however, may be a very ordinary person or character in a story whom they wish to imitate, and who can help them to grow in responsible decision-making and in overcoming hatred, selfishness, loneliness, bewilderment and pain.

Reference to the overt religious dimension of heroism need to be handled very sensitively in the classroom. Tragically, the history of religions and religiously committed people is shot through with fanaticism, hatred and persecution as well as loyalty and bravery. Frequently the villain must be studied with the hero, and the younger child is seldom able to avoid making generalisations resulting in sterotyping, misunderstanding and prejudice. He does not have the knowledge to view people 'in the round', to set actions against a backcloth of environment, culture and politics. He does not have a fully developed concept of time and therefore cannot adequately understand that situations change. He cannot make those allowances which are necessary for mature judgement. He cannot fully wrestle with the concept of forgiveness and the difference between justice and vengeance. Therefore it is difficult to find suitable material for the primary years, and the teacher must be fully aware of the pitfalls if he is to help the children to avoid them, and he must have adequate background knowledge and understanding to help them to exercise both justice and mercy.

Assembly books and collections of brief biographies often provide material, but used in isolation they can present a very distorted picture of a race or group — particularly in terms of religious persecution. The *Heroes of Islam* series provides one possible model, speaking not only of great warriors who possess praiseworthy qualities other than bravery on the battlefield (the portrait of the Mahdi is especially interesting) but also of the scholar Ibn Rushd ('When I am kind to my friends I am not doing anything good. When I am kind to my enemies, I *am* doing something good'), the explorer and historian Ibn Battutah, the philosopher Ibn Sina and the father of Arab medicine, Al Razi — all good stewards of the gifts that Allah has given them. All stories of those who fight with the sword for freedom and justice might be placed within the context of a famous *hadith* telling of Muhammad's reply to an army commander who had come to announce a great victory — 'You have won the lesser fight. Now go and win the greater fight' — the struggle against sin, selfishness and evil.

If the stories are to help children to grow towards responsible choice then they must stress the decisions involved more than the actual actions taken. The story of the Buddhist convert Ashoka shows the courage of one who admits he has been wrong. Stories of Martin Luther King, Gaudhi and Dom Helder Camara can gradually lead to an understanding that there are different ways to choose from in responding to violence.

For many primary children, however, courage will be most meaningfully studied in the context of themes on identity, relationships, caring, etc. The terms 'black heroes' and 'religions' must be interpreted very literally if they are to have relevance to what young children read and appreciate. The great lives approach — if pursued rather than touched upon — is of limited appeal and then only to the top age group. Black fictional heroes therefore may be defined as important characters having much in common with minority groups resident in this country, e.g. Caribbean, African and Asian. Although three thousand children's books are published annually in the UK, those with minority group themes are still hard to find despite greater availability and a welcome change of approach in the last decade. Ten years ago there were more poor books to criticise and fewer good ones to praise. *Books for Keeps* and *Books for Young Children* are useful sources of reference, and the most comprehensive booklist is that of the National Book League, which has a travelling exhibition, frequently updated as opinions in this particular area of literature continue to change rapidly (which can create difficulties), and relatively cheap for teachers' centres and schools to borrow.

The black writers Petronella Breinburg and Errol Lloyd have produced attractive illustrated books for the very young, telling of the uncomplicated adventures of a young black hero, Sean. Relationships, decision-making and courage are gently explored as he faces up to the trauma of his first day at school (*My Brother Sean*) and saves up for an exciting new possession (*Sean's Red Bike*). His attraction lies in his natural good humour. He is a small black boy being funny as opposed to the too familiar picture of a funny little black boy. The distinction is important. The bold, colourful illustrations have an urban British setting.

The American Ezra Jack Keats was a pioneer in including illustrations of black children in picture books. Stories such as *Goggles* and *Pet Show* are still worth consideration. His principal character, Peter, lives and plays with friends in the bleak surroundings of a decaying urban neighbourhood. Keat's drawings and dialogue, however, lack Breinbuurg's realism and there is often a sameness about his characters.

Kathleen Herson's *Maybe it's a Tiger* is fun! Joseph is a small black British boy living in a multi-racial city area — it could be Manchester. With his friends he creates an imaginary zoo. The illustrations of Nick Daly are lively and individual. Imagination and courage may often be linked together creatively, and imagination is one of the constituents of the soil from which religious growth springs. Another delightful example is *Josephine's Imagination* — but beware the school caretaker's wrath if all his sweeping brushes become dolls'.

Sultan's Elephants in the McDonald Starter Series tells of an Asian family in charge of the elephant act in a British travelling circus with a cosmpolitan membership. By contrast, the *Jafta* stories have as their eponymous hero a small African boy from a rural background. The stories are simple and touching, the illustrations magnificent. *Swarpu Returns* explores the courage needed by those in poor circumstances to return money given to them by mistake, a decision which involves an extra-long and tiring journey. *Balloon Travel* explores the area of foolish examples of courage, but illustrates the courage of clear thinking and calmness in a frightening situation. Its young hero, doubtless a future Indian scientist (whose family owns a car!) is carried away by gas-filled balloons after jumping from the roof! The delightful story of *Mahagiri* explores the courage necessary to accept pain rather than hurt others when a village elephant refuses to place a flag pole into a hole into which a kitten has fallen.

Most children enjoy folk tales, myths and legends. For young children Anansi the Spiderman is a mischievious rascal, clever and crafty but never evil. Whether he is Kwaku Anansi of the original Ashanti Stories, or Brer Anansi of the West Indian versions, he rarely ceases to entertain. Very gently, against the background of laughter, we can begin to explore an order of priorities re 'hero-worship' and to question if all acts of bravery, etc. show true courage. East and West Africa are fruitful sources of stories about folk heroes like Jaja of Opobo, Dirobi (the principal character of an African Garden of Eden legend), Omolo and Kakara. From South-West Africa comes *The Great Thirst*, the adventure story of an African boy faced by disasters to himself and his tribe. *Mogo's Fuite* tells how a frail village Kenyan boy discovers who he is, and the purpose of his life, as he seeks the answer to the riddle 'What is good to have, better to lose and best to find again?'

The Indian sub-continent is even more rich in folklore. Stories of gods and heroes abound. Many tell of Rama and Sita. There are also accounts of folk heroes like Raja Rasalu and ordinary people like the station master of Guntakal, who had the ability to cure snake-bites by the power of prayer.

During the late 1960s and early 1970s a number of books with a Caribbean background were published in this country. Their authors were often West Indians writing authentically about their homeland. They give older children a chance to explore relationships, often between black and white, whether read by the children themselves or retold by the teacher.

Outstanding contributions have been made by Andrew Salkey and Everard Palmer. Salkey's portraits of Jamaican youth coping with both natural and man-made disasters are convincing, particularly when the context is urban Kingston. The caricature-like illustrations of Papas enhance the humour which is rarely far beneath the surface and which creates a relaxed atmosphere in which class discussion can take place. By contrast, Palmer writes of lively adolescents living in the Jamaican countryside.

Theodore Taylor's *The Cay* received several awards for the way it tackled the problem of racial prejudice through the co-operation, in adverse circumstances, of an old black man and a young white boy, but recently there has been strong criticism of the contrast between the simple unlettered black man and the privileged white boy.

Many books have been written to give back the American Negro his pride in his race and himself. The teacher might like to introduce biographies and stories against the background of such books as *First Book of American Negroes* and *They had a Dream*. These tell of many black Americans who have overcome the barrier of prejudice to give invaluable service to their people, nation and the world, service in the fields of exploration, philosophy, invention, science, poetry, education, the theatre, church leadership, music, sport, politics, etc. The teacher might then share with his class *Underground to Canada*, in which Julilly, sold to a cruel slave trader in the deep south, again and again shows courage and refuses to lose her pride and identity. Eventually she travels the underground railway to Canada and freedom. *The Girl called Moses* tells of Harriet Tubman, who led over 300 slaves to 'the promised land' along the same railway. Her Christian commitment gave her incredible courage as she clung to the belief that freedom was a right all men should enjoy.

Two books older children might read for themselves are *Marchers for the Dream* and *Roll of Thunder, Hear my Cry*. In the former, eleven-year-old Bethany goes with Gran on the Poor People's March to Washington. She tries to find the answer to the use of violence or non-violent action in the fight for justice. Everyone she meets in Resurrection City is full of courage — but will she be truly courageous if she stays and is arrested during a demonstration, or if she goes back to look after Gran? In *Roll of Thunder* all children will identify with

Cassie in the Mississippi of the 1930s as she seeks to understand why she is considered inferior. Gradually she learns when to fight for a principle — and when to remain silent. 'We have no choice of what colour we're born or who our parents are or whether we're rich or poor. What we do have is some choice over what we make of our lives once we're here.'

Ishi, Last of his Tribe illustrates the incredible courage of an Amerindian boy who tried to remain true to the gentle ways of his ancestors. This is the true story of a tribe destroyed by white men in search of gold. Before he dies Ishi seeks to leave a record of his religion, language and culture for mankind.

The wealth of Indian myths and legends is not matched by a similar output of contemporary fiction. Suffice to mention three stories. *Shanta* is a delicate and sensitive story of a twelve-year-old Indian girl's first visit to the city, and the way in which she faces tragedy when she returns home. *The Peacock Garden* tells of a Muslim family who refuse to leave their home in the Punjab after partition. *A Garland for Gandhi* tells of Tara who gradually comes to understand why Gandhi chooses the path of non-violence as he attempts to secure dignity and humanity for his people.

Most of today's minority children are British-born, often viewing Africa, Asia and the West Indies through the mirror of their parents' nostalgia. It is fitting that a number of writers introduce us to these young people against a British urban background. Few, however, match at primary level the amusing and irreverent tales which Farukh Dhoudy creates for older pupils. One might use *Hackney Half-term Adventure*, telling the story of a multi-racial group in the capital, a theme repeated by both Petronella Breinburg and Buchi Emecheta. Terry, Brinsley and May, respectively, are exuberant and full of fun. Membership of their gangs depends on these qualities, not upon skin colour. Bernard Ashley, a London headmaster, has created a convincing West Indian hero in *The Trouble with Donovan Croft*, and an Asian heroine in *A Kind of Wild Justice*. *My Mate Shofiq* by Jan Needle is sited in north-west England.

We need more black heroes in books for primary children, so that they may follow the gentle religious path leading to the second road, where they will have to cope with more specific ways of asking and answering religious questions. Two things are certain, however. Today's heroes are more natural and far less awkward and self conscious than their predecessors, so that we can identify and grow with them, not just read about them. This means, however, that the teacher must work harder to identify the religious path for himself and his children.

BIBLIOGRAPHY

General

Bull, N., *One Hundred Great Lives,* Hulton Education, 1972
Carr, F., *One Hundred and One Assembly Stories, Foulsham*, 1973
Kennedy, M., *They Lived Dangerously,* Carousel, 1972
Prescott, D., *Readings for Senior Assembly,* Blandford, 1965
——, *Stories of Great Lives,* Blandford, 1977
African Historical Biographies, Heinmann
African Heroes Series, Oxford University Press
Round the World Series of Black Heroes, Hulton Educational
Amar Chitra Katha, Picture Strip Series
Heroes of Islam, Abouferakh, M. (ed), Islamic Information Services

Picture Books

Breinburg, P. and Lloyd, E., *My Brother Sean,* Bodley Head, 1973
——, *Doctor Sean,* Bodley Head, 1974
——, *Sean's Red Bike,* Bodley Head, 1975
Breinburg, P. and Murray, D., *Sally Ann's Umbrella,* Bodley Head, 1975
Cooper, E. and Ward, N., *Sultan's Elephants,* MacDonald, 1980
Dobrin, A., *Josephine's Imagination,* Scholastic Book Services
Fuller, L. H., *Swarup Returns,* Children's Book Trust, 1968
Hemalata, *Mahagiri,* Children's Book Trust, 1969
Herson, K. and Daly, N., *Maybe it's a Tiger,* Macmillan, 1981
Jafa, M., *Balloon Travel,* Children's Book Trust, 1972
Lewn, H. and Kopper, L., *Jafta — My Father,* Evans, 1981

Myths and Legends

Alagao, J. G., *Jaja of Opobo,* Longman, 1972
Appiah, P., *The Pineapple Child and Other Stories,* André Deutsch, 1969
——, *Tales of an Ashanti Father,* André Deutsch, 1974
Harmon, H., *More Tales told near a Crocodile,* Hutchinson, 1973
Makhanlall, D. P., *The Best of Brer Anansi,* Blackie, 1973
——, *The Invincible Brer Anansi,* Blackie, 1974
Seed, J., *The Great Thirst,* Hamish Hamilton, 1971
Seeger, E., *The Ramayana,* Dent, 1975
Shorlock, P., *West Indian Folk Tales,* Oxford University Press, 1973
Steel, F., *Tales of the Punjab,* Bodley Head, 1973
Troughton, J., *The Story of Rama and Sita,* Blackie, 1975

Zinkin, T., *The Faithful Parrot and Other Stories*, Oxford University Press, 1968

Stories from Africa and Asia

Desai, A., *The Peacock Garden*, Heinemann, 1979
Evans, B., *Gotama: The Indian Prince*, Galliard, 1979
——, *Muhammed: The Arab Boy*, Galliard, 1979
Jaeob, H. P., *A Garland for Gandhi*, Parnassus, 1968
Ruben, H., *The Calf of the November Cloud*, Collins, 1977
Sidhu, G. S., Sivia, G. S. and Singh, K., *Guru Nanak for Children*, Sikh Missionary Society, 1970
Stockum, H. V., *Mogo's Flute*, Knight, 1972
Thøger, M., *Shanta*, Puffin, 1961
Wylam, P., *Guru Nanak*, Children's Book Trust, 1969

Other Homelands

Palmer, C. E., *Big Doc Bitteroot*, André Deutsch, 1968
——, *The Cloud with a Silver Lining*, André Deutsch, 1968
——, *The Sun Salutes You*, André Deutsch, 1970
——, *A Cow called Boy*, André Deutsch, 1973
——, *Basa and Mr Big*, André Deutsch, 1974
——, *My Father Sun-Sun Johnson*, André Deutsch, 1974
Salkey, A., *Earthquake*, Oxford University Press, 1966
——, *Hurricane*, Oxford University Press, 1969
——, *Drought*, Oxford University Press, 1972
——, *Riot*, Oxford University Press, 1972
Taylor, T., *The Cay*, Puffin, 1973

North America

Carlson, N. S., *Marchers for the Dream*, Blackie, 1969
Kroeber, T., *Ishi, last of his Tribe*, Oxford, 1964
Petry, A., *The Girl called Moses*, Methuen, 1960
Reasone, G. and Patrick, S., *They Had a Dream*, Signet, 1969
Smucker, B., *Underground to Canada*, Puffin, 1978
Taylor, M. D., *Roll of Thunder, Hear my Cry*, Puffin, 1960
Young, M. B., *The First Book of American Negroes*, Franklin Watts, 1966

British Background

Ashley, B., *The Trouble with Donovan Croft*, Oxford University Press, 1974

——, *A Kind of Wild Justice*, Oxford University Press, 1978

Breinburg, P., *Brinsly's Dream*, Puffin, 1980

Emetcheta, B., *Nowhere to Play*, Allison and Busby, 1980

Needle, J., *My Mate Shofiq*, André Deutsch, 1978

Worpole, K. and Boler, J., *Hackney Half-term Adventure*, Centerprise, 1972

Information

A Wider Heritage: a selection of books for children and young people in multi-cultural Britain — available from National Book League, Book House, 45 East Hill, London SW18 211Z.

Books for Keeps: published 6 times p.a. by School Bookshop Association, 1 Effingham Road, Lee, London SE12 8NZ.

Books for Children: published 3 times p.a. by Slate House Farm, Papwith, Ashbourne.

Independent Publishing Co, 38 Kennington Lane, London, SE11 4LS.

New Beacon Books, 2 Albert Road, London, N4 3RW.

Hand in Hand Assembly Book, V. Bishop and R. Profitt, Longman, 1983.

APPENDIX 1: DEAR SIR OR MADAM . . .'

Scarcely a week goes by without some teacher or pupil writing to ask for help. During teaching practice or at the time when students are preparing to write their special studies the number of letters grows, but never reaches the proportions faced by the staff of CEM or some Jewish and Muslim agencies. We all like receiving these letters; after all we are in the business of fostering the study of religion and we would be foolish to turn away those who want to study or teach it better. However, attempts to help are often thwarted by the seekers themselves. Sometimes the content of the letter is literally 'I am doing a CSE project on Judaism, can you please help me?' An intending teacher once wrote 'I begin my teaching practice in a middle school next Monday and have to teach some RE, can you suggest some books and a suitable topic?'

Let me begin by trying to help pupils to send helpful letters, that is, ones which enable people like myself to send helpful replies.

ALWAYS include the following information:

The purpose of the study, e.g. O level project;
Its length, e.g. a five-hundred word-topic;
As precisely as possible the area to be covered, e.g. Jewish Sabbath in the home;
The O level board examining the project;
Books you have already used;
The kind of school to which you go (it may have Jewish pupils or teachers in it who could give help). Is it multi-faith?
The district of the town in which you live and/or go to school. Parts of Leeds are as mono-cultural as Chichester;

In addition,

Ask your teacher to read the letter before you send it. He/she may be able to provide additional helpful information;
Enclose a stamped and addressed envelope;
Do not expect an immediate reply. Very few of the people who deal with these queries do it as part of their jobs. It is usually a spare-time activity so they may not get round to replying for a week or two. Also when they receive hundreds of requests a year they cannot afford the postage, hence the need to remember the s.a.e. (And if I'm tired at the end of a day's work, a helpful letter with s.a.e. is something that usually wins my sympathy and a speedy reply. The other sort only adds to my irritation. Well, we've only human — at the best of times.)

328

My request to teachers and to students on teaching practice is very similar to what has already been given — with an emphasis upon time and timing. Late August or New Year's Day are not the best times to seek help for courses to be taught at the beginning of the following term. I like to enjoy a holiday as much as everyone else — and I have probably left my own preparation to the last minute, so I haven't much time to give to others! As for information it always helps to know as much about the school as possible.

Is it multi-cultural?
Is it primary, middle or secondary?
Is RS an O or A level subject, and, if so, which board?
Can visits to synagogues and other places of worship be made?
Is the use of videos, television and radio programmes possible?
Is a slide projector available?

Answers to these questions enable me to put RS into its context in the school.

Next, it is helpful to know the size and composition of the class(all boys, or e.g., mixed with fifteen Muslim girls, five Muslim boys and six boys from Irish Catholic backgrounds). Without this knowledge my postal suggestions might be a recipe for disaster. How many lessons a week, how long the topic is expected to last and what has already been taught to the class is also essential information. A student has been known to plan an excellent series of lessons on the five pillars of Islam only to discover that most of it was covered last term in a topic on worship. Finally, of course, it is necessary to know the ages of the pupils and whether they are of mixed ability or streamed in some way. If the teacher has some sets of books available or some money to spend on half a dozen of this or a dozen of that and some slides it is always useful to be told of these things.

It may seem that my request is putting a great demands upon teachers and others seeking help (including, sometimes, graduates looking for something to research), but if individuals and the 'useful addresses' mentioned in this book are to be useful enquirers must be prepared to give as much time to the exercise of asking as they expect others to give to the task of replying.

APPENDIX 2: MULTI-CULTURAL LEA RESOURCES CENTRES IN THE UK

A guide to centres offering support on ESL, language development and or multi-cultural education. (*= denotes centres offering publications lists: send s.a.e. for details.)

1. Avon	Multi-Cultural Education Service, Bishopston School Site, Bishop Road, Bishopston, Bristol BS7 8LS (Tel.: 0272 427636).
*2. Avon	Resources for Learning Development Unit, Bishopston School Site, Bishop Road, Bishopston, Bristol BS7 8LS (Tel.: 0272 428208).
3. Barking	Language Unit, London Borough of Barking and Dagenham, Station Parade, East Street, Barking, Essex (Tel.: 01–594 9830).
*4. Bedfordshire	Resources Centre, Acacia Road, Bedford MX42 0HU (Tel.: 0234 64475).
*5. Bedfordshire	Multi-Racial Education Resources Centre, Tennyson Road Primary School, Tennyson Road, Luton LU1 3RS (Tel.: 0582 26880)
6. Berkshire	English Language Centre, Lydford Road, Reading RG1 5QH (Tel.: 0734 61595).
7. Berkshire	Co. Ord. For Multi-Cultural Education, Thomas Gray Centre, Queens Road, Slough, Berks SL1 3OW.
*8. Birmingham	Multi-Cultural Support Service, Bordesley Centre, Camp Hill, Stratford Road, Birmingham B11 1AR (Tel.: 021 772 7676).
9. Blackburn	Blackburn Language Centre, Accrington Road, Blackburn, Lancs BB1 2AS.
*10. Bradford	(a) Multi-Cultural Education Service, T. F. Davies Teachers' Centre, Rosemount, Clifton Villas, Bradford BD8 7BY (Tel.: 0274 493771). (b) Keighley In-Service Base, Old Swire Smith Building, 1st Floor, Marlborough St, Keighley, West Yorkshire (Tel.: 0535 63410).
11. Bradford	Multi-Cultural Education Unit, Bradford College, Great Horton Road, Bradford, West Yorkshire BD7 1AY (Tel.: 0274 34844).
12. Brent	Multi-Cultural Resources Centre, c/o Brent Teachers' Centre, Ealing Road, Alperton, Wembley HAO 4QL (Tel.: 01–903 0661).

13. Burnley	Language Centre, Stoneyholme School, Burleigh Street, Burnley, Lancs.
*14. Cambridgeshire	National Extension College, Publications Dept, 18 Brookland Avenue, Cambridge CB2 2HN (Tel.: 0223 316644).
*15. Cambridgeshire	The Resources Centre for Multi-Racial Education, 165A Cromwell Road, Peterborough, Cambs (Tel.: 0733 62877).
16. Cardiff	Adult and Community Centre, 28 The Parade, Cardiff, Wales (Tel.: 0222 495578).
*17. Clwyd	Centre for Education Technology, County Civic Centre, Mold. Clwyd CH7 1YA (Tel.: 0352 55105).
*18. Coventry	Community Education Development Centre, Publications Section, Briton Road, Coventry CV2 4LF (Tel.: 0203 440814).
*19. Coventry	Minority Group Support Service, South Street, Hillfields, Coventry CV1 5EJ (Tel.: 0203 26888).
20. Croydon	St James Language and Reception Centre, c/o Woodside Junior, Morland Road, Croydon CR0 6NF (Tel.: 01–656 6679).
21. Croydon	ESL Advisory Service, Davidson High School, Davidson Road, Croydon CR0 6DD (Tel.: 01–656 0913).
22. Derby	Multi-Cultural Education Support Service, Dairy House Road, Derby, Derbyshire.
23. Ealing	Centre for Reading and Language Development, Stanhope School Site, Mansell Road, Greenford, Middlesex.
24. Enfield	English Language Centre, Tile Kiln Lane, London N13 6BY (Tel.: 01–803 4460).
25. Glasgow	Language Teaching Centre, 39 Napiershall Street, Glasgow, Scotland.
26. Halifax	Immigrant Teaching Service, West House, Kingcross Street, Halifax, West Yorkshire HX1 1EB.
27. Hampshire	English Language Resources Centre, Mount Pleasant Middle School, Mount Pleasant Road, Southampton S09 3TQ (Tel.: 0703 331741).
28. Hampshire	Sopley Education Centre, Sopley Reception Centre, Bransgore, Near Christchurch, Dorset (Tel.: 0425 73509).
29. Harringey	English Language Resources Centre, Tottenham Green Education Centre, Town Hall Approach,

Tottenham, London N15 4RY (Tel.: 01–801 1086).

30. Harringey	Multi-Cultural Curriculum Support Group, St Mary's C. of E. Junior, Rectory Gardens, London N8 7PJ (Tel.: 01–348 2827).
31. Harrow	Multi-Cultural Support Service, Little Stanmore First and Middle School, St David's Drive, Edgware, Middlesex HA8 6JH.
32. Hounslow	Primary ESL Unit, Smallberry Green Centre, London Road, Isleworth, Middlesex TW3 4DN.
33. Hounslow	Schools Language Unit, Smallberry Green Centre, London Road, Isleworth, Middlesex TW3 4DN (Tel.: 01–568 0551).
*34. ILEA	Learning Materials Service, Publishing Centre, Highbury Station Road, London N1 1SB (Tel.: 01–226 9143).
*35. ILEA	Centre for Language in Primary Education, Ebury Teachers' Centre, Sutherland Street, London SW1 4LH (Tel.: 01–828 8734).
*36. ILEA	The English Centre, Sutherland Street, Victoria, London SW1 (Tel.: 01–828 4906).
*37. ILEA	Centre for Urban Educational Studies, Top Floor, Robert Monte Fiore School, Underwood Road, London E1 5AD (Tel.: 01–377 0040);
*38. ILEA	Afro–Caribbean Education Resources (ACER) Project, c/o Centre for Learning Resources Service, 275 Kennington Lane, London SE11 (Tel.: 01–582 2771).
*39. Institute of Education, London University	Centre for Multi-Cultural Education, Institute of Education, London University, Bedford Way, London WC1H 0AL (Tel.: 01–636 1500).
*40. Kirklees	Reading and Language Centre, Hopton, Mirfield, West Yorkshire (Tel.: 0924 497949).
*41. Leeds	The Printed Resources Unit for Continuing Education, 27 Harrogate Road, Leeds 7 (Tel.: 0532 623308).
42. Leeds	John Taylor Teachers' Centre, 53 Headingley Lane, Leeds LS6 1AA.
43. Leicester	Rushey Mead Language Centre, Harrison Road, Leicester, LE4 7PA (Tel.: 0533 680224).
44. Liverpool	English Language Centre, c/o Paddington Comprehensive School, Mount Vernon, Liverpool L7 3EA (Tel.: 051 709 5820).

45. Liverpool	Centre for Multi-Racial Education, c/o Paddington Comprehensive School, Mount Vernon, Liverpool L7 3EA (Tel.: 051 709 8763).
46. Manchester	Birley High School ('Multi-Cultural Education in the 1980's'), Chichester Road, Hulme, Manchester, M15 5FU (Tel.: 061 226 4358).
47. Manchester	Multi-Cultural Development Service, 11 Anson Road, Manchester M14 5BY (Tel.: 061 225 8319).
*48. Manchester	The Centre For the Study of Religion and Education in the Inner City, Sacred Trinity Centre, Chapel Street, Salford M3 7AJ (Tel.: 061 832 3709).
49. Middlesbrough	Centre for Multi-Cultural Education, c/o Victoria Road Primary School, Victoria Road, Middlesbrough, Cleveland TS1 3AF (Tel.: 0642 219050).
50. Newham	Centre for English As A Second Language, In-Service Education Centre, New City Road, London E13 9PY (Tel.: 01–552 5719).
51. Northampton	The Advisory Teacher for Multi-Cultural Education, Teachers' Centre, Barry Road, Northampton NN1 5JS (Tel.: 0604 22547).
*52. Nottingham	The Language Centre, Goldswong Terrace, Cranmer Street, Nottingham NG2 4HB (Tel.: 0602 620946).
53. Oldham	Multi-Cultural Education and Language Service, Greengate Centre, Greengate Street, Oldham 0L4 1RY (Tel.: 061 665 3734).
54. Oxford	Centre for Multi-Cultural Education, Oxford First School, Union Street, Oxford, Oxon (Tel.: 0865 723580).
55. Rochdale	English Language Support Service, English Teaching Centre, Castlemere School, Tweedale Street, Rochdale, Lancs (Tel.: 0706 47078).
*56. Sandwell	Materials Production Unit, Ethnic Minority Support Service, Teachers' Centre, Churchbridge, Oldbury, Warley, West Midlands B69 2AX (Tel.: 021 552 55112).
*57. Walsall	Multi-Cultural Education Support Services, Education Development Centre, 36 Wolverhampton Road, Walsall, West Midlands (Tel.: 0922 613125).
58. Waltham Forest	English Language Centre, Markshouse Road, London E17 8BD.
59. Waltham Forest	Waltham Forest Teachers' Centre, Queens' Road, Walthamstow, London E17 8QS.

60. Wolverhampton Multi-Cultural Education Service, Resources Centre, Beckminster House, Birches Barn Road, Penn Fields, Wolverhampton WV3 7BJ (Tel.: 0902 337244).

(The Editor is indebted to Graham McFarlane of the Bedfordshire Multi-racial Education Resources. Centre for providing this list. It is reprinted with permission of the Chief Education Officer.)